Comparative Social Recognition

Comparative
Social Recognition

Patrick Colgan
Queen's University at Kingston
Ontario, Canada

A Wiley-Interscience Publication
JOHN WILEY & SONS
New York · Chichester · Brisbane · Toronto · Singapore

Copyright © 1983 by John Wiley & Sons, Inc.

Library of Congress Cataloging in Publication Data:

Colgan, Patrick W.
  Comparative social recognition.

  "A Wiley-Interscience publication."
  Bibliography: p.
  Includes index.
  1. Social behavior in animals.   I. Title.
II. Title: Social recognition.
QL775.C576   1983   591.51   82-17345
ISBN 0-471-09350-5

Printed in the United States of America

10   9   8   7   6   5   4   3   2   1

Pro Ethometrica

Preface

How is a female dove able to discriminate castrated from intact potential mates simply by watching them? What makes a nesting male sunfish change from attacking a female to courting her? By what means do tadpoles and bees distinguish siblings from nonsiblings? How do cockroaches find their position in a pecking order? Why do humans have initial difficulty in distinguishing individuals of unfamiliar racial groups? These questions all belong under the topic of social recognition. This book deals with this key topic and employs the comparative approach by exploring the similarities and differences in the biology of different social species. In focusing on social recognition, the treatment will not deal with interspecific phenomena such as mimicry, symbiosis, and predator–prey relations, with habitat recognition, or with other aspects of animal communication. This aperitif volume is intended for students and researchers exploring all aspects of the social behavior of animals.

The organization of this book is based on the answer to the question, What processes are operative in what species to produce what recognition behavior? The processes may be those operating during a particular instance of recognition, that is, sensory processes. Or they may be those that operate over an animal's lifetime, such as learning and imprinting. Or, finally, they may be those that operate over evolutionary time, namely, genetic and ecological processes. Thus, the first chapter reviews the evidence for different types of recognition behavior and the next three consider the three types of processes involved.

The first chapter surveys the acts by which social partners recognize each other during encounters. Just as every animal is constantly categorizing the features of its nonsocial environment (is that object edible? a predator? a potential nesting site?), so it identifies and pigeonholes each new conspecific as it is encountered (is it a potential mate? a rival? an ally?). The patterns involved in recognition interactions are reviewed, patterns ranging from the claw-waving displays of fiddler crabs to the head-bobbing of ducks.

The second chapter considers the sensory processes of social recognition. The operative discriminatory process may involve one or more of the basic sensory modalities. Across animal groups there is a differential use of different modalities. Vision plays a major role in many vertebrates and insects and in some crustaceans. Electroreception, foreign to humans, is highly developed in some families of fish. The choruses of frogs, crickets, and geese rely on audition. Among mammals, chemical sensation is important, and among arthropods, tactile sensation. Central to the operation of these sensory processes are the modes of pattern and form recognition whereby critical labeling features of the perceived animal are extracted.

The ontogeny of social recognition, that is, the development of these discriminations during the lifetime of the animal, is considered in the third chapter. First, the basic processes of habituation and learning are discussed. Imprinting, a developmental process of special importance in some groups of animals, especially birds, is reviewed next. Finally, general aspects of socialization are covered in relation to the ontogeny of recognition behavior and the development of social structures.

The fourth chapter examines the genetic and ecological processes of recognition behavior. The behavioral genetics of recognition behavior is reviewed, followed by an analysis of species recognition in relation to hybridization and speciation. Between two closely related species, failure to discriminate members of the two groups can lead to hybridization, or genetic exchange, and possible merging of the two populations over evolutionary time. Next are discussed the ecological conditions producing the diversity of observed social systems and the extent to which communication should be viewed as information or propaganda. This discussion leads to consideration of the functions of groups (colonies, flocks, schools) and the evolution of consciousness, aggressive relations (territoriality and dominance hierarchies), and reproductive relations (sexual selection, mating strategies, and assortative mating). In each case, functional interpretations of the observed recognition abilities are provided, together with genetic consequences for the population, such as inbreeding, which is reproduction by individuals with a shared ancestry. It is from this evolutionary perspective that the phylogenetic development of recognition behavior is analyzed.

Focusing on recognition behavior enables the development of a theme linking many contemporary issues in ethology and related fields. The diversity of species, sensory modalities, and social systems that need to be considered throughout each section of the book indicate the multiplicity of routes that have evolved as solutions to the problem of social recognition. This multiplicity reflects the importance of the topic as a key link between the general perceptual and motor integrative physiology of an animal and its social biology of interactions with its conspecifics.

PATRICK COLGAN

Kingston, Canada
January, 1983

Acknowledgments

I am extremely grateful to many persons for aid in the writing of this book. The Natural Sciences and Engineering Research Council and the administrators of my University cast bread upon the waters. Librarians, both here at Queen's (especially J. Stevenson, Biology Department Librarian) and at Toronto and McGill, suffered my myriad enquiries with cheerfulness. (Serving as a test case for the crushing capacity of the movable high-density book storage units in the bowels of the Sigmund Samuel Library had its compensations.) Two assistants shared the effort of preparation with me. J. Cross performed numerous valuable library errands. B. Silburt drove our text processor and tempered my phraseology and abhorrence of prolixity. For suggestions to the literature I thank R. Brown, B. Frost, J. Fullard, L. Geyer, J. Hamann, W. Honig, R. Kerbal, D. Kiez, M. Pereira, J. and S. Schmutz, D. Watler, R. Weisman, and G. Wyatt. M. Diamond, N. Flood, Z. Halprin, G. Martin, P. McArthur, E. Rissman, R. Porter, I. Rooke, G. Stratton, and W. Searcy kinkly supplied preprints of their research. Portions of the manuscript were read by J. Brown, F. Cooke, J. Eadie, L. Machlis, R. Rockwell, and B. Silburt. Members of the University of Toronto Animal Behaviour Research Group, especially M. Daly, J. Hogan, N. Lester, F. Pringmill, and D. Sherry, provided their usual acerbic comments. Above all, I benefited from the constructive criticism of my colleagues in our Bionomics Group, particularly J. Brown, D. Clark, F. Cooke, J. Eadie, J. Geramita, A. Hurly, R. Robertson, A. Salmon, J. Schmutz, and P. Taylor, and in the Animal Behavior Society (especially the 190-proof Fish Symposium) and the Association for the Study of Animal Behaviour. The Parnassian Hagiarchy and Magni Systemae also provided their support. Finally, I deeply appreciate the forebearance of my family and friends for this and other projects, most particularly the wishbone from Andrew and Jeffrey "because you wish the book done."

P.C.

Contents

Comparative Social Recognition

1

Evidence for Recognition Behavior

Students of animal mind continue to be impressed by the ancient epigram of Chuang-tzu and Hui-tzu on the bridge over the Hao River. Observed Chuang-tzu "See how the minnows are darting about! That is the pleasure of fishes." "You not being a fish yourself," said Hui-tzu, "how can you possibly know in what consists the pleasure of fishes?" "And you not being I," retorted Chuang-tzu, "how can you know that I do not know?" Indeed, what do we know? "Recognition," like "behavior," is a term used at several levels of organization. At the biomolecular level we speak of the recognition of foreign proteins by immunological antibodies, and at the sociological level, of an aspiring political group seeking recognition. In the area of artificial (machine) intelligence, pattern recognition of, say, faces, fingerprints, and speech is an active area of research (e.g., Haken, 1979; Levinson and Liberman, 1981). The exact location of the demarcation point between two levels of organization is to some extent uncertain. Sperm in the surrounding water cause gravid sea urchins to release their eggs for fertilization. This response indicates a simple type of species and sex recognition. Consider also the selective manner in which sea anemones use their acrorhagi (hollow structures encircling the oral disc beyond the tentacles) in aggression, avoiding clone mates and group mates while preying on others (Bigger, 1980). Such selection certainly falls within the province of ethology. Indeed, apparently distinct levels may prove to be closely linked. The *H-2* genetic locus in mice, important in immunological identification, also figures in mating preference at the

1

behavioral level (Yamazaki et al., 1976; discussed in Chapter 3, Genetic Aspects).

As Armstrong (1963) admits, "'recognition' is difficult to define." "Recognition" is used operationally in this book to describe discriminative behavior related to social categories and not as a theoretical term for some process independent of stimulation and subsequent response (cf. Crane, 1949). Perhaps because of such posible connotations, "recognition" has been used in quotes or avoided altogether by some researchers. On the other hand, it is more than simple habituation (discussed in Chapter 3), as implied by Kroodsma (1976). Mayr's (1970) definition for species recognition as the exchange of appropriate stimuli and responses between male and female and Kirkman's (1937) conclusion that "recognition is an elementary process common to most animals" reflect the same behavioral framework as that adopted here.

At the level of behavior, what are the kinds of evidence indicating that animals are discriminating group members from nongroup members, whether that group be mates, family, clan, sex, caste, nest, colony, population, morph, or species? Data may be collected from animals under unrestrained situations, either the natural environment or, increasingly as *Homo sapiens* enhance their dominion of the world, seminatural zoos, and conservation areas. For instance, sequences of spontaneous behavior may be analyzed for discrimination of social categories by examining the occurrence rates of different acts in response to various other individuals. Or observations may be made under controlled laboratory conditions through experiments in which test animals choose between alternatives such as familiar versus unfamiliar conspecifics. The use of stimulus dummies with fixed or variable characters is often valuable (Figure 1.1). Experiments involving conditioning (discussed in Chapter 3) can be used to assess discriminatory powers. The results of such experiments must be interpreted carefully so that the range and kinds of social stimuli among which animals *can* be trained to discriminate is not mistaken for those that it *does* discriminate in its normal behavior. In VonUexkull's (1957) terminology, the animal's *Merkwelt* (perceptual world) must not be confused with its *Umwelt* (functionally relevant world). VonUexkull also employed the term *Kumpan* (companon) for a conspecific that is responded to as an identified whole within one functional system (Figure 1.2). (Consider such role identities as tennis partners or drinking buddies.) This concept was used and made famous in Lorenz's celebrated 1935 paper on role companions as factors in the social environments of birds (see Lorenz, 1970). It will be useful to bear this concept in mind while examining the various social categories covered in this chapter.

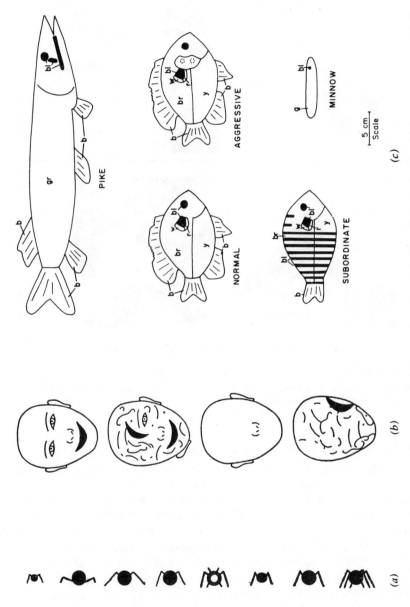

Figure 1.1. Stimulus dummies were used to assess (*a*) courtship in spiders, (*b*) smiling in infants, and (*c*) aggression in sunfish (from Land, 1969; Haaf and Bell, 1967; and Colgan and Gross, 1977, respectively). The letters indicate colors.

3

Figure 1.2. The four role companions of Lorenz's jackdaw, Jock: Lorenz as a mother companion, the maid as a love companion, a young jackdaw as an adopted companion, and crows as flight companions (from VonUexkull, 1957).

The experimental assessment of recognition is sometimes made difficult by the confounding influences of other factors. For instance, attachment to a common nest could produce behavior falsely indicative of individual recognition of the mate. Individual recognition implies an independence of the behavior from geographical location. Such recognition also implies discrimination of pairs of stimulus animals but the converse is not necessarily true. Again, affinity for heterospecifics could reflect a general social tendency to approach other animals, not a discriminated recognition, if the alternative presented was an empty area rather than conspecifics. Similarly, preferences may be obscured by dominance relations among the stimulus animals (e.g., Ferno and Sjolander, 1976; discussed in Chapter 3, Sexual and Filial Imprinting). Studies of, say, mother–

offspring recognition via calls can be confounded by the spatial relations of the individuals. If the distances between the test mother and the two offspring (her own and a control) whose calls are used as stimuli are not equal on average, any differences in her responses may simply reflect orientation. Experiments in which song dialects are played to test birds often confound similarity to the local song with geographical location of the playback, as discussed in Chapter 3, Song Imprinting. Finally, whether animals show recognition behavior also depends on the response studied and how it is measured. For instance, Shugart (1977) has argued that rejection of foreign young placed in the nests of birds is inappropriate to track the development of adult recognition (as can be shown through alternative choice tests) due to the broodiness of the parent which masks the recognition ability.

Choice of response measure is also often critical to detect recognition. Species recognition in damselfish is well measured by attraction but not by aggression (Katzir, 1981a, 1981b). All these problems call for careful experimental designs and critical interpretation of data. For instance, collapsing data from several animals in order to achieve a "sufficient sample size" may be inappropriate if there are large differences reflecting an underlying function of individual recognition (cf. Slater, 1981b). Unfortunately, ethologists as a group display a woeful lack of statistical expertise even though such expertise is generally essential for appropriate understanding of the phenomena under study. Indeed, there is serious doubt that many aspects of animal behavior are amenable to adequate investigation due to inherent limitations of data (Machlis, personal communication).

On interpretation, calls from aficionados of the cognitive richness of animal mind (e.g., Popper and Eccles, 1977; Griffin, 1976) threaten a return to the metaphysical swamps of Romanes and Spencer. It is well to keep firmly in sight Occam's razor that entities are not to be multiplied without necessity (a maxim not actually found in Occam's works) and its methodological offspring, Lloyd Morgan's (1909) canon that "in no case may we interpret an action as the outcome of the exercise of a higher psychical faculty, if it can be interpreted as the outcome of the exercise of one which stands lower in the psychological scale." A recent popular example of anthropomorphic overinterpretation in recognition behavior is Ardrey's (1966) discussion of the prairie-dog greeting kiss: "The kiss came about, I should assume, as a means of identification in the dark recesses of one's burrow to make sure by proper flavor that no stranger has sneaked in. Whatever its origin or selective value may be, when two members of a coterie meet, they exchange what is very nearly a human kiss, open-mouthed, and they seem to enjoy it." Shades of Lorenz' "jealous" geese!

Given that science is studied by humans, it is often important to calibrate the ability of scientists to recognize individual animals, as Batéson (1977) has done in a study with one of his graduate students, Scott. (Those familiar with the charming style of scientific reports of yesteryear will delight in the "It was a sunny, frosty morning in January..." to be found in this recent article.) Through testing using photographic slides of different animals, Bateson corroborated objectively Scott's claim of excellent recognition ability. As Bateson concludes, with such results "even the most sceptical armchair critic must surely accept that at least part of the apparatus necessary for such a field study is in good working order." In a different vein, it is sometimes methodologically prudent to run experiments "blind" (i.e., the researcher gathering and/or analyzing the data is unaware of which experimental treatment the animal he is observing belongs to). This is especially the case in work with higher primates (e.g., macaques, Wu et al., 1980; humans, Amsterdam and Greenberg, 1977).

This chapter focuses on the social categories used by different species in their recognition behavior. Included in this analysis is recognition of one life stage by another, such as eggs by parents or adults by larvae. The emphasis in the scientific literature on adult behavior probably reflects the life stage of the researcher more than the importance of that stage in the biology of the animal. Beyond social categories, animals often additionally recognize the state of a particular individual: the arousal level of a rival, the intensity of sexual motivation of a mate, or the emotional attitude of a parent. Among higher mammals that often play (see, e.g., Fagen, 1981), recognition of a playful state is important. Evidence for such state recognition will also be considered below.

It should be noted that a single behavior or sensory modality may be used by an animal to convey information on more than one of the social categories used to organize the material of this chapter. For instance, the complex calls of the neotropical frog *Hyla ebraccata* carry separate aggressive and sexual messages to males and females (Wells and Greer, 1981). Similarly, the song of a bird can identify the species, sex, and aggressive state of a territorial male. As West et al. (1981) have discussed for the brown-headed cowbird, different processes can underlie such simultaneous recognition of different social categories. Conversely, different behaviors or modalities may be used simultaneously or successively in recognition, especially as the distance between individuals changes. For instance, in much insect courtship, calls and then contact pheromones are employed. Popular literature on human behavior abounds with discussions of "body language," which modifies verbal communication.

The bias in this chapter for reporting studies with positive results, given that they are methodologically sound, with less emphasis on negative results, reflects the general belief that there are many more ways to miss an effect than to find it. Nevertheless, it will be seen that available evidence is generally too scanty to produce well supported generalizations. Throughout the text, significant results from some treatment should be taken to be in comparison with an untreated control group unless otherwise noted. Finally, while the evidence for recognition behavior is reviewed using a comparative (taxonomic) basis in this chapter, other perspectives are also useful. One of these, focusing on recognition in different social systems, is considered in Chapter 4.

SPECIES AND MORPHS

On account of its fundamental importance, species recognition has long been an area of intense interest, particularly as it functions as an isolating mechanism to decrease the likelihood of hybrids (discussed in Chapter 4). For instance, A. R. Wallace (1889) argued that "the wonderful diversity of colour and of marking that prevails, especially in birds and insects, may be due to the fact that one of the first needs of a new species would be to keep separate from its nearest allies, and this could be most readily done by some easily seen external mark of difference." He went on to discuss species recognition in a variety of ungulates, birds, and insects, with handsome accompanying figures (Figure 1.3). [The group selection (see Chapter 4, Ecology of Social Systems) nature of this argument is irrelevant

C. forbesi.　　　　Charadrius bifrontatus.　　　　C. tricollaris.

Figure 1.3. Species recognition marks involving the head and throat in three African plovers (from Wallace, 1889).

for present purposes.] Species recognition is particularly important for species involved in mimetic relations with other species and for species living in ecologically packed communities containing similar forms. With regard to the latter, Williams and Rand (1977) have analyzed the importance of the dewlap and associated behavior in species recognition in lizard communities. When the fauna is small, the dewlap plays at most a minor role in recognition but figures largely in communities with a diverse fauna. More generally, a germane phenomenon from community ecology is that of character displacement, referring to the observation that for similar species with partially overlapping ranges, character differences tend to be larger in the region of overlap (see Brown and Wilson, 1956). This competitive phenomenon is relevant to recognition behavior in the case of frog mating calls, as Blair (1974) has discussed for the North American fauna. Fruit-fly courtship behavior also shows character displacement (Markow, 1981b). In general, the sexual displays of many species, including both visual signals and auditory calls, serve the dual function of identifying species membership and of attracting mates (whose recognition will be discussed in the next section). Aspects of species recognition in various vertebrates are reviewed in Roy (1980).

The fundamental methodology of research into species recognition is to examine preference behavior on the part of each sex in the species of interest when presented with conspecific and heterospecific alternatives. The preferences may be measured in terms of social affinity (e.g., proportion of time spent near each alternative) or, very often, sexual choice, measured as the number of copulations completed, or in terms of the quantitative distribution of courtship behavior between the alternatives. For fruit flies, Wallace and Felthousen (1965) have suggested mating interference as a test of sexual isolation. They argue that the elapsed time before copulation should be lengthened if there are interspecific interactions, and hence that this time be the measure of isolation. Such a measure may often be appropriate, but caution is due since, as Hay (1976) argues, the overall "behavioral phenotype" of an animal must be considered in mating behavior, of which mating speed is but one component.

It should be noted that species isolation can involve behavioral differences that do not involve species recognition, such as differences in the habitat selected. Such habitat differences may be very subtle. For instance, in two European chironomid fly species, *Chironomus piger* swarm high above light markers while *Ch. thummi* swarm at lesser heights above dark markers (Miehlbradt and Neumann, 1976). More generally, any behavior producing spatial and/or temporal differences between closely related species can achieve species isolation without any species recognition *per se*. Thus, the mechanisms for species isolation differ across species.

The variation in appearance of members of a species is not always continuous. Polymorphism is the existence within a single population of two or more discontinuous forms at frequencies above those expected by genetic mutation (see review by Mayr, 1970). Morph recognition has generally been studied in connection with assortative mating (see Chapter 4, Reproduction) but, at least conceptually, is closely allied with species recognition since morphs are subsets within species. It also has ramifications for social organization beyond mating. For instance, groups in the dimorphic lesser snow goose are positively assortative (i.e., like associate with like) even if allowance is made for the pattern of positive assortative mating (Colgan et al., 1974). Thus, predominantly white flocks have more white birds in them than would be expected from a random mixing of white and blue birds, even taking into account the fact that white birds tend to mate with white birds. Polymorphic species pose intriguing evolutionary problems, and such species have been closely examined in te investigation of such major topics as imprinting (considered in Chapter 3). The problem of species recognition in species that are polymorphic due to mimicry is discussed in Chapter 4, Species Recognition and Hybridization.

Invertebrates

Species recognition is known for several noninsect invertebrates. When maintained as a single population, two species of flatworms (*Planaria gracilis* and *Cura foremani*) form separate aggregations using chemical cues (Reynierse, 1967) (Figure 1.4). The terrestrial snail *Achatina fulica* preferentially orients to mucus trails of conspecifics over heterospecifics (Chase et al., 1978). In the predaceous marine snail *Faciolaria tulipa*, both species and size recognition are mediated via pheromones (discussed in Chapter 2, Chemosensation) (Snyder and Snyder, 1971). Ensuing captures may lead to cannibalism or copulation. In a complex of North Atlantic isopods, recognition is mediated by species-typical displays in males and reactivity in females (Solignac, 1981). Crane has provided detailed comparative data on communicative patterns enabling species recognition in salticid spiders (1949) and fiddler crabs (1975) (Figure 1.5). Males of two closely related wolf spiders court females indiscriminantly by stridulating the substrate but females respond only to conspecific males (Stratton and Uetz, 1981; Uetz and Denterlein, 1979). Despite rich descriptive research, nothing definite is known about the role of

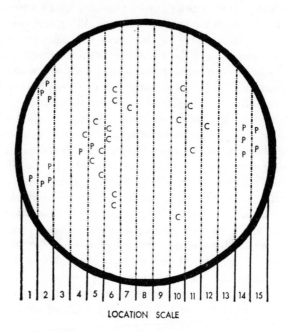

LOCATION   SCALE

Figure 1.4. Experimental bowl with location scale used to score the aggregations of two species of flatworms, *Planaria gracilis* (P) and *Cura foremani* (C) (from Reynierse, 1967).

courtship behavior in species recognition among araneid spiders (Robinson and Robinson, 1980). A social spider that lives in communal webs discriminates between conspecifics and prey animals on the web (Burgess, 1979). Much other arachnid research has recently been reviewed in the volume by Witt and Rovner (1982). In crayfish, recognition of conspecifics is mediated by chemical cues (Rose and Casper, 1980).

Species recognition can be expected to be a critical matter for an enormously diverse group such as the insects. [There are about 280,000 species of beetles (Coleoptera) alone. When J. B. S. Haldane was asked what his studies of nature had informed him about the Creator, he replied "the Creator, if He exists, has a special preference for beetles" (Slater, 1951).] Species recognition is the rule among dragonflies, although hybrids and heterospecific mating pairs are found (Corbet, 1980). Among swarming dipterans (flies), visual and auditory cues from the females are inadequate for species recognition, and are aided by specificity of the assembly station, where the flies gather, and, possibly, additional cues upon contact (Downes, 1969). The chironomid case cited above illustrates

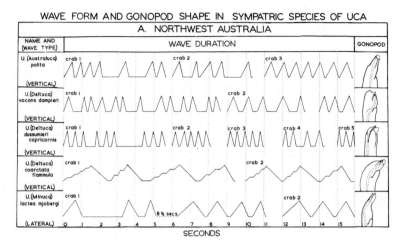

WAVE FORM AND GONOPOD SHAPE IN SYMPATRIC SPECIES OF UCA

A. NORTHWEST AUSTRALIA

Figure 1.5. Gonopodial waving in some fiddler crabs, with the base line representing periods between waves and the apex representing the peak of the wave (from Crane, 1975).

the role of such a station. Among bioluminescent insects, species-typical information, together with mimicry of prey species, is encoded in the flash patterns (Lloyd, 1966, 1971, 1980). Stridulation similarly mediates species recognition in scolytid beetles (Oester and Rutowsky, 1979).

Among hemipterans (bugs), stridulation of the forelegs against sharp edges of the head enables species recognition in waterbugs of the genus *Cenocorixa* (Jansson, 1973). Like the social spider cited, the backswimmer *Notonecta glauca* discriminates between prey and conspecifics by means of surface wave frequencies (Lang, 1980). Interspecific song differences isolate a complex of closely related planthopper species (Booij, 1982). In two species of periodical cicadas (*Magicicada septendecim* and *M. cassini*), the courtship patterns of both sexes differ in both behavioral and acoustical components (Dunning et al., 1979). Female preferences for conspecific sounds underlie species recognition and thus species isolation.

Among crickets (Walker, 1957; Bigelow, 1964; Shuvalov and Popov, 1973a, 1973b; Dathe, 1974; Hoy, 1974; Stout and McGhee, 1980) and grasshoppers (Perdeck, 1958; Bailey and Robinson, 1971; Otte, 1972; Hartley et al., 1974), song differences are important for species recognition. Females of the cricket *Gryllus bimaculatus* move toward male sounds in a Y-maze choice between the male's call and a silent maze arm (Dathe, 1974). Although distinction between the calls of *G. bimaculatus* and *G. campestris* is imperfect, at close range females approach conspecific calls more quickly than those of the heterospecific. Both sexes of *Teleogryllus oceanicus* prefer conspecific over heterospecific songs (Pollack, 1980) and isolation from the closely related *T. commodus* is achieved through selectivity by females in responding to male calls (Hill et al., 1972). Beyond song differences, male crickets of the genera *Acheta* and *Gryllus* distinguish species by odor (Otte and Cade, 1976). Such olfactory species recognition is elaborated among butterflies and moths where in many species one sex, generally the female, releases pheromones (e.g., clearwing moths, Greenfield and Karandinos, 1979). (Pheromones are discussed in Chapter 2, Chemosensation.)

Sexual pheromones also enable species recognition in slave-making ants. In such ants, colonies of a dominant species raids those of a subordinate species and gang press individuals of the latter as workers. Females of *Harpagoxenus canadensis* and *H. sublaevis* emit the same pheromone but discriminate behaviorally between males of the two species (Buschinger and Alloway, 1979). Males of a third species do not respond to the pheromones, and so species isolation is maintained among all three species. [Besides the interspecific interactions of slave-making ants, symphily, such as the dwelling of beetles within the colonies of ants, raises problems of species recognition. These topics are discussed by Holldobler (1971), Wilson (1971), Alloway (1980), and Buschinger et al. (1980)]. Pheromones also play important roles in non-slave-making species of ants as early investigated by Fielde (1904). Among fire ants the substances laid along foraging trails out of the colony are highly species-typical (Wilson, 1962). Daily activity rhythms, perennial mating sites, and surface pheromones in the females are all species-typical in harvester ants and so enable species recognition (Holldobler, 1976b).

The large literature on fruit flies (Drosophilidae) has been reviewed by Parsons (1973) and Spieth (1974), and many studies (e.g., Dobzhansky et al., 1968; Narda, 1968; Ohta, 1978) report on preference behavior between conspecifics and heterospecifics. The family contains about 2000 species, one-quarter of which are endemic to the Hawaiian islands. Within *Drosophila melanogaster*, individuals can discriminate between flies from other strains and cultures (Hay, 1972). In crosses between ancestral and derived species, asymmetric mating preferences are found, as discussed further in Chapter 4, Species Recognition and Hybridization. Among South American forms, courtship behavior is similar but quantitatively different (Koref-Santibanez, 1963). Both males and females show specific discrimination, the strength of the discrimination varying with the species. From the *D. melanogaster* group, Schilcher and Dow (1977) have gathered data to support their hypothesis that in some cases females are responsible for sexual selection and males for sexual isolation of the species (both discussed in Chapter 4, Reproduction). In the sibling species pair, *D. melanogaster* and *D. simulans*, the males differ in the amounts of scissoring and vibration displays that they produce during courtship (Manning, 1959). It seems likely that the proximate mechanism for species isolation in such species is a change in the reaction thresholds for courtship display, enabling the development of species-typical courtship behavior. The role of the male in maintaining ethological isolation is highly variable across species (Wood and Ringo, 1980). *Drosophila simulans* shows strong interspecific discrimination whereas *D. melanogaster* exhibits poor discrimination, with the hybrids intermediate. Within the *D. melanogaster* and *D. obscura* groups, species recognition is achieved by differences in the songs emanating from male wing beating during courtship. Schilcher (1976) has shown the importance of the pulse song in species recognition in the *D. melanogaster* group, and in the genus *Zaprionus* song also functions in species isolation (Bennet-Clark et al., 1980). Chemical cues figure in species recognition in some cases (Averhoff et al., 1979) while characteristic body markings of the male are found in other instances (Lambert, 1982). Jointly, these numerous studies reveal the nature of species recognition in this diverse group and the proximate behavioral mechanisms which are operative.

In insects showing brood care, the question of species recognition of larval stages arises. Worker ants of *Myrmica rubra* discriminate between conspecific larvae and larvae of the congeneric *M. scabrionodis* (Brian, 1975). Workers of *Tapinoma erraticum* distinguish their own brood from *Solenopsis* larvae, which are smaller, but less well from similarly sized *Tetramorium* larvae (Meudec, 1978). Discrimination of cocoons of different species develops over the first couple of weeks of adult life in workers of *Formica polyctena* (Jaisson, 1975).

Amphibians and Reptiles

Species recognition based on differences in male courtship calls has been shown in many anuran amphibians (frogs and toads, Table 1.1; reviews by Blair, 1968; Littlejohn 1969). For example, green and pine barrens tree frogs are easily crossed in the laboratory but are ecologically segregated in the field (Gerhardt, 1974a). Females allowed to choose between the songs of males of the two species showed preferences for conspecific calls. However, discrimination between the calls of different species is not always found. Awbrey (1968) found no discrimination by females of

Table 1.1.   Anuran Studies on Species Recognition via Calls

Genus	Locality	Source
Crinia	Southern Australia	Littlejohn (1959, 1964) and Littlejohn and Watson (1974)
Hyla	Eastern United States	Gerhardt (1974a, 1974b, 1976, 1978)
	Central United States	Johnson (1966) and Littlejohn et al. (1960)
	Western United States	Ball and Jameson (1966) and Littlejohn (1971)
	Costa Rica	Duellman (1967)
	Tenerife	Gerhardt and Schneider (1980)
	Southern Australia	Littlejohn (1965) and Littlejohn and Loftis-Hills (1968)
Microhyla	Central United States	Blair (1955)
Pseudacris	Eastern United States	Martof and Thompson (1964)
	Central United States	Littlejohn and Michaud (1959) and Michaud (1962)
Rana	Central United States	Littlejohn and Oldham (1968)
Scaphiopus	Central United States	Forester (1973)

Scaphiopus couchii and *S. h. hurterii* to the calls of males of the two species that do have overlapping geographical ranges. Mating calls are the chief source of ethological isolation in 10 Costa Rican hylids (Duellman, 1967). Other possible sources of isolation such as differences in body size and calling and oviposition sites are less important than these behaviorial differences. Thus courtship calls play a prominent role in species recognition among frogs.

Red-backed and Shenandoah salamanders show a preference for their own substrates only when also exposed to substrates of conspecific males (Jaeger and Gergits, 1979). In interspecific tests, each sex of each species avoided substrates of congeners although red-backed females did not avoid Shenandoah males.

Among reptiles, the importance of the dewlap and associated behavior (Williams and Rand, 1977) has already been mentioned. In the morphologically similar *Sceloporus torquatus* lizard group, specific head bobbing patterns, as well as tasting enable species recognition (Hunsaker, 1962). In tests in a compartmented cage, two species of this genus preferred to share a compartment with a conspecific over a heterospecific (Pyburn, 1955). Male side-blotched lizards in Colorado exhibit more courtship behavior to conspecific females than to females of three sympatric species (Ferguson, 1972). Further, Colorado and Texas populations have strikingly different color patterns, and males preferentially court females of their own race (Ferguson, 1969). Five-lined and ground skinks react to the odors of conspecifics but behave randomly in response to heterospecific odors (Duvall et al., 1980) (Figure 1.6). Similarly, male snakes discriminate among the skins of conspecifics and heterospecifics (Noble, 1937). Water snakes avoid areas soiled by conspecifics, while garter snakes prefer such areas when a clean area is the test alternative (Porter and Czaplicki, 1974). Neither species distinguishes clear areas and areas soiled by the other species. Neill (1964) has reviewed the variety of courtship mechanisms enabling species recognition in snakes, such as species-typical scent trails emitted by estrous females. Sexually active, territorial males of two South American tortoise species categorize other turtles as either conspecific males or not through reciprocal head movements (Auffenberg, 1965) (Figure 1.7). Conspecific females are recognized by their cloacal odors.

Birds

Avian species recognition is of interest to ornithomaniacal "life listers" and to the birds alike. In his classical work, Lorenz (1970) reports on recognition in many species. Hochbaum (1959) described a territorial blue-winged teal male that responded vigorously to conspecifics over a

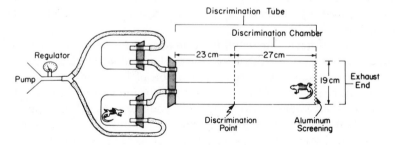

Figure 1.6. Olfactometer used for odor discriminations by skinks (From Duvall et al., 1980, by permission of the Society for the Study of Amphibians and Reptiles).

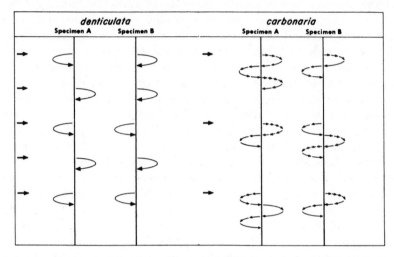

Figure 1.7. The South American tortoise *Geochelone denticulata* responds with a single smooth lateral head movement (indicated as an unbroken trajectory) in response to a visual stimulus (indicated by the arrow) whereas *G. carbonaria* responds with a few jerky movements (indicated by the broken trajectories) (from Auffenberg, 1965).

wide area but ignored nearby green-winged teal. Among four species of Arctic gulls, eye ring color is critical for species recognition, operating at two stages in reproduction (N. G. Smith, 1966; Figure 1.8). During pair formation, a female chooses a male with similar eye–head contrast, and in mated pairs a male copulates only with a similar female. Wing tip pattern and size differences supplement the eye ring color in achieving species recognition. These intriguing results warrant further investigation. Among estrildid finches, the red beak of *Pytilia lineata* isolates it from *P. phoenicaptera* by influencing both aggressive and sexual behavior (Nicolai, 1968).

Many studies have elucidated the role of song in species recognition by noting responses to broadcasts of conspecific and other calls (Table 1.2). The studies on sparrows reveal recognition of both species and dialect groups within species. French herring gulls do not respond to the food-finding calls of their North American counterparts. Three species of French crows similarly do not respond to alarm calls of the American species, and react to the latter's assembly call as to their own distress calls. American crows generally ignore broadcasts of French calls. Such species recognition often involves song imprinting, discussed in Chapter 3 together with song dialects.

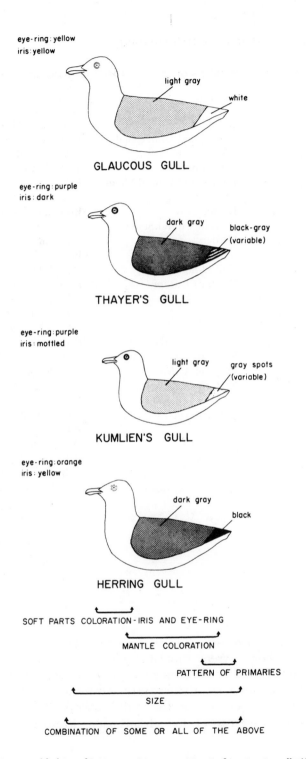

eye-ring: yellow
iris: yellow

light gray

white

GLAUCOUS GULL

eye-ring: purple
iris: dark

dark gray

black-gray
(variable)

THAYER'S GULL

eye-ring: purple
iris: mottled

light gray

gray spots
(variable)

KUMLIEN'S GULL

eye-ring: orange
iris: yellow

dark gray

black

HERRING GULL

SOFT PARTS COLORATION-IRIS AND EYE-RING

MANTLE COLORATION

PATTERN OF PRIMARIES

SIZE

COMBINATION OF SOME OR ALL OF THE ABOVE

Figure 1.8. Features likely mediating species recognition in four Arctic gulls (from N. G. Smith, 1966).

Table 1.2.   Avian Studies on Species Recognition via Calls

Taxon	Locality	Source
Prairie grouse	Central United States	Sparling (1981)
Gulls	France and United States	Frings et al. (1958)
Barbets	Tropical Africa	Wickler (1973)
Woodlarks	Germany	Tretzel (1965)
Crows	France and United States	Frings et al. (1958)
Creepers	Germany	Thielcke (1962)
Wrens	France	Bremond (1968b, 1978)
Thrushes	Eastern United States	Dilger (1956)
	Mexico	Raitt and Hardy (1970)
	France	Bremond (1968b)
Flycatchers	United States	Stein (1963)
Warblers	Western Europe	Becker (1976); Bremond (1968a, 1976); Lemaire (1977); G. Schubert (1971)
Ovenbirds	Eastern Canada	Falls (1963)
Blackbirds	Eastern United States	Beletsky et al. (1980)
Cordon bleus	Tropical Africa	S. M. Evans (1972)
Towhees	Eastern United States	Ewert (1980)
Buntings	Eastern and Central North America	Emlen (1972); Shiovitz (1975); Shiovitz and Lemon (1980); W. L. Thompson (1969)
Sparrows	North America	Baker et al. (1981a); Dooling and Searcy (1980); Falls (1963); Goldman (1973); Milligan (1966); Milligan and Verner (1971); Peters et al. (1980); Pleszcynska (1980); Searcy and Marler (1981); Searcy et al. (1981a)

Besides song broadcasts, mounted specimens of birds can be used as test stimuli. Male house wrens copulate with female mounts of both conspecifics and of winter wrens, but generally avoid long-billed marsh wren mounts (Noble and Vogt, 1935). Territorial flycatchers of four species discriminate between conspecific and heterospecific songs (Lanyon, 1963) and react aggressively to such specimens, irrespective of species, if conspecific playback is associated with them. Territorial male blue-winged warblers on Long Island discriminate visually and acoustically between their own species and golden-winged warblers (Gill and Lanyon, 1964). In contrast to Gill and Lanyon's two-stimulus technique, Ficken and Ficken (1969) used a single-stimulus method and found strong responses to conspecific song. Responsiveness to heterospecific song varied with the population. A Maryland blue-winged population with some introgressive golden-winged genes gave weak but significant responses to golden-winged song, but a West Virginia pure golden-winged population showed no responsiveness to blue-winged song. (Introgression is discussed in Chapter 4, Species Recognition and Hybridization.) Thus, both the methods used and the populations examined differed in these two studies.

Species recognition of other life stages also confronts adult birds. Adult sooty terns discriminate sooty and noddy tern chicks (Lashley, 1915). Eggs substituted into the nests of a variety of perching species were sometimes accepted and sometimes induced desertion of the nest (Rensch, 1925). The discrimination of one's own eggs from those of brood parasitic species such as cuckoos (e.g., Harrison, 1968) is a problem for host species (review by Payne, 1977). The victimized species of the brown-headed cowbird of North America divide into some "acceptors" and many "rejectors" which reject foreign eggs whether these are more, equally, or less numerous than the host eggs (Rothstein, 1975). For her part, a female cowbird adopts a copulatory posture in response to the songs of conspecific males but not to those of other species (King and West, 1977; West et al., 1981). The eggs of African village weaver birds vary in ground color and spotting pattern, and females reject from their nests eggs differing from their own, and so defend themselves against the brood parasitic didric cuckoo (Victoria, 1972). The eggs of the red-headed duck, which is a brood parasite on canvasbacks and mallards as well as other red-headeds, are accepted by hosts if similar in size and color to the other eggs in the nest (Weller, 1959). Dissimilar eggs are ejected or buried during the egg-laying period of the host but accepted during incubation. The eggs of the parasitic South American black-headed duck do not seem to be distinguished by hosts (Weller, 1968).

Vocally mimetic species also provide species recognition problems. The mimetic thrushes (Mimidae) include the brown thrasher, catbird, and mockingbird. Brown thrashers discriminate their songs from those of catbirds but not of mockingbirds, while catbirds recognize conspecific songs as being different from the other two species (Boughey and Thompson, 1976). Playback experiments with variously modified calls reveal that frequency modulation in syllables is important for species recognition in the catbird (Fletcher and Smith, 1978). Some mimetic species are brood parasites. Brood parasites among the African viduine finches include indigo birds and paradise whydahs. Mimetic songs are used in the reproductive behavior of these parasitic species (Nicolai, 1964, 1967). In response to this parasitic selection pressure, young of the host estrildid finches have distinctive gape markings to which parents are highly selective in responding, and which are mimicked in the gape of the young parasite. Indigo birds parasitize fire finches and females respond selectively to the vocal mimicry of their own species (Payne, 1973a). Similarly, female paradise whydahs approach in response to the songs of the host malba finch, which they mimic, more than those of a host congener (Payne, 1973b). The females do not discriminate between the host songs and mimic songs by their own males. These mimics thus present the intriguing case of species recognition in a parasitic species group being mediated via discrimination of host songs.

Species recognition is not restricted to adult birds. Domestic chicks and mallard ducklings discriminate the maternal call of their species from among those of several species (Gottlieb, 1966). Indeed, incubator-raised wood duck embryos distinguish calls, increasing bill-clapping in response to conspecific calls and decreasing to mallard calls (Heaton, 1972). In both wood and mallard ducklings, auditory cues promote visual imprinting and subsequent species recognition (Gottlieb, 1968; discussed in Chapter 3, Sexual and Filial Imprinting).

The diversity of breeds in domestic species, which stimulated Darwin toward his arguments for natural selection, also provide opportunities for examining morph recognition. Among birds, domestic fowl breeds have been used for such an examination. Bantams and leghorns raised in mixed groups of equal numbers of each breed learned an operant food-reinforced, shock-punished discrimination of the arms of a Y-maze with birds of each breed serving as cues (Howells and Vine, 1940). Learning was faster in the half of the experiment in which a bird of the same breed was a positive cue than in the half in which a bird of the other breed was a positive cue. Members of two breeds, New Hampshire and Barred Plymouth Rock, react to each other not as individuals but as breed types, as indicated by subsequent responses after experience with the opposite breed (Hale, 1957). In four strains with colorations black, red, and two white, young birds tended to interact more with birds of other strains than with those of the same strain (McBride, 1964). Members of the two white strains interacted more strongly with birds of the other white strain than with those of different colors. More recent work (Lill, 1968a, 1968b) using older test animals from different strains has shown sexual preferences in both cocks and hens for the same strain. Breed recognition in fowl is further considered below in connection with dominance hierarchies. The light and dark color morphs of western grebes show strong preferences for the calls of their own morph (Nuechterlein, 1981a, 1981b).

Mammals

Studies demonstrating species recognition in mammals appear few, but the rarity of hybrids found between closely related species which overlap ecologically suggests that species discrimination is excellent, as would be expected based on the complex behavior this group shows in other respects. It is interesting to note that bison cows often fail to suckle their calves sired by domestic bulls (Berlioz, 1933). As in strains of domestic fowl, there is breed recognition among varieties of sheep (Shillito Walser, 1980). From a visible stimulus group of ewes of Clun Forest, Dalesbreed, and Jacob breeds, lambs choose ewes of their own breed. Audition alone is unsufficient, as shown by the lack of choice if the stimulus group is hidden by a canvas. Male pigtail and rhesus monkeys show longer latencies in responding sexually to heterospecific females compared to conspecific females (Bernstein and Gordon, 1979). While lar gibbon groups respond strongly to playbacks of conspecific calls, they do not respond to those of the pileated gibbon (Andelman, 1980). Southern right whales distinguish broadcasts of conspecific calls from those of humpback whales as well as water noise and 200 Hz tones (Clark and Clark, 1980).

Rodents have provided information on species recognition, as on so many other matters. Both audition and especially olfaction are employed. King (1963) suggested that "differences in the squeaks of different species and subspecies of [deer] mice may provide a clue for maternal recognition of the young." More recently, species-specific calls have been described in a family of North African rodents (George, 1981). Gerbils distinguish between the odors of conspecifics and four other small rodent species when tested in a T-maze (Dagg and Windsor, 1971). Wild and domestic guinea pigs discriminate each other and their hybrids by urine and perineal scent gland cues (Beauchamp et al., 1979; Wellington et al., 1979) (Figure 1.9). Voles of the genera *Microtus* and *Clethrionomys* react differentially to conspecific and heterospecific odors, generally avoiding the latter (Jonge, 1980). Similarly, house mice discriminate between conspecifics and deer mice (Bowers and Alexander, 1967). Odors play an important role in species recognition among lemmings (Huck and Banks, 1980a, 1980b) and pygmy and house mice (Quadagno and Banks, 1970). In kangaroo rats, odors deposited at sandbathing sites permit species recognition (Randall, 1981). A paper by Murphy (1978) is abstracted by its title: "Oestrous turkish hamsters display lordosis toward conspecific males

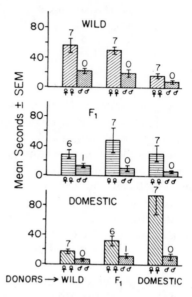

Figure 1.9. Mean number of seconds (+ standard error of the mean) for which domestic, hybrid (F_1), and wild guinea pigs investigated female urine of the three taxa (from Beauchamp et al., 1979). Note the preference for the urine of their own taxon.

but attack heterospecific males." (Lordosis refers to arching of the back to expose the genitals in sexually receptive female mammals.) Finally, the various effects of odors from the males of different strains in mice (Lott and Hopwood, 1972; Parkes and Bruce, 1961) reveal recognition of different morphs. In particular, the Bruce effect refers to the abortion, or the failure of the blastocyst to implant in the uterine wall in the first few days following mating, which occurs if the female is exposed to a male of another strain or to his urine or odor. Besides house mice, the effect is known or suspected in deer mice (Bronson and Eleftheriou, 1963), collared lemmings (Mallory and Brooks, 1980), and four species of voles (Clarke et al., 1970; Clulow and Clarke, 1968; Clulow and Langford, 1971; Stehn and Richmond 1975). There is evidence that the effect occurs in natural populations of meadow voles (Mallory and Clulow, 1977), and its possible function is discussed in Chapter 4, Reproduction. The role of the *H-2* genetic locus in mate preference among mouse strains is discussed in Chapter 4, Genetic Aspects.

Fish

At the peak of the scale of organic grandeur (Figure 1.10) fish demonstrate great versatility in the means by which they achieve species
recognition. Arctic charr show a preference for conspecific odors over no
odor (Hoglund and Astrand, 1973) and an avoidance of heterospecific
odors (Hoglund et al., 1975). Red shiners and European eels are attracted
to water in which conspecifics have lived (Asbury et al., 1981; Pesaro et
al.; 1981). The Siamese fishing fish discriminates water conditioned by
ripe females of species in its family from that of nonfamily species (guppy
and goldfish) (Ingersoll and Lee, 1980). Gouramis and damselfishes can

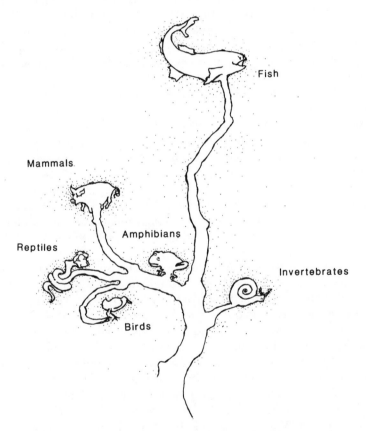

Figure 1.10.   Ichthyophilic evolutionary tree (*Scala unnaturae*).

distinguish between conspecifics and heterospecifics by vision alone (Picciolo, 1964; Thresher, 1976; Katzir, 1981a, 1981b). Sympatric species of Texan shiners and Caribbean damselfish discriminate by means of sounds (Delco, 1960; Myrberg and Spires, 1972; Spanier, 1979) while South American gymnotoids and African mormyrids use electrical signaling (Hopkins, 1972, 1974a, 1974b; Hopkins and Bass, 1981; Kramer et al., 1981; Serrier 1979). Blennies discriminate species by using both vision and pheromones (Todd, 1971). European minnows react to species-specific odors and can be trained to distinguish various fish and amphibian species through conditioning (Goz, 1941; Wrede 1932).

Species recognition often involves behavioral differences. Among four Guyanese species of the guppy family (Poeciliidae), species-typical displays and unlearned female selective responsiveness enable species recognition (Liley, 1966). In the genus *Poeciliopsis*, there are all-female unisexual forms as well as the usual bisexual forms (i.e., forms with females and males) (McKay, 1971). The unisexual females require sperm for reproduction although the sperm is excluded from the genome of the daughters. As expected, males prefer bisexual females over the parasitic unisexual ones. In other bisexual–unisexual species in the family, males are indiscriminate but the nearest neighbors of females tend to be females of the same form (Balsano et al., 1981). Also in the guppy family, males of gambusiine species generally discriminate well between conspecific and heterospecific females (Hubbs and Delco, 1960, 1962). Similar behavioral differences, especially during the early stages of courtship, mediate species recognition and isolation in the Nicaraguan cichlid pair, *Cichlasoma citrinellum* and *C. zaliosum* (Baylis, 1976). The African mouth-brooder cichlid, *Sarotherodon mossambica*, recognizes and prefers conspecifics in tests involving three other test species (Russock and Schein, 1978).

Species-typical groups are found among many schooling species such as young cichlids (Noble and Curtis, 1939). In a study in which stimulus dummies were presented to convict cichlid fry, Hay (1978) found that species-typical cues such as the dark bars seen in parents were important in eliciting responses. Young midas cichlids prefer urine solutions from conspecific adults, but not the mucus of the mother or urine from the predator *Cichlasoma nicaraguense*, over water (Barnett, 1981). A number of species, such as the characid *Pristella riddlei*, preferentially approach schools of their own species over heterospecific schools (Keenleyside, 1955). Other species, such as the three-spined stickleback, do not show this preference. Many species of the minnow order recognize injured conspecifics via an alarm substance. Such substances, known in a diversity of animal groups, are discussed in Chapter 2, Chemosensation.

Although sunfishes are known to hybridize extensively, species recognition is not absent. For instance, in a study of four species in which 12 ponds were stocked with each of the possible crosses (and hence conspecifics were not available as possible mates), only three produced large F_1 populations (Childers, 1967). Males of three species distinguish conspecific and heterospecific females (Keenleyside, 1967), revealing a choosiness to be expected by animals who make heavy parental investments. Female sunfish also recognize specific differences among potential mates (Steele and Keenleyside, 1971). Species-typical calls, discovered in several species (Gerald, 1971; Ballantyne and Colgan, 1978a, 1978b, 1978c) as well as quantitative behavioral differences (Clarke and Colgan, in preparation) (Figure 1.11), contribute to species recognition in this group. Musicians may wince at the results of experiments in which recorded calls were played back to test animals: "While there was a strong positive response to both *L. megalotis* and *L. humilis* calls, the fish completely ignored exerpts from the Finale of Grofe's Grand Canyon Suite indicating that they are not attracted by all sound disturbances in their vicinity" (Gerald, 1970). Field-caught yearling rockbass prefer conspecifics to similarly sized pumpkinseed sunfish (Brown, personal communication).

Species recognition of different life stages has been reported in some cichlids. Although egg discrimination is at best poor, discrimination of young is quite good (Baerends and Baerends-VanRoon, 1950). Jewel fish show no discrimination between the eggs of different cichlid species (Noble and Curtis, 1939). Experienced, but not inexperienced, parents distinguish their own young from those of other species. Underlying this distinction, two mechanisms lead to a vicious circle of behavior: the parents are visually attracted to attack the strange young, but as soon as these are taken into the mouth, tactile stimulation leads to their ejection. Both adults and young which are newly free swimming prefer the water from conspecifics over heterospecifics (Kuhme, 1963). In tests involving various cichlids, Myrberg (1964, 1975) found some ability for egg discrimination, and acute distinctions among young.

The role of imprinting as a mechanism underlying species recognition in many vertebrates is considered in Chapter 3.

SEX AND MATES

Some happy species are synchronous hermaphrodites (i.e., have both male and female reproductive systems active during the same breeding period). For the rest of us, recognition of the sex of conspecifics and of potential

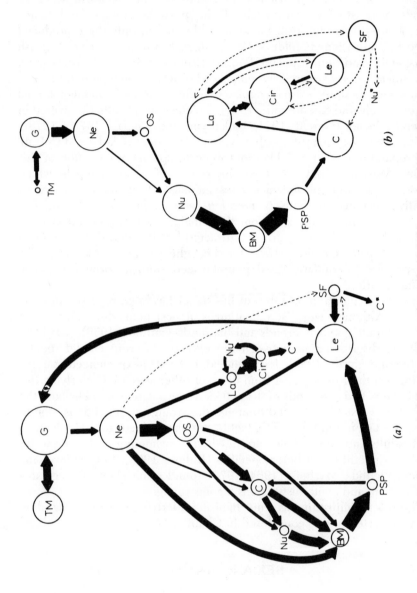

Figure 1.11. Male courtship is quantitatively different in (*a*) pumpkinseed and (*b*) bluegill sunfish (from Ballantyne and Colgan, 1978a, copyright Masson S. A. Paris). The areas of the circles and the thicknesses of the arrows indicate the frequencies of the acts and transitions, respectively.

mates among the opposite sex is of fundamental importance to biological fitness. It would make an interesting comparative study to investigate how much neural organization is required, and with which sensory modality, in order to improve on an indiscriminant "mount first and see what happens" strategy. In many species, morphological and behavioral cues combine to enable sex recognition. Mating systems vary across species from promiscuity through polygamy to monogamy. Polygamy has two aspects, polygyny (in which a males mates with multiple females) and polyandry (in which a female mates with multiple males). For many species, sexual dimorphism facilitates sex recognition, whether the dimorphism has evolved for this, or other, functions. For animals which form pair bonds, recognition of the mate in a crowd is also vital.

Pseudomale and pseudofemale behavior, the performance of courtship acts which are part of the repertoire of the opposite sex, is known in a variety of animals including insects, birds, mammals, and fish. Such behavior does not imply a lack of sex recognition, but rather reflects either behavioral "errors" due to high arousal or an alternate reproductive strategy. Morris (1955) has presented an ethological analysis of such behavior in terms of conflicting behavioral tendencies. The adaptive function of pseudofemale behavior, together with the question of behavioral optimality and "errors," is considered in Chapter 4.

The existence of sexual selection in which individuals of one sex choose among those of the other for their mates implies discrimination of potential mate quality. Mate choice has become the focus of much research since it represents an intersection of behavioral and ecological interests (see, e.g., Bateson, 1982; Janetos, 1980). For instance, monogamous feral pigeons prefer mates with greater reproductive experience, although pigeons over 7 years old are discriminated against (Burley and Moran, 1979). Sexual selection and the related topic of assortative mating are discussed in Chapter 4, Reproduction.

A central problem is the analysis of the recognition abilities operative in the process of pair formation. In his *Kumpan* analysis of such formation in birds, Lorenz (1970) distinguished three types, labeled after the three groups in which they were found in "purest form:" lizard-, labyrinth fish-, and cichlid fish-types. In the lizard-type, females flee in the face of male displays and are pursued and "raped;" in the labyrinth-type, displays are made, and reacted to, by both sexes, and the male dominates the female; in the cichlid-type, displays are mutual and there is no dominance relation between the pair members. This trichotomy has been criticized by researchers studying cichlids (Baerends and Baerends-VanRoon, 1950) and birds (ravens: Gwinner, 1964; European robins: Lack, 1939; passerines generally: Tinbergen, 1939) and Lorenz himself points out its shortcomings. Nevertheless, it is a worthwhile task for those undeterred by the problems of analogizing behavioral processes (see Lorenz, 1974, versus Cohen, 1975) to seek generalizations for the process of pair formation in terms of the recognition behavior involved, especially in the context of evolutionarily stable strategies (see Chapter 4). A widely found pattern in sex recognition by territorial species is the change from initial aggression toward both sexes on the part of the defender, generally the male, to subsequent recognition and courtship of females (e.g., snow buntings and passerines generally: Tinbergen 1939; sunfish: Ballantyne and Colgan, 1978a). Stimulus dummies are useful to detect the recognition features underlying this pattern. The detection task is complex because each sex may use different features and weight them differently, as is clear in the studies reviewed below.

The Coolidge effect refers, in promiscuous species, to the reinstatement of copulatory behavior in a previously satiated male by presenting a new mate. The label immortalizes an observation made by an American president while touring a barnyard and first appeared in the literature in Wilson et al. (1963). Ironically, subsequent research has involved mammals although this limitation seems unnecessary (as discussed in Chapter 4, Reproduction). The proximate mechanisms involve dishabituation in the male and differential behavior by mated and unmated females, the latter enhancing performance more than the former. To be more comprehensive, experiments should also allow for any possible similar effect in females, but virtually no research has been done in pursuit of this possibility, perhaps reflecting a sexist scientific establishment. Research must distinguish between animals seeking copulations and animals seeking a variety of mates. Dewsbury (1981) has reviewed the literature, analyzing the different senses in which the effect has been invoked and the variety of experimental paradigms: the effect itself, changes of female prior to satiety, changes of environment and females between tests, and choice situations with more than one female present. The outcomes of these paradigms depends on many factors and varies across species and test conditions. Overall, although novelty has important effects on mating, the Coolidge effect is not a simple, clear-cut phenomenon.

Invertebrates

Sex and mate recognition have been investigated in a number of noninsect invertebrate species. Octopuses can discriminate both the sex and the state of sexual arousal of other individuals (M. J. Wells, 1978) (Figure 1.12). The amphipod *Gammarus duebenii* courts only mature premolt

Figure 1.12. Sex recognition in octopus may be facilitated by the male displaying the large suckers on the second and third pairs of arms (from M. J. Wells, 1978).

females (Hartnoll and Smith, 1980). Although the cues from the female are unknown, a contact pheromone seems likely. Similarly, males of the isopod genus *Asellus* can recognize the reproductive stage of potential mates (Manning, 1975; Thompson and Manning, 1981). Pair-bonding desert wood lice exhibit individual recognition of their mates, probably through chemical cues (Linsenmair and Linsenmair, 1971). Seibt and Wickler (1972) showed this also to be the case with the monogamous Indopacific shrimp *Hymenocera picta*, and Johnson (1977) has reported such recognition for a Hawaiian shrimp. The fiddler crabs *Uca pugnax* and *U. pugilator* discriminate conspecific males and females readily (Aspey, 1971). Males of the former species display agonistically to heterospecific stimuli while those of the latter court heterospecific female stimuli and respond aggressively to male stimuli about two-thirds of the time. In blue crabs sex recognition is aided by pheromones (Gleeson, 1980). Among fiddler crabs (Crane, 1975) and spiders (Crane, 1949; Robinson and Robinson, 1980) elaborate diplays aid sex recognition.

Among nematodes, several cases of sex attraction mediated by chemical cues and facilitating reproduction have been reported. In this group of animals it is particularly important to distinguish sex attraction from migration by both sexes to an optimal habitat. In two species of root nematodes, male orient to females (Green, 1966) while in the trichina worm (of trichinosis fame) both sexes are attracted to each other (Bonner and Etges, 1967). Similarly, both sexes emit chemical attractants in *Panagrolaimus rigidus* and, once contact is made, tactile and probably chemical cues from the female enable species recognition by the male (Greet, 1964). A water-soluble attractant is secreted by receptive females of *Pelodera teres* which activates and attracts adult males (Jones, 1967).

Turning to the insects, sex recognition among dragonflies is chiefly visual and is assisted by precopulatory courtship displays (Corbet, 1980). In the checkered butterfly sexual dimorphism in the ultraviolet reflectance of the wings underlies distinction of the sexes (Rutowski, 1981). Pheromones are important for orienting males and females in many species of moths and butterflies (e.g., Conner et al., 1980) and in at least some ants (Buschinger and Alloway, 1979; Holldobler and Wust, 1973; Holldobler and Haskins, 1977; Haskins, 1978). Odor cues are also important in the mating reaction of male *Habrobracon* wasps (Grosch, 1948) and harvester ants (Holldobler, 1976b). Among bioluminescent insects, the flash pattern often includes sexual cues (Lloyd, 1966, 1971, 1980). Stridulations by both males and females enable sex recognition among water bugs of the genus *Cenocorixa* (Jansson, 1973). Water striders use surface waves for sexual recognition (Wilcox, 1972, 1979). In cockroaches, pheromones from females attract males from a distance while at closer range movements of the female and antennal sparring permit sexual recognition (Roth and Willis, 1952; Tobin, 1981). Besides calls, crickets use odor cues (Otte and Cade, 1976) and contact chemoreception (Rence and Loher, 1977) to distinguish sex.

Sex recognition and mate preferences have been widely reported in fruit flies (reviews by Parsons, 1973; Spieth, 1974). In *Drosophila melanogaster*, sex recognition by the male requires touching and/or orientation to an individual (Shorey and Bartell, 1970). In the genus *Zaprionus* sex-typical songs aid sex recognition (Bennet-Clark et al., 1980) (Figure 1.13). In *D. mojavensis*, females from the mainland population discriminate against males of outlying populations of the same species. This is probably due to the evolution of sexual isolation from the sibling species, *D. arizonensis* (Zouros and d'Entremont, 1980; discussed in Chapter 4, Species Recognition and Hybridization). Discrimination of sex, like that of species and strain, is complex in *Drosophila*, with different modalities functioning for different types of recognition in different species (Averhoff et al., 1979). These researchers argue that the antennal arista is an olfactory receptor, not an auditory one as previously thought. The intensity with which the analysis of the relevent cues in *Drosophila* courtship is pursued may come as a surprise to the nonspecialist, but the letter by Bennet-Clark et al. (1976) and the ensuing reply by Averhoff and

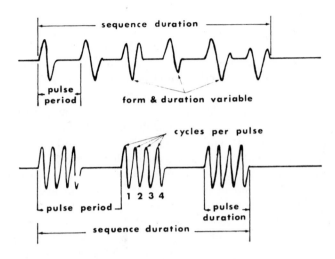

Figure 1.13. Measures which can be taken from recordings of fruitfly songs to quantify these sex-typical signals (from Bennet-Clark et al., 1980).

Richardson (1976) bear witness to the heat and passion with which fruit fly orgies are scrutinized by the initiated. The sociologists of science would love it! The rare male effect, in which the mating success of males of a given strain depends on the frequency of their strain in the population, is discussed in Chapter 4, Reproduction.

Amphibians and Reptiles

In the North American wood frog, sex recognition is achieved by a male after embracing another individual. He continues to embrace females ripe with eggs but releases spent females and males who may emit warning croaks (Noble and Farris, 1929). Pacific tree frog females prefer males who initiate bouts of calling by a group of males (Whitney and Krebs, 1975). Territorial male bullfrogs visually recognize the sex of conspecifics introduced into their areas (personal observation). For their part, females exert sexual selection in many frog species by discriminating among male calls which provide cues on the caller's size, as discussed in Chapter 2, Audition.

Among reptiles, male snakes distinguish the skin odors of males and females (Noble, 1937). Similarly, blind and common snakes of three families follow the pheromone trails of conspecifics of the opposite sex further than those of the same sex (Gehlbach et al., 1971). Among lizards, sex recognition is chiefly behavioral, as for example in the *Sceloporus torquatus* group of species (Hunsaker, 1962). In a choice behavior study in which normal and altered film loops of a displaying male were shown to female anolis lizards, the test animals approached the normal image more as the altered image contained more changes (Jenssen, 1970). In the six-lined racerunner, chase and retreat behavior is likely important for sex recognition (Carpenter, 1960). Similarly, resident male side-blotched lizards discriminate nonresidents sexually by their behavior and color pattern (Ferguson, 1966). Unlike females, male ground skinks approach female odors, while both sexes avoid male odors (Duvall et al., 1980). In the western fence lizard, males perform more substrate licks and tongue flicks to male-labeled surfaces than female-labeled surfaces. Females do not exhibit this distinction. In the American chameleon, territorial males challenge all intruders and subsequent distinctive responses by the intruder permit sex recognition (Greenberg and Noble, 1944). The striking male dewlap appears to be a result of sexual selection. In two South American tortoises, conspecific males exchange reciprocal head movements while females are recognized by odors from the cloacal region (Auffenberg, 1965).

Birds

Among avian studies, the pioneering work of Whitman (1919) provides detailed descriptions of sex recognition in pigeons. This work shows that the behavior of the stimulus bird is highly important for recognition of both sex and sexual status. Similar results have been found for penguins (Roberts, 1940), lovebirds (Dilger, 1956), canvasback ducks (Hochbaum, 1959), and song sparrows (Nice, 1937). Female ring doves can detect the sexual state of males simply by watching them through a glass partition (Erickson and Lehrman, 1964). Females observing castrated males have significantly lighter median oviduct weights, and fewer of them ovulate, than those observing intact males. Much of the early literature on perching birds has been reviewed by Nice (1943).

Postural cues involving the feathers and other behaviors including song underlie sex recognition in many species (e.g., European robins: Lack, 1939). Gentoo penguins rely on behavioral cues for sex recognition (Roberts, 1940). In her classical work on song sparrows, Nice (1937) found that a trapped bird attracts the pair member of its own sex when placed in the territory of a neighboring pair. Sex recognition is achieved visually at close range by red-necked phalaropes (Tinbergen, 1935). In Jackson's whydah, males alighting in a neighbor's territory with the two conspicuous outer plumes raised are attacked, but are courted if the tail is folded (Van Someren, 1944). Sex recognition in shags is also based on postural cues (Snow, 1963). Sexual responses of domestic cocks vary with the form and posture of the stuffed hen presented, with the body and head the key releasing stimuli (Carbaugh et al., 1962). In terns, a territorial male recognizes the sex of an intruder through behavior including posturing and a pecking ceremony in which he presents a fish to a female who begs (Palmer, 1941). This fish ceremony is the prelude to nutritionally important feeding of the female by the male during incubation. In the laughing gull, a male initiates a "pairing charge" toward conspecifics to which males and females react differently (Noble and Wurm, 1943). Similarly, the progress of aggressive encounters in the glaucous-winged gull is influenced by sex recognition (Amlaner and Stout, 1978).

Discriminative responses to stuffed dummies indicate that behavior is not necessary for sex recognition in some species. Early in the breeding season before the migratory arrival of females, male red-winged blackbirds and northern yellow-throats discriminate the sexes of mounted conspecifics (Noble and Vogt, 1935). Territorial male savannah sparrows similarly discriminate between male and female dummies (Weatherhead and Robertson, 1980). Calls can also provide information on sexual identity. Within any particular dialect group of the Indian hill mynah, the call type indicates the sex of the caller (Bertram, 1970). Interspecifically, human chicken sexers respond with high accuracy to unknown Gestalt features of the young birds.

Recognition of the sex of young shortly after hatching by parental zebra finches has been reported by Burley (1981a). The mechanism is unknown but the suggested function is the manipulation of the sex ratio of the clutch toward the sex of the more attractive parent. The report suffers from several major inadequacies, some of which are discussed in Burley (1982).

Many species of birds also show acute mate recognition. In one of his classic studies, Heinroth (1911) reported a male swan who attacked his mate when her head was under water, but stopped as soon as her head appeared. Lorenz (1970) described the personal recognition of the sexual *Kumpan* in many species, and Roell (1978) has followed up the work on jackdaws. European robins recognize their mates at 10 m in bushes (Lack, 1939), pintails at 100 m (Hochbaum, 1959), and terns in the air (Marples and Marples, 1934; Palmer, 1941). Both canvasback ducks (Hochbaum, 1959) and marsh tits (Morley, 1942) recognize their mates (and familiar humans) individually. Mate recognition is also served by nest-relief ceremonies described for so many avian species. In geese, the triumph ceremony in which partners exchange greetings is important in maintaining the pair bond (Fischer, 1965). The ceremony, which consists of the two elements, rolling and cackling, permits mate recognition. Similar mutual displays are found in parrots (Serpell, 1981a; Figure 1.14). VanTets (1965) has presented a detailed comparative analysis of the derivation of mate recognition behavior from other responses among the members of the pelican order. Black-headed and herring gulls also exhibit excellent mate and colonial neighbor recognition (Kirkman, 1937; Tinbergen, 1953). There is also good mate recognition in Adelie penguins (Penney, 1968), western grebes (Nuechterlein, 1981a), sandpipers (Oring, personal communication), and pied flycatchers (Curio, 1959), and bullfinches immediately recognize their mates after a 6 month separation (Nicolai, 1956).

Different species variously employ vision and audition for mate recognition. Yellow head markers on females disrupt pair bonds during first breeding attempts of mourning dove pairs, but not the pair bonds of experienced birds (Goforth and Baskett, 1965). Other colors of markers, and markers on males, do not have any effect. Among four Arctic gull species, individual recognition of mates is achieved via body shape (N. G. Smith, 1966). In Bewick's swans (Bateson et al., 1980) and shags (Snow, 1963) mates are recognized via facial characters. In anis, a cuckoo subfamily, mates are recognized by individual appearance (Davis, 1942).

Figure 1.14. Exaggerated peering, a cooperative display of pair-bonded parrots (from Serpell, 1981a).

In other species, vocal signals permit mate recognition (Table 1.3; Figure 1.15). Turnstones discriminate the calls of mates and conspecific intruders while a female hawfinch responds selectively to the single call note of her mate. In nocturnally active manx shearwaters, females recognize the cries of their mates as they approach the burrow nests. An Indian hill mynah distinguishes a call from its mate from the same call produced by a neighbor. The calls of reproductively active male pheasants in Tadjikistan are very distinct to human observers and, apparently, to hens, who are always seen in the company of the same male (Kozlowa, 1947). A male budgerigar attacks a mate whose cere (a beak region) has been painted blue but desists as soon as she calls (Cinat-Tomson, 1926). Antiphonal singing, which functions to maintain pair bonds, is discussed in Chapter 2, Audition.

Mate discrimination and choice has been closely studied in members of the pigeon family, beginning with Whitman's (1919) work. In ring doves, previously paired males and females who were separated for up to 7 months remated when released into large outdoor cages in groups of three pairs (Morris and Erickson, 1971). Twelve of 15 females, offered a choice between previous mates and strange males, laid eggs near the former mate and otherwise behaved reproductively toward him. Such results are consistent with the hypothesis of individual recognition of mates. Feral pigeons choose mates by using several characters including plumage, age,

Table 1.3. Avian Studies on Mate Recognition via Calls

Taxon	Locality	Source
Penguins	Antarctica	Jouventin et al. (1979)
Shearwaters	England	Brooke (1978)
Petrels	Antarctica	Guillotin and Jouventin (1980)
Gannets	Scotland	White (1971)
Turnstones	Finland	Bergman (1946)
Terns	Eastern United States	Moseley (1979)
	England	Hutchison et al. (1968)
Gulls	England	Wooller (1978)
Peking robins	Asia	Thielcke and Thielcke (1970)
Mynahs	India	Bertram (1970)
Finches	Western United States	Samson (1978)
	Europe	Marler and Mundinger (1975); Mountfort (1957)
	Australia	Miller (1979b)

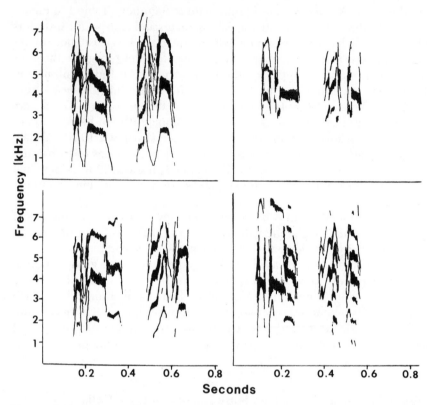

Figure 1.15. Sonograms (frequency–time plots) of vocalizations by four individual least terns (from Moseley, 1979). Variation in the first portion of the call enables mate recognition.

social status, and reproductive experience (Burley, 1981b). Characters vary in their importance in mate choice. Females are more selective than males and weight characters differently. Preferred individuals are more selective and use more characters in evaluating mates. These results are in accordance with sexual selection theory. This theory, and further aspects of mate selection, are discussed in Chapter 4, Reproduction.

Mammals

Mammalian sex recognition is generally straightforward due to dimorphisms of morphology and odor (Blaustein, 1981) together with behavioral cues. This is true even in those species, such as the spotted hyaena, in which there is genital mimicry of one sex by the other, which is linked with dominance behavior (see Gould, 1981). Mammals also demonstrate acute sensitivity to the sexual state of potential mates. (Mae West once quipped "Are you pleased t'see me or d'you have a gun in your pocket?") Many mammals, particularly ungulates, employ flehmen, a behavior involving sniffing and lip curling to facilitate olfaction, as discussed in Chapter 2, Chemosensation. Sexual swellings and lordosis by females and penile displays by males also aid in state recognition.

The odoriferous sexual world of rodents has been explored by a number of researchers. Gerbils distinguish between male and female conspecifics olfactorily (Dagg and Windsor, 1971) as do kangaroo rats at sand bathing sites (Randall, 1981). Guinea pigs can discriminate both the sex and the sexual state of other individuals (Beauchamp et al., 1979; Ruddy, 1980). When presented with unfamiliar anaesthetized conspecifics or their odors, both sexually experienced and inexperienced male hamsters preferred females over males, but did not distinguish between receptive and unreceptive females (Landauer et al., 1978). Subsequent work (Johnston, 1980) has shown that male hamsters do react differentially to females in different reproductive states. Sex recognition involves a combination of modalities in this species and is also influenced by recent heterosexual experience (Carmichael, 1980). In eastern chipmunks, each sex spends more time investigating the odors of the other sex than odors of the same sex (Keevin et al., 1981). The production of ultrasounds by male European wood mice reflects olfactory discrimination of the sexes and of the sexual state of females (Gyger and Schenk, 1980). Adult male rats (LeMagnen, 1952) and mice (Bowers and Alexander, 1967; Chanel and Vernet-Maury, 1963, Dixon and Mackintosh, 1975; Nyby et al., 1977) discriminate males and sexually receptive and unreceptive females by smell. Intact and gonadectomized rats, of either sex, learn equally well to discriminate between individuals of the opposite sex which differ in sexual state (Carr and Caul, 1962). As might be expected in a species showing the Coolidge effect, male rats distinguish between familiar and novel females by odor (Carr et al., 1980). Mice prefer the odor of unstressed over stressed males (Carr et al., 1980) and readily discriminate the sex of unfamiliar conspecifics (Poole and Morgan, 1975). In a comprehensive study comparing his own results with previously reported data, R. E. Brown (1977) has scaled the odor preferences of naive, experienced, and gonadectomized rats of each sex. While male mice are indiscriminant between females, females prefer males with the odor of their parents (Mainardi et al., 1965).

Normal, but not anosmic, rams discriminate estrous from nonestrous ewes (Lindsay, 1965). In the domestic cat, the sexual state of females is discriminated via chemical cues (Verberne and DeBoer, 1976). In choice experiments, estrous female beagles prefer males to females (Dunbar, 1977, 1978). Males spend more time visiting females or odorous materials, such as urine, from females, especially estrous females, than males. The lemur *L. fulvus* distinguishes males and females by scent (Harrington, 1977) and squirrel monkeys use urine cues (Candland et al., 1980). Male rhesus monkeys in an operant situation bar press to gain access to estrous females, but not if anosmic (Michael and Keverne, 1968). Like antiphonal bird pairs, monogamous siamang partners maintain their bond by duetting with long-range calls (Lamprecht, 1970). Male and female lar gibbons respond differently to playbacks of a male conspecific (Andelman, 1980). Besides vision and audition, odor is useful in human sexual recognition. In an experiment in which married test subjects wore shirts for 7 nights and were then tested for olfactory discrimination among them, about a third could identify their own odor, and a similar fraction the odor of their spouse (Hold and Schleidt, 1977; M. Schleidt, 1980). Correct identification was higher for women than men. About a third of the subjects could distinguish the odors sexually. Similar discrimination of T-shirt odors with respect to sex has been reported by Russell (1976). The role of individualization in human sexual relations is discussed by Campbell (1966).

Fish

Sex recognition has been studied in many fish species, including European minnows (Goz, 1941), gouramis (Picciolo, 1964), sunfish (Noble, 1934); Gerald, 1970, 1971; Ballantyne and Colgan, 1978a, 1978b, 1978c), Siamese fighting fish (Robertson and Sale, 1975; Robertson, 1979), and a number of cichlids (e.g., Noble and Curtis, 1939; Baerends and Baerends-VanRoon, 1950; Terami, 1977). Results on gobies (Tavolga, 1958; Todd, 1971), blennies (Todd, 1971), and shiners (Stout, 1963) reveal that in different species various combinations of vision, audition, and olfaction function for sex recognition. Distinction of the sexes in the cichlid *Astatotilapia strigigena* and the cardinal fish *Apogon notatus* results from sequences of exchanged stimuli and responses (Seitz, 1940; Usuki, 1977). In goldfish, discrimination of the sexes is mediated via a hormone-dependent pheromone from the kidneys (Yamazaki and Watanabe, 1979). The cave dwelling tooth-carp *Poecilia sphenops* can distinguish conspecifics sexually in the dark (Parzefall, 1973). Similarly, the California blind goby uses chemical cues for sexual recognition (MacGinitie, 1939). Males and females of two Texan shiner species produce distinct sounds (Delco, 1960). In the South American electric fish *Sternopygus macrurus* males selectively respond to artificial signals in the frequency range of females (Hopkins, 1972, 1974b). Reactions to stimulus dummies show that male rainbow trout recognize females by their proximity to the spawning substrate and their posture (Newcombe and Hartman, 1980).

Mate choice behavior has been investigated in several fish species. In Johnny darters, females choose to mate with males who defend a relatively large area around their nest (Grant, 1980). The mate choice behavior of female spotted sculpins has been modeled by computer simulation (L. Brown, 1981). An adequate model is one which assumes that females have short memories of males and mate with a male which is larger than the previous one encountered. Mate recognition is found among fish species which pair for extended periods of time, such as many cichlids (e.g., Noble and Curtis, 1939; Baerends and Baerends-VanRoon 1950) and some butterflyfish (Reese, 1975) whose "greeting ceremonies," analogous to the famous exhanges between greylag geese, maintain the pair bond. Individual recognition is important in the long-term association of male–female pairs in glandulocaudine fish (Nelson, 1964). The mate is individually recognized in the monogamous Red Sea reef fish *Amphiprion bicinctus*, which dwells among the tentacles of sea anemones (Fricke, 1973). Similarly, in groups of the damselfish *Dascyllus aruanus*, which consist of a large male and several smaller females with a linear, size-dependent rank order, members recognize each other (Fricke and Holzberg, 1974).

PARENTS, OFFSPRING, AND OTHER RELATIVES

Shakespeare's Falstaff, impersonating Henry IV, declares to the Prince "that thou art my son, I have partly thy mother's word, partly my own opinion, but chiefly a villainous trick of thine eye and a foolish hanging of thy nether lip, that doth warrant me." Recognition of kin, both direct offspring and other relatives contributing to an individual's "inclusive fitness" (Hamilton, 1964; see Chapter 4, Groups), is a valuable ability, as is recognition of parents. Many species that have been investigated reveal such ability. One might expect such recognition in reproductively active species where mixing of broods is relatively common, while location cues alone could serve when such mixing is rare. This expectation has inspired much of the avian research considered below. Again with emphasis on birds, Lorenz (1970) has stressed the personal recognition of parental, offspring, and sibling *Kumpan* in many species. The development of recognition of relatives is considered in Chapter 3.

Other

Among invertebrates, the discrimination between clone mates and group mates versus other anemones in the aggressive behavior of *Anthopleura krebsi* reflects an elementary form of ethological discrimination based on relatedness (Bigger, 1980). In the cockroach *Byrsotria fumigata*, in which a mother cares for her brood, first instar nymphs discriminate her from other mothers (Leichti and Bell, 1975). Among desert wood lice, family-specific chemical badges enable recognition of family members (Linsenmair, 1972).

Genetically, colonies of social insects are extended families and hence belong to the present case. The recognition behavior of social insects, along with many other aspects of their biology, has long been of interest (see, e.g., Fielde, 1904) and is thoroughly reviewed by Wilson (1971). Discrimination between colonies is often acute, as seen in, for instance, honeybees, leaf-cutting ants (Jutsum et al., 1979), and South American army ants. In the latter group, nest odors have been described as meaty, musky, fetid, and resembling potato blossoms (Schneirla, 1971). Some ant species of the genus *Leptothorax*, however, do not exhibit closed societies, and introduced workers are accepted (Provost, 1979). In an African weaver ant, the territorial pheromones are colony-typical, with alien odors eliciting aversive and aggressive behavior and recruitment of colony mates (Holldobler and Wilson, 1977). In an area impregnated with its odor, a colony has an initial advantage in aggressive encounters with other colonies. Similarly, the trail pheromones of the ant *Lasius neoniger* are colony-typical, with workers of a colony discriminating their own phero-mone from that of conspecifics (Traniello, 1980). Harvester ants lay trails using recruitment pheromones from the poison gland and orientation pheromones from Dufour's gland (Holldobler and Wilson, 1970). In primitively eusocial sweat bees, colony member recognition is achieved via odor cues (see Chapter 2), although noncolony members are sometimes admitted to the nest (Michener, 1966; Kukuk et al., 1977). Kin recognition in these and other bees has both genetic and experiential aspects, as discussed in Chapter 3, Learning, and Chapter 4, Groups.

A number of studies have examined recognition of life forms, such as brood and queens, in social insects, as well as age discrimination and discrimination of dead individuals. Workers of the ant species *Tapinoma erraticum* show nest discrimination in their transport of brood from their own and other nests (Meudec, 1978). Among army ants, callows (newly emerged workers) artificially removed from their cocoons are accepted in other colonies while older callows are attacked (Schneirla, 1941). Presumably the latter pick up the odors of their home colonies via ingestion and these are detected by members of other colonies. In fire ants, brood recognition is mediated via a pheromone spread over the preadult cuticle which is shed at eclosion (Walsh and Tschinkel, 1974). In the ant *Myrmica rubra*, workers recognize queens by both topographical and chemical cues (Brian, 1973) and discriminate between small worker-biased and large queen-potential larvae (Brian, 1974, 1975). Worker honeybees distinguish queens from workers by means of contact phero-mones (Simpson, 1979) and discriminate their own from other queens by using hive odors (Boch and Morse, 1974). Also in honeybees, the shaker dance involves one worker vibrating against another (Gahl, 1975). Shaking is performed nonrandomly with respect to the age of the recipient, suggesting age discrimination that probably depends on physio-logical variation in bees of different ages. In fire ants, dead individuals are recognized by contact chemical cues which are absent at death but develop over the first hour postmortem (Howard and Tschinkel, 1976). The cues release necrophoric behavior in which the corpse is carried away from the nest.

Tadpoles of the American toad and the Cascade frog associate pref-erentially with siblings (Blaustein and O'Hara, 1981; O'Hara and Blaustein, 1981; Waldman and Adler, 1979; Waldman, 1981; discussed in Chapter 4, Groups). Isolated toad tadpoles prefer full-siblings over paternal half-siblings, but not maternal half-siblings, a result suggesting a nonchro-mosomal maternal label for sibling recognition.

Birds

As expected, parent and offspring recognition is a common finding among colonially nesting birds in which mixing of families is likely. Nice (1943) has reviewed much of the early research on perching birds. Noddy and sooty terns were early studied by none other than J. B. Watson and Karl Lashley. Alteration of the visual appearance (hue, brightness, and mark-ings) of the eggs of nesting birds affected sooties but not noddies. Neither species recognized its own egg (Watson, 1908). Similarly, in subsequent work Lashley (1915) showed that sooties, unlike noddies, discriminate both the species of chicks and the number of chicks in the nest. As with eggs, however, neither species discriminates between conspecific chicks of similar ages during the first few days after hatching. These specific differences probably relate to the nesting patterns, noddies nesting in bushes and sooties in dense colonies on the ground. Nesting site also influences parental recognition in herring gulls (VonRautenfeld, 1978). Unlike ground-nesting pairs, cliff-nesting pairs adopt introduced chicks after the first week of life.

Although eggs are less mobile than hatched young, parental birds require sufficient recognition abilities to respond to them appropriately. The readiness of greylag geese to incubate an enormous variety of egg substitutes (Lorenz and Tinbergen, 1957) has provided ethology with its classic case of a supernormal stimulus. Hence, with respect to intraspecific brood parasitism, or dumping (reviewed by Yom-Tov, 1980), it is not surprising that there is no evidence that host parents discriminate dumped eggs from their own in snow geese (Cooke, 1978). Gulls, too, show great tolerance in incubating egg substitutes (review in Thorpe, 1963). Herring gulls allow alterations in color, spotting, and size, but not shape (Tinbergen, 1953). Although laughing gulls fail to discriminate their own from conspecific eggs which differ in color and pattern, they do distinguish them from artificial eggs which match them closely in form and color, suggesting that texture is an important cue (Noble and Lehrman, 1940). Black-headed gulls exhibit catholic incubation behavior, sitting on their own eggs when brightly colored, on large, white domestic duck eggs, as well as various egg substitutes including china and wooden eggs, wooden blocks, golf balls, and tin boxes (Kirkman, 1937). Atlantic murres recognize their own eggs and ignore those of neighbors (Johnson, 1941; Tschanz, 1979). Black-crowned night herons give no indications of recognition of eggs or young (Allen and Mangles, 1938/1939). Some birds lay eggs in communal nests. South American groove-billed ani females toss eggs out of the nest only before they initiate their own laying, suggesting a lack of recognition of their own eggs in a mixed clutch (Vehrencamp, 1977). In Masai ostriches, the major hen of a nest does recognize her own eggs by unknown means (Bertram, 1979). She pushes the eggs of other hens out of the nest, with the consequence that her eggs have double the survival advantage of the eggs of the other hens.

The calls of young in many avian species (e.g., chickens: Bermant, 1963; Impekhoven, 1973) are behavioral traits available for the evolutionary development of individual recognition of offspring. Razorbill parents recognize their chicks by both auditory and visual cues (Ingold, 1973). Along with differences in cue modalities is a diversity in developmental patterns, generally grouped as altricial (parents feeding young, which are poorly developed at hatching, in the nest until the young are nearly adult in size), semiprecocial (young remaining in the nest for only a few days during which they are fed), or precocial (young with well-developed locomotory abilities at hatching, leaving the nest quickly and free feeding). Whatever the developmental pattern and cue modalities, parental recognition, if it is to operate, must be accomplished by the time the young become mobile. Beginning first with some altricial cases, parental carrion crows show no evidence of egg recognition, and chick recognition develops only late in the breeding season (Yom-Tov, 1976). Shags accept strange chicks for the first month after hatching, but then become more discriminating (Snow, 1963). Bank swallows react aggressively to strange young which wander into or are placed in their burrows, and preferentially feed their own young (Hoogland and Sherman, 1976; Beecher et al., 1981a). Misplaced young are often recognized by their parents who feed them and attempt to coax them to leave the strange burrow. Parents also recognize their offspring in flight. Recognition errors do occur, especially by males, but on less than 1% of the feeding bouts. Unlike colonial bank swallows, noncolonial rough-winged swallows do not appear to discriminate their own and unrelated offspring. In tree and barn swallows, recognition of eggs and young nestlings is absent and parent–chick recognition begins only near the time of fledging (Burtt, 1977; Grzybowski, 1979). Recognition of fledglings and parents seems to be lacking in the European robin (Lack 1939). In three hawks of the genus *Buteo*, experiments in which young were added to nests to test the ability of parents to feed extra mouths revealed no discrimination between own and added offspring (Schmutz et al., 1980). The same is true of other raptors (Martin and Ruos, 1976; see also Mueller, 1980).

Among semiprecocial species, colonial herring gull parents accept strange chicks when these are only a few days old but not thereafter, probably basing this discrimination on both appearance and calls (Tinbergen, 1953). More recently, nonexperimental observations revealed that 10 of 19 chicks of varying ages which transferred to new territories were adopted (Graves and Whiten, 1980). They remained initially near the nest which led to the inhibition of attack in adults. Detection of discrimination by parents thus requires more detailed data such as feeding latencies toward adopted and own chicks. Unlike ground-nesting gulls who distinguish their young in a few days, no recognition of young by parents is seen in cliff-nesting kittiwakes at least up to 4 weeks of age (Cullen, 1957).

Crested terns do not recognize their own eggs or newly hatched chicks, but do learn to recognize the chicks within 2 days following hatching (Davies and Carrick, 1962). In densely nesting royal terns, parents distinguish their own egg, if it becomes displaced into an adjacent nest, as well as their own chicks (Buckley and Buckley, 1972). The "fish call" enables recognition of parents and young in sandwich terns (Hutchison et al., 1968). Parental Caspian terns discriminate between their own and strange 2- to 3-day-old chicks (Shugart, 1977).

Parental gentoo penguins distinguish among young only if newly hatched chicks are replaced with chicks at least 2 weeks old (Roberts, 1940). Additionally, young do not seem to recognize their own parents. In the more discriminating Adelie penguin, parents reject foreign chicks increasingly over the period from 8 to 17 days posthatch (Penney, 1968; Thompson and Emlen, 1968). Chicks leave the nest at about 21 days, with both parents and offspring demonstrating good recognition. In oyster-catchers parents and young become selectively responsive to each other during the period of parental feeding (Norton-Griffiths, 1969). Evans (1980a) has reviewed family recognition in seabirds, and vocally mediated cases of parental recognition in precocial species are considered in Chapter 2, Audition. Overall, these avian studies, in which recognition is tested by means of nestling substitution, corroborate Heinroth's (1911) early conclusion that the behavior of a young bird is a critical factor for recognition by its parents. Young birds that are ambivalent in their behavior tend not to be accepted.

For their part, the young of many avian species learn to respond to their parents. Recognition between family members in several domestic species has been shown by Ramsay (1951). Domestic chicks discriminate between maternal feeding and distress calls without training (Bruckner, 1933; Snapp, 1969). The feeding call produces an end to locomotion and calling while the distress call enhances these activities. Chicks develop selective approach and feeding responses to individual maternal vocalizations and this selectivity helps maintain the family unit (Cowan and Evans, 1974; Evans and Mattson, 1972; Falt, 1981). Adult laughing gulls also have a repertoire of calls eliciting various reactions by chicks that recognize their parents by call and behave in a manner in which enables the parents to identify them as their own (Beer, 1969, 1970b, 1970c, 1979; Impekhoven 1976). By 4–5 days of age, ring-billed gull chicks recognize parents and brood mates as individuals (Evans, 1970a, 1980b). Black-billed gull young soon come to recognize the parental mew call (Evans, 1970b). Recognition of parental over strange adult calls has also been found in young of the Arctic and common terns (Busse and Busse, 1977; Stevenson et al., 1970). Parents and young recognize each other when the latter are 5 days old (Palmer, 1941). Parental recognition seems unlikely in wood ducks based on the small amount of variation between maternal calls (Miller and Gottlieb, 1976). In gannets there is weak recognition of the parents by young but this recognition ability is in any case not critical for survival (White, 1971). Juvenile Canada geese recognize their siblings at a few days of age (Radesater, 1976) and similar recognition abilities maintain the integrity of the family in snow geese (Prevett and MacInnes, 1980). Murre chicks discriminate both parents and helpers acoustically (Tschanz,

1968, 1979). Common eider ducklings appear capable of recognizing their mothers by the latters' calls and by 8 weeks of age form stable groups (Schmutz, personal communication, Munro and Bedard, 1977a). These observations suggest individual recognition. Young coots distinguish their parents by 3 weeks of age who themselves discriminate between their own and foreign young by at least 2 weeks of age (Alley and Boyd, 1950). As nestlings, blackbirds recognize their mother's food call, and as fledglings, their father's song (Messmer and Messmer, 1956; Thielcke-Poltz and Thielcke, 1960). In pinon jays, which form creches, parents and young come to recognize each other over the first 3 weeks of life through individually characteristic calls (McArthur, 1982). Chiffchaffs when fledged recognize their mothers (Gwinner, 1961). When perched 2m distant, parental horsefield bushlarks are distinguished from sparrows by their nestlings (Bourke, 1947). Nestlings of the galah, a cockatoo, recognize their parents' calls in the fifth week of life (Rowley, 1980). By about 40 days posthatch, a week before fledging, both parents and offspring recognize each other well. Songs possibly enable kin recognition in Bengalese finches (discussed in Chapter 3, Song Imprinting).

Mammals

Despite William James's (1890) famous description of the world of the newborn infant as a "blooming, buzzing confusion," mammalian young, like other young, soon begin to discriminate the components of their environment, including their parents, particularly their mothers, who also learn to recognize them. As in many mammals, mothers and infants of the New Guinea gliding phalanger recognize each other by odor cues (Schultze-Westrum, 1965). Maternal recognition in sheep and goats and in moose and elk have been reviewed by Hersher et al. (1963b) and Altmann (1963), respectively. Postpartum separation easily disrupts parental attachment, leading to rejection of young, in some mammalian groups such as ungulates. This process is discussed in Chapter 3, Offspring Imprinting. Reindeer cows and calves use their voices for individual recognition (Espmarck, 1971, 1975). Extensive research has investigated ewe–lamb recognition in sheep (Lindsay and Fletcher, 1968; Morgan et al., 1975, Poindron et al., 1980; Poindron and Carrick, 1976; Shillito Walser, 1980; Shillito Walser and Alexander, 1980; Alexander and Stevens, 1981; Shillito Walser et al., 1981; review by Poindron and LeNeindre, 1980). Dams recognize their lambs by vision and audition at a distance and by olfactory cues at close range. For their part, lambs identify their mothers by individual call characters. In cattle all these modalities contribute to the recognition processes between cow and calf (Schloeth, 1958). Especially interesting is the finding that in herds containing monozygotic twin cows, the preferred grooming partner is the twin (Wood, 1977). In horses, visual or olfactory cues enable recognition between mares and foals (LeBlanc and Bouissou, 1981; Wolski et al., 1980). While mares show evidence of distinguishing the calls of foals, the reverse is not the case.

Infant guinea pigs recognize classes of adults at a distance (e.g., male, lactating female, nonlactating female) but individuals only when in close contact (Berryman and Fullerton, 1976). Maternal behavior, especially retrieving, as well as predatory and sexual responses, are elicited in adult and juvenile golden hamsters of both sexes when offered pups, implying different recognition reactions (Rowell, 1961). In precocial spiny mice, females who have given birth either within 12 hours or 8 days earlier nurse unfamiliar, newly born pups as frequently as their own, but unfamiliar 8-day-old pups less frequently (Porter et al., 1980). Sibling recognition develops over the first week or so of life based on a modifiable attraction using odor cues (Porter et al., 1978; Porter and Wyrick, 1979). Familiar littermate siblings share food more than unfamiliar, unrelated mice (Porter et al., 1981a). However, experience is not always necessary for the recognition of kin. In white-footed mice individuals of both sexes discriminate related and unrelated strangers (Grau, 1982).

Maternal recognition, and subsequent suckling, is facilitated by nest and nipple odors in several rodent species (Geyer, 1981). Factors influencing maternal behavior, as reflected in the survival and weights of introduced pups, has been examined in rats by Denenberg et al. (1963). Survival and weights decreased as the prior period of lactation by the foster mother increased. Survival of pups was better if the pups were introduced with their placentae or if the mother received an estradiol injection. Results such as these indicate the proximate physiological mechanisms underlying maternal recognition in rats. A fecal pheromone from the mother also attracts young (Moltz and Lee, 1981). The pheromone facilitates fecal eating which promotes growth. Both field observations and laboratory tests reveal parental recognition in the females of Richardson's ground squirrel (Michener, 1973; Michener and Sheppard, 1972). In the field mothers engage in nasal and cohesive contacts with their own young but fight with other young. Similar behavior has been found in laboratory pairings of mothers and young, with the mothers treating male and female offspring differently. Identification involves the behavior of the animal, and juveniles are 6–7 weeks old before they can identify adults independent of location cues.

Northern elephant seal mothers recognize pups individually through their vocalizations (Petrinovich, 1974) while Alaskan fur seal mothers use odor (Bartholomew, 1959). Both sounds and smells mediate mutual mother–young recognition in southern fur seals and sea lions (Trillmich, 1981; Vaz-Ferreira and Achaval, 1979). Identification of pups by maternal harp seals on the shifting ice floes is not an easy task, and distinctions are achieved only at close range through vision, audition, and olfaction (Terhune et al., 1979). Individual recognition of young by mothers has been found in both the pallid bat (P. Brown, 1976) and a species of leaf-nosed bat (Porter, 1979). In a species of European bat, mothers and their young recognize each other by ultrasonic sounds and odors (Kolb, 1977).

Primate mothers and young take some time to come to recognize each other. In a study with samples of two and three individuals, mothers in two galago species required a few days before they could discriminate their own from alien young (Klopfer, 1970) (Figure 1.16). Similarly, pigtail macaque mothers take about a week to discriminate between their own and other infants as measured by the amount of pacing of their mother when separated from, but with a view of, the infant (Jensen, 1965). As is generally the case, the age at which discrimination is detected is partially a function of the response examined. In vervet monkeys, the scream calls of infants enable maternal recognition (Cheney and Seyfarth, 1980). Conversely, juvenile rhesus monkeys respond selectively to calls from their mothers (Hansen, 1976) and 2-week-old langur infants recognize their mothers at distances of several meters (Jay, 1963). Infant squirrel monkeys distinguish their mothers from other females chiefly by odor cues (Kaplan, 1978; Kaplan and Russell, 1974; Kaplan et al., 1977). By 3 months of age bonnet and pigtail macaques, especially females, prefer their mothers to strangers (Rosenblum and Alpert, 1977). However, as with the white-footed deer mice discussed above, kin recognition among primates does not require prior association. Young pigtail macaques prefer half-siblings over equally strange unrelated conspecifics in test choices (Wu et al., 1980).

Beyond distinguishing spouses, as discussed above under Sex and Mates, members of human families can identify each other by odors alone (Porter and Moore, 1982). Mothers and siblings recognize T-shirts worn by children and parents distinguish the odors of their children. Experiments using sensitive measures have shown early maternal recognition by infants. By 6 weeks of age, babies react differently to the odors of breast pads from their own mother versus a strange mother (Russell, 1976). Mothers distinguish the cries of their infants from those of others (Morsbach and Bunting, 1979) and babies only a few days old discriminate their mothers' voices from those of strange females as shown by conditioning of the sucking response (DeCasper and Fifer, 1980; Mehler et

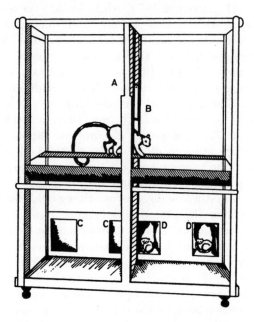

Figure 1.16. Apparatus for studying maternal recognition in galagos (from Klopfer, 1970). Available sensory cues can be varied by changing the fronts of the infant boxes (C and D) from wire mesh to opaque.

al., 1978; Mills and Melhuish, 1974). Subsequent development is considered in Chapter 3, Socialization. Equal opportunity demands equivalent experiments with paternal cues! In terms of appearance, newborn infants are much more frequently reported to resemble the father rather than the mother (Daly and Wilson, 1982). This difference can be interpreted in terms of confidence of paternity, as discussed in Chapter 4, Reproduction.

Fish

The seminal work by Noble and Curtis (1939) and Baerends and Baerends-VanRoon (1950) stands at the head of research on recognition of parents and offspring among cichlid fishes. (The possibility of imprinting of cichlid parents on young is discussed in Chapter 3.) Jewel fish visually recognize eggs, and accept conspecific fry of other broods if these are of a similar age to their own (Noble and Curtis, 1939). They can discriminate between water from their own brood and that from another conspecific brood of the same age (Kuhme, 1963). Parental behavior facilitates general orientation of the brood to adults. For instance free swimming young of the orange chromide respond to their parents when the latter flicker their dark pelvic fins (Cole and Ward, 1970). Young midas cichlids discriminate between plain water and that from their own or another mother, but not between mothers or between plain water and that from their father (Barnett, 1977a). Such observations do not imply individual recognition of parents, but rather recognition of femaleness. For their parts, parents discriminate their own broods from other conspecific broods and the broods of other cichlid species (McKaye and Barlow, 1976). Nevertheless, in brood exchange experiments, parents accept new broods provided they are reproductively motivated and the members of the new brood are not older than their own brood (Noakes and Barlow, 1973; Watanabe and Tamoto, 1981). The males of some species are more discriminating. A male desert pupfish can distinguish between eggs fertilized by him and those fertilized by other males (Loiselle, personal communication).

In certain mouth-brooding African cichlids, the male has spots on the anal fin, resembling eggs, which facilitate mating (see Wickler, 1968) (Figure 1.17). During spawning, the female is attracted to these and, while

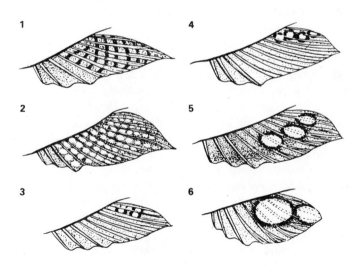

Figure 1.17.   Evolutionary series of egg dummies on the anal fins of various African cichlid species (from Wickler, 1968).

attempting to take them into the mouth, engulfs sperm which fertilize the eggs. Axelrod and Burgess (1976) has put forth the alternative suggestion that the spots function in species recognition but provide no experimental evidence for this.

RIVALS

While the fabled Don Quixote has entertained generations by tilting at windmills, real animals must be more discriminating in recognizing rivals. In aggressive situations, recognition behavior is important at two stages: the recognition of an animal as a rival and, as the encounter draws to a conclusion, the recognition of a winner and loser. The class "rival" may encompass several species, as in the case of interspecifically aggressive animals (reviewed by Murray, 1981), or only a subset of conspecifics, such as similarly sized individuals of the same sex. Rival recognition will thus generally involve species and sex recognition while recognition of a victor will depend on finer cues involving size, strength, and, very importantly, aggressive state. Winston and Jacobson (1978) have noted that recognition can be based on physiognomic and/or behavioral characters, and they restrict "individual recognition" for recognition using only the former type of character. As will be seen in the summary of the literature which follows, such as individual recognition of territorial neighbors via song in birds, this restriction runs counter to common usage. Indeed, it is difficult to classify such characters as postures or pheromone releases as physiognomic or behavioral. Barnard and Burk (1979; discussed in Chapter 4, Aggression) have pointed out that any attempt to distinguish between individual recognition and discrimination using simpler cues in the assessment of the probable outcomes of agonistic encounters is fallacious.

Recognition of aggressive state has several aspects. The signals may involve specialized morphological characters such as the enlarged chelipods waved by fiddler crabs (Crane, 1975). The "eye-spots" of the firemouth cichlid intimidate adversaries (Radesater and Ferno, 1979). Recognition often emerges from a complex interplay of acts between the antagonists, as in Siamese fighting fish (M. J. A. Simpson, 1968). Aggressive interactions between spiders that build funnel-webs proceed through several stages (Riechert, 1978). Assessment of the relative weights of the opponents is achieved by movements on the web, and determines later behavior which can be viewed as alternate aggressive strategies (discussed in Chapter 4, Evolutionarily Stable Strategy Approach). In many species there is a prior residency effect: animals are more likely to win an encounter if they have previously spent time in the area. The effect is probably mediated via behavioral confidence by the resident. Between rival male grasshoppers, chirp rate patterning and dominance are associated (A. J. Young, 1971). Aggressive displays between similarly sized red deer involve roaring contests and parallel walks (Clutton-Brock and Albon, 1979). Conversely, submission signaling in mule deer decreases the likelihood of continued aggression from the victor (Koutnik, 1980). In the Panamanian poeciliid fish *Neoheterandria tridentiger*, aggression is inhibited by a black midlateral spot, which probably evolved as a species recognition mark and is seen on juveniles, losers of fights, and mature males attempting copulation (McPhail, 1978). Such results on submission signaling support Darwin's (1872) Principle of Antithesis: "Certain states of the mind lead . . . to certain habitual movements which were primarily, or may still be, of service; and we shall find that when a directly opposite state of mind is induced, there is a strong and involuntary tendency to the performance of movements of a directly opposite nature, though these have never been of any service" (Figure 1.18).

Aggressive state can be assessed experimentally by presenting fixed stimulus dummies to test animals and monitoring the elicited responses. For instance, the aggressive state of male pumpkinseed sunfish varies greatly over the typical ten days of the nesting cycle (Colgan and Gross, 1977) (Figure 1.19). Dummies with variable characters can be used to discover to what features of a rival an animal responds. In glaucous-winged gulls, dummies with relatively higher head-neck levels are attacked before dummies with lower levels (Galusha and Stout, 1977). The analysis of the recognition of aggressive state in terms of evolutionarily stable strategies (e.g., Maynard Smith, 1979) is considered in Chapter 4, Aggression.

The following review discusses territoriality and dominance hierarchies separately, but it should be kept in mind that both are social ranking structures and that intermediate cases are known (e.g., cockroaches: Ewing 1972; black lizards: Evans, 1951; starlings: Davis 1959).

Territoriality

The establishment and maintenance of a territory, by which is meant dominance over rivals in a particular area, requires the recognition of intruders, generally conspecifics of the same sex. The discrimination of neighboring and strange conspecifics was first described by Fisher (1954) as the dear enemy effect in his examination of the evolution of avian sociality.

Figure 1.18. The contrasting (*a*) aggressive and (*b*) submissive postures of a dog support the Principle of Antithesis (from Darwin, 1872).

> [T]*he effect of the holding of territory by common passerines is to create "neighbourhoods" of individuals which are masters of their own definite and limited property, but which are bound firmly, and socially, to their next door neighbours by what in human terms would be described as a dear enemy or rival friend situation, but which in bird terms should more safely be described as mutual stimulation.*

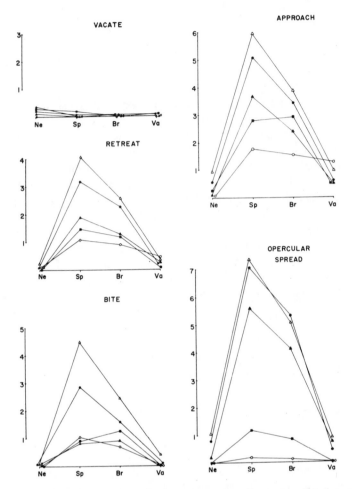

Figure 1.19. Change in the aggressive state of male pumpkinseed sunfish over the nesting cycle (from Colgan and Gross, 1977). Numbers of bites elicited by various stimulus dummies (see Figure 1.1) during the nesting (Ne, 2 days), spawning (Sp, 3 days), brooding (Br, 4 days), and vacating (Va, 1 day) periods.

Such discrimination has now been reported in a variety of species, as described below.

Satellite males are found in some territorial, and hierarchical, social systems (see review in Bateson, 1982). Such males do not hold territories themselves, but their presence is tolerated by territory owners. Satellite males may or may not sneak fertilizations from owners, as discussed in

Chapter 4, Reproduction. The existence of satellites indicates that territory owners make categorical distinctions among fellow owners, satellites,
and strangers.

Other

Among social insects, territorial African weaver ants use colony-typical
pheromones to mark their territories, resulting in aversive and aggressive
behavior from ants belonging to other colonies (Holldobler and Wilson,
1977). Such ants also recruit nest mates to the site. In encounters between
colonies, impregnation of the area with the pheromone of one colony
provides that colony with an initial advantage over its rival. Other ants
(e.g., *Lasius neoniger*: Traniello, 1980; *Myrmica rubra*: Cammaerts et al.,
1977), as well as anthophorid bees of the genus *Centris*, also chemically
mark territories (Raw, 1975).

Among amphibia, red-backed salamanders tap the substrate to facilitate
olfaction which mediates intraspecific communication. Territorial salamanders tap more in response to the odor of a conspecific to which they
have been repeatedly exposed than to that of a novel animal (McGavin,
1978). They also demonstrate dear enemy recognition by being less
aggressive toward familiar neighbors compared to strangers (Jaeger,
1981). Although a number of frog species are territorial (e.g., bullfrogs:
Emlen, 1976; Howard, 1978; Ryan, 1980b), there appears to be no
information on recognition of territorial neighbors. The same applies for
reptiles.

Birds

As shown by decreased responsiveness to the calls of neighbors compared
to those of strangers, neighbor recognition is mediated via song in many
territorial birds (Table 1.4; review by Falls, 1978). Territorial birds also
discriminate among dialects (whose acquisition is discussed in Chapter 3,
Song Imprinting). For example, territorial male cardinals respond more
intensely to local than strange dialect songs as measured by approaches to
the playing speaker and by singing rates (Lemon, 1967). Neighboring
black-crested titmice tend to sing the same songs and to reply to tape
recorded songs by repeating the song pattern (Lemon, 1968a). Similar
matching occurs in cardinals and pyrrhuloxias (Lemon, 1968b; Lemon and
Herzog, 1969). The role of antiphonal singing in territorial recognition is
discussed in Chapter 2, Audition.

Table 1.4. Avian Studies on Neighbor Recognition via Calls

Taxon	Locality	Source
Grouse	Western Canada	Falls and McNicholl (1979)
Magpies	Australia	Falls and Brooks (1965)
Tits	England	Krebs (1971)
Wrens	Western United States	Anderson and Anderson (1957)
	South America	Wiley and Wiley (1977)
Warblers	Eastern Canada	Wunderle (1978)
Ovenbirds	Eastern Canada	Weeden and Falls (1959)
Meadowlarks	Eastern Canada	Falls and D'Agincourt (1981)
Buntings	Eastern United States	Emlen (1971)
Sparrows	North America	Baker et al. (1981b); Brooks and Falls (1975a); Falls and Brooks (1965, 1975); Kroodsma (1976); Searcy et al. (1981b)

Visual presentations of neighbors is far less experimentally tractable than playbacks of their songs, but it is known that recognition of territorial birds involves vision in many cases (e.g., marsh tits: Morley, 1942). Male red-winged blackbirds which are muted or tranquilized with reserpine or whose epaulets are dyed black are less successful in defending their territories (Peek, 1972a, 1972b; D. G. Smith, 1972, 1976, 1979). The number of vocal and visual advertising displays of the test birds decreased under such treatment, territories were lost, and rates of trespassing increased. Interestingly, birds with blackened epaulets could still attract and mate with females. In anis, territorial intruders are recognized first by behavior and then by appearance (Davis, 1942). Herring gulls are selectively aggressive toward conspecifics in reproductive condition and, like black-headed gulls, also discriminate territorial neighbors from strangers (Tinbergen, 1953).

"Lek" is a Scandanavian term referring to clusters of males defending small, contiguous territories solely for the purpose of attracting and fertilizing females. The ruff is exemplary for the lek system (VanRhijn, 1973). In a display area of about 15 m², typically seven males with great plumage diversity occupy positions, which are very constant with respect to each other, for about 40 days. Individual recognition of neighbors, with whom aggressive interactions occur, seems certain. Such recognition probably also occurs in many lekking species (review by Wilson, 1975): other birds (Lill, 1974a, 1974b; Robel and Ballard, 1974; Wiley, 1974), insects (Alcock, 1981; Alexander, 1975; Campanella and Wolf, 1974; Holldobler, 1976b; Kimsey, 1980), amphibians (Emlen, 1976; Wells, 1977), mammals (Bradbury 1977, Leuthold 1966), and fish (Loiselle and Barlow, 1978).

Mammals

In many mammalian species, territorial recognition is mediated via odor cues deposited by the defending individual (e.g., rabbits: Mykytowycz, 1968; viverrids and felids: Verberne and Leyhausen, 1976; canids: Barrette and Messier, 1980; Bekoff, 1979; Graf and Meyer-Holzapfel, 1974; Heimburger, 1959; Lamprecht, 1979; Peters and Mech, 1975; review by Johnson, 1973). Wolves use howling as a short-term mechanism, and scent marking as a long-term mechanism for territory maintenance (Harrington and Mech, 1979). The dear enemy effect is pronounced in wildebeest in which neighboring males engage in ritualized interactions such as the grooming step (Estes, 1969). Both the territory and other group members are marked in the New Guinea gliding phalanger (Schultze-Westrum, 1965).

Territoriality is a dominant feature of rodent social systems. Flank marking of territories is a frequent activity in hamsters (Johnston, 1975). Similarly, scent marking underlies territoriality in gerbils (Thiessen et al., 1970; review by Thiessen and Yahr 1977). Gerbils discriminate individuals based on olfaction (Dagg and Windsor, 1971; Halpin 1976) and overmark alien odors, especially from the same sex (Biben, 1980; Kumari and Prakash, 1981). the role of this recognition ability and marking behavior has been demonstrated in the territorial family system which exists under natural conditions (Agren, 1976). Intruders into territories are attacked by the resident and, after several attacks, seldom mark (Yahr, 1977). The important result seems to be the defense of food resources. Adult Columbian ground squirrels react differentially to the odors of familiar and unfamiliar males (Harris and Murie, 1982). In mice, territorial recognition depends on visual recognition of landmarks as well as olfactory cues (Mackintosh, 1973; Harrington, 1976c). Healey's (1967) study on aggression and its impact on population regulation in deer mice reported evidence for neighbor recognition. Field caught males from the same or adjacent sites were observed during ten minute arena encounters with each other and with strange males from a laboratory stock. Neighbors made an average of 2.45 aggressive responses during the encounters while strangers made 9.22. Observations on encounters between distant field males and between laboratory males would have been useful as controls for strain differences in aggressiveness. Vestal and Hellack (1978) did not find such recognition in a different subspecies of deer mice, but wood mice neighbors interacted with less aggression and more investigation than strangers when tested in similar arena trials.

Fish
Among coral reef fish, territorial adult threespot damselfish discriminate between neighboring and strange conspecifics, presented simultaneously in pairs of bottles in the territory (Thresher, 1979). This is evidenced by more vigorous attacks against the strangers of either a congener, the dusky damselfish, or a surgeonfish, the blue tang. The reduction in aggression toward conspecifics extends only to immediate neighbors or individuals immediately beyond them. Intruder location and color pattern cues are important in this discrimination, whereas size and behavior are less so.

Territorial fish habituate to features of a territorial neighbor in a highly specific fashion and can therefore respond on an individual basis. Territorial sticklebacks habituate to both the location and identity of presented intruders (Peeke and Veno, 1973). Nesting male bluegill sunfish react strongly to neighbors whose appearances have been altered, and then habituate to these alterations (Colgan et al., 1979). R. J. Miller (1979) reports a dear enemy effect in a Pacific damselfish, and territorial rockfish also discriminate between neighbors and conspecifics (Larson, 1980). Among territorial gobies there is evidence, based on the outcomes of staged encounters, for short-term individual recognition lasting at least 1 hour but less than 24 hours (Gandolfi et al., 1973).

Dominance Hierarchies

Dominance hierarchies are social status structures in which the relation of "is boss of" is established for all pairs of animals. The hierarchies are often quite linear: A bosses everyone else, B bosses everyone except A, and so forth. The peck orders of domestic chickens [described in Schjelderup-Ebbe's (1921, 1922) originating articles], the ant *Leptothorax allardyce* (Cole, 1981), guinea pigs (Coulon, 1975), squirrel monkeys (Clark and Dillon, 1974), and guppies (Gorlick, 1976) are of such a type. It has sometimes been claimed that individual recognition is necessary for the formation and maintenance of dominance hierarchies. Guhl (1953) stated that "the existence of a peck-order is evidence that birds recognize one another. Without recognition, pecking would be promiscuous and uni-directional pecking would not occur." Hamilton (1964) suggested that "animals capable of forming a social hierarchy presumably have some ability to recognize one another as individuals." Lorenz (1971) has asserted that "personal recognition of individual animals is a prerequisite for . . . the internal rank-order prevailing between group members." And recently, "any species capable of forming a dominance hierarchy is capable of individual recognition" (Gallup et al., 1980). But individual recognition is not essential for a dominance hierarchy as shown, for instance, by wasps of the genus *Vespula* (see Wilson, 1971). Animals may well respond to some relatively simple cue as the size of a weapon such as antlers (e.g., reindeer: Espmark, 1964) without any recognition of in-dividuals as such. Indeed the distinction between recognition of in-dividuals and the use of simpler cues is an arbitrary one (Barnard and Burk, 1979; discussed in Chapter 4, Aggression). On the terminological front, Hazlett (1969) has proposed "that only orders based on specific within-group experience be termed dominance hierarchies and that arrangements of relationships not proved to be based on such experience be termed simply 'aggressive orders.' " Finally, in some species (e.g., lions: Bertram, 1975; chimpanzees: Goodall, 1968) coalitions of males achieve dominance in a group. The operation of such coalitions implies recog-nition of the other members of the coalition. Given kin selection (dis-cussed in Chapter 4, Groups), it is not surprising that the members are often related (e.g., brothers) and hence kin recognition aids recognition of coalition members.

Other

Chemically mediated individual recognition is found in the dominance relations of stomatopods (Caldwell, 1979). Individual recognition based on behavioral cues underlies the dominance hierarchies of hermit crabs (Hazlett, 1969; Winston and Jacobson, 1978) and possibly those of the hairy crab as studied with successive removals and replacements of animals in established hierarchies (Lobb, 1972). In one species of hermit crab a white patch on the enlarged left chela correlates with body size and obscuring the patch with dark paint results in losses in agonistic en-counters (Dunham, 1978). Mixed sex groups of four or eight crayfish form dominance hierarchies (Lowe, 1956). Larger animals dominate and in-dividual recognition appears to operate. The dominance hierarchies of the ant *Leptothorax allardyce* cited above are unique in that diverse group. The dominance hierarchies of male cockroaches consist of three classes of individuals with no finer discrimination occurring (Ewing, 1972). Females distinguish between the odors of dominant and nondominant males (Breed et al., 1980). The grasshopper *Chorthippus brunneus* has an acoustically mediated male hierarchical system in which the dominant individuals are the ones who chirp last in a rivalry sequence (Young, 1971).

The stable dominance relations existing between resident black lizards suggest that individual recognition of neighbors is very probable (Evans, 1951). The population studied lives in an agricultural area, and this hierarchical social system has probably evolved from individual territoriality of an earlier period.

Birds

Beginning with Schjelderup-Ebbe's work, there have been many studies on the recognition process underlying avian dominance hierarchies in domestic fowl (review by Guhl and Fischer, 1969). Experiments with white leghorns in a discrimination pen indicate that birds of both sexes could respond according to individual differences and to previous interactions (Guhl, 1942, 1953). Plumage changes, such as dying, especially of the head and neck region, combine, along with behavior, in their overall effect on recognition (Guhl and Ortman, 1953). Hens of seven different breeds show differences in their dominance behavior and, at least under certain conditions, respond to the breed of a stranger and not to a stranger as an individual (Potter, 1949). Subsequent research in which hens of five breeds were observed in three successive contests produced a variety of results indicating that experienced hens use breed-typical cues in their reactions to unfamiliar hens of different breeds (Potter and Allee, 1953). Just as facial features are important in mate recognition in some species (see Sex and Mates, above), so in chickens these features, especially the comb, beak, and wattle, are used for individual recognition and maintenance of the dominance hierarchy (Candland, 1969). The relation of the number of aggressive interactions to time after flock formation is similar for control and dubbed (comb and wattles removed) flocks over the first year although there are more interactions in the latter (Siegel and Hurst, 1962). Comb size, an indicator of androgen (male hormone) output, is known to be a factor of major importance in the outcome of initial dominance encounters (Collias, 1943). Consonant with this result is the finding that dubbing leads to a low rank in the hierarchy (Guhl, 1953; Marks et al., 1960). Beyond visual and auditory cues, social recognition in fowl also requires physical contact involving ritualized behavior in which the dominant head-thrusts and the submissive bows (Maier, 1964). The free movement of birds in large flocks likely indicates that individual recognition fails to operate among such "lonely crowds," as is expected (Hughes et al., 1974).

Turning to other avian species, individual recognition among the male turkeys of a flock is mediated via gobbling calls (Schleidt, 1964). In Canada geese, although dominance in large flocks is dependent on postural and threat intensity cues, dominance rank orders based on individual recognition could exist (Raveling, 1970). Certainly recognition among family members occurs. Experimental flocks of white-throated sparrows form linear dominance hierarchies when numbering three to five, but triangles (A bosses B who bosses C who bosses A) in groups of six (Wessel and Leigh, 1941). Caged flocks of ring doves maintain dominance hierarchies and recognize each other by their behavior, with alterations of plumage color or contour having only minor effects (Bennett, 1939). Dominance in Harris sparrows is recognized by the amount of black feathering on the crowns and throats, as shown by manipulation experiments in which plumage was either dyed or bleached (Rohwer, 1977; discussed in Chapter 4, Aggression).

Mammals

Among mammals, the males of elephant seal colonies maintain hierarchies and recognize vocalization differences involving the pulse structure (LeBoeuf and Peterson, 1969; Sandegren, 1976; Shipley et al., 1981). Dominant males are also more active than subordinate ones. Individual recognition is also operative among the males of guinea pig colonies (Coulon, 1975), buffalo herds (McHugh, 1958), and in many primate groups (e.g., squirrel monkeys: Clark and Dillon, 1974; chimpanzees: Goodall, 1968). Among group living primates, sociosexual mounting behavior often indicates dominance. Status recognition among humans reflects the extreme perversity of the species: in classical Rome, a *puella candida* who did not have to work in the fields sported her pale pelage proudly whereas today tans are widely prized among indoor Caucasians. In black-tailed prairie dog families, individuals recognize each other, and a dominant male controls the group and prevents the intrusion of strangers (King, 1955). In genets, individual recognition and recognition of the physiological state of females are mediated olfactorily, and the amount of marking by males increases with social status (Roeder, 1978, 1980). Similarly, in the mongoose (Gorman, 1976) and gliding phalanger (Schultze-Westrum, 1965) individual recognition is achieved via distinctive odors. In pigs, pheromones are important for hierarchy formation while vision is not necessary for hierarchy maintenance (Ewbank et al.,

1974). Hierarchies in farm animals have recently been reviewed by Syme and Syme (1979).

Fish

Individual recognition is operative in the dominance hierarchies of glandulocaudine fish (Nelson, 1964). This is most clearly shown by consistent differences in behavior toward different group members over periods of several months. Recognition of individual odors is found among yellow bullheads (Todd et al., 1967; Todd, 1971). Social units of the damselfish *Dascyllus aruanus* consist of a large male and a linear, size-dependent dominance hierarchy of females, all of whom recognize each other individually (Fricke and Holzberg, 1974). Several species of the guppy family have also yielded information on individual recognition in hierarchies. Guppy hierarchies may involve individual or role recognition (Gorlick, 1976). In platies, fish introduced to a group are reacted to on an individual basis and the maintenance of the hierarchies involves similar recognition (Braddock, 1945). Members of pairs of swordtail–platy hybrids can recognize each other independent of environmental cues, probably through subtle behavioral and morphological cues (Zayan, 1974). The prior residency effect is inhibited by this recognition (Zayan, 1975).

GROUPS AND SELF

The nexus of relations and behavioral patterns underlying the dynamics of social groups presents to the aspiring ethologist a veritable Gordian knot. Beyond the types of recognition discussed earlier in this chapter, there is operative additional recognition behavior involving the overall social states of the interacting individuals. The very formation and continuance of groups implies some basic social recognition. Individual recognition is common in vertebrate groups which persist for long periods of time. An important subset of such groups in birds (e.g., Mexican jays, reviewed by J. L. Brown, 1978) and mammals (e.g., black-backed jackal: Moehlman, 1979) are those exhibiting cooperative breeding, in which sexually mature, nonbreeding individuals assist the raising of other individuals' (often their parents') offspring. A general analysis of the problems associated with the study of individuals in their social settings has been presented by M. J. A. Simpson (1973).

What is the evidence for self-recognition? Clear operational definitions of terms are especially important in the evaluation of evidence for this

Reprinted by permission of Tribune Company Syndicate, Inc.

type of recognition. Rudimentary knowledge of one's own characters is suggested by assortative mating, species recognition, discrimination of one's own from other odor cues, and selective aggression, as in that of the sea anemones described above. A pathological aspect of self-recognition is a phantom limb in which the amputee still "feels" the limb. Self-recognition is obviously a multifaceted ability, which can be variously assessed with different experimental procedures. Like other complex traits it surely has a gradual ontogeny and phylogeny. With regard to ontogeny, human infants less than a day old stop crying when recording of their own cries are played to them, but not in response to the cries of other babies (Martin and Clark, 1981). Young sunfish switch from avoiding older conspecifics, who prey on them, to interacting socially with them as they grow (Brown and Colgan, in preparation). This switch indicates recognition of body size.

In a discussion of the proximate mechanisms of self-recognition, Parr (1937) outlined what he termed individual self-recognition and social self-recognition, the latter being the recognition of one's self as one's social partners do. Individual self-recognition involves the coordination of different sensory modalities, such as simultaneously seeing and touching a body part. The development of such self-recognition takes time: dogs stop chasing their own tails. Many animals, such as most fish, the group of interest to Parr, are limited in the cross-modal sensory integration they can achieve. Social self-recognition, by requiring individual self-recognition, is therefore impossible for many species. Social responses are therefore mediated, not by social self-recognition, but by mechanical reaction complexes which, to avoid the hoary old term "instinct," Parr calls synaprokrises. Perhaps not surprisingly, this neologism has not become widely adopted.

Imitative behavior, by reflecting the ability of an animal to produce behavior of its own similar to other animals, is also evidence for some degree of self-recognition. Thorpe (1963) defines imitation as "the copying of a novel or otherwise improbable act or utterance, or some act for which there is clearly no instinctive tendency." He discusses the problems of distinguishing imitative behavior from social facilitation and local enhancement, and the particular difficulty associated with bird song mimicry. [Social facilitation refers to the performance of a response, already present in the repertoire of an animal, due to such performance by others (consider contagious yawns). Local enhancement refers to responding to some part of the environment due to the responses of others to this part, such as avoiding dangerous areas avoided by others.] Human infants imitate facial and manual gestures at three weeks of age (Meltzoff and Moore, 1977, 1979). Imitative behavior has been reported in cats and chimpanzees (see Thorpe, 1963). The evidence for the observational learning underlying imitation in birds and mammals is reviewed by Klopfer (1973) and Mackintosh (1974) (see also reports on red-winged blackbirds: Mason and Reidinger, 1981; quail: Sanavio and Savardi, 1980; cats: Chesler, 1969; baboons: Jouventin et al., 1977; macaques: Strayer, 1976; squirrels: Weigel and Hanson, 1980; and rats: Zentall and Levine, 1972). Among fish, a study of the firemouthed cichlid did not find observational learning (Haeson and Wijffels, 1967). A classical associative analysis of such social learning has been made by Miller and Dollard (1941). As discussed generally in Chapter 3, the problem of whether observational learning is one of several basic forms of learning or one aspect of a single form remains unresolved.

Mirror tests have been extensively used as evidence for self-recognition. In tests with mirrors, orangutans and chimpanzees show self-recognition in their reactions to color marks placed on parts of their bodies which are visible only with the mirror by directing behavior to such marks (Lethmate and Ducker, 1973). By contrast, gibbons and five species of monkeys tested show only social reactions to their mirror images, treating them as unfamiliar conspecifics. Similar results have been reported by Gallup (1970, 1975, 1977b, 1979a, 1979b). Chimpanzees born in captivity and reared in social isolation do not recognize themselves in mirrors (Gallup, 1977a). Even if single rhesus monkeys show no self-recognition, cagemate pairs with access to a common mirror might be expected to since they will see the reflection of a familiar conspecific. However, this is not the case (Gallup et al., 1980). A laboratory-reared gorilla recognized herself in a mirror and related photographs of objects to the objects themselves (Patterson, 1978). In a picture sorting task, Viki, a home-raised chimpanzee, placed a picture of her father in the animal pile but one of herself in the human pile (Hayes and Nissen, 1971). In human infants, there is a gradual development from 6 to 24 months of age with a succession of reactions to mirror images including playfulness, wariness, and embarrassment (e.g., Amsterdam, 1972; Amsterdam and Greenberg, 1977; Bertenthal and Fischer, 1978).

Self-recognition is a topic particularly prone to highlight differences in methodological and metaphysical positions. For instance, to contrast with

Gallup's approach, Epstein et al. (1981) trained pigeons to use a mirror to locate blue dots, located on their bodies, which were not directly visible. They provide a "nonmentalistic" interpretation of their results in terms of environmental controlling variables. The onus is thus on the "mentalists" to demonstrate the need for concepts such as "self-awareness." In response, Gallup has suggested a similar experiment using a conspecific as the stimulus cue. As with all work in this problematic area, such an experiment would likely be open to different interpretations from different viewpoints.

Interpreted as consciousness, self-recognition has long been a central concern to philosophers, medics, and psychologists (e.g., Jaynes, 1976; Davidson and Davidson, 1980). But even laid end to end they are unable to reach any conclusion. Ethologists have joined this interest group under the influence of an expansive *Zeitgeist* (spirit of the times) epitomized by Griffin's (1976) provocative volume on the question of animal awareness. The heated and muddled discussions that are usually generated in the consideration of this question indicate the need for well-defined terms and a dispassionate posture by the discussants. Some speculations on the evolution of consciousness are presented in Chapter 4, Groups.

Other

Among insects, much general social recognition is mediated via chemical cues. Pheromones produce dispersal of cricket groups with each sex responding more negatively to the dispersant of its own sex than to that of the opposite sex (Sexton and Hess, 1968). Pheromones also facilitate aggregations in an aposematic lycid beetle (Eisner and Kafatos, 1962) and in locusts (Nolte et al., 1970, 1973). (Aposematic animals are distasteful to predators and bear warning coloration.) Individual recognition in social insects is discussed in Chapter 4, Groups.

Aggregations of blind and common snakes form by individuals following pheromone trails (Gehlbach et al., 1971).

Birds

Among birds, group recognition often involves song dialects, discussed in Chapter 3, Song Imprinting. Individual recognition of group members is found among geese (Heinroth, 1911; Lorenz, 1970), Indian hill mynahs (Bertram, 1970), a number of corvids (jackdaws: Roell, 1978; pinon jays: Berger and Ligon, 1977; Mexican jays: J. L. Brown, 1963; and crows: N. S. Thompson, 1969), and other perching birds (review by Nice, 1943). In flocks of Stellar's jays recognition is mediated through vocalizations, postures, and movements (J. L. Brown, 1964b). In ravens, plasticity of behavior enables individual recognition through the communication of subtle social signals (Gwinner, 1964). Three of these signals are sex-typical and there are also three patterns of agonistic display. Displays vary in their frequency, amplitude, orientation, and sequencing. Strangers to ani groups are recognized first by behavior and then by appearance (Davis, 1942). Based on extensive studies, Whitman (1919) concluded that although pigeons did not recognize their offspring as such, they could distinguish among all members of the flock. The stable heterospecific families of ducks and fowl reported by Cushing and Ramsay (1949) reflect the strength of social bonds involving imprinting (discussed in Chapter 3).

In the New Holland honeyeater, group members are distinguished from nongroup members (Rooke, 1979). After a separation, group members perform a corraboree, a display involving wing flutter, open beak, low bow, and call. Plumage alterations do not affect recognition but the behavior of the other bird does, as shown by the lack of recognition when the stimulus bird is fitted with opaque contact lenses. The difference in the behavior of resident and stranger birds is obvious to a human observer as well as to conspecifics. In valley quail coveys, members and nonmembers are discriminated, with new members being gradually accepted as they develop the "confident" behavior of full members (Howard and Emlen, 1942). Creches of young from several broods form in some duck species, such as the common eider (Munro and Bedard, 1977a, 1977b; Schmutz, personal communication). In the shelduck the protecting parents do not attack ducklings joining the creche provided that they are of the same general size as the young of the parents (Williams, 1974). In both species, adults tend to care selectively for certain ducklings in the creche.

Parrots, hawks, domestic fowl, and some anatids recognize some humans individually (Burtt, Johansen, Mueller, personal communications; Heinroth, 1911) and Thorpe (1963) reports instances of such recognition by a number of other species, some of these accounts (e.g., Morley, 1942) making delightful reading. Avian signals often involve feather postures (Morris, 1956). While the primary functions of feathers are flight, temperature regulation, waterproofing, and brooding, secondary signal functions reveal fear, aggression, sexual arousal, and conflicts of these motivational factors. The behavioral integration of bird groups is thus frequently modulated through postural cues.

Mammals

Ewer (1968) has reviewed the behavior associated with recognition in a variety of mammals, complete with amusing anecdotes. Individual recognition is found in gliding phalangers (Schultze-Westrum, 1965) and in several rodents: mice (Bowers and Alexander, 1967; Kalkowski, 1967; Hahn and Simmel, 1968; Hahn and Tumolo, 1971; Poole and Morgan, 1975), prairie dogs (King, 1955; Smith et al. 1973), eastern chipmunks (Keevin et al., 1981), and marmots (Armitage, 1962, 1965). Young house mice discriminate between stressed and nonstressed adult conspecifics (Carr et al., 1980). Similarly, the activity of rats is affected differently by odors from the body or blood of stressed conspecifics compared to unstressed animals (MacKay-Sim and Laing, 1981a, 1981b). The odors are found on the body surface and in urine, but not in feces, and are dependent on the type of stress applied to the rat. (The closely related topic of alarm pheromones is discussed in Chapter 2, Chemosensation.) Strange rats introduced into established groups induce increased olfactory contacts among all animals, the enhancement dependent on the sex and sexual status of the stranger (Sokolov et al., 1979). As in fire ants (see Parents above), so in rats there is olfactory discrimination of dead individuals, with freshly dead, but not moribund, animals being distinguished from live controls (Carr et al., 1981). Nonagonistic marking facilitates social organization in the Bahaman hutia (Howe, 1974). Individual recognition is found among small permanent ungulate herds such as muntjacs (Barrette, 1977). Among the pheromones of the black-tailed deer the tarsal scent is particularly important for sex, age, and individual recognition (Muller-Schwarze, 1971, 1972; Volkman et al., 1978).

Carnivores exhibiting individual recognition include lions (Schaller, 1972), wolves (Klinghammer, 1975). bat-eared foxes (Lamprecht, 1979), and black-backed jackals (Moehlman, 1979). Wolves recognize each other by both olfaction (Mech, 1970) and howls (Theberge and Falls, 1967). Male dogs living in colonies investigate urine from other colony members more, and that of strange males even more, than their own urine (Dunbar and Carmichael, 1981). Even "solitary" species like the red fox and raccoon exhibit recognition of neighbors (Barash, 1974). Individuals of these species trapped close to one another show more initial status-related behavior and less high intensity aggression than animals trapped far apart. Members of dwarf mongoose groups recognize each other individually (Rasa, 1977). Among sea mammals, spotted dolphins recognize each other individually via signature whistles (Caldwell et al., 1973) which bottlenosed dolphins can also be trained to distinguish (Caldwell et al., 1971). The celebrated songs of the humpback whale certainly enable individual recognition and may serve to assist group cohesion (Payne and McVay, 1971).

Groups of primates with complex behavioral repertoires manifest acute recognition behavior (see DeVore, 1965). Individual recognition is evident in orangutans (Mackinnon, 1974) and chimpanzees (Goodall, 1968). In chimpanzees, Yerkes (1943) early emphasized the great individual variation of the species. Among Siamang family groups, subtle visual signals and loud and complex calls mediate social recognition (Chivers, 1976). The Venezuelan weeper capuchin uses at least eleven vocal and seven visual displays (Oppenheimer and Oppenheimer, 1973). Pygmy marmosets recognize each other individually via contact calls (Snowden and Cleveland, 1980). Similarly, playback experiments show that forest monkeys recognize group members individually (Waser, 1976). Sounds have also been investigated by Rowell (1972), Marler (1973), Green (1975), Marler and Hobbett (1975), Beecher et al. (1979), and Jurgens (1979). Humans can discriminate individuals by odors from the hand (Wallace, 1977), a result consonant with the findings on olfactory recognition of spouses and family members cited above. The discrimination is stronger between unrelated individuals and individuals on different diets.

Recognition of group members can be effectively studied by introducing strangers. Wade (1976) has carried out such work with rhesus groups with discriminate between group members and strangers, and between strangers of each sex. Rhesus males associate with particular individuals, not indiscriminately with members of a certain sex or rank category (Kaufman, 1967). Urine cues identify group members in squirrel monkeys (Candland et al., 1980).

The recognition of emotions in mammals has been a focal topic for workers from Darwin (1872) to Young (1943) and Eibl-Eibesfeldt (1972). Socio-sexual signaling and recognition of emotional state is highly evolved in many primates (Wickler, 1967). Facial displays of catarrhine monkeys and apes reflect different motivations (VanHooff, 1967). Threat is displayed with a tense-mouth face, fear with bared teeth and teeth chattering displays, and approach and mating motivation with lip smacking and a protruded-lips face. Redican (1975) has extended the analysis to a finer level, while Emory et al. (1979) have described a nonplay, status related use of the "play face" in long-tailed macaques. Analysis of the seven discrete facial expressions used by the brown capuchin shows that these animals provide accurate motivational information to other group members (Weigel, 1979). Facial recognition in humans is extremely acute and develops over the first several months of life (discussed in Chapter 2, Vision, and Chapter 3, Socialization). As Galton long ago suggested, attractive human faces are more typical and hence more difficult to remember (Light et al., 1981). Facial expressions can also be recognized interspecifically. Clever Hans was a turn-of-the-century German stallion famous for his arithmetic and linguistic skills. With a front hoof on a board, he tapped out responses to questions from his owner, VonOsten, or from other persons. Pfungst (1965) showed that Hans was cued by the behavior of his questioner or owner, who relaxed after the correct number of taps.

While fans of Swift's Houyhnhnms may be disappointed by this finding, they can be consoled by his acute recognition abilities. Zoo animals, too, often discriminate among different humans (Hediger, 1942) as do various domesticated species.

From the arctic Inuit to the patagonian Kawashka, human tribes tend to identify themselves as "the people" and to refer to other tribes with such deprecatory labels as "eskimo" ("eater of raw meat," applied by the Algonquins to the Inuit). Somalis discriminate between "tight hairs" and "flat noses" in their neighbors. Such recognition labels reveal the antiquity of human racism. For the human ethologist secret societies abound with recognition behavior, including ceremonies such as the following nineteenth century oriental one:

> Set aromatic tea on the table, and when offering it, hold the edge of the cup between the thumb and forefinger, with the middle finger touching the bottom of the cup (Chesneaux, 1971)

providing rich material for the researcher. Finally, graphologists claim to recognize personality features in handwriting but supporting evidence is wanting, just as it is in phrenology and palmistry.

Fish

In persistent fish groups, as found among Japanese medakas (Ono, 1955), glandulocaudines (Nelson, 1964), and parrot fish (Dubin, personal communication), for instance, individual recognition is operative. Anthouard (1973) has reached the tentative conclusion that goldfish can distinguish members of their own living groups from strange conspecifics. Bluegills, in a laboratory operant test situation, appear gradually to learn over many trials to discriminate between individual conspecifics (Butler and Johnson, 1972), a result consistent with their territorial behavior discussed above. In bluegills and rockbass, yearling individuals tested in a choice situation after a week of living in homospecific groups prefer group members to strange conspecifics of similar size (Brown, personal communication). European minnows can be conditioned to distinguish individual conspecifics of both sexes (Goz, 1941).

2

Sensory Processes

The question of why a given animal exhibits recognition behavior has both proximate and ultimate interpretations. Ultimate interpretations require a functional examination of the selection pressures for recognition behavior and are considered in Chapter 4. Proximate interpretations involve a reductionist study of the sensory mechanisms and developmental processes which are responsible for the behavior. Overall, such study lags behind the collection of behavioral data. It is one thing to observe recognition behavior, but quite another to reveal the underlying mechanism and processes. In this chapter the roles of the different sensory modalities are discussed, and in the next chapter attention focuses on developmental processes. It will become clear that many of the issues raised in this chapter are subsets of more general problems in perceptual psychology. For instance, facial recognition, discussed below, includes the perception of static features (such as the shape of the nose), constancies (such as full face versus three-quarters pose), and dynamic features (such as expressions).

In most recognition situations, several sensory aspects play a role. Male ground crickets respond to chemical stimuli from females by calling (Paul, 1976). Lashley (1915) early emphasized the importance of such a stimulus complex in his work on terns. Parental terns react to alterations in the visual appearance of their chicks. However, the ongoing, normal behavior of the chicks comes to override this alteration and parental treatment ensues. Recognition between ewes and their lambs involves vision, audition, and olfaction (see, e.g., Shillito Walser, 1980; Shillto Walser and Alexander, 1980). The recognition of conspecifics for the aggressive reaction of European robins depends proximately on flying away movements by the intruder, a robin shape, a red breast, and song (Lack, 1939).

69

In avian imprinting, visual and auditory cues interact to produce the subsequent species recognition (Gottlieb, 1968; Johnston and Gottlieb, 1981a, 1981b; discussed in Chapter 3, Imprinting). The roles of different modalities in recognition behavior among fish has recently been thoroughly reviewed by Myrberg (1980).

The unraveling of the components of the stimulus complex remains an unexplored problem in almost all areas of recognition behavior. The comparative variability of different characters that are possibly used in recognition, such as facial features, song parameters, fin lengths, and egg colors, may indicate the relative importances of these characters. Characters with little interindividual variability would not be useful in recognition. It must be borne in mind, of course, that the characters may have high or low variability due to functions other than recognition behavior. Schleidt (1976) has provided a theoretical analysis of how inter- and intraindividual variation along the various dimensions of a behavioral pattern can achieve individuality of displays. He concludes that optimal distinctiveness is achieved through the use of a few characters of low intraindividual variability, and not by a single character of very low variability or many characters of moderate variability. It would seem worthwhile to test these ideas in actual cases.

VISION AND ELECTRORECEPTION

The aged St. Mael of France's *L'Ile des Pingouins* baptized penguins, a failure in species recognition with grave theological implications. In this case and many others, vision is a critical modality for much recognition behavior. In particular, color vision has evolved independently in a number of phylogenetic lines, with different species sensitive to different portions of the spectrum. Recent general reviews of the importance of vision in social behavior are by Hailman (1977) and Burtt (1979).

Other

In octopuses, elaborate chromatophore displays facilitate sex recognition (Wells, 1978). Complex visual displays have also evolved among salticid spiders (Crane, 1949) and fiddler crabs (Crane, 1975). The white patch on the enlarged left chela of the hermit crab signals body size to agonistic opponents (Dunham, 1978).

The visual system of jumping spiders is similar to that of mammals and unlike that of most arthropods (Land, 1969). The side eyes, corresponding

Figure 2.1. Flight paths and flashes by males in several species of fireflies (from Lloyd, 1966).

to peripheral retinal areas in mammals, detect motion while the antero-median eyes, corresponding to central retinal areas, evaluate details and so enable the recognition of prey versus conspecifics. As in mammals, these spiders execute saccades, fast eye movements bringing a stimulus into the center of the visual field where it can be scanned for recognition. Any small object that has just moved is attacked as prey unless it has a pair of legs on either side in which case it is courted by males. Land discusses how this discrimination could be achieved through the detection of contours by oriented rows of visual receptors.

Vision plays a dominant role in both species and sex recognition among dragonflies (Corbet, 1980). Light-producing fireflies employ complex flash patterns for similar recognition in courtship communication (Lloyd, 1966, 1971, 1980; Lall et al., 1980; Figure 2.1). The ecological adaptiveness of the signals involved has been shown in particular for *Photinus pyralis* (Lall, 1981). In this species the elctroretinogram is sensitive in the yellow region of the spectrum, in which region the insect also produces its light. The insensitivity to green functions to remove foliage-produced green noise at dusk, thus enhancing detection of the signal. Many insects are sensitive to wavelengths in the ultraviolet. In checkered white butterflies both sexes discriminate each other through differences in ultraviolet reflectance of the wings, as shown by presenting stimulus dummies with wings treated in ammonia to alter their reflectance (Rutowski, 1981).

Light is necessary for successful courtship and mating in some *Drosophila* species (review by Spieth, 1974). In *D. melanogaster*, vision is relatively unimportant, females being chiefly stimulated by antennal reception of the wing display of the courting male (Manning, 1959). By contrast, in the closely related *D. simulans* the visual aspects of courtship, especially the wing display termed scissoring, are very important. Grossfield (1971) has identified three classes of species based on the effect of light on their reproductive behavior: those unaffected by the presence or absence of light, those inhibited by darkness, and those whose mating is completely blocked by darkness. These classes can be related to their biogeographical and genetic characters. Recently, Lambert (1982) has shown that courting males of the *D. nasuta* complex display species-typical body markings to potential mates.

The visual appearance of other individuals mediates the formation of aggressions among tadpoles of *Xenopus laevis* (Wassersug and Hessler, 1971). Among lizards and tortoises, visually distinct displays are important in species and sex recognition (Greenberg and Noble, 1944; Carpenter, 1960; Hunsaker, 1962; Auffenberg, 1965; Figure 2.2).

Birds

Vision is the effective modality for many types of recognition behavior in birds. Baerends and co-workers (e.g., Baerends and VanRhijn, 1975) have greatly extended the line of research into the visual stimulus features such as color and spotting pattern that function in egg recognition among gulls.

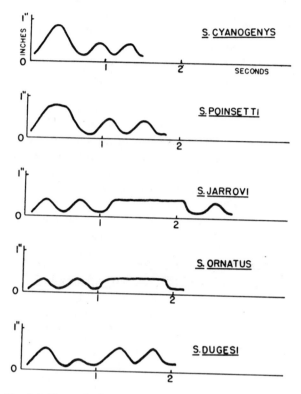

Figure 2.2. Head bobbing displays in various *Sceloporus* lizards mediating species recognition (from Hunsaker, 1962). Head height is plotted against time.

Species recognition in ducks (Gottlieb, 1968) and mate recognition in sooty and noddy terns (Watson, 1908) involve visual cues. Such cues underlie all of species, sex, and individual recognition in gulls (N. G. Smith, 1966). Gape markings in young African estrildid finches are species-typical and are mimicked by brood parasitic viduine finches (Nicolai, 1964). "Whiteness" is an important cue for identifying conspecifics in mute swans (Norman, 1977). Plumage differences underlie many of the cases of imprinting and assortative mating (discussed in Chapters 3 and 4, respectively). Individual recognition in budgerigars (Trillmich, 1976), sex recognition in red-necked phalaropes (Tinbergen, 1935), and chick recognition by parental razorbills (Ingold, 1973) are chiefly visual. Ring-billed gull parents often attack chicks 12 to 20 days old with altered plumage and facial patterns but they do not attack muted ones (Miller and

Emlen, 1975). The attacks decline over a few hours, and the behavior of the chicks likely plays a role in this. (The markings used to alter the appearance of the offspring are not in themselves releasers for aggression, as shown by the lack of attacks against marked 3- to 4-day-old chicks.) Postures and movements enable individual and aggressive state recognition in Stellar's jays (J. L. Brown, 1964b).

Facial features serve as discriminative stimuli in much avian recognition. Beak morphology and color are critical in viduine and estrildid finches (Nicolai, 1967, 1968) as well as in the famous Galapagos finches (Lack, 1945). The red spot on the bill of a herring gull cues recognition by its chicks (Hailman, 1967). The visually distinctive faces of Bewick's swans play a role in mate choice (Bateson et al., 1980) and Heinroth's observation on facial recognition within swan pairs, cited in Chapter 1, Sex and Mates, also demonstrates this role. Variable facial features in Japanese quail also seem likely to facilitate individual recognition (Bateson, 1980). Pair bonds are disrupted by head marking in doves (Goforth and Baskett, 1965) and beak painting in budgerigars (Cinat-Tomson, 1926). Similarly, male flickers chase mates marked with the "moustache" characteristic of males (Noble, 1936). The dominance hierarchies of domestic chickens involve the visual discrimination of several facial regions, as well as general plumage (Guhl, 1953; Guhl and Ortman, 1953; Potter, 1949; Marks et al., 1960; Candland, 1969).

Mammals

Although olfaction is the dominant recognition modality in many mammals, vision is also important. Ewes recognize their lambs chiefly by vision (Lindsay and Fletcher, 1968). In horses, tests of mares with foals of different coat colors reveal the role of vision in recognition at a distance (LeBlanc and Bouisseau, 1981). Among primates, facial expressions and postures enable the recognition of the social status and motivation of group conspecifics (e.g., VanHooff, 1967; Redican, 1975; Weigel, 1979). Subtle visual signals which integrate siamang family groups include facial expressions and expressive gestures (Chivers, 1976).

As indicated by the vast array of cosmetic unguents and dyes employed by *Homo sapiens*, recognition of age of conspecifics can be of great interest, especially the age of potential mates among species with long-term associations. Form vision is important in perceiving human aging (Todd et al., 1980), as shown by judgments on cranial silhouettes made different by various mathematical strain transformations (Figure 2.3). Of the five transformations used, only the cardioidal and spiral strain trans-

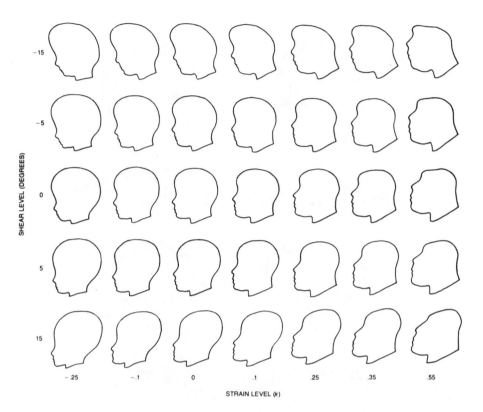

Figure 2.3. Stimulus silhouettes with varying levels of strain and shear used in age judgment experiments (from Todd et al., 1980, copyright Scientific American, Inc.).

formations were interpreted as reflecting growth. [When the Cartesian coordinates (x, y) of a point in a plane are expressed as polar coordinates, $x = r \sin \theta$ and $y = r \cos \theta$, cardioidal strain is given by $r' = r(1 - k \cos \theta)$ and spiral strain by $r' = r(1 + k|\theta|)$.] It seems that these transformations model cranial growth patterns, and it is intriguing to speculate how they may also be used to model perceptual mechanisms of form, in the best tradition of D'Arcy Thompson (1961) and his morphological ordinations. Recognition of age also involves perception of other form features such as posture, as well as other characters such as behavior and skin features.

The distinctiveness of various aspects of the human face is proverbial. The lower lip of the royal family of the Austrian empire was so protuberant that it became known as the Hapsburger Lippe. In censored photographs of contemporary news media, the region of the eyes is often

Figure 2.4. Drawings by face-reconstruction artist (from Harmon, 1973). Upper left: photograph. Upper right: portrait based on written description and selections from a catalog of facial features. Lower left: portrait modified by verbal corrections. Lower right: portrait from photograph.

blocked out. Face-reconstruction artists can generate with a high level of validity portraits of police suspects from descriptions provided by witnesses (Harmon, 1973) (Figure 2.4). Block portraits consisting of grids, each square of which is shaded with one of a number of grays, can be surprisingly coarse and yet recognizable. The experimental techniques of computer blurring reveal that low-frequency information on head shape, neck and shoulder geometry, and gross hairline, alone, is adequate for good recognition among individuals in small groups. The results provide further support for the flattering conclusion that "the human viewer is a fantastically competent information processor." However, humans are not unique in facial recognition ability. Rhesus monkeys learn facial discriminations and are not confused by alterations in size, posture, orientation, color, or illumination (Rosenfeld and VanHoesen, 1979). Indeed, there appear to be cortical cells in the temporal lobes which are selective in their responsiveness to faces (Perret et al., 1979). Four-month-old boys fixate longer at head-shaped stimuli the more these resemble a face, thus revealing a facial dimension in their visual perception (Haaf and Bell, 1967). Finally, as suggested by the use of the drug belladonna ("beautiful lady," whose active ingredient, atropine, dilates the pupils), pupil size is an important visual cue in state recognition (Hess, 1975). Of two portraits of a woman differing only in pupil size, the one with larger pupils is ranked higher in terms of positive attributes. Adults, but not subjects between 9 and 15 years of age, draw larger pupils on a cartoon of a happy face compared to a scowling one. The gradual development of facial recognition is discussed in Chapter 3, Socialization.

Fish

For the large number of fish species which live in well-lighted waters, vision is an important modality. For schooling species, visual marks often facilitate maintenance of the school. Such marks are important for the characid *Pristella riddlei* in distinguishing conspecific from heterospecific schools (Keenleyside, 1955). A second schooling species, zebra danios, in a choice situation with photographic stimuli, prefers stimuli of the same size over different sizes and, additionally, stimuli with stripes over uniform intermediate gray stimuli (McCann et al., 1971).

Both species and sex recognition often involve vision, as in the case of anabantid fishes (Picciolo, 1964). Since males discriminate between species with similar behavior, visual stimuli other than behavior are important. Visual cues are also important in species recognition among sunfishes (e.g., Steele and Kennleyside, 1971). Red-eared male sunfish hybridize with bluegill females only when the conspicuous red opercular flaps are removed (Childers, 1967). Also in bluegills, the caudal fin dark spot may function in species recognition (Stacey and Chiszar, 1978). In the orange chromide cichlid, "black belly" is a mate-directed signal (Rechten, 1980). In the jewel fish, vision is the chief modality for both sex and mate recognition as shown, for instance, by the effects of various alterations of the appearance of the mate's head (Noble and Curtis, 1939). Color patterning is also important in the monogamous Indopacific reef fish *Amphiprion bicinctus* (Fricke, 1973). In the related damselfish *Dascyllus aruanus*, vision is sufficient for species recognition, with the three bars, especially the central one, playing key roles (Katzir, 1981a, 1981b). Similarly, body form and color patterning mediate individual and species recognition in the Carribean threespot damselfish (Thresher, 1976, 1979).

Vision also figures largely in agonistic behavior, such as habituation to aggressive stimuli in sticklebacks (Assem and Molen, 1969; Peeke and Veno, 1973) and bluegills (Colgan et al., 1979). Parr marks are important in the territoriality of Japanese salmon (Maeda and Hidaka, 1979). In the dominance hierarchies of green sunfish rank and coloration correlate perfectly (Howard, 1974). Generalized visual cues are important in the aggressive behavior of glandulocaudine fishes (Nelson, 1964). The "eye-spots" of fire-mouth cichlids intimidate adversaries during agonistic encounters (Radesater and Ferno 1979; Figure 2.5). Conversely, the black midlateral spot of *Neoheterandria tridentiger* acts to inhibit aggression (McPhail, 1978).

Reproductive recognition also relies heavily on vision. Eggs, young, and parents are recognized visually in a variety of cichlids (Noble and Curtis, 1939; Baerends and Baerends-VanRoon, 1950; Myrberg, 1966, 1975). In the jewel fish social responses of the young are dependent on visual features and can be elicited by dummies with two facing eyes (Coss, 1978, 1979).

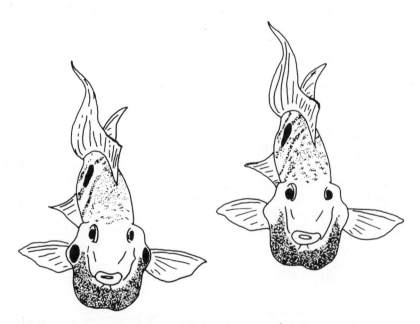

Figure 2.5. "Eye-spots" of fire-mouthed cichlids (from Radesater and Ferno, 1979, copyright Elsevier Scientific Publ. Co.). Spots of right fish have been scraped.

According to an Oriental proverb, "though the distance between the ear and the eye is very small, the difference between hearing and seeing is very great." A *fortiori*, the small distance between the receptors belies the gulf between the two modalities of electromagnetic radiation, vision and electroreception. Electroreception serves the nonsocial function of geo-orientation in organisms as diverse as bacteria, honeybees, pigeons, and some sharks and rays (see, e.g., J. L. Gould, 1980). The social use of such reception for purposes of recognition is known only in the African mormyrid and the Central and South American gymnotoid fishes, which generate and detect weak electric fields. (The fields are weak compared to the strong fields generated by predaceous species such as the electric eel and catfish.) Such electric signals can serve species, sex, and rival recognition functions (Figure 2.6). Species recognition in mormyrids is achieved with temporal cues involving the wave form of the signal (Hopkins and Bass, 1981; Kramer et al., 1981; Serrier, 1979). The two sexes of one gymnotoid, *Sternopygus macrurus*, have discharges with the same wave form and polarity but different frequencies (Hopkins, 1972,

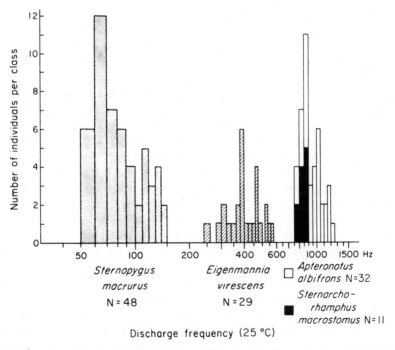

Figure 2.6. Variation in electric discharge frequency in four sympatric Amazonian gymnotoids (from Hopkins, 1974b).

1974a, 1974b). Frequency rises and discharge interruptions are given only by males during the breeding season to passing females, and therefore appear to serve a courtship function. Males may be able to discriminate reproductive from nonreproductive females by the amplitude of their signals, which vary with body size. Males and females have been observed to adopt frequencies an octave apart. In such a relation, is the male blind to the female or, to the contrary, are they engaged in a rapturous duet?

AUDITION AND TACTILE SENSATION

In Solzhenitsyn's *The First Circle*, Volodin is convicted with a voice print of a telephone call he made, a grim example of the usefulness of audition for individual recognition. Audition plays a major role in much recognition behavior in many animal groups. Many vocal species have distinct calls for distinct functions, such as spacing males and attracting females (e.g., katydids: Spooner, 1964).

Like audition, the tactile modality rests fundamentally on mechano-receptors. Recognition with the tactile modality can be via some medium or directly between individuals. Some spiders and water striders use webs and water, respectively, as a medium analogous to that used for audition. By sensing vibrational patterns, web-spinning spiders, some of which are solitary and some communal, can discriminate male and female con-specifics as well as prey animals (e.g., Burgess, 1979). Species recognition in wolf spiders is mediated via substrate vibrations (Uetz and Denterlein, 1979; Stratton, 1979; Stratton and Uetz, 1981). Surface waves mediate recognition behavior in an Australian water strider (Wilcox, 1972). Vision is necessary for neither precopulatory behavior nor oviposition. Males produce wave patterns that attract females that can discriminate wave frequency differences as low as 2 Hz. Males of a North American speices, when blinded with masks, treat females as males when the females are artificially made to broadcast computer-generated male surface wave signals at about 90 Hz (Wilcox, 1979). When not made to broadcast such signals, the females are treated as females. Similarly, the backswimmer discriminates between prey and nonprey species, including conspecifics (Lang, 1980).

Direct tactile contact plays an important role in the recognition of sexual state in many species. Among many insects antennal contact is found in advanced stages of courtship (e.g., ants: Holldobler and Wust, 1973; fruitflies: Spieth, 1974; wasps: Grosch, 1947). In connection with an analysis of lateral displays in vertebrates, Chiszar (1978) has argued that body rubbing coordinates the release of gametes in externally fertilizing species or the acceptance of the male or his spermatophore (sperm package) in internal fertilizers. Such rubbing may be reciprocal or executed by the male alone.

Other

Among insects, temporal rather than frequency components of a call tend to carry its information content (review by Alexander, 1967). This is the case for species recognition in both parental and hybrid crickets (Bigelow, 1964; Dathe, 1974; Hoy, 1974; Hoy et al., 1977). Females of each species show a preference for the calls of conspecific males as measured by performance on a Y-maze. Hybrid females prefer the songs of hybrid males, suggesting a genetic linkage of song production in the male and reception in the famale (see Chapter 4, Genetic Aspects). Among *Gryllus* species the recognition reaction to the song is mediated by its rhythmical structure, particularly the frequency of pulse repetition, as well as the signal intensity (Shuvalov and Popov, 1973a, 1973b). While both sexes of th cricket *Teleogryllus oceanicus* prefer conspecific to heterospecific calls, tests with synthetic songs showed that females most prefer the chirp portion and males the trill portion (Pollack, 1982). This difference suggests that male–female and male–male differences are mediated by different song components. Females distinguish a song in which the stereotyped sequence of interpulse intervals has been randomized (Pollack and Hoy, 1979). This result indicates that recognition is not achieved by matching input to an internal template as has been sometimes hypothesized. Similar research using modified songs with *Acheta domestica* has revealed that females are sensitive to many call features and strongly prefer songs within the normal range for the species (Stout and McGhee, 1980). In terms of physiological mechanisms, the abdominal cerci of crickets have sense organs which are sensitive to the temporal patterning of the low-frequency components of cricket calls (Kamper and Dambach, 1981). Nerve cells from these organs synapse with giant interneurons centrally to mediate species, sex, and status recognition, which is conveyed through calling, rivalry, and courtship songs. Among other orthopterans, grasshopper females respond only to conspecific songs by attending to their temporal features (Otte, 1972; Hartley et al., 1974; Helversen, 1972, 1979).

Both sexes stridulate in the water bug genus *Cenocorixa*, enabling species and sex recognition (Jansson, 1973). In a complex of planthopper species, song differences, especially among males, achieve similar recognition (Booij, 1982). Stridulation and pheromones mediate species recognition in scolytid beetles, and behavior and song in periodical cicadas (Dunning et al., 1979). In *Drosophila*, male courtship pulse songs convey species-typical information. The important stimulus dimensions of these songs are the frequency within the pulses and the intervals between them (Waldron, 1964; Ewing and Bennet-Clark, 1968; review by Spieth, 1974). In contrast to pulse songs, sine songs (a humming sound with a frequency close to 160 Hz) function to prime the sexual receptivity of the female (Schilcher, 1976). In the related genus *Zaprionus*, both males and females produce their own songs during courtship (Bennet-Clark et al., 1980).

The auditory modality is dominant in much frog recognition behavior. Reproductively active female *Pseudacris streckeri* show a strong preference for conspecific calls over those of sympatric *P. clarki* or *P. triserata* (Littlejohn and Michaud, 1959). Pulse repetition frequency conveys information on species in Australian (Littlejohn, 1965) and Texan (Johnson, 1966) hylids. In the latter case, the trill rates of *H. versicolor* males lie in the range of 17 to 35 Hz while those of *H. chrysoscelis* are between 34 and 69 Hz. These frogs are thus instances of ethospecies (discussed in Chapter 4, Species Recognition and Hybridization). In the North American green tree frog, the low frequency components of the male call attract the female at a distance while the high frequency components permit species recognition at a closer range (Gerhardt, 1976). Females respond most readily to synthetic calls with a waveform periodicity of approximately 300 Hz (Gerhardt, 1978). They discriminate strongly against calls with frequencies of 100 Hz or below and respond with intermediate strength to 225 and 900 Hz calls. Female choice in the neotropical frog *Physalaemus pustulosus* is cued by the frequency of the male advertisement call (Ryan, 1980a). Females choose larger males by responding to calls with a lower fundamental frequency. Similar size preference in mates has been found in bullfrogs (Howard, 1978). In laboratory studies, bullfrogs have been found to discriminate mating calls very critically (Capranica, 1966). To the calls of 34 species, they responded only to those of certain conspecifics. Using findings on the physiology of the auditory system, Capranica has produced a model call yielding this specificity. Male size in Fowler's toad is mediated by pulse rate (Fairchild, 1981). The attractiveness of the call depends not only directly on the size of the male but also inversely on body temperature. Indeed large males enhance their sex appeal by thermoregulating behaviorally through occupying relatively cooler areas of the pond.

Birds

Swans may well sing at the approach of death, as Aristotle claimed, but contemporary reviews (e.g., Armstrong, 1963; Beer, 1970a; Hinde, 1969; Thorpe and Hall-Craggs, 1976) report only on other aspects of birdsong. The present discussion will be restricted to the functional role of song in recognition behavior, with emphasis on recent work. Many cases, besides those cited here, of the role of song in recognition behavior are considered in Chapter 1. Different parameters of song provide information on different types of recognition (e.g., of species and individuals) (Marler, 1960; Falls, 1969; Brooks and Falls, 1975b). For instance, in red-winged blackbirds, the narrow frequency band between 2.5 and 4.0 kHz in the trill portion of the advertisement song elicits species-typical territorial responses over at least 100 m, whereas the higher frequency portion, as well as the introductory notes, attenuate over distance and do not produce responses (Brenowitz, 1982).

Frequency modulation and repetition rate are important features of maternal song for species recognition in mallards (Miller and Gottlieb, 1978). To wood ducklings, synthetic calls incorporating a descending frequency modulation are as attractive as natural maternal calls (Gottlieb, 1974). In the common yellowthroat, synthetic songs containing doubled internote time intervals or songs whose frequency range is lowered by 1 kHz are less effective in eliciting responses than synthetic normal songs (Wunderle, 1979). Removing hooks on notes which slur the frequency of the note does not alter the effectiveness of the song. Species recognition minimally requires a two-note (one an upstroke, the second a downstroke) repeated phrase song with a frequency range of 2 to 6 kHz. In the golden-winged warbler, features of the song such as frequency and number of syllables per trill probably enable individual recognition while broader aspects of these parameters mediate species recognition (Ficken and Ficken, 1973). Both syllabic structure and temporal patterning enable females of song and swamp sparrows to discriminate conspecific from heterospecific songs (Searcy and Marler, 1981; Searcy et al., 1981a). Females use these cues, along with others such as the variety of song types, to exhibit a preference for males of their own species, which is advantageous to both sexes. In ovenbirds and white-throated sparrows, dimensions of song that are important for species recognition include pitch, form, and arrangement of the component sounds and the temporal patterning of these components (Falls, 1963). Indigo buntings recognize syllables as approximations of culturally transmitted song types (Shiovitz and Lemon, 1980). This recognition involves many cues, some of them adding together in their effectiveness. In the greater prairie chicken and the sharp-tailed grouse, audition is important in the preference which each sex shows for conspecifics over heterospecifics (Sparling, 1981). Highly developed vocal mimicry serves species recognition in some brood parasitic species such as African viduine finches (Nicolai, 1964). Audition also functions in other ways in species recognition. The allied wood hewer discriminates the sound of its mate alighting near by from that of other species (Skutch, 1945).

Sex and mate recognition are often mediated by song. Call variation in male brown-headed cowbirds reflects social status and so enables females to select dominant mates (West et al., 1981). In gannets, changes in the amplitude envelope incorporate information on the individual (White and White, 1970; White et al., 1970) (Figure 2.7). For this discrimination, the first part of the call is used while frequency and time parameters are of little value. However, temporal patterning of calls is important in mate recognition in colonial snow petrels (Guillotin and Jouventin, 1980). The "fish-call" of sandwich terns shows variation in its features to enable mate, parents and offspring recognition (Hutchison et al., 1968). The call consists of three sound segments, and features of each segment, such as duration and pitch, vary as does the overall patterning of the call. In least terns, temporal and spectral characters of the first note of the nest approach call change across individuals but those of the second note do

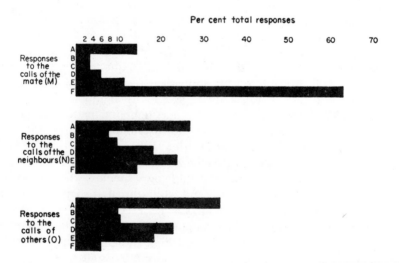

Figure 2.7. Responses by gannets to broadcasts of calls of mates, neighbors, and others (from White, 1971). Responses ranged from A (no response) to F (sustained response).

not (Moseley, 1979). The former functions for individual identification while the latter plays a role in courtship. In Cassin's finch, individual variation in songs enables mate recognition (Samson, 1978). Similarly, in the dimorphic western grebe there is variation in the advertising call across color morph, sex, pairing status, individuals, and the season (Nuechterlein, 1981a, 1981b). The chief difference in call between the morphs is the number of notes: one in the light morph, two in the dark (Figure 2.8). Unpaired males respond to the calls of unpaired females of the same color morph while ignoring the calls of other birds. Paired birds engage in shorter bouts of one or two calls, alternating with the mate. In geese, cackling combines with the behavior, rolling, to produce the triumph ceremony, which maintains pair bonds, family integrity, and dominance relations (Fischer, 1965). The ability to analyze the fine structure of a call enables an Indian hill mynah to distinguish a call from its

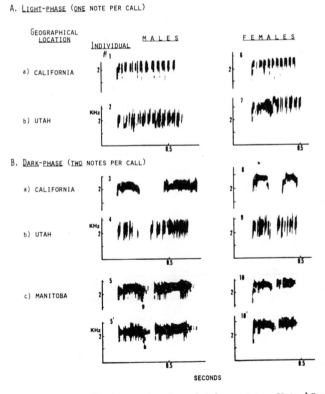

Figure 2.8.   Sonograms of two light morph male grebes from western United States and two dark males from Manitoba (from Nuechterlein, 1981a).

mate from the same call from a neighbor (Bertram, 1970). The pertinent structural features are timing, minor components of the call, and soft preceding sounds.

Antiphonal singing, which is highly developed in many human cultures, especially Western music (Figure 2.9), has been interpreted as serving in some bird species to maintain contacts and bonds between pair members and to advertise territorial possession (Wickler, 1980, criticized by Serpell, 1981b). Payne (1971) and Thorpe (1972) have provided detailed analyses and general reviews of antiphonal singing in African birds (Figure 2.10). Usually pair members alternate different vocalizations, which may be sex-typical, although there are exceptions such as the African forest weaver in which pairs sing in unison (Wickler and Seibt, 1980). The duetting birds, rather than responding to each other, are actually executing two programs synchronously. In d'Arnaud's barbet, the male portion of the duet is derived from the begging call of the young and the response time between the alternations of the partners, which ranges from 33 to 400 msec, is slower than the fastest possible physiological reaction time and probably reflects ritualization (Wickler and Uhrig, 1969). [Ritualization is "the adaptive formalization or canalization of emotionally motivated behavior, under the teleonomic pressure of natural selection so as: (1) to promote better and more unambiguous signal function, both intra- and inter-specifically; (2) to serve as more efficient stimulators or releasers of more efficient patterns of action in other individuals; (3) to reduce intraspecific damage; and (4) to serve as sexual or social bonding mechanisms" (Huxley, 1966). See also Chapter 4, Communication.]

Duets also accompany the mutual displays in pairs of monogamous parrots (Serpell, 1981a). In the Australian eastern whipbird, the male song consists of two components, an individually variable introduction and a

Figure 2.9. Opening bars from Janequin's (1485–1558) antiphonal "Le Chant des Oyseaux" (from Janequin, 1965).

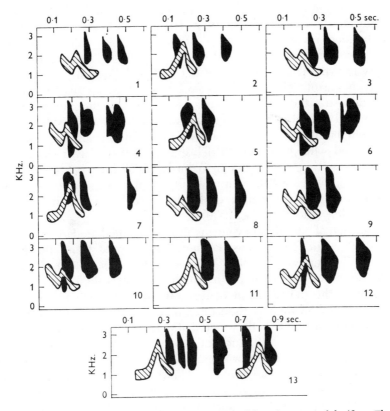

Figure 2.10. Antiphonal duets (black and crosshatched) by African gonoleks (from Thorpe, 1972).

species-typical whip-crack (Watson, 1969). Female song shows both geographical and individual variation. Ontogenetically, the antiphony develops slowly in juvenile pairs. In experiments with the African thrush *Cossypha heuglini*, Todt (1975) demonstrated that antiphonal coordination enables a female to distinguish her mate from another male. The occurrence of song elements within the structured duets of African drongos and slate-colored bou bou shrikes depends on the singer's preceding element and that of its partner, as well as the repertoire of neighbors (Helversen and Wickler, 1971; Wickler, 1972). Neighboring pairs of shrikes share almost all their elements, but the structures of their duets are different. The temporal synchronization of duets in Aldabra white-throated rails is not precise. Nevertheless, variation in song components across individuals and differential responsiveness to playbacks of calls indicates acute mate recognition (Huxley and Wilkinson, 1979).

Pair-bonded ravens and shamas often emit their calls when their partners are absent (Gwinner and Kneutgen, 1962). The absent partner prompty returns. The authors point out that such "naming" is similar to "speech" in parrots. The underlying sensory mechanisms involved in song recognition are indicated by further work with the latter species (Kneutgen, 1964). Upon presentation to test birds, tonal stimuli containing few harmonics release "motive-song" which is also harmonically impoverished, while harmonically rich stimuli elicit similarly rich subsong. Indeed, presenting these stimuli to birds while they are singing can precipitate a switch to the harmonically similar song type. Male and female Peking robins recognize each other through their rich variety of songs (Thielcke and Thielcke, 1970).

Recognition of parents and young is also vocally mediated in many avian species (e.g., Adelie penguins: Penney, 1968; arctic terns: Busse and Busse, 1977; domestic species: Ramsay, 1951; Falt, 1981). Heinroth (1911) described the manner in which the soft calls of parents are important in the development of recognition by the young. Deafened turkey poults follow their mothers more than control poults, but deafened mothers kill their poults as they would attack a predator approaching the nest (Schleidt et al., 1960). Incubator reared willow grouse chicks are attracted to some synthetic brooding calls and repelled by others, but prefer none to the genuine hen call (Allen, 1977, 1979). In choice tests between calls of their own and another hen, chicks removed from the nest at hatching prefer the former, while chicks that have spent most of a day in the nest before removal tend to avoid the latter (Allen, 1980). Vocal behavior in broods of mallard ducklings is maintained by the maternal assembly call and inhibited by the alarm call (Miller, 1980). As in the above cited work on mallard species recognition, repetition rate is a critical dimension of the vocalizations. When either call is played at 3.7 notes per second, the typical rate of assembly calls, duckling vocal behavior is excited, but is inhibited when either call is played at 1.4 notes per second, the alarm call rate. Nestling galahs (a cockatoo) recognize their parents by their calls (Rowley, 1980). Similarly, the individually characteristic feeding call notes of a maternal European blackbird are soon recognized by her nestlings (Messmer and Messmer, 1956). This species has a large and diverse vocal repertoire mediating many kinds of recognition behavior. The mutual recognition of parents and young in pinon jay creches is achieved through individual variation in many of the characters of the calls (McArthur, 1982). In nestling bank swallows, the replacement of an immature begging call with individually characteristic signature calls at about 2 weeks of age enables recognition by parents (Beecher et al., 1981b). Parent–offspring recognition in murres is primarily acoustic (Tschanz, 1968). Young murres approach a tape recorder steadily playing a parental call over an intermittently calling but visible parent. The greater interindividual than intraindividual variation in the key luring call is achieved through pitch, timbre, and volume differences.

Territorial song enables recognition of neighbors and strangers among many birds (review by Falls, 1978). Hazel grouse cocks tend to sing highly stereotyped songs but some intraindividual variation is achieved by dropping, adding, breaking off, or coalescing song elements (Bergmann et al., 1975). Interindividual variation is found in portions of the song after the first element and permits identification of the singing bird. Individual recognition of territorial male chiffchaffs is achieved through the frequency features of single notes, with amplitude modulation having no role (Becker et al., 1980). In white-throated sparrows, the first three notes of a song are sufficient to permit discrimination (Brooks and Falls, 1975b). Recognition of neighbors' songs is affected if the pitch of the song, or even of the first note, is changed by 5–10%. Yet the duration of a song or first note can be changed by as much as 15% without effect. Considerable powers of discrimination are indicated for song sparrows, who typically have repertoires of 10 songs and four to seven neighbors and yet react more strongly to songs of strangers than to those of neighbors (Kroodsma, 1976). Searcy et al. (1981b) tested the hypothesis that species song learning proceeds by a bird generalizing from its own output in swamp and song sparrows. No support was found for the prediction of the hypothesis that responsiveness to one's one song is stronger than to the song of a stranger. An additional finding from this research on sparrows, as from other work on meadowlarks (Falls and D'Agincourt, 1981), was that discrimination between neighbors and strangers is weaker in species with larger song repertoires. Such a finding could well result from memory limitations in territorial birds.

Song repertoire size has received attention for its role in recognition behavior. Wren's Beau Geste defended his fort at Zinderneuf by propping up the dead and wounded at appropriate places to impress the attackers with his strength. Krebs (1977) has suggested that avian song repertoires may owe their diversity to a similar strategy by territory owners. Intruders would then gain the false impression that competititon for territories is very high. This Beau Geste hypothesis of deceptive recognition has difficulties, however, at least for the well-studied chaffinch (Slater, 1978, 1981a). Many chaffinch song repertoires are very small, sometimes consisting of but one song. Some songs are very similar whereas the hypothesis implies that songs should be very different. While the hypothesis asserts that birds should switch often between song types, they in fact often repeat the same song. However, singing behavior by red-winged blackbirds is consistent with the hypothesis (Yasukawa, 1981). For instance, males often switch song types when they switch singing perches, and intraindividual variation in song repertoires is as great as interindividual variation. Finally, repertoires do not appear to be important for neighbor or kin recognition in birds (review by Krebs and Kroodsma, 1980).

Vocal individual recognition has also been found in several avian species which live in permanent groups (e.g., Indian hill mynahs: Bertram, 1970). In turkey flocks, gobbling calls identify males individually (Schleidt, 1964). In flocks of crows reliable interindividual differences in the durations of caws and intervals betweens them, as well as idiosyncratic temporal patterns such as an alternation of long and short intervals, enable individual recognition (N. S. Thompson, 1969). Among pinon jays 15 vocalizations with much variation both between and within calls enable a complex communication system and personal identification (Berger and Ligon, 1977). Vocalizations are important in the integration of agonistic behavior in Stellar's jays (J. L. Brown, 1964b). Individual recognition via distinctive flight calls occurs in flocks of cardueline finches (Mundinger, 1970). Song dialects are considered in Chapter 3, Song Imprinting.

Mammals

King's College Chapel choir aside, most mammal vocalizations lack the aesthetic appeal of birdsong but nevertheless figure predominantly in much recognition behavior. Spotted dolphins have individual signature whistles, and can be personally identified by Atlantic bottle-nosed dolphins (Caldwell et al., 1971, 1973). Humpback whales communicate information about species, sex, sexual readiness, and individuality in their elaborate songs, (Payne and McVay, 1971; Tyack, 1981). Southern right whales distinguish humpback calls from those of their own species (Clark and Clark, 1980). Male elephant seal roars are unique to the producer (Sandegren, 1976; Shipley et al., 1981) and mothers recognize their pups vocally (Petrinovich, 1974). Interindividual variation in pup attraction calls also assists the mutual recognition of mothers and young in southern fur seals and sea lions (Trillmich, 1981; Vaz-Ferreira and Achaval, 1979). An overview of marine mammal sounds has been provided by W. E. Evans (1967). In sheep, voice is important for the recognition of the lamb by its dam (Poindron and Carrick, 1976; Shillito Walser et al., 1981) and vocal differences enable individual recognition in reindeer cows and calves (Espmark, 1971, 1975). Wolf howls are characteristic of individuals in the pack (Theberge and Falls, 1967; Harrington and Mech, 1979) and, of course, the RCA phonograph mutt recognizes "his master's voice."

In the higher frequency ranges above 10 kHz, bats use a variety of recognition signals, differing in their volume, duration, and rate of frequency modulation, which are distinct from predatory echolocating cries. Infant calls enable maternal recognition in the pallid (P. Brown, 1976), mouse-eared (Kolb, 1977), and leafed-nose (Porter, 1979) bats. Also at high frequencies, a variety of male rodents emit cries in agonistic and sexual encounters, and females do so if disturbed or deprived of their litters (Geyer, 1979; Graham and Thiessen, 1980; Gyger and Schenk, 1980; Nyby et al., 1977; Sales, 1972a, 1972b). Female hamsters, in the best tradition of sirens, emit calls when in heat. At lower frequencies, North African rodents emit species-typical calls in the range of 1 to 6 kHz (George, 1981).

Among primates, vocalizations are important in the discrimination of young by galagos (Klopfer, 1970) and vervets (Cheney and Seyfarth, 1980). In the latter species, group members look at the mother in response to playbacks of infant screams, independent of the behavior of the mother, indicating a recognition by members of the social relations existing in the group. Struhsaker (1967) has noted that vervet infants produce a "Lost rrr" call when separated from their mothers. The Lost rrr tends to be given in call sequences containing other types of Lost calls. In one monkey group a particular type of scream was given by infants 1 to 4 months old toward an adult male that had recently joined the group. The scream elicited retrieval by the infant's mother. Since other males did not precipitate this call, it seems that the infants recognized this particular male as an individual. Juvenile rhesus monkeys recognize their mothers' calls as shown by their vocalizations and locomotor behavior (Hansen, 1976). Human infants as young as 3 days suck more on an experimental teat when the mother's voice is contingent on sucking than when the voice is of a strange female (DeCasper and Fifer, 1980; see also Mehler et al., 1978; Mills and Melhuish, 1974). Obversely, 22 of 27 mothers correctly recognized their own week-old babies from a tape recording of babies' cries (Morsbach and Bunting, 1979).

The calls of forest monkeys, like wolf howls, permit individual recognition. Similarly, personal identity is encoded in the distinctive features of the two contact calls produced by pygmy marmosets (Snowden and

Cleveland, 1980). The long-range pant-hooting vocalizations of chimpanzees show sufficient spectrographic variation that the sources are most likely individually identifiable (Marler and Hobbett, 1975). Siamangs also have very loud and complex calls (Lamprecht, 1970; Chivers, 1976). In red-tailed and blue monkeys, specific distinctiveness characterizes the calls of adult males which space and rally groups (Marler, 1973). By contrast, alarm calls are very similar across species. The vocal systems consist of five and seven basic, discrete, and nonoverlapping calls in the two species, respectively. Marler argues that this is to be expected in arboreal species with poor visual communication, and that nonarboreal, open-country primates will use graded visual and auditory communication systems. In a manner similar to the antiphony of birds, monogamous Siamang pairs carry on long duets of long-range calls (Lamprecht, 1970). Calls from each partner are interlaced and at various points the progression of the duet hinges on the call from the partner. Between these points, the animals apparently follow an internal program. The calls may also assist territorial defense. Similarly, the calls of gibbons permit both species and sex recognition (Andelman, 1980).

In the Japanese macaque, vocal pattern varies widely with the social situation (Green, 1975). Perceptual selectivity of conspecific vocalizations in this species has been examined by Beecher et al. (1979). Experimental animals were subjected to food-reinforced discrimination training together with animals from three control species. Field-recorded calls were presented to left or right ears in order to assess neural lateralization. While experimentals discriminated two functional classes of calls faster than they discriminated the same calls grouped into low- and high-pitched categories, the reverse result was obtained for the controls. Further, the Japanese macaques demonstrated a right-ear (and hence left cerebral hemisphere) advantage for the functional discrimination but not for the pitch discrimination. Japanese macaques thus show selective attention and neural specialization for auditory signals which are important in conspecific recognition, just as in humans.

State recognition is easily attained with diverse and graded vocalization systems. For instance, in the squirrel monkey Jurgens (1979) has described five classes of calls that serve as emotional indicators and are associated with different social contexts. Cranial self-stimulation, in which test animals can control electrical stimulation to brain sites eliciting specific calls, enables detection of the aversiveness or attractiveness of different calls. Such an approach promises to be valuable in the study of emotional states and thus state recognition.

Finally, the entire post-Babel diversity of human tongues rests on only some 90 phonemes, the smallest speech units distinguishing utterances (such as *b*an and *p*an). The interaction of recognition behavior and language is a dominant theme of much of psycholinguistics and the philosophy of language.

Fish

As with insects, temporal patterning is important in fish sound recognition behavior (see Tavolga, 1976, 1977). Sound communication mediates species recognition in four Caribbean damselfishes which are reproductively active at the same time (Myrberg and Spires, 1972; Spanier, 1979). The chirps produced by the fish have similar frequency and amplitude characteristics but differ in the temporal features of the pulse interval and duration and the interpulse interval (Figure 2.11). Playback experiments in both the laboratory and the field demonstrate species recognition, with pulse interval and number of pulses as the significant variables. Sexual and territorial recognition are aided by the sounds produced by male gobies (Tavolga, 1958). In the satinfin shiner, sounds

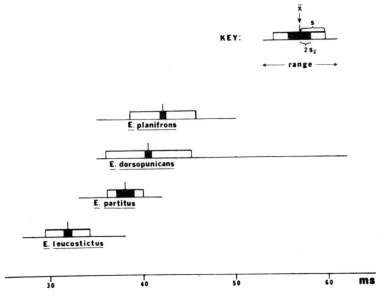

Figure 2.11. Pulse interval differences among calls of four damselfishes (from Spanier, 1979).

produced by males when either fighting another male or courting a female enhance intermale aggressive behavior (Stout, 1963). Similarly, in two species of Texan shiners, sound production serves species and sex recognition (Delco, 1960). Among sunfish, sounds provide information on species identity as well as aggressive and sexual state (Gerald, 1970, 1971; Ballantyne and Colgan, 1978a, 1978b, 1978c).

CHEMOSENSATION

Perfumeries use, for their most alluring products, natural resources as diverse as oakmoss, civet musk, khuskhus, and champac. Yet these materials scarcely indicate the vast diversity of compounds produced by animals to function in recognition behavior. Much information on chemosensation has been drawn together by Ritter (1979) and the role of odors for individual recognition has been reviewed by Halpin (1980).

Like Bethe's (1932) earlier term of "ectohormone," "pheromone" was defined by Karlson and Butenandt (1959) as "substances that are secreted by an individual to the outside and cause a specific reaction in a receiving individual of the same species, for example, a release of certain behavior or a determination of physiologic development." Thus, pheromones can have both releasing and priming functions. It is the release of recognition responses which is of interest in the present context. Pheromones have been reported for a large number of insect and mammalian species, as well as some fish and other invertebrates (e.g., blue crab: Gleeson, 1980; crayfish: Thorp and Ammerman, 1978; Rose and Casper, 1980), and hence comprise an important class of chemical communication substances. Pheromones may be typical of a species or of smaller groups such as individual ant colonies (Holldobler and Wilson, 1977) or even individuals, as in yellow bullheads (Todd, 1971). The existence of a pheromone is proved by demonstrating that a particular secretion reliably elicits a specific reaction in at least some class of conspecifics. Identification of the pheromone is often very difficult, especially in mammals, and has been accomplished only for certain insect cases. Long-range pheromones are usually emitted by the sex making the larger metabolic investment in reproduction. Generally this is the female, which is producing eggs, but in hanging flies it is the male, which provides his mate with a nuptial meal of prey, which emits a pheromone (Thornhill, 1980). Pheromones loom large in the area of reproductive strategies. Beside their role in the Bruce and related effects, pheromones serve to depress reproduction in female sexual competitors in both honeybees (Wilson,

1971) and Mongolion gerbils (Payman and Swanson, 1980). General reviews of pheromones have been made by Johnston et al. (1970), Birch (1974), Shorey (1976), Muller-Schwarze and Silverstein (1979), and, for vertebrates, Gleason and Reynierse (1969).

Other

To begin with nematodes, in the trichina worm both sexes are attracted to each other chemically (Bonner and Etges, 1967). Males of two species of the root nematode genus *Heterodera* are attracted to females by a chemical released by them (Green, 1966). Perception is gustatory and orientation is achieved via klinokinesis and klinotaxis. [Klinokinesis is an orientation response involving random turning of the body at a rate dependent on the intensity of stimulation, while klinotaxis involves turning oriented with respect to the source of stimulation (see Gunn, 1975).] Ripe females in the namatode *Pelodera teres* also secrete a water soluble sex attractant (Jones, 1966).

Among stomatopod crustaceans, individual recognition is mediated via chemical signals (Caldwell, 1979). In a monogamous desert wood louse, chemical cues enable mate and family recognition (Linsenmair, 1972; Linsenmair and Linsenmair, 1972), as they also do in two species of shrimps (Seibt and Wickler, 1972; Johnson, 1977). Discrimination of the reproductive condition of females among isopods and amphipods relies on similar cues (Hartnoll and Smith, 1980; Thompson and Manning, 1981). Chemotaxis underlies species-typical aggregations in planaria (Reynierse, 1967) and species and size recognition in snails (Chase et al., 1978; Snyder and Snyder, 1971).

The role of pheromones in insect behavior has been reviewed by Jacobson (1972) and Shorey (1973). Pheromones figure prominently in the species and sex recognition of many moth and butterfly species (review by Roelofs and Carde, 1977). Clearwing moths achieve species recognition via species-typical pheromones (Greenfield and Karandinos, 1979). Females in the arctiid moth *Utetheisa ornatrix* release a sex attractant in pulses, at a rate of about 1.5 pulses per second, which facilitates the orientation of males (Conner et al., 1980). Females of the tsetse fly, a severe tropical pest, also emit a sex pheromone (Langley et al., 1982). The precision of pheromonal responses in insects is exemplified by a pair of ambrosia beetle species which use two enantiomers (compounds that are mirror images of each other) as pheromones (Borden et al., 1980). One species responds to one enantiomer only and not to a mixture of the two, while the reverse is true for the other species. In the aposematic beetle *Lycus loripes* a pheromone promotes aggregation, which enhances the aposematic effect (Eisner and Kafatos, 1962).

Among the orthoptera (grasshoppers and crickets) pheromones are common. A pheromone-like dispersant is found in crickets (Sexton and Hess, 1968) while in locusts the pheromone locustol, a degradation product of the metabolism of plant lignin, facilitates gregariousness (Nolte et al., 1970, 1973). Both contact chemoreception and long-distance pheromones released by the female are important in sex recognition by male cockroaches (Roth and Willis, 1952; Tobin 1981) and crickets (Rence and Loher, 1977). Indeed, in crickets, odor cues provide distinction of both sex and species (Otte and Cade, 1976). The sex pheromone from American cockroach females produces responses in males at three different levels, arousal, running, and courtship (Rust, 1976). Female cockroaches discriminate the dominance status of males through odor cues (Breed et al., 1980). Contact chemoreception of a fecal pheromone enables first instar Cuban burrowing cricket nymphs to identify their brood-caring mothers (Liechti and Bell, 1975).

Short-range pheromones are important in the ethological isolation of closely related *Drosophila* species such as *melanogaster* and *simulans* (Manning, 1959) and *pseudoobscura* and *persimilis* (Mayr, 1950), although only in the latter case is this discrimination affected by removing the antennae of the females. Averhoff et al. (1979) have considered the role of the antennal arista in chemical signaling which is important in species, strain, and mate recognition. The stimulation of male courtship behavior by female pheromones in *D. melanogaster* has been described by Shorey and Bartell (1970), and Spieth (1974) has provided a comprehensive review. Members of this species also discriminate between conspecifics from different cultures of the same strain (Hay, 1972). Such an environmental effect could facilitate recognition of different genotypes and hence may play a role in the rare male effect (discussed in Chapter 4, Reproduction).

Pheromones and odor cues play important recognition roles among both lower and higher social insects (reviewed by Wilson, 1971; Noirot et al., 1975). A number of ant species emit sex pheromones. Among primitive ants females release sex pheromones from their tergal glands (Holldobler and Haskins, 1977; Haskins, 1978). In another ant, *Monomorium pharaonis*, a short-range pheromone from Dufour's gland and bursa pouches (in the reproductive tract) attracts males to females and subsequent courtship continues as the female signals the male by touching him with her antennae or presenting herself to him (Holldobler and Wust, 1973).

Pheromones contribute to the ethological isolation of slave-making ants of the genus *Harpagoxenus* (Buschinger and Alloway, 1979). Similarly, surface pheromones on the female enable species recognition in harvester ant species while stimulation pheromones regulate the sexual behavior (Holldobler 1976b). In the wasp *Habrobracon juglandis*, olfaction is a crucial stimulus modality for the mating reaction of the males that respond sexually to extracts of a female adbomen, but not of a head or thorax (Grosch, 1948).

Colony identity and territoriality are also conveyed via phermones as, for instance, in leaf-cutting ants (Jutsum et al., 1979). Fielde (1904) demonstrated the inheritance of such odors in several ant species. In his classic studies of South American army ants, Schneirla (1941, 1971) revealed the importance of colony odors for integrated social recognition and activity. Fire ants leave their nest and follow trails marked with species-typical pheromones (Wilson, 1962). Similarly, the pheromonally marked trails of harvester ants excite workers to follow them, to forage, and to defend the territory of the colony (Holldobler, 1976a; Holldobler and Wilson, 1970). In *Myrmica rubra* the secretions from Dufour's gland stimulate recruitment activity for about three minutes and continue to have a large lasting territorial effect (Cammaerts et al., 1977). Persistent territorial pheromones originating in the hind gut are used to mark areas in African weaver ants (Holldobler and Wilson, 1977). The pheromones are colony-typical, as are the trail pheromones of *Lasius neoniger* (Traniello, 1980), which, however, unlike the former, do not elicit aggressive reactions when presented to alien colonies. Anthrophorid bees of the genus *Centris* mark their territories with secretions from mandibular or hind femoral glands (Raw, 1975). Pheromones even mediate interspecific aggression in stingless bees (Johnson and Hubbell, 1975).

Recognition of caste, the brood, and dead conspecifics involves chemosensation in a number of ant species studied. Fire ants use chemical cues in removing dead from the nest (Howard and Tschinkel, 1976) and recognize brood members via a nonvolatile contact pheromone that is distributed evenly over the preadult cuticle and is effective until the pupal skin is shed at adult emergence (Walsh and Tschinkel, 1974). Odor cues are important in the release of brood transport responses in workers of *Tapinoma erraticum* and assist in discrimination from *Solenopsis* brood (Meudec, 1978). In *Myrmica rubra,* abdominal secretions from the queen are part of the stimulus complex by which she is recognized by her workers (Brian, 1973). As in fire ants, in this species the brood is recognized by a chemical signal that is widely distributed over the body surface (Brian, 1975). Hive odors adsorbed over this surface also enable worker honeybees to distinguish their own queens from others (Boch and Morse, 1974, 1979). Similarly, workers use contact pheromones to distinguish queens from workers (Simpson, 1979).

Individual odor differences are also important in the social organization of many hymenoptera. The primitively social sweat bees of the family Halictidae, chiefly *Lasioglossum zephyrum*, which live in small nests, have been the object of considerable study (Barrows, 1975; Barrows et al., 1975; Kukuk et al., 1977). A behaviorally specialized female guards the nest and males leave it upon reaching maturity. The female guard displays acute discrimination between nest mates and nonnest mates. Generally adults less than 2 days of age are accepted into a nest but older adults are not. Since discrimination by the guard is maintained even with bees killed by freezing, contact chemoreception or olfaction must be the operative modality. Individuals introduced into nests of genetically related bees are accepted but are usually rejected by unrelated bees, indicating a genetic basis to the odors. However, since guards discriminate between nest mates and nonnest mates in nests of bees from diverse sources, they must recognize the odors of individuals. Several manipulations have failed to show acquisition of distinctive odors by the bees from the environment. Nest mates removed from the colony and later reintroduced show that the guards remembered individual odors for up to 7 days. Such discrimination of nest mates from nonnest mates obviously serves to maintain the integrity and functioning of the colony, just as it does in the much larger colonies of honey bees.

Male sweat bees also show discriminatory powers. Presented with tethered females, they habituate to them over the course of two 5-minute periods of presentation. Although attracted to papers impregnated with female odors, males also exhibit habituation to them. However, responsiveness, as measured by pounces on the papers, increases when papers from novel females are presented, thus demonstrating that males can discriminate among females. The males show this discrimination whether the different females providing the papers are from the same nest (and therefore presumably sisters) or different nests. The males' memories of female odors persist at least an hour despite experience with the odors of other females in the interim. The adaptiveness of such habituation by males to females is perhaps the saving in time of not pursuing nonreceptive females. It is interesting to compare the time scale of memory in the two sexes: an hour for males, a week for females. The role of these odor discriminations in kin selection among sweat bees is considered in Chapter 4, Groups.

Among herpes, chemical signals mediate individual, neighbor, and species recognition in red-backed and Shenandoah salamanders (McGavin, 1978; Jaeger, 1981; Jaeger and Gergits, 1979). In snakes, pheromonal trails enable species and sex recognition and facilitate the formation of aggregations (Gehlbach et al., 1971; Neill, 1964; Noble, 1937; Porter and Czaplicki, 1974). In skinks and fence lizards, species and sex recognition are achieved via odor cues (Duvall, 1979; Duvall et al., 1980; Figure 2.12). In the latter species, such cues alone can release the push-up display, which plays an important role in much social communication. Females of two South American tortoises are recognized by cloacal odors (Auffenberg, 1965).

Mammals

As any hound dog can testify, mammals shed bounteous odors, which can serve recognition behavior. Kalmus (1955) showed that trained dogs can even distinguish the odors of identical twins. Reviews on mammalian chemical communication and pheromones include Bronson (1971), Eisenberg and Kleiman (1972), Johnson (1973), Mykytowycz (1972), Ralls (1971), and Thiessen and Rice (1976). Olfaction and mammalian sexual behavior, including ovulation and pregnancy effects mediated by olfaction, have been reviewed by Keverne (1978) and Parkes and Bruce (1961). Blaustein (1981) has summarized numerous indications of the role of odors in sexual selection. Recognition of group members often involves odors (review by Ewer, 1968). In the gliding phalanger of New Guinea, odor cues from several glands mediate every aspect of social recognition: territory, dominance, mate, offspring, group, and individual (Schultze-Westrum, 1965). The topics of maternal imprinting on young and sexual imprinting on specific odor cues are considered in Chapter 3, Imprinting.

Because of their convenience, rodents have been extensively studied. In a variety of species, maternal odor facilitates recognition and subsequent suckling (Geyer, 1981). Suckling is decreased when nipples are cleaned with organic solvents. In gerbils, pups prefer the odor of lactating females to nonlactating ones, or to ones whose scent glands have been removed (Gerling, 1980). Mothers are not discriminated from other lactating females, but are preferred to a maternal and paternal pair. Strange parental pairs are less preferred to a pup's own parents. Individual recognition of males is achieved by urine odors (Dagg and Windsor, 1971; Halpin, 1976), and alien conspecific odors are overmarked (Biben, 1980; Kumari and Prakash, 1981). After attacks from a territorially dominant animal, subordinated males are inhibited from scent marking in that

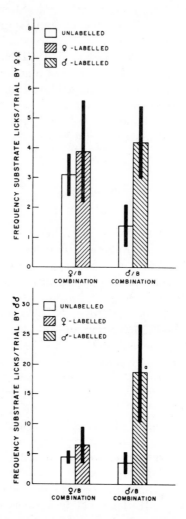

Figure 2.12.   Responsiveness in fence lizards to odor combinations of female-labeled and blank surfaces or male-labeled and blank surfaces (from Duvall, 1979).

territory (Yahr, 1977). Baran and Glickman (1970) showed that marking is almost completely eliminated by olfactory bulbectomy and that, beyond olfaction, visual and cutaneous feedback also contribute to a multimodal control of marking behavior. Similarly, in both sexually naive and experienced male hamsters, bulbectomy eliminates sexual behavior (Murphy and Schneider, 1970). Androgen injections reinstate such behavior in castrated control animals but not bulbectomized individuals. Sex recognition and recognition of sexual status by male hamsters is mediated via odors and ear gland secretions (Landauer et al., 1978, 1980; Johnston, 1980). Dominant hamsters also flank-mark their home range through which they move freely, unlike subordinate individuals (Johnston, 1975).

Olfactory cues underlie species recognition and avoidance in three species of European voles (Jonge, 1980). Male European wood mice distinguish the sexes and the sexual status of females by smell (Gyger and Schenk, 1980). Males from stocks of wild, domestic, and hybrid guinea pigs can distinguish sex and species by urine and perineal scent gland odors (Beauchamp et al., 1979; Wellington et al., 1979). In the domestic species, both males and females can discriminate individuals, and the sexual status of females, using perineal odors (Ruddy, 1980). Odor cues mediate species, sex, and individual recognition in lemmings (Huck and Banks, 1979, 1980a, 1980b), kangaroo rats (Randall, 1981), Columbian ground squirrels (Harris and Murie, 1982), eastern chipmunks (Keevin et al., 1981), and pygmy and house mice (Quadagno and Banks, 1970). In the gregarious Bahaman hutia, a rare hystricomorph rodent, olfactory recognition and scent marking are important for social organization.

Carr (1974) has reviewed the large literature on pheromonal sex attractants in rats, and R. E. Brown (1977) has constructed odor preference and urine marking scales for both sexes, including the effects of gonadectomy and experience, based on data of his own and other researchers. Discrimination of the sexual status of individuals of the opposite sex is independent of the gonadal state of the test animal for both males and females (Carr and Caul, 1962). Male preference for novel over familiar female odors, but the reverse preference in females for male odors, reflects the importance of odor cues in mate selection (Carr et al., 1980a). Odor cues mediate recognition of stress (MacKay-Sim and Laing, 1981a, 1981b) and the reception of strangers into established groups (Sokolov et al., 1979). A fecal pheromone from maternal rats attracts offspring (Moltz and Lee, 1981).

Olfactory cues in mice have been shown to play dominant roles in the recognition of strain (Mainardi et al., 1965a), sex (Chanel and Vernet-Maury, 1963; Nyby et al., 1977), individuals (Bowers and Alexander, 1967; Hahn and Simmel, 1968; Hahn and Tumolo, 1971; Kalkowski, 1967), and territories (Harrington, 1976c). In aggressive situations, mice rely heavily on odor cues, and their discriminating powers are interfered with when antagonists are sprayed with commercial human deodorants (Lee, 1970; Ropartz, 1969). Similarly, aggression is reduced when the antagonists are scented and disappears entirely after olfactory bulbectomy. Both the preputial glands and urine are sources of aggression-promoting odors (Mugford and Nowell, 1971). The urine source is effective only within a strain but is not indicative of individuals (Jones and Nowell, 1974). Young house mice can distinguish odors from stressed and nonstressed adults (Carr et al., 1980b). Female urine has an inhibitory effect on male aggression, while an additional urine factor primes sexual behavior (Dixon and Mackintosh, 1975). This latter effect, unlike that on aggression, is dependent on the sexual status of the female. Odors from various parts of the bodies of females elicit ultrasonic (70 kHz) courtship calls from males (Nyby et al., 1977). Much research has been carried out on the manner in which olfaction mediates the Bruce effect (see Chapter 1, Species and Morphs). For instance, Lott and Hopwood (1972) have provided evidence to support the hypothesis that the stud male sensitizes the female to stimulation by alien males. Pregnancy blocking in females exposed to the stud male for only 3 hours is less than in those exposed for a day or more.

Among ungulates, the black-tailed deer has several pheromones that give social information (Muller-Schwarze, 1971; Volkman et al., 1978; Figure 2.13). Tarsal scent is informative of sex, age, and individual identity while metatarsal scent is associated with fear. Urine cues attract males to females and rub-urinating, in which the hooves are rubbed together while urinating on them, is a distress signal in fawns and a threat signal in adults. Age and dominance relations among males are mediated with forehead gland and preorbital sac contents. Wildebeest luxuriate in an odorous collage of dung, urine, and preorbital gland secretions (Estes, 1969). In the primitive muntjac, olfaction is more important than vision or audition for recognition, and involves nose-to-nose sniffing as well as sniffing of the head, tail and other body parts (Barrette, 1977). Maternal bonding to, and recognition of, young is achieved via odors in a number of species such as goats (Klopfer and Bamble, 1966) and sheep (Morgan et al., 1975). Odors also enable the discrimination of estrous and anestous ewes by rams (Lindsay, 1965), a discrimination that anosmic rams fail to make.

Flehmen is a behavior involving lip curling and sniffing, chiefly by males to detect odor cues from females (see, e.g., Ritter, 1979). The behavior facilitates the passage of air over the vomeronasal, or Jacobson's, organ, which contains a specialized portion of the olfactory epithelium and which connects with either the main nasal cavity or the mouth through ducts. Flehmen has been reported in a wide variety of mammals including marsupials (see Coulson and Croft, 1980), goats (Ladewig and Hart, 1980), Thomson's gazelle (Walther, 1978), cats (Verberne, 1976), tigers (Whittle, 1981), wildebeest (Estes, 1969), buffalo (McHugh, 1958), and the ring-tailed lemur (Bailey, 1978).

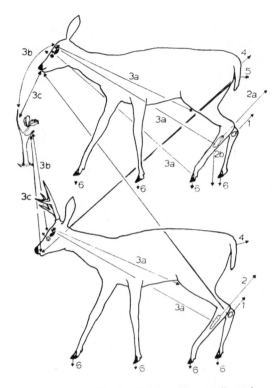

Figure 2.13. Social pheromones in black-tailed deer (from Muller-Schwarze, 1971). Scents of tarsal organ (1), metatarsal gland (2a), tail (4), and urine (5) are air-borne. Interdigital glands (6) and, during reclining, metatarsal gland (2b) touch ground. Forehead (3a) is rubbed by hindleg and then over twigs (3b) which are sniffed and licked (3c).

Carnivore use of olfaction for both territorial and individual recognition has been reported for coyotes (Barrette and Messier, 1980), domestic dogs (Bekoff, 1979; Graf and Meyer-Holzapfel, 1974), wolves (Mech, 1970; Peters and Mech, 1975), foxes (Heimburger, 1959; Lamprecht, 1979), raccoon dogs and jackals (Heimburger, 1959), mongoose (Gorman, 1976), and viverrids and felids generally (Verberne and Leyhausen, 1976). [Rabbits also mark territorially with scents from anal and subcutaneous chin glands (Mykytowycz, 1968).] In genets, social status and amount of scent marking by males are correlated (Roeder, 1978). Individual recognition and recognition of the physiological state of females is mediated olfactorily (Roeder, 1980). Similarly, urine odor cues provide information on colony membership, sex, and sexual state in beagles (Dunbar, 1977, 1978; Dunbar and Carmichael, 1981). Alaskan fur seal and South American sea lion mothers recognize their pups by smell (Bartholomew, 1959; Vaz-Ferreira and Achaval, 1979). Olfactory cues for mother–young recognition have been reported for the pallid (P. Brown, 1976) and mouse-eared (Kolb, 1977) bats.

For primates, too, the *Umwelt* is richly odoriferous. Young galagos can be discriminated by their mothers using only olfactory cues (Klopfer, 1970). Group members, as well as territorial features are marked in, for example, the ring-tailed lemur (Schilling, 1976). Anosmic male rhesus monkeys, unlike intact ones, show no operant behavior to gain access to estrous females (Michael and Keverne, 1968). Subsequent work demonstrates that short-chain aliphatic acids in the vaginal secretions of the females are the operative pheromones (Michael et al., 1971). In *Lemur fulvus*, scent also permits sexual and individual identification (Harrington, 1976a, 1976b, 1977). In squirrel monkeys urine cues identify group members and facilitate sexual recognition (Candland et al., 1980) and olfaction seems to be a more important cue than vision in the discrimination of mothers by infants (Kaplan and Russell, 1974; Kaplan et al., 1977). Infants choose their own anesthetized and hooded mothers over similarly presented females, but the preference disappears if the stimulus females are washed (Kaplan, 1978). The anesthesia and hooding eliminate behavioral and facial cues.

The best efforts of deodorant manufacturers notwithstanding, even humans apparently still show olfactory recognition. After all, Jacobson, an eighteenth century Dutch physician, first described the olfactory organ named after him from a wounded soldier! Some members of married couples can identify their own odors and those of their spouses from a set of such stimuli (Hold and Schleidt, 1977; Schleidt, 1980). Russell (1976) has demonstrated olfactory discrimination of sex by adults and of own versus strange mothers by infants. Parents and children can also recognize each other (Porter and Moore, 1982). The finding that discrimination of hand odors is stronger between unrelated individuals, compared to related ones, parallels Kalmus's (1955) results with dogs, as well as those with bees, discussed in Chapter 4, Groups. American female undergraduates living in either all-women or coeducational dormitories show synchrony in their menstrual cycles (McClintock, 1971; Quadagno et al., 1981). Further evidence for human pheromones is reviewed in Comfort (1971) and in Birch (1974) and Shorey (1976). Blind humans are particularly acute with olfactory discriminations. Helen Keller (1968) wrote that "everyone has a particular person-odor different from everybody else's."

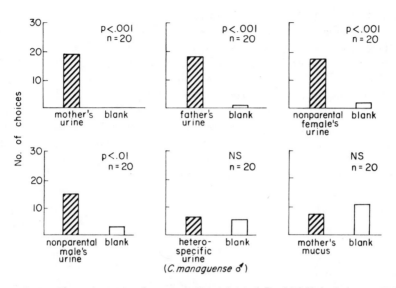

Figure 2.14.   Chemosensory preferences in fry of the midas cichlid (from Barnett, 1981).

Fish

Barnett (1977b), Liley (1982), and Saglio (1979) have reviewed the increasing information about chemical communication, especially phero-. mones, in fish. In most areas, too little research has yet been carried out to decide if generalized chemical cues or specific pheromones underlie the wide variety of chemcically mediated recognition behavior known for the group. Odors underlie species recognition in blennies (Todd, 1971), European minnows (Wrede, 1932) and eels (Pesaro et al., 1981), red shiners (Asbury et al., 1981), and Arctic charr, with juveniles preferring water current bearing intraspecific odors over currents free from smell (Hoglund and Astrand, 1973). The preference disappears when the olfactory organ is removed. Juveniles also tend to avoid currents containing the odors of white fish, cisco, and brown trout (Hoglund et al., 1975). Chemical cues mediate sexual recognition in the California blind goby (MacGinitie, 1939) and in the goldfish (Yamazaki and Watanabe, 1979). Male *Haplochromis burtoni* discriminate the sex and breeding condition of conspecifics chemically (Crapon de Caprona, 1980). Unlike visual stimulation by itself, the odor alone of a gravid female stimulates reproductive activity in males for several days. Recognition of parents and young is mediated by odors in a variety of cichlids studied (Barnett, 1977a; Kuhme, 1963; McKaye and Barlow, 1976; Myrberg, 1966, 1975). In the midas cichlid, peptide chains and steroid titers in the urine possibly mediate species and sex recognition respectively (Barnett, 1981; Figure 2.14). Among the toothed carps, chemical recognition of females by males is widespread. Postpartum females with everted genital papillae are particularly attractive. In the guppy, males and androgen-treated females and juveniles are attracted to water in which females have been living, and their similar response to solutions of 17β-estradiol suggests that this may be the active component of a close range pheromone (Johansen, personal communication). In the cave dwelling *Poecilia sphenops*, sex recognition is achieved in the dark by the male tasting the genital area of the female (Parzefall, 1973). Female goldfish release a pheromone in the ovarian fluid shortly after ovulation, enabling males to identify olfactorily females who have ovulated (Partridge et al., 1976). Pheromones mediate individual recognition among yellow bullheads (Todd et al., 1967; Todd, 1971) and European minnows can be trained to discriminate the odors of individual conspecifics (Goz, 1941).

Alarm substance, or *Schreckstoff*, is released from epidermal club cells when the skin of schooling fish in the order including minnows and their relatives is broken by a predator (R.J.F. Smith, 1982). The ensuing alarm response includes dramatic behavior such as excited swimming, sinking to the substrate, and fleeing to the surface. It is interesting to note that in the fathead minnow alarm substance is absent during the reproductive season in which abrasive breeding behavior takes place. Sensitivity to alarm substance may be a preadaptation for individual recognition by olfaction as seen in catfish (Todd, 1971) and European minnows (Goz, 1941). [A preadaptation is a character capable of shifting into a new function without interference with the original function (see Mayr, 1970).]

Alarm pheromones and consequent species recognition are also known in a number of other animal groups. Galton (1908) long ago noted fear reactions in cattle passing the locations of conspecific fatalities. An alarm pheromone is known in black-tailed deer (Muller-Schwarze, 1971) and alarm reactions have been reported in rodents in response to injuries and to the odors of stressed conspecifics (review by R. E. Brown, 1979). In view of these results, further mamalian research would be worthwhile. American toad tadpoles release an alarm pheromone when injured (Waldman and Adler, 1979). Among invertebrates, the sea urchin *Diodema antillarum* displays strong escape responses to conspecific juices but weak or no responses to other urchins (Snyder and Snyder, 1978). In a sea anemone, an alarm pheromone, named anthopleurine, has been identified (Howe and Sheikh, 1975). Finally, nest defense in the social insects is integrated via alarm pheromones (see Wilson, 1971). The evolution of such pheromones is considered in Chapter 4, Groups.

Overall, it is clear that the efficacy of different sensory modalities is dependent on many interacting factors, some of which are intrinsic to the animal and some are properties of its environment. In frogs body size determines the fundamental frequency of call notes and this fact is important in the recognition of mate size. The surroundings of an animal provide noise that interfere with the signals it produces. These surroundings also affect the suitability of different modalities. In open, well-lighted areas, vision is quick and rich in its information content. But at night all cats are black, and in such obscured areas, acoustical and electrical signals are more useful. While electromagnetic and auditory signals disappear quickly after their broadcast, chemical cues remain for some time. These differing features of modalities have permitted the evolution of the current diversity of sensory processes.

3
Developmental Processes

In many species, recognition behavior changes during an animal's lifetime. Such changes may be the result of maturation, involving growth and the onset of nervous and hormonal mechanisms, and/or of experience gained from individual social encounters. Experimental manipulations enable analysis of the relative roles of maturation and experience, thus operationally solving the "nature-nurture" dilemma of the extent to which behavior is "learned" or "innate." The basic methodology in developmental studies is to expose adequately sized groups of individuals to experimental treatments of interest, and then to compare the subsequent behavior (such as mating preference, approach to conspecifics, and aggressive interactions) with the behavior of one or more control groups. Sometimes the experimental treatment is to raise individuals in social isolation, such individuals often being referred to as Kasper Hauser individuals after an early nineteenth century "wild boy" in Nuremburg who apparently grew up without human contact until the age of 17 years. Another common experimental design is that of (interspecific) cross-fostering, in which broods of related species are exchanged and their subsequent species and sex recognition behavior examined.

Behavioral ontogeny is, of course, only one aspect of the overall ontogeny of an organism and must often be considered in this broader context. For instance, in a number of mammalian species recognition of status differences between males involves neoteny (the retention of formerly juvenile characters by adult descendants produced by retardation of somatic development) (Gould, 1977). Bighorn sheep become

sexually mature at 2.5 years but continue to develop over many succeeding years, with the horns growing in both size and curvature (Geist,
1971). The resulting differences in appearance between age classes
facilitate dominance recognition. Similarly, among African bovids, growth
is almost complete at maturation in territorial species, but is prolonged in
nonterritorial ones where absolute dominance is vital to reproductive
success (Estes, 1974).

Research on developmental processes in recognition behavior has
progressed on several fronts. Nevertheless, it is far from clear how many
distinct mechanisms exist, despite the widespread use of a number of
customary labels such as "imprinting" and "conditioning." The details of
the neural and hormonal bases of recognition behavior, as of behavior
generally, are lacking. In gerbils, territorial marking is under hormonal
control (Lindzey et al., 1968). Sexual recognition disappears in forebrainless
cichlids (Ribbink, 1972). A school of forebrainless minnows accepts
strangers more readily than a school of intact ones (Berwein, 1941). (A
single forebrainless minnow tends to lead a school of intact ones, an
uncomfortable finding for observers of the contemporary political arena!)
Imprinted reactions in young turkeys and Nile mouthbrooders have been
reported as chemically transferable (Schulman, 1972; Zippell and
Langescheid, 1973). Turkey poults receiving intraperitoneal injections of
brain homogenates from trained donor birds performed more key pecking
to view an imprinted stimulus than did controls receiving injections from
untrained birds. The result is not due to an overall increase in general
activity. Similarly, intramuscular injections, from donors who are imprinted on a spherical dummy, into unimprinted cichlid recipients after
the end of the critical period promote responsiveness to the dummy.
Injections from nonimprinted donors do not have any effect. Further work
using different dummies could investigate the specificity of the effect.
Finally, there is the clinical condition of prosopagnosia in which lesions in
the temporal and occipital lobes have the consequence that patients can
identify objects by sight and persons by voices but not persons by their
faces. All these preliminary results only indicate further avenues for
research. As Bullock (1965) points out, the gap between physiology and
ethology is the widest found between disciplines in science.

Conventional ethological wisdom asserts that when an animal responds
differently to the same stimulus, the underlying process may involve
either a structural change (such as maturation, learning, or imprinting) or
a motivational change (a nonstructural change due to drive level
variation). The distinction is thus between changes in mechanisms and
changes in the activation of mechanisms. The time scale of structural

changes tends to be longer than that of motivational changes, but separation is not always easy. For instance, the great alterations in the hormonal and nervous systems over the reproductive cycle, which have important consequences for recognition behavior, doubtless include both structural and motivational changes. Imprinting processes are clearly structural, but the changes in the way pumpkinseed sunfish (Colgan and Gross, 1977) and savannah sparrows (Weatherhead and Robertson, 1980; discussed in Chapter 4) react to stimulus dummies over the nesting period are likely motivational. Watanabe and Tamoto (1981) have shown the central role of reproductive motivation in the parental reactions of an African mouthbrooding cichlid. The duration of parental care depends on the state of the female, not the developmental stage of the brood. In newly formed pairs of mourning doves yellow head markers disrupt pair bonds but not in pairs incubating eggs or brooding squabs (Goforth and Baskett, 1965). Is this change due to learning or motivation?

The internal state alters the perceptual world. Lorenz has cited an instance of this realization in Goethe: "With this drink inside you, you will soon see Helen in every woman." Recognition behaviors are among those affected when parental behavior is induced in previously nonparental animals by the presentation of eggs or young (e.g., sticklebacks: Iersel, 1953; gouramis: Kramer, 1973; chickens: Burrows and Byerly, 1938; hamsters: Noirot and Richards, 1966; mice: Noirot, 1969; rats: Rosenblatt, 1967). Unlike virgin females, lactating guinea pigs vocalize in response to the calls of infants (Berryman, 1981). Olfactory discrimination, which underlies sexual recognition in rats and mice, is dependent on the state of maturity and gonadal condition of both the donor and recipient animals (Carr and Caul, 1962; Chanel and Vernet-Maury, 1963). For their part, the recognition behavior of offspring also changes greatly over early ontogeny both from maturational processes and specific experiences, structurally and motivationally.

The taxonomy of the motivational and structural processes involved in the ontogeny of recognition behavior is obviously murky. Developmental ethologists are like the proverbial blind men, each touching and describing one part of the elephant, with consequent confusion and conflict. It is small wonder that one frustrated reaction to this situation has been "Under precisely controlled conditions an animal does as he damn pleases" (Dubos, 1971). Against this unsettling background, the available evidence on structural changes is reviewed. General treatments of behavioral ontogeny are available (Burghardt and Bekoff, 1978; birds: Kruijt, 1962; mammals: Denenberg, 1972). For purposes of organization, this chapter considers habituation and learning (processes involving distinct changes in stimulus–response relations, at any time in an animal's life once it has developed sensorimotor integrity, consequent to specific experience), imprinting (developmental changes restricted to certain stimuli during certain critical, or sensitive, periods), and socialization (more general aspects of the ontogeny of social recognition).

Habituation and Learning

The closely related processes of habituation and learning are both involved in recognition behavior. Habituation is "the waning of responsiveness to repeated or constant stimulation" (Peeke and Herz, 1973). The meaning of "learning" unfortunately varies with the user but generally refers to a long-term change, in the likelihood of a particular response following a particular stimulus, over successive associations of the stimulus and response ("when followed by appropriate reinforcement" according to reinforcement theorists). Learning is generally explained as the outcome of classical and operant conditioning. In classical conditioning, such as with Pavlov's dogs, an initially ineffective stimulus, such as a tone, is paired with one, such as a puff of meat powder on the tongue, which is effective in eliciting the response, salivation. Over successive pairings, the tone comes to elicit salivation when presented alone. Operant conditioning refers to instrumental responding such as maze running described for domestic fowl in Chapter 1, Species and Morph Recognition. Learning researchers disagree on whether these conditioning paradigms reflect fundamentally different processes, and on whether all learning is based on these processes. It is thus largely a matter of definition to what extent the distinction between "habituation" and "learning" is maintained (cf. Mackintosh, 1974; Petrinovich and Patterson, 1979). Should the physiological mechanisms underlying these behavioral processes differ, then the distinction could gain more importance. But our knowledge of these processes, as discussed above, is as yet very incomplete.

Habituation is likely operative in reproductive recognition behavior such as the Coolidge effect (Chapter 1, Sex and Mates), the rare male effect (Chapter 4, Reproduction), and sexual imprinting on female morphs (Gallagher, 1976), as well as the recognition of parasitic eggs by host bird species (Rothstein, 1978), colony recognition among army ants (Schneirla, 1941), the decrease in aggression by parental ring-billed gulls towards chicks with altered appearance (Miller and Emlen, 1975), odor responses in dogs (Dunbar and Carmichael, 1981), and the waning of recognition smiling responses in human infants (Ambrose, 1961; Figure 3.1). By contrast, sensitization, taken as the reverse of habituation, has been invoked as a mechanism in recognition behavior development only

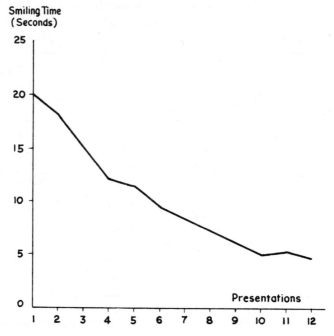

Figure 3.1. Habituation in the smiling response of human infants to an adult face (from Ambrose, 1961).

in connection with the Bruce effect (Lott and Hopwood, 1972; discussed in Chapter 2, Chemosensation) and some aspects of imprinting (Gallagher, 1976).

The role of habituation in the recognition of aggressive rivals has been shown in several species of birds (e.g., white-crowned sparrow: Petrinovich and Peeke, 1973) and fishes (e.g., sticklebacks: Assem and Molen, 1969; Peeke and Veno, 1973, 1976; Peeke et al., 1979; bluegills: Colgan et al., 1979), and likely underlies the dear enemy effect (discussed in Chapter 1, Territoriality) in which responsiveness to territorial neighbors is less than to strangers. Estes (1969) describes the habituation of aggressive responses to newcomers by established male territorial wildebeest underlying the dear enemy effect in that species. It might be expected that habituation would be less in those bird species in which song repertoires are relatively large. Nevertheless, Kroodsma (1976) has shown differential responses to neighbors and strangers in a population of song sparrows in which repertoire size was about 10 songs and territorial males typically had four to seven neighbors. On the other hand, other data are in agreement with this expectation. Differences in responses to neighbors and strangers are larger in swamp sparrows than song sparrows, which have a larger repertoire (Searcy et al., 1981b).

As Wilson (1975) points out, the dear enemy effect may also involve two other processes besides habituation. The first process is the increase in the attractiveness of an object by repeated exposure to it, as reported by Zajonc (1971) in rats, responding to music, and humans, to nonsense words. The second process is the convergence of the dialect used by long-term neighbors so that more elements are shared more often (e.g., Indian hill mynahs: Bertram, 1970; cardinals: Lemon, 1968b). Like forgetting, habituation enables an animal to ignore past or repetitive changes in its environment and to turn its attention, always finite in scope, to new events.

The issue of constraints on learning is relevant to recognition learning. This issue is important because recognition behavior often involves complex learned responses, in social situations, strongly constrained by selection pressures (e.g., species, mate, and offspring recognition). The constraints issue embodies the realization that learning is dependent on, not only stimulus and response, but also reinforcer, species, and context (see Hinde and Stevenson-Hinde, 1973). It thus represents one of an increasing number of points of fusion between the historically but artificially distinct disciplines of ethology and psychology. Knowledge of constraints is scarcely recent. Heinroth (1911) reported on the differential ease of cross-fostering young in different anatid species.

It appears worthwhile to investigate further possible extensions of concepts between ethology and psychology. For instance, ring-necked pheasants are more similar in appearance to golden pheasants than are silver pheasants. Golden males show more interest in a mounted female ring-necked than a silver (Noble and Vogt, 1935). Such a finding suggests exploring recognition errors in terms of stimulus generalization, a key psychological concept. Similar mechanisms probably underly facial recognition by humans (e.g., Light et al., 1981) and species recognition and mate choice in many other visually oriented species. Operant psychologists have used discrimination procedures to investigate "natural concepts" in pigeons (e.g., Herrnstein and DeVilliers, 1980). These birds learn to distinguish bodies of water, trees, fish, and individual persons. Such an approach suggests an additional experimental technique by which could be investigated the social categories which various species recognize. Further, cognitive psychologists employ the concept of a chunk, a stimulus unit familiar to the subject. Humans involved in cognitive tasks such as arithmetic can hold only a few chunks in their immediate memory simultaneously. Chunks reflect previous learning. The product of 7×5 is a chunk, but not that of 123×45. To speakers of English, the name Cartwright is easily recognizable but Nakazono is not. To what extent can animal recognition behavior be analyzed in terms of chunks?

Species

Learning experience enhances species recognition and hence ethological isolation (discussed in Chapter 4) in groups from *Drosophila* (Parsons, 1973) through lizards (Ferguson, 1969) and grebes (Nuechterlein, 1981b) to guppies and their relatives (Liley,1966; Kennett and McKay, 1980). Such learning, in the usual psychological sense of the association of stimuli and responses, is doubtless of great importance in many species independent of imprinting processes which may also be involved. Since it appears that species learning and imprinting lie on a single continuum of behavioral modifiability, they are discussed together under Sexual and Song Imprinting below.

Sex and Mates

Learning plays a role in sex discrimination. Discrimination by male red-winged blackbirds in their nuptial plumage is inferior to that of fully adult birds (Noble and Vogt, 1935). This difference could arise from learning or maturation. In a choice situation involving anesthetized males and females as test stimuli, sexually experienced male hamsters direct more movements to the anesthetized females than do inexperienced males (Landauer et al., 1978).

Learning is also operative in the recognition of mate quality necessary for sexual selection. In *Drosophila pseudoobscura* 11-day-old females have been reported to mate preferentially with orange-eyed males only when they have had previous copulatory experience with males of this type (Pruzan, 1976). However, females that did not copulate initially with such males were discarded from the sample, and so this result may reflect only a constant preference in some females for these males, and not a learning effect. Female bullfrogs learn to choose fitter mates (Howard, 1978). While younger females are more variable in mate choice, older females consistently choose the oldest and largest males in the population. Among monogamous feral pigeons, inexperienced females, and especially males, are less consistent in their mate choice behavior than are more experienced birds (Burley and Moran, 1979). Intact and gonadectomized

rats, of either sex, learn equally well to discriminate between individuals of the opposite sex which differ in sexual state (Carr and Caul, 1962). The importance of learning for recognition reactions in many species should not be overemphasized, however. For instance, in female hampsters, heterosexual contact experience is not necessary for sex discrimination (Carmichael, 1980). Overall, these studies on diverse species indicate that learning can serve to improve mate selection over an individual's lifetime.

Relatives

The role of learning in the development of the recognition of relatives was pointed out by Hamilton in his key 1964 paper (discussed in Chapter 4, Groups). He concluded that "if [an individual] could learn to recognize those of his neighbours who really were close relatives and could devote his beneficial actions to them alone an advantage to inclusive fitnes would at once appear." Abundant evidence supports this conclusion. For nest mate recognition abilities in sweat bees, genetic homogeneity accounts for much of the behavior but early larval conditioning and adult learning also contribute to the ontogeny of the discrimination (Kukuk et al., 1977). In early work on the ability for recognition learning, Fielde (1904) concluded that "if [the ant] has not reason and imagination, she has at least the ground on which to exercise both, cognoscence of past experiences." Tadpoles of American toads and Cascade frogs when reared alone or with siblings preferentially associate with siblings over nonsiblings, in contrast to those reared with both siblings and nonsiblings which show no preference (Waldman, 1981; Blaustein and O'Hara, 1981). Thus, experience is not necessary for sibling recognition, but early experience can alter preferences.

Recognition learning involving parents, eggs, and young has been especially studied in birds. The development of the parental ability to discriminate offspring often coincides with that of increased mobility on the part of young. Bank swallows begin to discriminate young when these become mobile at just over 2 weeks of age through the development of signature calls which replace the begging call (Hoogland and Sherman, 1976; Beecher et al., 1981b). Sooty tern chicks are not distinguished by their parents until 4 or 5 days after hatching (Lashley, 1915; Palmer, 1941). Similarly, in ring-billed gulls, parents take 7–9 days to come to recognize their young individually (Miller and Emlen, 1975). Parents presented with normally advancing-age chicks on each of the first 8 days do not reject such substitutes at any point. Parental razorbills do not

distinguish the leap calls of their own versus other chicks at 4 days of age but do so at 10–18 days (Ingold, 1973). Carrion crows show no development of egg recognition, and recognition of chicks occurs only late in the breeding season (Yom-Tov, 1976).

Young birds also learn about their parents. In at least two species prenatal experience has been shown to influence later behavior. In laughing gulls, parent-hatched chicks show increased activity in response to "crooning" calls whereas incubator-hatched chicks do not (Impe-khoven, 1976). Similarly, while in the egg, murre chicks come to discriminate the luring calls of their parents and of any helping adult over the successive contacts with it (Tschanz,1979). Indeed, the young can learn two luring calls prior to hatching and hence recognize both parents (Tschanz, 1968). Additionally, the vocalizations of incubating female common eiders during late incubation are probably important in the development of recognition of the mother by the ducklings (Schmutz, personal communication). Gull chicks learn to recognize their parents vocally. Laughing gulls distinguish parents from neighbors (Beer, 1970c) and ring-billed gulls learn to identify the mew calls, which are associated with feeding, as demonstrated by their approaching and vocalizing when such calls are followed by food reinforcement (Evans, 1980b). Hailman (1967) has detailed the ontogeny of the pecking response of gull chicks through which they are fed by their parents (Figure 3.2). Nestling galahs come to recognize their parents through their calls by the fifth week after hatching, and by a week prior to fledging (at about 46 days posthatch) both parents and offspring recognize each other well (Rowley, 1980). In pinon jays, which form creches, mutual learning of the calls of parents and offspring goes on over the third week of life of the nestlings (McArthur, 1982). The calls of the young vary over time, and thus require tracking by the parents. European blackbird nestlings distinguish the characteristic feeding notes of their mothers (Messmer and Messmer, 1956). This learning process can be used in artificially reared birds to yield selective responsiveness to pure tones and whistled melodies.

The ontogeny of recognition behavior is complex in both mammalian mothers and young over the reproductive cycle. In southern sea lions and fur seals, recognition of pups by mothers develops over the first few hours after birth while the reverse recognition requires up to several days (Trillmich, 1981; Vaz-Ferreira and Achaval, 1979). Adult female Richardson's ground squirrels discriminated their own and unrelated young between 3 and 7 weeks old when paired with them in an experimental observation box (Michener, 1974). Even before their eyes opened, the young also distinguished among adults, responding cohesively to mothers and submissively to unrelated adults. In the field, juveniles take 6–7 weeks

PECKS/30 SEC

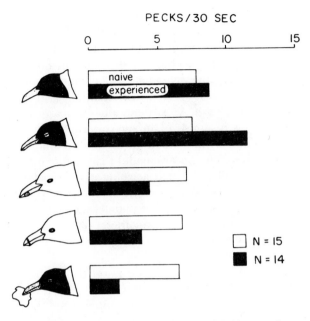

Figure 3.2. Experienced gull chicks peck at the most adult-like stimuli more than naive chicks (from Hailman, 1967).

before they can consistently identify adults independent of the location of the encounter (Michener, 1973). In precocial spiny mice, sibling recognition arises during early development from exposure learning of the odors of siblings mediated through the mother (Porter and Wyrick, 1979; Porter et al., 1978, 1981b). The attachments are modifiable by subsequent experience and so do not appear to involve imprinting. Cross-fostered young prefer foster siblings to related siblings, and spend no more time with strange siblings than with strange nonsiblings. Thus, in this case there is no evidence for any inborn ability for sibling recognition. The role of learning in kin recognition has also been demonstrated in white-footed mice raised under one of four conditions; kin socialized, nonkin socialized, kin nonsocialized, and nonkin nonsocialized (M.D. Hoffman, 1981). When separated at weaning and tested for social preferences at 2–3 months of age, mice spent more time near individuals with whom they had socialized, whether kin or not. Similar early learning permits the evaluation of the degree of kinship in other rodents (e.g., Gilder and Slater, 1978). The necessity for learning in kin recognition can lead to errors, as discussed for Belding's ground squirrels in Chapter 4, Reproduction.

Parental learning of young primates (e.g., galagos: Klopfer 1970; pigtail macaques: Jensen, 1965) is matched by learning of parents by young (e.g., pigtail and bonnet macaques: Rosenblum and Alpert, 1977). Porter and Moore (1982) argue that learning of odor cues in human recognition parallels such learning in other mammals. The development of recognition smiling in infants involves operant conditioning, with handling as a reinforcer (Brackbill, 1958). As is generally the case in operant conditioning, the smiling response of infants intermittently reinforced for smiling waned less quickly in extinction (the period following acquisition and in which no reinforcements are made) than that of infants reinforced for each response. Finally, although learning plays a major role in much mammalian recognition behavior, genetic components remain important, as demonstrated by the preference of pigtail macaques for strange half-siblings over similar unrelated conspecifics (Wu et al., 1980) and the discrimination of related from unrelated strangers by white-footed mice (Grau, 1982).

Among cichlid fishes, five of six male jewel fish, removed from their spawn and replaced 24 to 28 hours later, resumed guarding the eggs (Noble and Curtis, 1939). The authors interpreted this outcome as indicating memory of the spawn. Experienced jewel fish parents distinguish their own young from those of other species whereas inexperienced parents do not. Myrberg (1975) paired chemical stimuli of conspecific young with visual stimuli of young of the same or a different species for 15–19 hours. Under such stimulation female convict cichlids show preference for such young by visual cues alone for at least 5–7 hours after the chemical stimuli have stopped. In the midas cichlid, parents learn to recognize young over the parental cycle and display a moderately short-term memory (Noakes and Barlow, 1973). Parents accept conspecific fry providing they are not older than their own, and substitutions with successive broods can greatly extend the parental period.

Closely related to the topic of learning in parent and offspring recognition is that of imprinting, discussed in the next section.

Aggression

Recognition learning is also important in agonistic relations. The individual recognition underlying crayfish dominance hierarchies is retained for up to 5 days, but the cues used remain to be elucidated (Lowe, 1956). Hens learn to be submissive in their hierarchies (Ratner, 1961) and pair relations once established are usually carried over to subsequent encounters (King, 1965). After winning in a contest against a particular breed, hens show a decreased latency for displaying dominance behavior to a second hen of that breed (Potter and Allee, 1953). Guhl (1953) concluded that white rock hens display good learning and memory of ther individuals in their flocks. In young chicks, social discrimination develops quickly after a few hours of cohabitation (Zajonc et al., 1975). The opportunity to peck during exposure to companions seems necessary for discriminating these companions from strangers. An unusual population of rufus-sided towhees revealed the role of associative learning of territorial songs (Richards, 1979). Some male towhees sing songs resembling those of Carolina wrens. Such songs played to neighbors of these birds elicit strong responses while playbacks to nonneighbors elicit only weak responses. Thus, neighbors learn to associate the wren songs with their conspecifics. Further aspects of song learning in birds are considered below in Song Imprinting.

In domestic mice, the response of adult males to the odors of urines from other dominant and subordinate males is partially a function of experience with such odors during the first month of life (Hennessy, 1980).

Memory of rivals in the territorial and dominance hierarchy systems of fish seems to be short-lived. In a territorial goby, such memory of rivals lasts for an hour between succeeding tests, but not for 24 hours (Gandolfi et al., 1973). Small differences in morphology and/or behavior are the features which underlie similar learning in the dominance hierarchies of hybrid platies (Zayan, 1974).

Individual

The role of learning in individual recognition behavior can be appreciated in the results of a variety of studies ranging from tightly controlled laboratory studies to field observations on behavioral differences as a function of experience. The contributions of genes and experience to kin and individual recognition in the social insects is discussed in Chapter 4, Groups.

Following removal from a group, canvasback ducklings are treated as familiar by their associates if returned in a few days, but as strangers after a week or more, probably due to the rapid change in appearance at this stage of life (Hochbaum, 1959). By 8 weeks of age, groups of common eiders form stable groups, suggesting individual recognition (Munro and Bedard, 1977a). Performance in a Y-maze reveals good ability in budgerigars of both sexes to recognize individuals (Trillmich, 1976). Adults of many social birds and mammals recall individuals even after removals of several months. In domestic chickens, a separation of 2–3 weeks generally leads to a forgetting of former pen-mates (Guhl, 1953, Schjelderup-Ebbe, 1935). Learning of new flight calls mediates individual recognition in flocks of cardueline finches (Mundinger, 1970).

In mammals, recognition of not only individuals but also the state of those individuals depends on learning. Experience with adults during rearing is important in the discrimination of stressed and nonstressed adult conspecifics in young house mice (Carr et al., 1980b). At 48 days of age, mice prefer the odors of nonstressed individuals while at 24 days no preference is found. Male–female pairs of collared lemmings were housed together for 30 days and then tested for odor recognition after varying intervals of separation (Huck and Banks, 1979). Both sexes preferred the odors of their partners over that of a stranger after 1 day. Females, but not males, exhibited this preference after 12 days, and neither sex showed any preference after 24 days. In New Guinea gliding phalangers, young members of the group first learn to recognize others, besides their mother, as members of the group, and later come to recognize them on an individual basis (Schultze-Westrum, 1965).

Among fish, the rate of learning for individual recognition is quite variable. Bluegill sunfish in an operant task showed only slow acquisition of the ability to discriminate between individuals (Butler and Johnson, 1972). But the individual characters of the anemone dwelling fish *Amphiprion bicinctus* are learned in 24 hours and retained for at least 10 days (Fricke, 1973). European minnows retain the memory of individual conspecifics 15 weeks after conditioning (Goz, 1941).

IMPRINTING

In many vertebrate species, the development of recognition of conspecifics is limited to a brief critical period early in life. Few terms in behavioral biology have been so widely used and abused as "imprinting" to label this process. Lorenz introduced the term in connection with the development of avian sexual preferences (as discussed below). "Imprinting" has since been applied to many types of behavior in many species in which early, and often short, social experience has a relatively long-lasting influence on subsequent social recognition behavior. (Habitat imprinting is an additional, nonsocial form of imprinting found in some species.) Consequently the term now doubtless encompasses behavioral phenomena which are heterogeneous with respect to both mechanism and function. For instance, Sambraus and Sambraus (1975) report that in domestic farm animals there is no brief critical period as in birds. Although imprinting was originally contrasted with traditional learning as understood in the laboratory, it is now realized to share many features with such learning, as discussed below in the following response of birds. Together with the issue of learning constraints (see above), this realization makes evident a spectrum of behavioral modifiability ranging from very rigid acts with high genetic determination to very labile acts permitting great ontogenetic plasticity. Many general reviews of the Byzantine literature on imprinting and associated critical periods are available (Bateson, 1966, 1978b, 1979; Beach and Jaynes, 1954; Hess, 1973; Immelmann, 1975a, 1975b; Matthews and Hemmings, 1963; Scott, 1978; Scott et al., 1974; Sluckin, 1970; and, for domestic animals, Denenberg, 1969). Research has focused on offspring imprinting, sexual and filial imprinting, and song imprinting.

Offspring

In offspring imprinting, parents come to recognize and be attached to their offspring at either the first breeding or at each successive breeding. In the ant *Formica polyctena* the development of the discrimination of cocoons of different species shows many similarities to cases of vertebrate imprinting (Jaisson, 1975; Jaisson and Fresneau, 1978). Workers exposed to cocoons of a given species during the first 2 weeks of adult life subsequently care for this species and eat the cocoons of other species. Workers with no exposure fail to care for any cocoons. The first 2 weeks are a sensitive period for the establishment of this discrimination, which is still evident after months of hibernation.

Offspring imprinting has been investigated in several bird species. Northern orioles reject the eggs of the brood parasite, the brown-headed cowbird, from their nests. Rothstein (1978) has provided data supporting the hypothesis that orioles imprint on their own eggs during a sensitive period which begins when they lay the first egg in their first nest. Subsequently they reject all eggs that are sufficiently different from their own in color and spotting. Parental lovebirds imprint on their young, which have either red or white down depending on the species (Dilger, 1960). Experienced adults do not feed young of the other down type, but adults breeding for the first time do. Since plumage is so critical, it is curious that foster parents raise well-feathered young of different lovebird species, which appear dissimilar. These two studies by Rothstein and Dilger indicate how diverse avian species become imprinted on their offspring.

Among many mammals postpartum contact between mother and young is important for appropriate recognition and subsequent nursing (e.g., moose and elk: Altmann, 1963; Alaskan fur seal: Bartholomew, 1959). In domestic cattle the first 3 hours postpartum are critical for maternal acceptance of the calf (LeNeindre and Garel, 1976). Similarly, in goats, immediate separation of does and kids for as little as an hour leads to rejection, but this is prevented by a brief period of contact (as short as 5 minutes) which enables olfactory identification (Klopfer et al., 1964; Klopfer and Gamble, 1966). Does do not discriminate between their own young, but do distinguish between strange kids and their own. Alien kids can be successfully substituted for a doe's own newborn immediately after parturition, showing that birth fluids themselves are not necessary for the bonding (Klopfer and Klopfer, 1968; Klopfer, 1971). More recent work (Gubernick, 1980, 1981; Gubernick et al., 1979), however, indicates that bonding takes longer than a few minutes and that a doe labels her kid via licking and milk, and subsequently learns to recognize these labels. Does who are separated from their kids for an hour immediately after birth nurse their own and alien kids equally in succeeding months (Hersher et al., 1958). This lack of discrimination contrasts with normal does who nurse their own kids preferentially. It is also possible to foster cross-species adoptions between goats and sheep by enforcing early contact between a lamb or kid and a mother restrained in a harness (Hersher et al., 1963a, 1963b). In sheep, although similar recognition behavior underlies attachment (F.V. Smith, 1965), separation for a few hours has less effect than in goats (F.V. Smith et al., 1966). Bubenik (1965) observed maternal bonding in two tamed females of each of red and roe deer. Maternal recognition develops in both species, with red deer having more complex doe–fawn relations and primiparous and multiparous females showing behavioral differences. Overall, offspring imprinting contributes to the elaborate maternal care which typifies mammalian reproduction.

A number of cichlid studies have investigated the possibility of adult imprinting on eggs. Some data from several species have suggested the existence of egg imprinting (Myrberg, 1964, 1966). However, both experienced and inexperienced pairs of jewel fish and black acaras readily accept replacement eggs, wrigglers, and free-swimming young of the other species providing the replacement offspring are age matched to those being replaced (Greenberg, 1963). Similarly, exchanges of wrigglers (but not eggs) are generally successful between *Aequidens latifrons* and *Tilapia sparrmani*, providing the replacements are size matched (Collins, 1965). Again, the breeding history of the parents makes no difference to their response. Hence these studies fail to indicate a mechanism of imprinting although species recognition of different life stages is acute in several species studied (discussed in Chapter 1, Species and Morphs).

Sexual and Filial

Birds

The vast literaure on avian sexual and filial imprinting attests to William McDougall's (1923) conclusion that "the problems of bird-behavior are innumerable." Recognizable accounts of such imprinting can be found in Book 10 of the Roman natural historian, Pliny the Elder, in the writings of Reginald, a medieval monk in Durham, and in Book 3 of Thomas More's "Utopia" written in 1515:

> Men hatch the eggs, not hens, by keeping them in a warm place at an even temperature. The chicks, as soon as they come out of the shell, recognize and follow men instead of their mothers.

Systematic observations were first reported by Spalding (1873), tutor of Bertrand Russell until his early death from tuberculosis. (For Spalding's unique relations with his employers, see Russell's *Autobiography*.) One can only dream of the effect on ethology had Spalding lived longer and perhaps turned Russell's interests to the discipline!

The erroneous imprinting of birds on humans is well documented. Contemporary accounts are given by Raber (1948) and Lorenz (1970). Bullfinches raised in isolation from conspecifics may become attached to humans (Nicolai, 1956). Reflecting the usual behavior between bonded conspecific mates, females attack humans vigorously while males attempt to feed them. Additional evidence of recognition is that males reared by men prefer them to women. Sexual attachment to humans by brown leghorn chickens follows early experience and persists throughout at least the first year of life (Guiton, 1962).

Excellent general reviews on sexual imprinting have been given by Bateson (1972, 1973), Gottlieb (1971), and Immelmann (1972). (Song imprinting is considered in the next section.) Certain findings suggest that it is appropriate to group research into investigations focusing on sexual attachments and those on the following response, or filial imprinting. For instance, the critical period for sexual attachment in ducks persists over the first 2 months after hatching whereas that for the following response is limited to the first few days or even hours (Schutz, 1965, 1971). In domestic cocks attachment as measured by the following response is not identical with subsequent sexual preferences (Vidal, 1980).

The development of adult sexual attachments was central in the original work by Lorenz who was inspired by earlier work of Heinroth (1911) who had raised a great diversity of the European avifauna. He concluded that early experience during the first few hours or days posthatch stamped in permanent species preferences which expressed themselves at maturity, and hence used the term *Pragung*, also used for the stamping of coins, to describe the process. Lorenz emphasized the differences between imprinting and associative learning as studied by those benighted stimulus–response psychologists, but it now seems more realistic to see both processes as members of a spectrum of acquisition processes, as discussed above.

Lorenz maintained that sexual imprinting was restricted to a critical period early in the lifetime of the bird, and obversely that subsequent experience did not influence the resulting preferences. Evidence for such critical periods has come from several studies. In one such study Japanese quail males were exposed to adult female albinos for 10 days at different periods in early life while controls were reared with normal age mates for 10 days (Gallagher, 1977). The behavior of the experimental birds in a choice situation between normal and albino females revealed a critical period during the first 2 weeks posthatch. The existence of such a period belies an associationist interpretation, which predicts that the time when responses can be acquired is not limited. However, the length of the period is longer than suggested by Lorenz. It seems that imprinting and habituation/sensitization mechanisms combine to produce sexual reactions in quail males (Gallagher, 1976).

On the obverse question of irreversibility, the preferences of some species do indeed seem irreversible. At 5 years of age, three turkeys imprinted on humans and three on conspecifics all consistently preferred the imprinted species for sexual behavior but would court either species (Schein, 1963). Cross-fostered drakes also reveal permanent effects of imprinting (Schutz, 1965, 1971, discussed below). In a study involving normal and white feathered zebra finch pairs, young were removed from the nest at 28 days and allowed to choose mates 8 weeks later (Walter, 1973). The young of normal and white parents chose mates like those parents. Sons of mixed parents chose at random while daughters chose normal mates. In all cases later experience had no influence on the initial mate preferences. Although later experience can influence sexual orientations in cross-fostered pigeon species, the influence of the early experience is never fully eradicated (Brosset, 1971).

However, other results indicate that the influence of early experience declines and that new experiences in later life alter preferences. In cocks of the Brown Leghorn domestic fowl strain, neonatal experience during the first 5 days of life produces strong and selective following responses, but by three months of age reactions to the imprinting stimuli are not detectable (Guiton, 1961). In the homogamy (choosing a mate with a similar appearance) of domestic hens, there is no clear evidence for a critical period, but heterosexual experience before 11 weeks of age is not sufficient for the expression of homogamy while such experience after sexual maturity enhances homogamy (Lill, 1968b). (The profound influence of early experience in the ontogeny of recognition behavior in the closely related junglefowl is discussed under Socialization below.) In mallards, both early and juvenile experiences affect mate preferences (Sherrod, 1974). This was shown by testing individuals of two varieties raised with both varieties or only their own variety during early and/or juvenile periods. In the dimorphic snow goose Cooke and McNally (1975) measured approach responses in young birds, association preferences over the first 2 years of life, and mate selection at sexual maturity. In their approach responses, birds chose stimulus birds whose color matched that of the parents. The choice could be modified by the color of the siblings, if different from that of the parents, and by removal of the parents during adolescence. The influence of sibling color and parental removal indicates the importance of recent experience over prior experience in mate preferences. Neither differences in the color patterns of the parents nor the playback of vocalizations altered the choice behavior. Birds associated with their peer group and, when associating with nonpeer group birds, chose individuals of the same color. At maturity, birds raised in large flocks in the absence of parents chose mates at random, as did birds in flocks with siblings of one color and foster parents of another. Thus, in snow geese long-term experience provided by the integrity of the family group influences mate choice. Similarly, in mallards the color of both the mother and siblings affect mate choice as demonstrated by Klint (1978) who raised young with normal or white mothers or siblings.

In many species, plumage differences are the chief sensory dimension in sexual imprinting. Such differences often underly homogamy, as in the cases discussed above. The role of plumage differences in imprinting has been extensively studied in domestic fowl. In hens, heterosexual experience with their own strain is important for the expression of homogamy (Lill, 1968b). In cocks, homogamy is slightly enhanced by experience with females, but not with males, of the same plumage type (Lill, 1968a). Males reared with females of their own and another breed show only weak homogamy, unlike males whose experience is restricted to females of their own breed (Lill and Wood-Gush, 1965). Kaspar Hauser cocks choose a sexual partner with plumage coloration similar to their own while control cocks choose one with coloration similar to their home pen conspecifics (Vidal, 1975). The perceptual bias toward one's own kind, as demonstrated by these isolates, has also been reported in other studies. Yellow and black chicks develop a preference for their own variety after 24–30 hours of experience with similarly colored chicks (Kilham et al., 1968). By contrast, chicks receiving experience with the other variety show no choice. Discriminations also develop in cocks raised with age mates ("peerprinting") or mothers ("damprinting")(Worsely, 1974a, 1974b). Individuals were exposed during the first 2 days after hatch to peers of their own or another breed and then raised in mixed groups. Those exposed to their own breed directed more aggression toward their own breed over the sixth to eleventh weeks of life, but not beyond this point. However, sexual behavior at maturity reflects the countinuing influence of peerprinting. Similarly, cocks raised with dams direct more aggression toward their own breed, but the behavior is influenced by breed, sex, and exposure to the other breed.

The development of avian sexual attachments can also be studied through cross-fostering experiments. Brood parasites, such as cuckoos, cowbirds, and viduine finches, provide natural cross-fostering experiments (in one direction only!) In the tradition of the early classic work by Whitman (1919), Brosset (1971) has cross-fostered among four pigeon species. Birds imprinted well on the foster species and courted accordingly, with the development of the imprinting varying across both species and sex. The resulting interspecific attachments led to hypersexuality and stable homosexual bonds. The color of the foster parent proved to be a key stimulus for sexual display, but the color of the siblings was not important. With regard to the organization of functional behavior systems, it is interesting that cross-fostered birds were aggressive toward conspecifics even though the fostering altered their sexual orientations. Such a differentiation is not seen in domestic fowl, however, which do direct aggressive responses toward stimulus dummies on which they have been imprinted (Guiton, 1961). Nicolai (1964) has shown that imprinting is important for fixation of African viduine finches on the appropriate estrildid host species on which they are brood parasitic.

Experiments that include cross-fostering treatments show that the following response (discussed below) is important in the development of familial recognition in domestic species (Ramsay, 1951). Among ducks, drakes raised with foster mothers of a different species court members of this species in later life (Schutz, 1965, 1971). Drakes raised with siblings of another species show similar behavior, but to a lesser extent. The effects of the imprinting are seen for many years, persisting despite lack of reproductive success. Rarely were the heterospecific mother or siblings courted, indicating that the attachment was not to particular familiar individuals. The ease with which imprinting occurs in cross-fostering experiments with ducks, fowl, and coots varies with the cross. Mallards are easy to imprint on other ducks but not on fowl and coots. Thus, here is yet another instance of a developmental constraint. In general, females recognize males regardless of how they were reared but males are subject to imprinting. Kaspar Hauser mallard drakes pair with conspecifics. In the Chilean teal, both sexes have dull plumage and are easily imprinted. Schutz suggests that recognition of the opposite sex can be achieved without experience when that sex is conspicuously colored but requires imprinting experience otherwise. The plumage dimorphisms could arise by sexual selection (discussed in Chapter 4, Reproduction).

Schutz's suggestion is corroborated by studies on mallards. Klint (1975, 1980) reared female mallards under a variety of conditions (e.g., with and without experience of males with white plumage, and as Kaspar Hauser individuals). The results indicate that experience is not necessary for a female to recognize a normal male, that plumage of the male is crucial for choice by the female, and that familiarity and individual recognition also play roles. For their part, male mallards of both wild and game-farm strains choose mates according to the strain of females with whom they are raised (Cheng et al., 1978, 1979). However, these latter studies also suggest that mallard females may be responding not to the plumage of the male but rather to his courtship behavior. When house and tree sparrows are cross-fostered, males strongly prefer the foster species whereas females, although initially attracted to the foster species, respond to displays of conspecifics (Cheke, 1969). In pigeons, parental color influences mate choice in later life by males but not females (Warriner et al., 1963).

However, sexual imprinting can occur in the females of both sexually monomorphic and dimorphic species. Among monomorphic herring gulls and lesser black-backed gulls, interbreeding is very rare but cross-fostering young results in much hybridization (Harris, 1970). Females, whether raised normally or by cross-fostering, usually mate only with males of the species which raised them, whereas males will mate with either species. This reduced choosiness of males is further discussed in Chapter 4, Reproduction. Females of dimorphic zebra finches, cross-fostered to Bengalese finches or raised normally as controls, show sexual preferences for the species by whom they were raised (Sonnemann and Sjolander, 1977). The authors indicate the critical importance of testing methods in such research. For instance, it is difficult to measure female preferences if she cannot avoid or invite males by her behavior. It is also important to note the ecological differences between species. In many duck species the father is not present when the young hatch whereas in zebra finches he is and feeds the young.

Hormones can be used to accelerate the course of sexual imprinting. Newly hatched chickens have been imprinted on one of two moving objects, in the manner used to study the following response discussed below, and then treated with androgens (Bambridge, 1962). In a later choice test, the birds displayed sexually to the imprinted object, whereas birds exposed to the object for an equal length of time outside the critical period did not. In a similar procedure, domestic cocks were raised either in isolation or communally during the first 3 weeks of life (Guiton, 1966). They subsequently lived individually and were injected with androgen. At 7 weeks of age the isolates, unlike communal birds, responded very little to a stimulus hen, offered in a choice with a human stimulus, but increased their responsiveness over 3 days of communal living. The isolates also reacted sexually to the human stimulus. By 6 months, all birds responded only to the hen. The timing of androgen injection in chicks is crucial. A 5-mg injection within 24 hours of hatching has no effect on imprinting of the following response on a visual flicker stimulus, but at 3 days of age a similar injection depresses the response (James, 1962). Androgen-injected male and female turkeys were raised in groups or as isolates, and were subsequently tested for sexual reactions to various stimuli, such as a poult body or the experimenter's hand (Schein and Hale, 1959). Although sexual behavior itself is independent of early experience, such experience modifies the value of stimuli as releasers of sexual behavior and hence recognition behavior. For instance, isolates preferred the experimenter's hand over other stimuli.

While the above studies have investigated the impact of early experience on subsequent sexual preferences, much researched, especially by animal psychologists, has involved short-term experiments in which preferences are measured while the subjects are still young by recording following responses to stimulus objects (Figures 3.3 and 3.4). Such research is thus related to that on conditioning and perceptual learning, as discussed below, and, while the time scale of such studies may enable the researcher to meet his grant deadline, the identity of the attachments underlying sexual imprinting and following responses is an empirical question. As discussed above, following responses and sexual attachments do not always match (Schutz, 1965, 1971; Vidal, 1980).

Many studies have examined experimental aspects of the acquisition of the following response (review by Sluckin, 1964). Research with mallards (e.g., Fabricius, 1951; Ramsay and Hess, 1954) has shown that the visual and auditory cues summate in their effectiveness to produce following, and that such following can be elicited during only a relatively brief period in early life. Much work has been done with visual stimuli presented to domestic chicks. Important stimulus dimensions include size, motion (including rotation and intermittency), and angle of regard (Smith, 1960; Smith and Hoyes, 1961). With a stationary or moving box as the stimulus, the incidence of the following response depends on the amount

Figure 3.3. Duckling following decoy in laboratory imprinting apparatus (from Hess, 1973, copyright American Association for the Advancement of Science).

of stimulus exposure and the age of the test bird (Salzen and Sluckin, 1959). The critical period can persist for up to a week, and responsiveness declines after the first day although retention is better after later imprinting (Jaynes, 1957). Visual flicker is an unconditioned stimuls for imprinting (i.e., chicks will move so as to maintain contact with such a stimulus) (James, 1959). Similarly, in mallards motion of a stimulus suppresses distress calls, and static features of the stimulus can be conditioned as suppressors through movement (Hoffman et al., 1972).

There are reports that later experience can reverse preferences established during the critical period (e.g., Salzen and Meyer, 1967). However, recent work shows that such reversals are not permanent (Cherfas and Scott, 1981). Along similar lines is an experiment in which chicks had either experience with another chick, experience with a guinea pig, or no experience at all (Hindman, 1981). Experience with a different companion subsequent to initial experience decreases social preferences but does not reverse them.

Chicks also learn the details of their isolation pens, as shown by faster responding to stimuli similar to the stripe pattern of the pen than to dissimilar stimuli (Bateson, 1964). Chicks isolated from one another and from humans do not show the usual cessation of the following response

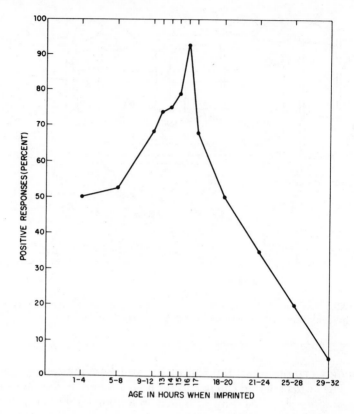

Figure 3.4. Responses to imprinting stimulus as a function of age of imprinted duckling (from Hess, 1973, copyright Brooks/Cole Publ. Co.).

after 3 days (Guiton, 1958). Even birds communally reared for 3 or 4 days and then isolated for 5 will produce following responses. Similarly, the critical period in mallards can be extended by housing the ducklings in a visually diffuse environment (Moltz and Stettner, 1961). These results are reminders that in isolation experiments it must always be specified from what the test animals are isolated. Further, mallard ducklings imprint on a second visual stimulus even though they can discriminate it from an initial imprinting stimulus (Hoffman and Ratner, 1973). Thus familiarity with the first stimulus is not sufficient to produce avoidance of the second. Ratner and Hoffman (1974) went on to show that the ability of test ducklings to flee from an unfamiliar stimulus is important in the measurement of critical periods. Thus, experimental situations must not be so confining as to prevent natural responses.

Physiological aspects of the development of following responses include the effects of drugs and cold shock, as well as hormones as discussed above. Hess (1957) investigated the effects of drugs on both the acquisition and the later occurrence of following responses. Meprobomate, which reduces emotional behavior such as fear, prevents imprinting but does not interfere with imprinting responses already acquired. Chlorpromazine, by contrast, does not block imprinting. Cold shock can kill embryos less than 24 hours old. It has therefore been used to decrease variation in the developmental age of eggs and thus to deal with the problem of whether the measurement of critical periods should be from the start of incubation or from hatching. However, there are species differences in the effects of cold shock. Chick embryos, but not those of ducks, are killed (Hailman and Klopfer, 1962). Beyond these physiological aspects, the relation of all these results on following responses to those from more natural studies must be ascertained.

Much attention has been paid to the process(es) underlying the following response (e.g., Fabricius, 1964; Figure 3.5). In an epigenetic (developmental) approach, Moltz (1963) argued that attachment develops in the early part of the critical period by modulation of stimulation and is later maintained by fear reduction. Salzen (1970) has speculated on possible underlying neuronal mechanisms. A variety of studies indicate that classical conditioning (Hoffman and DePaulo, 1977; Hoffman, 1978) and operant conditioning (Bateson and Reese, 1969; Peterson, 1960) are involved. Additionally, acquisition of the following response shares features with perceptual learning such as the importance of prior exposure to stimuli (Klopfer and Hailman, 1964; Kovach, 1979; Kovach et al., 1966). All these analyses indicate more in common between acquisition of the following response and traditional learning than has been suggested by ethologists such as Lorenz (1970) and Hess (1973).

The close linkage among the topics of species recognition, perceptual learning, and imprinting is clear in the series of reports on the embryonic development of species identification in mallard ducklings by Gottlieb (1968, 1975a, 1975b, 1975c, 1978, 1979, 1980a, 1980b, 1981). (Perceptual learning refers to the acquisition of information about the environment in the absence of obvious reinforcement.) Key acoustic features of the maternal call are repetition rate and frequency components. Experimental ducklings are muted and isolated so that they do not receive the experience of high-frequency calls from themselves or sibs. Experimental and control ducklings are subsequently tested for responsiveness to both normal maternal calls and calls with missing spectral portions. The auditory deprivation results in a perceptual deficiency which is selectively confined to the higher frequency components of the maternal call

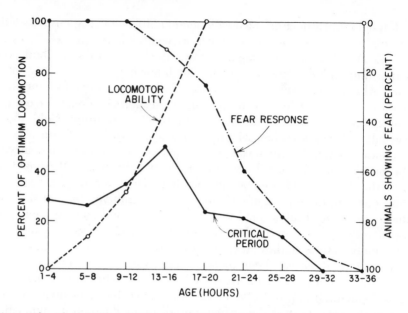

Figure 3.5. The critical period for imprinting lies between the onset of locomotor ability and the development of fear responses (from Hess, 1973, copyright Brooks/Cole Publ. Co.).

(1975a). Although experimental ducklings differentiate low-frequency attenuated mallard calls from normal calls as well as control birds, they are less discriminating between high-frequency attenuated and normal calls. This deficiency is eliminated by providing experimental ducklings with experience of maternal calls (1975b) and by maturational processes over the first 2 posthatch days (1975c). Similarly, duckling responses to the descending frequency-modulated call of the mother is dependent on prior experience with the duckling's own vocalizations (1980b). With regard to repetition rate, normal ducklings show a fairly narrow species-typical preference of about four to six notes per second. Experimental ducklings are less discriminating and so fail to distinguish between mallard and chicken maternal calls, which average 3.7 and 2.3 notes per second, respectively (1978). Embryonic auditory experience facilitates the development of high-frequency sensitivity and maintains repetition-rate specificity (1979). The specificity maintenance requires exposure to the species-typical rate of approximately four notes per second, other rates being ineffective (1980a). The exposure can be as brief as 5 minutes per hour for 24 hours, before or after hatching, providing testing does not take place sooner than 2 days later (1981). Embryonic experience of sounds has also been found to influence imprinting in chickens (Grier et al.,

1967). Chicks exposed to a patterned sound from days 12 to 18 of incubation show a preference for this sound after hatching in comparison to control birds.

Overall, the auditory specificity of the audiovisual perception of species recognition functions to focus the relatively undifferentiated visual component on the appropriate environmental stimuli (Gottlieb, 1968). Indeed, maternal calls are more important than visual experience in influencing preference behavior. Mallard ducklings visually imprinted on a stuffed dummy prefer a box from which such calls are broadcast (Johnston and Gottlieb, 1981a). Additionally, stuffed members of various duck species are less effective as stimuli in visual imprinting than the arbitrary stimuli (such as colored cubes) often used in laboratory experiments (Johnston and Gottlieb, 1981b). These results indicate the importance of investigating all the sensory modalities of the stimuli operative in the development of recognition. The combined roles of visual and auditory stimuli in leaving the nest by mallard ducklings has been studied by Bjarvall (1967). Exodus from a hole-nest occurs in response to auditory stimuli alone, but is later than that from the usual ground-nest in which imprinting to visual and auditory cues takes place.

The role of visual imprinting in facilitating the learning of auditory discriminations has also been investigated in several species by R. M. Evans and colleagues. In day-old domestic chicks, familiar visual stimuli aid discrimination learning of vocalizations which are important in the maintenance of the family group (Evans and Mattson, 1972). In other experiments, chicks were trained either with a parental call alone or a parental call paired with a visual stimulus (Cowan, 1974; Cowan and Evans, 1974). Only the latter group distinguished the parental call from a novel call, as measured both by the motor response to the parental call and by a lesser pecking rate in response to novel calls. These results therefore suggest that auditory discrimination learning involving visual stimuli as reinforcers is the underlying process, not auditory imprinting itself. Young quail also reveal recognition abilities by peeping more during the playback of familiar tones (Evans and Cosens, 1977). Both brood-parasitic redhead and the host canvasback ducklings imprint visually but only the canvasbacks learn auditory discriminations (Mattson and Evans, 1974). This difference is understandable in terms of subsequent development since the host family members remain together while the brood parasites leave. Auditory recognition is a well-developed faculty in arctic tern chicks which recognize parental calls from the second day after hatch (Busse and Busse, 1977). Young can be imprinted successively or simultaneously on two different parental pairs, and attachment behavior is influenced by further experience.

Overall, the research on avian sexual imprinting and following responses reflects a concatenation of problems in reproductive ecology, perceptual and learning psychology, and recognition ethology.

Mammals

Sexual attachment processes similar in many respects to those found in birds have been observed in many mammals. Mammalian imprinting has been reviewed by Cairns (1966a). Accidental imprinting of domestic and zoo mammals on humans (Grabowski, 1941; Hafez, 1969; Hediger, 1942; Sambraus and Sambraus, 1975) show that Mary was not alone with her little lamb. Morris (1979) amusingly recounts attempts to breed a human-imprinted female panda. The acquisition and extinction of responses to perceptually prominent objects by young lambs have been studied by Cairns (1966b). Sheep and goats reared with members of the other species for the first 8–9 months spend more time with stimulus members of that species than with conspecifics (Tomlinson and Price, 1980). Further, experimental sheep reared with conspecifics at 13 months of age for 1–3 months show a reversal of species preference. The reversal is greater the longer the time with conspecifics. Thus experience over a long period influences social preferences in these species.

Beauchamp and Hess (1971) reared guinea pigs with their own mother, a nonlactating adult female, or a young chick. During the first 3 weeks of life the pigs preferred the species with which they had been raised, but by 10–17 weeks all males preferred sexual contact with a female guinea pig. Unlike control animals, guinea pigs isolated from normal social contact at birth or at 5 days of age imprint on moving octagonal wooden blocks (Shipley, 1963). Attachments can be formed after several weeks of isolation and early imprinting responses persist for at least 40 days during isolation. Two brief sessions with the object in infancy produce a stronger response at 6 weeks than does one session, suggesting a gradually learned change in behavior. Experiments in which the odors of mothers and littermates are altered indicate a critical period for the influence of early experience on odor preferences (Carter and Marr, 1970). The preferences for the odors experienced increased with exposure during the first 3 weeks of life, but by 60 days of age the general preference was for the natural odor. Guinea pigs cross-fostered with rats show divided social and sexual preferences (Rossetto et al., 1980). Males reared with both species showed social preferences for rats but sexual ones for conspecifics. Overall, these ontogenetic processes in guinea pigs resemble those in birds in many respects, with differences in such features as the time scale of the critical period.

Sexual attachments have also been studied in other rodent species through cross-fostering experiments. Cross-fostered lemmings show an increased preference for heterospecific odors and engage in more sexual behavior with heterospecifics compared to control animals either non-fostered or intraspecifically fostered (Huck and Banks, 1980a, 1980b). Similarly, cross-fostered house and pygmy mice react more positively to heterospecifics than do controls (Quadagno and Banks, 1970). Scorpion and white-footed mice also show a decreased preference for conspecific odors following cross-fostering (McCarty and Southwick, 1977). Male and female voles differ in their responses to cross-fostering. Normally reared control males of both mountain and gray-tailed voles prefer conspecific females while experimentals who have been cross-fostered show no preference (McDonald and Forslund, 1978). The only preference among control or experimental females of either species is by mountain experimentals for the foster species. The effect of early experience of odors on later sexual preferences has been demonstrated in mice, when the parents of the experimental group are perfumed with "Violetta di Parma" (Mainardi et al., 1965a). As predicted by the theory of sexual selection (discussed in Chapter 4, Reproduction), males show no effect but experimental females prefer perfumed males. However, this preference by the females depends on their strain (Alleva et al., 1981). D'Udine and Partridge (1981) also found that the effects of cross-fostering were dependent on the strain of mouse.

Imprinting plays a role in the formation of caravans in shrews in which a line of young follow the mother (Zippelius, 1972). Imprinting occurs with any surrogate object when the young are 6–7 days old but from the eighth day the odor of the species must be present. After the second week, following behavior is shown only in response to the mother or siblings.

Overall, sexual imprinting in birds and mammals share many features but the developmental processes in mammals allow new experiences to influence recognition behavior for a relatively longer period.

Fish

The imprinting of intraspecific sexual preferences has been investigated in several polymorphic fish species, especially cichlids. In platyfish, males become imprinted on color morphs during a short interval after sexual maturity, whereas females show no imprinting (Ferno and Sjolander, 1973). The convict cichlid is a color polymorphic species but assessing experiential effects is difficult due to dominance relations between the two morphs which mask preferences (Weber and Weber, 1976). In an experiment in which the influence of such relations was avoided, sexual preference for the previously experienced morph was found when a large group of fish could pair freely (Ferno and Sjolander, 1976). In the similarly polymorphic midas cichlid, all individuals begin life as normal, and the offspring of gold parents metamorphose over a wide range of ages to gold (Barlow and Rogers, 1978). Data on female spawning indicate that imprinting experience and the female's own color influence the mate choice of the females. More generally, it would seem worthwhile to examine parallels between sexual imprinting and olfactory imprinting found among some migrating species such as salmon (e.g., Hasler et al., 1978).

Cross-fostering and isolation experiments reveal further aspects of sexual imprinting in fish. Males of the guppy genes *Poeciliopsis* must discriminate between normal bisexual females and parasitic unisexual ones (as discussed in Chapter 1, Species and Morphs). They do this increasingly well with experience, reflecting the importance of learning as an isolating mechanism (Kennett and McKaye, 1980). Males of the related genus *Gambusia* raised alone prefer conspecific females in choice tests while males reared in mixed cultures are less discriminating (Hubbs and Delco, 1962). Kaspar Hauser guppies, when tested, spend an increasing amount of time with conspecifics over testing whereas control fish raised in groups spend less time (Pinckney and Anderson, 1967). Isolate zebra danios spend less time near schools of conspecifics, in preference to schools of pearl danios, than zebra danios reared in groups (McCann and Matthews, 1974). The test situation, by involving a choice between two groups of stimulus fish, avoided the confounding of species identification with generalized attraction to groups. Such confounding is a problem in studies where test fish are presented with one group of stimulus fish and can "take them or leave them." In a subsequent study (McCann and Carlson, 1982), cross-fostered fish preferred their foster species at initial testing, and showed less species identification than did the isolates of the first experiment. After 30 days in conspecific groups, the pearl danios showed a considerably stronger conspecific preference, but the preference of the zebra danios shifted only a small amount. A lowered conspecific preference is also found in paradise fish fostered by blue gouramis (Kassel and Davis, 1975).

Yearling Kaspar Hauser rockbass spend no more time with conspecifics than similar-sized pumpkinseeds, unlike field caught yearlings (Brown, personal communication). Fernald (1980) has reported that male *Haplochromis burtoni* raised in isolation attack yellow and blue stimulus dummies of conspecifics with the species-typical black eye bar. Such a result would indicate genetic control of this pattern recognition. However, the experimental design and data analysis are not adequate for this conclusion. Members of this species raised with convict cichlids show a strong and lasting preference for this species over their own, unlike control fish who demonstrated no interest in convicts (Sjolander and Ferno, 1973). A similar and more recent cross-fostering study (Crapon de Caprona, 1982) with larger groups of animals also found that the effects of differential olfactory and visual experience were long lasting, suggesting an imprinting process. Two jewel fish raised from the egg stage to 160 days with *Tilapia mariae* showed a preference for individuals of this species over conspecifics for several months until the preference became undetectable (Kop and Heuts, 1973). Control fish raised with conspecifics showed no preference. However, both sexes of the Mozambique mouth-brooder prefer their own species whether they are raised with siblings, with siblings and mother, or alone (Russock and Schein, 1978). The fish were tested at maturity with fish of their own and three other species.

Taken together, these vertebrate results reiterate a common conclusion that different species of the same group exhibit different recognition development. Kaspar Hauser individuals may or may not exhibit preferences for conspecifics. Experience with heterospecifics, and possible subsequent sexual contact with conspecifics, may or may not alter such preferences. Investigation into the physiological and ecological causes of these differences is required.

Song

Birdsong has become an area of emphasis in imprinting research. Work has shown that the development of song production and recognition may or may not involve a critical period, or indeed may not be influenced by experience at all, depending on the species under study. The present section indicates tha diversity of these ontogenies. Song acquisition has been reviewed by Konishi and Nottebohm (1969), Marler (1970), Marler and Mundinger (1971), Nottebohm (1970), J. L. Brown (1975), and Kroodsma (1977, 1978).

Some species recognize songs independent of experience. Cross-fostered doves sing normally and show no influence of the foster parent (Lade and Thorpe, 1964). As is appropriate for a brood parasite, female brown-headed cowbirds raised in isolation display copulatory postures in response to the songs of conspecific males but not to those of other species (King and West, 1977). However, learning does play a role in song development in the two subspecies whose songs differ in the presence or absence of one element (King et al., 1980; West et al., 1981). Juveniles of the eastern subspecies do include this element if raised in isolation or in contact with adults of the southern subspecies. Females prefer songs of their own subspecies, as in species with dialects, discussed below.

In other species, a critical period for song imprinting has been found. Male white-crowned sparrows learn from older males in the first 100 days of life, but after this period new song stimulation is not assimilated (Marler and Tamura, 1964). Even during early life there are limits to what stimuli will be accepted. Alien white-crowned sparrow songs are learned but not those of Harris or song sparrows. Here is yet another example of constraints on learning. Elucidating the underlying sensory mechanisms of recognition poses an exciting challenge. In this connection, measurement of the cardiac orienting response has produced evidence for a sensory component in the development of song recognition in young swamp sparrows (Dooling and Searcy, 1980). With testing beginning at 20 days posthatch, individuals show a greater cardiac deceleration to conspecific songs than to those of sympatric song sparrows. [Cardiac changes in response to songs have also been recorded in European chiffchaffs (Zimmer, 1982).] The reviews cited above consider the roles of sensory experience, auditory feedback, and hormones on acquisition, and fixation into final form, of song in sparrows. In the Indian hill mynah, selective imitation of neighbors during the first few months of life leads to individually characteristic calls (Bertram, 1970). In terns, the critical period for song recognition begins before hatching (Busse, 1977). Eggs were exchanged between nests of common and Arctic terns and chicks were then tested at 1–3 days after hatching with the calls of both species. Chicks preferred the calls of the species which incubated them, although there was some indication of conspecific recognition independent of experience. In marsh wrens environmental factors influence the sensitive period (Kroodsma and Pickert, 1980). The period is dependent on photoperiod and the amount of adult song heard in the hatching year. These factors also affect learning ability during the next spring as well as the onset of adult song.

In yet other species, learning appears to go on over much of the lifetime of the bird. The role of parents and neighbors, usually male, is often large. Extensive call learning is found among numerous cardueline finches (Mundinger, 1979). New Zealand saddlebacks learn new songs over an indeterminate period (Jenkins, 1978). The complex adult song of European blackbirds undergoes an extended ontogeny (Messmer and Messmer, 1956; Thielcke-Poltz and Thielcke, 1960). The diverse vocal repertoire together with the learning ability of the birds combine to mediate much recognition behavior. Warblers learn to discriminate conspecific from heterospecific songs (Gill and Lanyon, 1964).

The role of the father in song acquisition has been shown in cross-fostering experiments with European sparrows (Cheke, 1969), bullfinches (Nicolai, 1959), and zebra finches (Immelmann, 1969). Sons learn the songs of their father even when conspecific males are also heard. Female zebra finches, also, prefer the song of their father to that of another adult male when separated from their parents at about 35 days and tested at about 100 days of age (Miller, 1979a). Likewise, bengalese females recognize the songs of their fathers, whether sung by the fathers or other males (Dietrich, 1981). Such singing thus provides a cue for the assessment of genetic relatedness in prospective mates (discussed in Chapter 4). Antiphonal singing (Chapter 2, Audition) clearly also involves much learning with the mate.

The influence of neighbors is seen in coordinated territorial singing in which a response tends to include phrases used by the first bird (e.g., black-crested titmice: Lemon, 1968a). Learning the songs of territorial neighbors may be linked to learning the song characteristic for the species. Searcy et al. (1981b) tested the hypothesis that a male learns to recognize the song of his species by generalizing from his own singing. The hypothesis predicts that, in a territorial situation, response to one's own song will be stronger than to the song of strangers, but results with song and swamp sparrows run counter to this. Further, the difference in responsiveness towards neighbor and stranger songs is less in song sparrows. This finding is consistent with the hypothesis that neighbor recognition is more difficult when repertoires are larger.

Mimetic species clearly demonstrate great learning ability. Among such species are some brood parasitic forms such as African viduine finches which learn the calls of their hosts (Nicolai, 1964). In one group of these finches, the indigo birds, the mimetic songs are probably learned from the host firefinch parents by the nestlings (Payne, 1973a). The songs determine both subsequent mate and host selection. The evolutionary consequences of such mimicry are discussed in Chapter 4, Species Recognition and Hybridization.

Local dialects can evolve if individuals tend to remain in, or after migration return to, the same area (review by Armstrong, 1963; Thielcke 1969). The function of these dialects is considered in Chapter 4, Assortative Mating. In a Maine population of song sparrows, the existence of dialects is shown by the distribution of song types (Borror, 1965). The most common song phrases in the study area have a lower incidence outside the area, with the prevalence of the song decreasing with increasing distance. Analysis of songs in wild and Kaspar Hauser cardinals reveals that dialects differentiate in this species as a result of repetition and a progressive change or drift (Lemon, 1971). Like Indian hill mynahs (Bertram, 1970) and white-crowned sparrows (Milligan and Verner,

1971), cardinals respond more strongly to songs of their own dialect than to those of other dialects (Lemon, 1967).

Several dialects are found among white-crowned sparrows in the San Francisco Bay area (Marler and Tamura, 1964) and in European blackbirds (Messmer and Messmer, 1956). Male white-crowned sparrows raised in isolation do not develop songs resembling their home dialects. Based on this kind of evidence it seems that learning is of major importance even though "dialect" refers to observed population differences without specifying the nature and nurture of the process. Female sparrows are also influenced by experience with their own dialect, as shown by the greater elicitation of copulatory postures in response to home dialect songs over those of alien dialects (Baker et al., 1981a). Methodologically, as Petrinovich and Patterson (1981) point out, the playback experiments widely used to study dialects generally confound the geographical location of songs and their similarity to the local song. This confounding must be removed if valid interpretations of results are to be made.

In general, birds with distinct dialects have but one song. The unique exception reported to date is the British corn bunting which displays both local dialects and repertoires of up to three song types (McGregor, 1980). Dialects are also found in d'Arnaud's barbet which sings antiphonally (Wickler and Uhrig, 1969). The nonmimetic songs of mimetic indigobirds reveal graded dialectic differences (Payne, 1973a). Individual males may have a repertoire of a dozen or more such songs, and the proportion of songs shared by two males decreases over increasing distance. Neither sex responds selectively to the nonmimetic songs of their own dialect or species. Hence the function of these large repertoirs of nonmimetic songs is unclear.

SOCIALIZATION

Socialization refers to the entire process of the development of appropriate social responses. This process no doubt involves experience with many particular stimuli in many specific situations, but the study of socialization focuses on the entire development in the social context. Although the elucidation of factors influencing socialization has been the objective of much research (e.g., Kuo, 1967; Roy, 1980; Schneirla and Rosenblatt, 1961; Mason, 1979), the discussion that follows will be limited to those studies in which recognition behavior is affected.

Insects do demonstrate some ontogenetic changes in behavior, including recognition behavior, contrary to their popular image as fixed instinctive automats. First instar cockroach nymphs prefer their own brood-caring mothers to other females, but second instars show no preference (Liechti and Bell, 1975). The well-documented role changes over the life of worker honeybees (see Wilson, 1971) also doubtless involve shifts in recognition.

Among birds, general aspects of socialization and associated recognition behavior have been considered by Collias (1952) who has discussed the interaction of hormonal mechanisms and social experience. Kruijt (1962, 1964, see also 1972) has provided an extremely detailed analysis of the ontogeny of social behavior and recognition in male Burmese junglefowl. He has paid particular attention to the manner in which different functional systems, principally sex and aggression, develop and interact. Kaspar Hauser males develop very aberrant aggressive and escape behaviors after 10 months of isolation, and successful copulatory behavior is very unlikely to occur. In closely related domestic cocks, males reared in social isolation show a higher incidence of a reversed position in initial mating attempts compared to normally raised birds (Vidal, 1975). Socialization is often initiated through imprinting in chickens and other avian species. Under normal circumstances, birds become imprinted on each other and thus become inhibited in their responses to unfamiliar objects unless there is a subsequent period of isolation (Guiton, 1959). In ring-billed gull chicks, imprinting, mobility, and social recognition develop concurrently (Evans, 1970a). For the first 3 or 4 days after hatch, chicks remain in, or on the edge of, the nest and are responsive to a wide range of stimuli. During the next 2 days, the chicks make temporary excursions from the nest and discriminate conspecifics from other stimuli. After this period, there is permanent emigration from the nesting area and the recognition of individuals.

Mammalian socialization and the development of recognition behavior are included in the topics covered by broad works such as Newton and Levine (1968) and Chevalier-Skolnikoff and Poirier (1977). In a comfortable fashion no longer tolerated by journal editors, McDougall and McDougall (1927) tell the story of the joint socialization and recognition behavior of two laboratory rats and a pet cat in their apartment. As a part of his epigenetic program for the analysis of behavior, Kuo (1930) continued this research with experiments raising cats under differing conditions. He showed the inadequacy of any attempt to describe the resulting behavior in terms of "instinct" or "learning." Notwithstanding the speedy development of recognition reported in the biblical blind man of Bethsaida, mammalian recognition ontogeny is an extended process. In his classic monograph, Hebb (1949) argued that "identity," a fundamental concept in recognition behavior, evolves only slowly as a result of prolonged experience in mammals. Scott and Fuller (1974) have reported extensive studies on the genetics and epigenesis of social behavior in dogs. The development of recognition behavior is a lengthy process in goats and sheep (Collias, 1956) and elephant seals (Bartholomew, 1959). As the young mammal grows, its social milieu expands from its mother alone to include a peer group, sexual partners, and rivals. Socialization produces different behavior in the different members of the socializing group. For instance, in shrews, the mother leads in the caravan behavior in which the young follow her, while males retrieve young who have fallen out of the nest but do not induce caravan formation (Zippelius, 1972). Like males, half-grown shrews drag young back to the nest in a nonspecific action without necessarily recognizing the nestlings as such.

In macaques, varying the amount of contact during early life drastically affects later social behavior. Infants repeatedly separated from their mothers during the first 8 months of life exhibit a syndrome involving heightened fear, compared to control animals, up to a year after the experience (Mitchell et al., 1967). Individuals raised either alone, in visual and auditory contact, or in normal contact, show preferences for individuals similarly raised, even when the stimulus animals are strangers (Pratt and Sackett, 1967). In a study in which macaques of three species were reared with one or more of these three species, attachments were formed during experience over the third to ninth months of life, but not the ninth to fifteenth (Chamove and Harlow, 1975). Beyond indicating the importance of the timing of experience, the results also revealed some preference for conspecifics independent of experience. Play occurred almost exclusively with conspecifics even when subjects still slept with their rearing partners.

In human infants, the development of social recognition responses, including smiling, has been extensively investigated. The roles of habituation and learning in smiling behavior have been cited above. As the months of infancy pass, a more and more lifelike stimulus is required by the baby for a smile to be elicited (Ahrens, 1954; Ambrose, 1961; Figure 3.6). In very young infants, smiles are elicited by dots, and then by the region around the eyes. At 5 months, a broadly drawn mouth is an effective stimulus and at 8 months a full face is necessary. By the end of this interval, the rudiments of adult facial discrimination are found (review by Fagan, 1979). The great variety of experiments reported for the ontogeny of this discrimination have revealed many interesting results. For instance, rotated faces are more difficult for infants to distinguish than

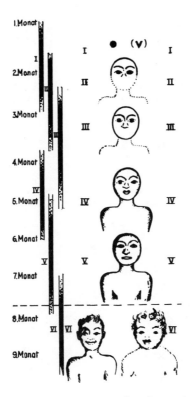

Figure 3.6. Increasingly lifelike stimuli are required to elicit smiling in human infants over the first months of life (from Ambrose, 1961).

when they are correctly oriented. This finding indicates that the pattern of the features in the faces are important, and not just, say, brightness cues. Three-month-olds are also sensitive to facial expressions, habituating differently to smiling and frowning stimuli, especially if these are of the mother (Barrera and Maurer, 1981). More generally, experience in the environment (e.g., home versus institution) influences the ontogeny of appropriate social responses in infants. For instance, smiling begins around 8 weeks for babies at home but not until 12 weeks for those in institutions. Yarrow (1967) has outlined the process by which the relation between an individual mother and child grows. A period of indiscriminate attachment behavior gives way during the third quarter of the first year to specific attachments to recognized individuals (Schaffer and Emerson, 1964). Although much of the work in this area is in the psychoanalytical

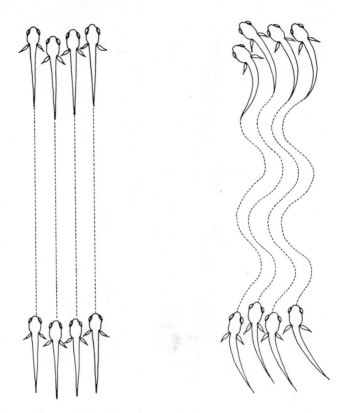

Figure 3.7. Compared to the straight paths of control schools of silversides (*a*), schools of isolates reflect aberrant lateral turning (*b*) (from Williams and Shaw, 1971).

tradition [e.g., much of Ainsworth's (1969) theoretical discussion], Bowlby (1980) has led the way out of this wilderness by incorporating an ethological approach in his penetrating analysis of the ontogeny of mother–infant recognition and attachment.

The development of self-recognition, or consciousness, has been considered by Humphrey (1980) as follows. As discussed in Chapter 4, it can be assumed that in many advanced social species with complex nervous systems, there are selection pressures favoring competency at the building of social models that include oneself. This reflexive inclusion produces self-recognition. From an ontogenetic perspective, the development of such competency is aided by play, parental manipulation, and dreams. In human cultures, these three mechanisms for enhancing competency are reinforced by sports, initiation rights, and drama, respectively. Humphrey's analysis provides insights to several aspects of human cognitive life such as why play is often so serious, why dreams loom so large in importance, and why drama has such an enormous appeal.

Among fish, the development of schooling, involving species recognition, has received considerable attention, especially from Shaw and her co-workers. In the Atlantic silverside schooling develops gradually from basic behavioral components of approach and orientation (Shaw, 1960). Fry under 12 mm in length do not school but above this length they do. While early work suffered from heavy mortality of isolated fish (Shaw, 1961), more resent research has shown that the normal development of schooling behavior is disrupted by isolation (Williams and Shaw, 1971). Withdrawal behavior from conspecifics, which typically decreases in grouped fish, continues, and aberrant lateral turning behavior is also observed (Figure 3.7).

Socialization and the development of recognition behavior has been studied in few fish species aside from a small number of reports such as Shaw (1962) dealing with the ontogeny of sexual behavior in platies. Mozambique mouthbrooders exhibit a complex behavioral repertoire. Orientation and approach to the mother are dependent on an initial perceptual schema that limits early responsiveness (Russock and Schein, 1977). Subsequent experience sharpens this responsiveness which finally detoriates at the end of the period of infancy when it becomes adaptive for the young to avoid mouth-sized holes! Extended parental care and changes in the responsiveness of fry to dummies is also found in convict cichlids (Hay, 1978).

4
Evolutionary Processes

Ecology and population genetics have a historical but artificial separateness only recently overcome under the aegis of ecological genetics (Ford, 1964). In this respect, the two areas are similar to ethology and psychology (see Chapter 3 on the issue of constraints on learning). This chapter considers the genetics and ecology of recognition behavior, and the consequences of this behavior for the evolution of populations. The topic is difficult to cover for two reasons. First, the various facets of this topic are intertwined, making organization of the material difficult. Second, several of these facets are of great contemporary interest and hence are developing very quickly. The chapter considers first the genetics of recognition behavior, and then the problem of species recognition and hybridization. Next is an overview of the ecology of social systems and strategies of communication within these systems. This overview leads to a discussion of the function and impact of recognition behavior in the activity of groups, in aggressive interactions, and, finally, in reproductive strategies.

GENETIC ASPECTS

How much is known about the genetic mechanisms underlying recognition behavior? Something is known about recognition behavior, but much work remains to be done, including a large amount of pure description. Less is known about the sensory aspects, developmental processes, and selection pressures involved. The genetics of recognition behavior, as of behavior in general, is a virtual *terra incognita* (cf. Ehrman and Parsons, 1976; Fuller and Thompson, 1978). Despite research efforts

146

such as Benzer's (1971) frontal assault on the genetic basis of fruitfly behavior, reductionist hopes must realistically be very low. The intricacies of the pathways from cistron to act, producing an enormously complex "epigenetic landscape" (Waddington, 1940), are daunting. (In this metaphor, the developing organism is likened to a ball running down a series of branching valleys. The path at such branch points is determined by the genome and environmental stimuli.) In the vast majority of cases, many genes contribute to the expression of a given act (polygeny) and a single gene influences many acts (pleiotropy). For instance, it is known that the retarded cognitive abilities of infants with Down's syndrome are correlated with poorer recognition memory of faces (Miranda and Fantz, 1974). (In most cases of Down's syndrome the child has three, rather than the usual two, copies of chromosome 21.) As in so many cases, it is difficult to imagine the landscape for this case. Fortunately, for the study of the genetics of recognition behavior, at least some researchers are not daunted by such difficulties. (With a candor not universal among scientists, Benzer admits about his research that "in any case, it is fun.")

The adapted coordination of sender and signaler in recognition behavior is a familiar phenomenon to ethologists aware of social releasers, which are morphological or behavioral features that function to signal other animals. Such coordination suggests the likelihood of an association of genes contributing to releasers with genes yielding sensitivity to these releasers. Evidence for such genetic organization comes from research into song production and species recognition in crickets (Hoy, 1974; Hoy et al., 1977; Leroy 1964a, 1964b; Figure 4.1). Males of *Teleogryllus oceanicus*, *T. commodus*, and their hybrids all have distinctive calls. Females prefer the calls of their own type, with the females of each of the two hybrid crosses (*oceanicus* male × *commodus* female and *commodus* male × *oceanicus* female) preferring males of the same cross. Such results imply that the timing elements for song production by males and song detection by females have a common genetic basis which is both polygenic and multichromosomal. Sex-linked genetic factors mediate differences between the hybrids such as the presence or absence of an intertrill interval. In analogous research, the hybridization experiments of Grula and Taylor (1980) have shown that the X chromosome largely controls both female choice and male courtship behavior in sulfur butterflies. Female hybrid wolf spiders, however, show no preference for courting hybrid males over males of the parental species (Stratton, 1979). The genetics of kin recognition in hymenoptera is discussed below in Groups.

A coordination of sender and signaler paralleling that of the crickets is found in cricket frogs (appropriately enough!) (Capranica et al., 1973). The spectral energy of the mating calls and the frequency sensitivity of

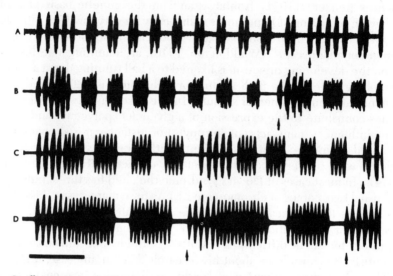

4.1. Oscillograms of calls of *Teleogryllus oceanicus* (A), *T. o.* female × *T. c.* male (B), *T. c.* female × *T. o.* male (C), and *T. commodus* (D) (from Hoy, 1974). Bar represents 0.5 seconds and arrows represent beginnings and ends of phrases.

the auditory nervous systems show matching geographical variation. The resulting dialect preferences resemble those of learned birdsong dialects (discussed in Chapter 3, Song Imprinting). In five dove species, cooing rhythmicity appears to be genetically patterned (Lade and Thorpe, 1964) and a study of song pattern preferences similar to the above cricket studies would be most intriguing.

Histocompatibility gene complexes are genetic loci which produce antigens important in tissue compatibility. In house mice, the major complex *H-2* has been found to play a role in mate preferences (Yamazaki et al., 1976). Males from inbred lines preferred a similar *H-2* type in one of six comparisons of females, and a dissimilar one in four of six. The preferences may be for the same or a different strain depending on the alternative offered. As in the insect cases discussed above, there appears to be a pair of linked genes, one for the receptor of the male and the other for the signal of the female. The mate preferences could function to maintain a heterozygosity in the gene complex which would be adaptive in immune responses to infections. Another promising avenue for genetic research into recognition behavior in this species stems from the finding that the imprinting of females on odor cues is strain dependent (discussed in Chapter 3, Sexual Imprinting).

In the light of these results with the *H-2* locus in mice, it is interesting to note Dawkins' (1976) green beard hypothesis. He has speculated that kin recognition would be enhanced if genes could produce distinct phenotypic effects, such as green beards, as labels. He suggests that such a green beard effect is unlikely due to genetic linkage producing multiple associations which would confound the labels. Additionally, it is improbable that a single gene would cause both appropriate recognition and helpful behavior. The possible routes for the evolution of green beard genes remain unclear (Ridley and Grafen, 1981; and see Getz, 1981). Nevertheless, the results concerning the *H-2* locus indicate that evolution may favor linked genes which mediate the recognition of, and response to, related individuals. More general aspects of the genetic basis of kin selection are considered under Groups below.

In many cases, the analysis of data in behavioral genetics seems particularly problematical (e.g., see Thiessen, 1971, versus Wilcock, 1971, on the value and interpretation of single-gene studies). Barash (1975) has reported on the inheritance of individual behavioral differences by comparing aggressive and sexual behavior in fathers and offspring (sex not reported) in the Mozambique mouthbrooder. He argues for the existence of a heritable behavioral polymorphism, with individuals belonging to genetic categories that are behaviorally homogeneous within themselves. However, two questions remain unanswered in the report. First, do the three categories of males which he distinguishes coincide with the three suppliers providing the fish? Second, mate choice on the part of females was obviously occurring, as evidenced by the difficulty in obtaining successful matings. It thus becomes as important to know the behavioral characters of the mothers as of the fathers. In view of such problems, the investigation of the genetic basis of recognition behavior must proceed with particular caution.

Lumsden and Wilson (1980) have undertaken to model the development of behavioral genetic tendencies in a cultural milieu. They have introduced the concept of "culturgen" to refer to both behaviors and artifacts transmitted between individuals during socialization in cultural species. In the case of incest avoidance among human siblings, biases regarding outbreeding and brother–sister incest are two such culturgens. The model suggests that the outbreeding bias is very strong, based on the ethnographic distribution of societies containing a stated number of nonincestuous members. More interestingly, "it also illustrates the very general principle that even fixed epigenetic (developmental) rules, provided they do not favor one culturgen absolutely, can be expected to yield substantial cultural diversity as measured by the variance of the ethnographic distributions. Put another way, the existence of a great deal of variation among societies in a particular behavioral category does not imply the absence of genetically prescribed bias in the epigenetic rules." The model thus refutes cultural anthropologists who have argued in this vein. Lumsden and Wilson (1981) consider the role of recognition behavior in such social systems which are the result of both genetic and cultural influences.

SPECIES RECOGNITION AND HYBRIDIZATION

Species recognition often plays an important role in ethological isolation, as is clear from Chapter 1, Species and Morphs. Hence species recognition and hybridization are inverse processes: when recognition functions well, hybridization is rare. The advantages of species recognition are several. When an individual is recognized as not being a conspecific, it fails to elicit species-appropriate behavior, especially courtship. The same applies in recognition of a unisexual in the case of species which have both unisexual and bisexual forms such as certain guppies (McKay, 1971). As Lorenz (1970) has stressed, the chief function of imprinting (Chapter 3) is the recognition of potential conspecific mates. Mayr (1970) has provided an excellent review of ethological isolating mechanisms as they operate in speciation. Such mechanisms are critical for species whose members are not reproductively isolated either geographically or temporally. In a-posematic species, such as the lycid beetle studied by Eisner and Kafatos (1962), the warning effect may be enhanced by species recognition and subsequent congregation. Aggregations of snakes, whose formations are facilitated by pheromone trails, reduce water loss and temperature fluctuations (Gehlbach et al., 1971). Species recognition may also assist in interactive ecological segregation, as Hoglund et al. (1975) have suggested to account for the odor aversion of related salmonids by juvenile Arctic charr. The same interpretation can be applied to Jonge's (1980) findings of interspecific avoidance in European voles. Similarly, female pheromones segregate species of clearwing moths (Greenfield and Karandinos, 1979). Sensory modalities provide sufficiently information-rich channels that species recognition is not obscured. Bremond (1978) has shown that masking of wren's songs by similar songs is extremely unlikely.

Selection for species recognition may often be in opposition to other selection pressures. In species where individual recognition is important, species recognition and individual recognition will influence inter-individual variability antagonistically. Species recognition can also be sharpened by closely related species. In *Drosophila mojavensis*, the mainland population has been selected for sexual isolation from the sibling species, *D. arizonensis* (Zouros and d'Entremont, 1980; Markow, 1981b). Consequently, mainland females discriminate against conspecific males of outlying populations. Ethological isolation between the two species results from behavioral differences at various courtship stages in both males and females. Similarly, among gambusiine fishes, greater discrimination is found in the males of species thought to have been sympatric with close relatives than in those from allopatric species (Hubbs and Delco, 1960).

Ever since Lamarck and Darwin, it has been clear that recognition behavior plays an important evolutionary role both in species isolation and as a source for adaptations in the formation of new species (reviews by Littlejohn, 1969; Spieth, 1958). Species differing chiefly in their behavior have been termed "ethospecies" by Emerson (1956) who cites several examples from the termites. Some ethospecific research has begun on such groups as crickets (Bigelow, 1964); spiders (Uetz, and Denterlein, 1979; Stratton, 1979; Stratton and Uetz, 1981), and snakes (Neill, 1964). The three groups of animals most extensively studied are fruit flies, birds, and fish. Fruit flies have the dual advantages of great abundance and diversity in the field and tractability in the laboratory. A large number of studies have examined ethological isolation among *Drosophila* species (e.g., *D. paulistorum* complex: Ehrman, 1964; *D. nasuta* complex: Lambert, 1982). One component of ethological isolation reported for many insect species is a difference in the times of day when mating occurs. For instance, such differences are found in the *D. melanogaster* group of species (Hardeland, 1972). The extent of ethological isolation between closely related species can be selected. Kessler (1966) selected for and against such isolation in *D. pseudoobscura* and *D. persimilis*. In the former species divergence of the lines was slower for the males than the females. In *D. persimilis* both sexes in the low isolation lines responded to selection, but only the females in the high isolation lines. Given that sperm is metabolically cheap, it is not surprising that males respond less well to this selection. Similarly, Ahearn (1980) has reported partial sexual isolation of a laboratory stock of *D. silvestris* from a natural population of the species, probably as a result of random genetic drift leading to a reorganization of the genetics of its sexual behavior. Finally, arguments have been presented for inferring the direction of evolution across *Drosophila* species from asymmetrical mating preferences. Some have suggested that females of derived species should discriminate more strongly against males of ancestral species than ancestral females against derived males, while others have maintained the reverse. A recent report based on experimental populations concludes that the direction of evolution cannot be inferred from mating preferences (Markow, 1981a). However, the presentation of data is unclear and it remains open whether these populations are good models of natural ones.

Birds also provide material for the role of recognition behavior in species isolation. Courtship behavior in hybrid mallard ducks includes the same elements as parentals but in altered sequences (Ramsay, 1961). Such data imply different genetic bases for the forms of the acts and their patterning. Behavioral differences are important in the isolation of greater prairie chickens and sharp-tailed grouse, between which species hybridization occurs in places (Sparling, 1981). A female marsh warbler was observed with a male reed warbler which had a mixed reed-marsh song repertoire (Lemaire, 1977). This hybridization illustrates how a breakdown in recognition behavior, mediated in this case by song, produces introgression. [Introgression is the introduction of the genes of one species into the gene pool of another species (Anderson and Hubricht, 1938).] In his study on nesting behavior in lovebirds, Dilger (1962) has provided one of the few reports on the development of behavior in hybrids. Similar developmental research into recognition behavior in hybrids would doubtless be most illuminating for revealing mechanisms operating in the parental species.

Brood parasites, including cowbirds, cuckoos, viduine finches, and possibly some cichlid fish, offer examples of the selection for species recognition independent of parental experience. This is not to say that social ontogeny does not occur in such species. Such ontogeny is in fact well established in, say, song development in brown-headed cowbirds (e.g., West et al., 1981). Song imprinting in mimetic brood parasites could lead to both recognition problems and subsequent speciation. Nicolai (1964) has analyzed the intertwined evolution of species recognition and diversity in African viduines and their host estrildid finches. Payne (1973a) has argued for the possibility of sympatric speciation in viduines. (Sympatric speciation refers to speciation while the populations of the incipient species overlap geographically. By contrast, if there is geographical separation, the speciation is termed allopatric.) Viduines learn the songs of their hosts and use these songs in their own courtship. Hence, the rare event of a female laying eggs in the nests of two different hosts could lead to two sympatric but reproductively isolated incipient species.

Advocates of allopatric speciation have long fretted over the embarrassing species diversity of many fish groups such as tropical cyprinids and characids and, most particularly, the cichlids of the great lakes of Africa. There appear to be too many species in these lakes to be the result of allopatric speciation. For instance, Lake Malawi contains some 200 species. Selective mating has been suggested as a key factor in the explosive speciation (Kosswig, 1947). More recently, in his controversy with Greenwood, Fryer (1977) has emphasized the manner in which behavioral modifications lead morphological ones in speciation, and the role of species recognition in the Lake Victoria fauna. Similarly, in his detailed study of four Guyanese poeciliids, Liley (1966) has stressed the importance of selection for reproductive isolation in the evolution of courtship behavior. In sunfish, problems of species recognition are linked to those of sex recognition, as discussed below in Reproduction.

Species recognition becomes difficult in polymorphic species evolving in mimetic complexes, such as butterflies (e.g., Turner, 1978). The two chief forms of mimicry are Batesian, in which a palatable species mimics the appearance of an unpalatable model species, and Mullerian, in which a number of unpalatable species come to resemble each other. The selective pressure driving the process is predation. Some mimetic species have morphs that mimic different models. In species with such multiple Batesian mimics, mimicry is often restricted to the females. Since females can be expected to be choosy about mates (as discussed in Reproduction below), males are monomorphic since deviants are selected against strongly. Additionally, the sensory modalities and ensuing signals used for species recognition are different from those used for the mimicry. Although predation and the early stages of courtship are mediated visually, odors are crucial in the advanced stages of courtship.

ECOLOGY OF SOCIAL SYSTEMS

The central tenet of the neo-Darwinian selectionist theory is that organisms exhibit the heritable phenotypic traits they do because these characters enhance fitness interpreted as their proportionate genetic contributions in succeeding generations. Regrettably, fitness is extremely difficult to measure (see Lewontin, 1974) and some substitute measure such as survival, number of matings, or number of offspring must generally be used. For many traits the presumed selection pressures appear to be not only unknown but unknowable. Theories are essential in science because facts become evidence only in the light of theory, and disconnected facts abound in science. Still, it is all too easy for even moderately imaginative adaptationists to produce daily before breakfast three different selection scenarios for virtually any character. Gould (1979) has called such scenarios "Just So stories" after Kipling's animal fables (see also Gould and Lewontin, 1979). As Humphrey (1982) has mentioned in another context, adaptationists would be well to recall the verdicts that medieval English grand juries could bring in: innocent or guilty (as with contemporary juries) but also *ignoramus* (we do not know). Nevertheless, the effort at specifying the pressures needs to be made. This section considers the ecology of social systems as the primary source of these pressures and the issue of communication strategies.

Behavioral Optimality

A central consequence of selection theory is the expectation that over generations various selected characters will alter so that maximal fitness results. This expectation has been dignified as the Principle of Optimal Design (see Rashevsky, 1960). Although behavior is selected, and often strongly, we should not expect the entire behavioral output of an animal over its lifetime to be optimal. Presumably behavioral propensities will under selection approach optima, but there are many reasons why any specific behavioral sequence may not be optimal. The effects of selection are limited by the time, population size, and genetic variation available. A population which has evolved to one local adaptive peak in its epigenetic landscape may be unable to reach a higher peak separated by a valley of lower fitness. In fluctuating environments, the optimum will in general fluctuate. But, at best, only behavioral propensities will be optimized, and behavioral "errors" can still occur under adequate conditions of external and internal stimulation. Janetos and Cole (1981) have considered models that incorporate simple rules and produce behavioral output that is nearly optimal. However, there are both biological and mathematical difficulties in their arguments (Montgomerie and Taylor, in preparation). Finally, there is no logical connection between the optimality of performance of some system and that of any of its subsystems. A well known ethological example has been reported in the study by Tinbergen et al. (1962) of egg shell removal by black-headed gulls, in which this behavior is concluded to be suboptimal because of a countervailing force. Egg shell removal functions to protect the brood from heterospecific predators but such removal is delayed because of predation by conspecifics on wet chicks. However, it is possible that this delay is due to disturbance from the observer.

Determinants of Social Systems and the Red Queen

Comprehension of the selection pressures favoring recognition abilities is aided by a brief examination of the diversity of the social systems in which they operate. The evolution of social systems is a topic of keen interest to contemporary biologists and has been considered in depth by Wilson

(1975), Emlen and Oring (1977), Wittenburger (1979), Crook et al. (1976), for canids and felids by Kleiman and Eisenberg (1973), for African bovids by Estes (1974), and for birds by J. L. Brown (1964a) (Figure 4.2). Beyond abiotic influences such as seasonality and consequent water and temperature fluctuations, the chief biotic determinants of social systems are those related to food (distribution, abundance, and predictability), reproduction (availability of mates and reproductive sites), and predation (intensity and variation with life stage). The interacting influences of these abiotic and biotic determinants govern the characters of the resulting social system. Groups vary in size, structure, and permanence. Feeding patterns may be social or individual, extensive or concentrated. The use of space may be random or territorial, or a dominance hierarchy may occur. Finally, the mating system may involve promiscuity, polygamy, or monogamy. In polygamy, multiple mates may be taken sequentially or simultaneously. Reproduction may be communal (i.e., parents may collaborate in raising broods) or cooperative (i.e., mature but nonbreeding adults may assist).

Clearly the features of a social system have direct consequences for the types of recognition behavior which will be selected. Species with intense conflict over resources such as food and mates (as in lekking species) can be expected to evolve acute abilities for the recognition of rivals. Where choice of mates is available, recognition of mate quality and receptivity is advantageous. Additionally, in species with long-term pair bonds, individual mate recognition is important. For species, such as many big cats and raptors, which are spaced over large distances, sex and species recognition may suffice for social interactions. For colonial species, such as gulls, seals, and sunfish, with more extensive social interactions, more acute types of recognition, such as of offspring and neighbors, enhance fitness. Species living in permanent groups, such as jays, wolves, and anemone fish, tend to evolve individual recognition. Overall, the great diversity of reproductive strategies (solitary, colonial, cooperative, communal, creching, brood parasitic) requires many different roles for recognition behavior.

VanValen's (1973) Red Queen hypothesis would appear to be relevant in considering the evolution of recognition abilities. VanValen has postulated that an evolutionary advance by one species leads to a deterioration of other ecologically similar species. Thus, evolutionary rates will remain high, with each species evolving quickly but none ever getting ahead. The allusion is to *Alice Through the Looking Glass* in which Alice makes a breathtaking dash with the Red Queen which apparently takes her nowhere, the Queen remarking "Now, here, you see, it takes all the running you can do, to keep in the same place." The assumptions

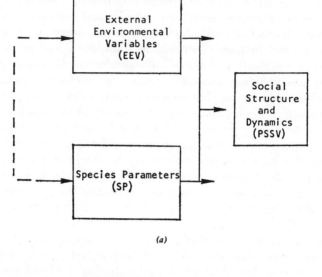

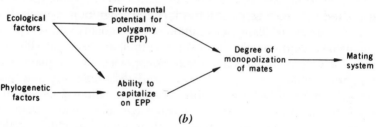

(b)

Figure 4.2. Models for social systems of (*a*) mammals, (*b*) mating, and (*c*) avian territoriality (from Crook et al., 1976; Emlen and Oring, 1977, copyright American Association for the Advancement of Science; and J. L. Brown, 1964a, respectively).

underlying the hypothesis have been examined by Maynard Smith (1976) and an intraspecific version has been considered by Dawkins and Krebs (1979) in terms of arms races between parents and offspring and between males and females, although the situation is complicated here because the competitors share the same gene pool. The central point of the hypothesis is that fitness is a measure relative to the other members of the population and that therefore the fittest value of any trait, whether that be a recognition ability or something else, will evolve.

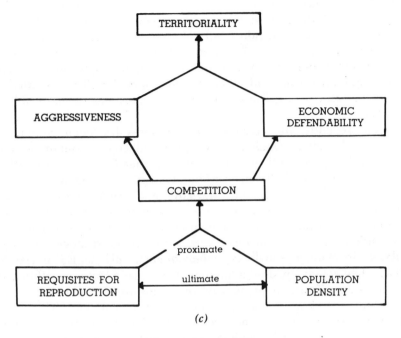

(c)

Figure 4.2 *(continued)*

Communication: Information or Propaganda?

Before considering the selection pressures acting on social recognition behavior, it is worthwhile noting the two frameworks within which animal communication generally has been examined. Classical ethology tended to view the communication process underlying recognition behavior as one in which information was exchanged about the respective motivational states of the interacting animals so that appropriate adjustments could be made in these states. Consequently, the behavioral sequence could advance to the resolution of the encounter, such as copulation in a reproductive case or victory in an aggressive one. This information exchange and the consequent resolution of the encounter were often explicated as being "good for the species." Such "group selectionist" arguments have a long history in zoology generally and in ethology specifically. Huxley (1914) concluded that courtship movements in the great-crested grebe were "of use to the species"; Tinbergen (1951) defined an instinct as involving "movements that contribute to the maintenance of the individual and the species"; and Lorenz (1966) in his discussion of aggression referred to "the selective pressure of a species-preserving function." Such arguments reflected the expectation of smooth and cooperative communication. The envisioned result was settled disputes between rivals, contented pairs of mates, and domestic bliss in families.

More recently, the communication process has been viewed as a propaganda battle. Paralleling interspecific deception (mimicry), intraspecific deception has begun to receive attention (e.g., B. Wallace, 1973). The new framework hinges on the concept of evolutionarily stable strategy (ESS) as developed by Maynard Smith (1979). A strategy is a set of rules for a course of action in a competitive situation. The strategy produces a particular payoff, measured in fitness, whose magnitude is dependent on the frequencies with which other strategies are being played. Speaking informally (i.e., nonmathematically), an ESS is a strategy that, when commonly used in the population, has a larger payoff than any rival strategy. This framework may appear anthropomorphic but in fact is not, and is finding increasing application in evolutionary biology (e.g., Dawkins, 1976; Dawkins and Krebs, 1978). Its relevance to recognition behavior is that it may be an ESS for an animal to send information about its size or strength but not about its motivations. It may even be part of an ESS to lie. Such behavior clearly contrasts with that expected under the classical ethological approach (cf. Caryl 1979, 1981). In place of the happy results envisioned under that approach, we now descry despotic dominance, mate manipulation, and parent–offspring conflict. Such antagonisms can produce the evolutionary intraspecific arms races in recognition behavior mentioned above (e.g., Dawkins and Krebs, 1979), especially recognition of state in aggressive and sexual encounters.

In a recent, careful review of these frameworks, Hinde (1981) has argued that ESS proponents have caricatured classical ethology, particularly on the issues of selection pressures and the information content of displays. He thus feels that a straw man has been set up. True to his own magistral synthesis of ethology and psychology (1970), he calls for an approach synthesizing ethology and ESS research. However, such a synthesis may be difficult since the two approaches qualify, if not as distinct Kuhnian paradigms (Kuhn, 1971) at least as very significant shifts in emphasis. Caryl (1982) has forcefully presented the differences in the approaches. These discussions have served to highlight the different meanings of "information," as in its cooperative or theoretical senses, and the consequent assortment of orientations taken by researchers.

In his discussion of the risks of lying, W. J. Smith (1977) concluded that "ethologists have not yet caught nonhuman animals in intentional acts of lying with display behavior." Hinde (1981) reaches a similar conclusion. It is difficult to deal with Smith's assertion scientifically since there is no generally accepted operational definition of "intentional acts." Nevertheless, results considered below do seem to embody such catches. For instance, courtship in the intensively studied three-spined stickleback may involve considerable deception (Rohwer, 1978a). In this species, nesting males aerate eggs by fanning. Fanning may be performed deceptively by males during courtship to convince females that eggs are already present and that the male is therefore a desirable mate. (Males generally fast during nesting but may eat eggs. Thus, the presence of eggs in a nest indicates to a female that her eggs are at low risk of being eaten.) Also, Coco, a gorilla tutored in sign language, is reported to lie (Patterson, 1978). In summary, as with the topic of constraints on learning, that of behavioral strategies is one of the clear points of contact between evolutionary ethology and traditional psychology, as seen in papers such as Carr et al. (1980a) in which the laboratory behavior of male and female rats is considered from a strategic viewpoint.

Blushing remains an outstanding problem in state recognition, and its analysis poses a problem for the student of communication. Darwin (1872) included a long chapter on the topic, discussing cross-cultural data and proximate mechanisms but not, unusually for him, adaptive function. Blushing scarcely seems propaganda, yet what information is advantageously broadcast by the sender? Is the occurrence of blushing dependent on the presence of others besides the person causing it? If so, is the signal directed toward these others? Does blushing manipulate by signaling submission for the present plus threat of aggression in the future if the receiver persists? Or is blushing simply an ephiphenomenon (i.e., a by-product of other responses, in this case autonomic vasodilation)?

GROUPS

This section considers the selection pressures favoring recognition in colonies of social insects, recognition of membership in a flock or school, as well as individual and self-recognition in long-term groups.

Colony Recognition

Among the hymenoptera (about 24,000 species of ants, bees, and wasps), males are haploid and females diploid. All the sperm of a male are consequently identical. Daughters of females who mate with one male will therefore on average share half of their genes with their mother but three-quarters with each other: all the genes from their father and half of the genes from their mother. Females who raise sisters rather than daughters are therefore rearing genetically more similar individuals. The inclusive fitness of an individual consists of both fitness achieved by personal reproduction and fitness achieved by helping relatives, weighted by the relatedness of those individuals. Female workers attain their fitness by raising closely related sisters. [Kin selection refers to the evolutionary advantages accruing from such efforts expended to benefit relatives. As defined by Maynard Smith (1964), it is "the evolution of characteristics which favour the survival of close relatives of the affected individual, by processes which do not require any discontinuities in population breeding structure."] This haplodiploid theory was formulated by Hamilton (1964) to account for the origin of sociality 11 independent times in the hymenoptera. In this key paper, Hamilton put forth a general genetic model for the evolution of social behavior centered around the concepts of kin selection and inclusive fitness. Typical of its precise conclusions is "the selective advantage when a benefit comes to be given to sibs only instead of to sibs and half-sibs indifferently is more than four times the advantage when a benefit of the same magnitude is given to cousins only instead of to cousins and half-cousins indifferently." The chief result germane to recognition behavior is that "the situations which a species discriminates in its social behavior tend to evolve and multiply in such a way that the coefficients of relationship involved in each situation become more nearly determinate." More recently, Getz (1981) has outlined a detailed model for the evolution of genetically based kin recognition systems in which alleles are expressed as identifiable labels such as odors.

Haplodiploid theory has received general support in broad outline and has implications for selection pressures for colony recognition. Nest mates should discriminate keenly between colony and noncolony members if the haplodiploid advantages are to accrue. This is indeed the case across the social insects (e.g., Schneirla, 1971; Wilson, 1971). Additionally, the theory predicts that workers will be able to identify their own queen since it is her daughters to whom they are related by three quarters. Boch and Morse (1974, 1979) have provided support for this expectation in honey bees, the discrimination resting in part on the detection of hive odor differences. Even when environmental sources of such differences are eliminated, the discrimination persists, indicating a genetic basis (Breed, 1981). Similarity of recognition odors varies with genetic similarity, and it takes hive workers some time to learn to recognize a new queen (Figure

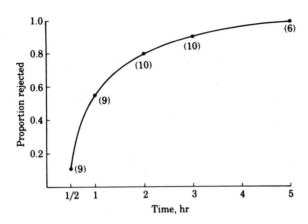

Figure 4.3. As honeybee workers are allowed more time to learn the odor of a new queen, the probability of rejecting a second queen increases (from Breed, 1981, courtesy of Michael D. Breed).

4.3). In contrast to queens, workers are rarely rejected from a hive. Proximately this may be due to a different recognition systems for queens and workers; ultimately the acceptance of (nonlaying) foreign workers does not lower the inclusive fitness of hive workers but rather in general increases it. By contrast, accepting a foreign queen does decrease fitness.

Similarly, a genetic basis for kin recognition has been found in 14 laboratory inbred lines of the primitively social sweat bee *Lasioglossum zephyrum* (Greenberg, 1979; Buckle and Greenberg, 1981). Guard bees at nest entrances were tested by presenting them with other bees of known relatedness. As Figure 4.4 shows, a larger proportion of introduced bees were permitted to pass into the nest as the genetic coefficient of relatedness increased. A likely operative mechanism is a genetically determined odor combined with learning of the odor of the home nest. Guarding bees accept or reject introduced bees on the basis of odor similarity to their nest mates, not to themselves. Evolutionarily, the recognition system could have begun as one whose function was the detection of the odors of other species, especially of parasites. Unlike the higher social insects where caste determination occurs during the larval stages, in this group caste determination occurs in the adult stage. It is therefore of great selective advantage for members of a colony to be able to recognize genetically similar bees who may subsequently become reproductively active. As in sweat bees, so in leaf-cutting ants there are both genetic and environmental aspects to the recognition of colony

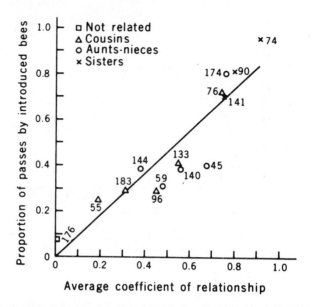

Figure 4.4.   More closely related sweat bees are more likely to be permitted to enter the nest (from L. Greenberg, 1979, copyright American Association for the Advancement of Science).

members (Jutsum et al., 1979). In yet another social insect, the wasp *Polistes metricus*, overwintered females prefer to associate on new nests with their former nestmates, which are likely sisters, rather than with nonformer nestmates (Ross and Gamboa, 1981).

Greenberg's study is important for demonstrating clearly an instance of an innate mechanism for distinguishing closeness of kinship. It thus parallels the work by Wu et al. (1980) on pigtail macaques. However, in many cases of kin recognition it is clear that learning plays a role since acquaintance with family and other related individuals is necessary for the discrimination of kin from nonkin. For instance, Gilder and Slater (1978) found that female mice, influenced by early learning, showed greatest interest in the odors of males of intermediate relatedness. Song learning among birds enables recognition of kin, as explored by Dietrich (1981) in Bengalese finches. In general, under natural conditions, kin become socialized together and so genetic and experiential mechanisms reinforce each other. These experiential aspects are exemplified in Porter's work with spiny mice, and the occasional errors which can occur are instanced in Belding's ground squirrel (discussed under Reproduction below).

In many vertebrates the recognition of kin and the consequent nepotism are important for enhancing inclusive fitness. This is the case in many social primates. Among baboons offspring tend to assume the status of their mothers in the troop (Hausfater, 1975). Rhesus brothers are also nepotistic (Meikle and Vessey, 1981). At sexual maturity males leave their natal groups and join nonnatal ones. Males tend to join groups with older, maternally related brothers, to form alliances with these brothers, and not to disrupt interactions between them and estrous females. In a different vein, increased food sharing among related spiny mice can clearly enhance inclusive fitness (Porter et al., 1981a). Alarm calls and kin recognition are also linked. The function of alarm calls has long been the focus of much dispute. Such calls serve to warn relatives in Belding's ground squirrels (Sherman, 1977, 1980). Distress screams in birds also appear to be kin selected (Rohwer et al., 1976). "Charity begins at home." Further work can elucidate the extent to which callers recognize the recipients as kin, since it might be in some cases that no recognition is involved, but rather that kin selection operates because kin tend to be in the same area.

Flocks and Schools

An understanding of the selection pressures for recognition of members of a flock or school necessitates analysis of, first, the function of such groups and, second, the importance of recognizing the appropriate features of the other members of that group. On the topic of group function, it is widely believed that many such groups function as "selfish herds" (Hamilton, 1971) in which those individuals are selected which locate themselves so that another member is between the individual and an attacking predator. Further, anonymity within the group is often enhanced by sharing characters with other members. Conversely, standing out in the crowd ("oddity") and hence providing a target for the predator is selected against. An individual may be odd because of its morphology, behavior, or spatial position. However, oddity is not always disadvantageous. For instance, rare small fish may be able to hide among larger ones. The frequency-dependent aspect of the effect immediately recommends an ESS analysis. Experimental support for selection against oddity comes from work reviewed by Curio (1976). More recently, Milinski (1977a, 1977b), Milinski and Lowenstein (1980), and Ohguchi (1981) have reported on selection by preying sticklebacks against water fleas exhibiting spatial, color, or motion oddity.

Avian creching is found in both solitarily and communally breeding species. Creches apparently serve different functions in different species. In penguins creches help to conserve body heat in a harsh environment. In the case of creches of shelduck broods it may be that the higher mortality associated with creching is offset by a higher growth rate due to enhanced foraging and hence greater likelihood of surviving to breed (Williams, 1974), or creching may be a result of high brood density (Patterson et al., 1982). Common eider ducklings in creches are less susceptible to gull predation (Munro and Bedard, 1977a, 1977b). Predation may also be the selective force for creching in pinon jays (McArthur, 1982). As in the case of the mixed cichlid broods discussed below under Reproduction, it may thus be advantageous for a parent to tolerate or even encourage other young to join the group while still treating offspring preferentially. Indeed, goldeneye ducklings in broods "parasitized" by hooded mergansers may have higher survival than unparasitized broods, apparently from a selfish herd effect (Eadie and Lumsden, personal communication). Alternatively, it may be that in some cases creche formation is fortuitous and serves no function.

On the topic of recognizing group members, discrimination of kin is often important. Selection favors associating with kin so that the advantages of flocking or schooling are shared with them and so inclusive fitness enhanced. This is what is found among aposematic tadpoles of the American toad (Waldman and Adler, 1979; Waldman, 1981). Tadpoles from each of two clutches were dyed red or blue and then allowed to mingle. Nearest-neighbor analysis showed that individuals were closer to siblings than nonsiblings. To control for the possibility that the tadpoles were choosing similarly colored individuals, single clutches were divided in half and dyed red or blue. No nearest-neighbor differences were found. The intriguing question of the operative mechanism of recognition remains unanswered. Like the alarm substance of fish, an alarm pheromone is released by injured tadpoles and may be kin selected. Kin recognition could have evolved if it prolonged the benefits of the aposematic black body color. Similar sibling recognition has been reported for the Cascade frog (Blaustein and O'Hara, 1981; O'Hara and Blaustein, 1981). Indeed, members of this species reared in isolation from the egg stage prefer siblings to nonsiblings. Furthermore, early association with nonsiblings does not affect recognition. Both of these results suggest a genetic basis to the recognition.

The evolution of alarm substances and associated responses in a large order of fish is an intriguing problem. It has even precipitated the comment that "the alarm substance does not protect the individual but serves for the protection of the school" (Pfeiffer, 1977). The release of an alarm substance is not exactly parallel to other alarm signals since in the latter cases the signals are given before, not after, the predators have struck. Barnett (1977b) and R. J. F. Smith (1982) have considered various possibilities. One likely scenario is an original repellent function for the substance to discourage predators, and subsequent kin selection acting through anticannibalism, thus preventing related individuals from preying on each other. Hymenopteran alarm pheromones are surely kin selected.

Individual and Self-Recognition

Kin selection can favor individual recognition in long-term groups. Enhancement of inclusive fitness results from assisting genetically related individuals and such assistance can be aided by individual recognition. In cooperative breeding systems, helpers gain indirectly by raising genetically similar offspring besides receiving direct benefits such as gaining experience and standing the chance of inheriting the territory.

Beyond kin selection, Trivers (1971) has argued that selection for reciprocal altruism favors individual recognition. He points out that among unrelated individuals in groups where cooperation is possible, there will be selection for the ability to recognize individuals who reciprocate assistance and to discriminate against cheaters who take but do not give. The cooperative acts occur over extended time, thus requiring good memory, and the benefits of receiving aid are assumed greater than the costs of providing it. Trivers considers the evolution of such reciprocal altruism at length with discussions of such cases as interspecific cleaning symbioses between coral reef fish, warning calls in birds, and human cooperation. It seems unlikely that the costs and benefits can be measured with any precision in most cases.

Rothstein (1980) points out that, assuming there is a genetic basis to behavior, individuals of the same species engaging in reciprocal altruism also share genes for such behavior. Therefore, reciprocal altruism and kin selection are not separable. Given this, he suggests a new definition for reciprocal altruism:

> Reciprocal altruism is reciprocity that is not maintainable (i.e. selected for) solely on the basis of the increases in inclusive fitness that are likely to occur in reciprocity and whose maintenance depends on the fact that the altruist will at a later time receive benefits from the individual he has aided.

He adds that "under this definition an individual who practices reciprocal altruism need not receive future direct benefits that outweigh the costs of the aid he has dispensed (cf. Trivers, 1971) because reciprocated aid is not the only benefit the individual receives. Aiding another reciprocal altruist aids the individual indirectly via an increase in inclusive fitness." Rothstein views reciprocal altruism as a genetic recognition system where the cue for recognition is the tendency to return aid. Reciprocal altruism between individuals of different species [e.g., cleaning symbioses and breeding cooperation as suggested by McKaye (1977), discussed under Reproduction below] is still possible. Rothstein's arguments would benefit from clarification on points such as who is a relative and what genetic mechanisms of behavior are being assumed, as well as examples of experimental situations which would distinguish kin selection from reciprocal altruism. The important point for the present discussion is that individual recognition abilities will frequently be favored in group-living species.

The problem of the evolution of human self-recognition (consciousness) is an intellectual quagmire that has caused otherwise sensible biologists to wax dangerously. Cued by Teilard de Chardin, Huxley (1961) has presented a metaphysical platform founded on fundamental levels of organization from the inorganic through the biological and psychosocial to the noetic (or knowing). On this platform he raises an exhilarating edifice of evolutionary ethics. Recently, Slobodkin (1978) has invoked self-awareness as a development liberating man from biological determinism, a claim of opaque scientific meaning. More satisfying are Humphrey's (1980) clear and cogent arguments on the problem. His analysis of the causation of self recognition is in ultimate terms, rather than the proximate ones considered by Parr (1937) and discussed in Chapter 1, Groups. Humphrey assumes that there is a significant selective advantage to being able to model reality, and goes on to point out that for highly social animals, the most important portion of reality to be modeled is the social group. Since such a group is composed of complex individuals, it is difficult to model, but the goal is achieved by use of the animal's own motives and behavior as a source of analogy. In brief, the animal introspects (cf. Lorenz, 1974). The need for the animal to include itself in its model leads to self recognition. Such speculation enables inferences on the distribution of consciousness across species, and Humphrey concludes:

> *If consciousness has evolved as a biological adaption for doing introspective psychology, then the presence or absence of consciousness in animals of different species will depend on whether or not they need to be able to understand the behavior of other animals in a social group. Wolves, chimpanzees and elephants, which all go in for complex social interactions, are probably all conscious; frogs, snails and codfish are probably not.*

Such consciousness is clearly a double-edged sword, producing art and science, but also metaphysics and religion! Additional dogmatic comments on the problem of consciousness are included in the Coda.

AGGRESSION

Evolutionarily Stable Strategy Approach

Much of the recent work on the selective advantages of aggression has been from an ESS viewpoint. Caryl (1979, 1981) has reviewed the available data on agonistic displays vis-à-vis predictions from games theory. The finding that displays do not always predict the likelihood of attack supports the War of Attrition model of the ESS approach (in which animals display until one gives up and accepts defeat) and not the contrasting and traditional ethological interpretation of signaling intentions. A variety of bird data reveals that displays are much better predictors of escape than attack. Results on display duration in several vertebrates require modifications of cost functions for the ESS models to apply. As Caryl indicates, the testing of ESS models is fraught with methodological difficulties (see also Hinde, 1981; VanRhijn, 1980) but the ESS approach is encouraging. For instance, it has provided a framework for the analysis of intermale aggression in red deer (Clutton-Brock and Albon, 1979; Clutton-Brock et al., 1979). One promising line of research is to present stimulus dummies in order to test animals. Such tests permit detection of different behavioral strategies in different individuals. Finally, kin selection predicts that less aggression should be directed toward related animals compared to unrelated animals. Consequently, recognition of relatives is advantageous, as exemplified by the work on sweat bees by Greenberg (1979; discussed above in Groups).

What role may individual recognition play in settling conflicts? Healey (1967), based on his study of deermice aggression, has suggested that individual recognition enables a better allocation of aggressive effort than would be achieved if animals could not distinguish individuals. Such a line of argument applies to all instances of the dear enemy effect. VanRhijn and Vodegel (1980) review the feasibility of individual recognition in many species of animals living in small groups. They argue that it can be expected that knowledge of individuals will be used for conflict settlements, yielding asymmetric contests (as opposed to symmetric contests where nothing is known about the opponent). Signaling of intentions can also be expected to be important when the individuals know each other. The authors provide the results of a number of simulations under the assumption that knowledge about the relative strengths of contestants is either perfect or learned over encounters. Various assumptions were made about the manner in which dominance relations were settled (e.g., by the outcome of the first conflict involving a dangerous act). The simulation results showed that being honest about one's intentions is not always an ESS. In the case of perfect knowledge about the attributes of the opponent, a "threat-right" strategy (i.e., threatening a submissive, and attacking if it does not retreat, and conversely retreating from a threatening or attacking dominant) is an ESS. In the case where learning occurs, other strategies have larger payoffs. Of particular interest is the impact of individual recognition on bluffing. Bluffing cannot be expected to evolve if bluffers are recognized! Andersson (1980) has expanded on this topic of bluffing in connection with the diversity of threat displays. He argues that as displays come to be used by bluffers, new displays which are better predictors of attack will evolve. The consequent frequency-dependent selection can be expected to lead to a proliferation of displays. It would be interesting to know the evolutionary lifespan of morphological cues for fighting ability, such as the white patch on the enlarged left chela of a hermit crab (Dunham, 1978).

Territoriality

The selective advantages of territoriality and the accompanying recognition behavior have been well documented in many species. Territories variously function to guarantee food supply, reproductive sites, and freedom from predation, disease, and competition. In lekking species, possession of a territory indicates the relatively superior prowess of the territory holder. Behaviors serving territory establishment and maintenance, including marking behavior and birdsong, will therefore be selected as will the ability to recognize the significance of these behaviors. In wolves it is generally the case that individuals that scent mark breed and those that do not mark do not breed (Rothman and Mech, 1979). Similarly, a territory is a prerequisite for male reproduction in wildebeest (Estes, 1969). In Mongolian gerbils, mutual marking and grooming, plus overmarking at specific sites, may serve to distribute a colony odor, consisting of the odors of the member individuals, and to reduce intracolony aggression (Roper and Polioudakis, 1977). The pheromonally-marked trails and resulting territories of harvester ants enable an efficient use of foraging areas (Holldobler, 1976a; Holldobler and Wilson, 1970). The recruitment pheromones facilitate retrieval of food sources too large to move in a single trip.

Recognition of the most dangerous rivals is advantageous so that an animal can allocate its aggressive efforts to greatest effect. The dear enemy effect (discussed in Chapter 1) is one consequent form of such selectivity: strangers elicit a stronger response than established neighbors. The selective aggression of herring gulls toward conspecifics in re-productive condition is adaptive since it is aimed at potential reproductive rivals (Tinbergen, 1953). Recognition between members of pairs in birds that sing antiphonally enables cooperation in establishing and defending a territory (Seibt and Wickler, 1977).

Establishment of territories via deceptive recognition has been sug-gested for various birds (Rohwer et al., 1980). The hypothesis is that in a number of species, males delay development of sexual plumage and thus, by mimicking females, avoid eliciting aggression from territorial males. They are then able to establish territories themselves which they maintain through site dominance. In support of this account is the finding that adult male territorial red-winged blackbirds are less aggressive to subadult males than to peers, even though subadults are poor female mimics (Rohwer, 1978b). This finding is congruent with those by Peek and Smith (discussed in Chapter 1, Territoriality) on this species. Data from purple martins also support the argument against an alternate hypothesis that the maturation of plumage is delayed to provide cryptic protection against predation during the first potential breeding season, during which sexual selection makes breeding unlikely (Rohwer and Niles, 1979). For in-stance, success at entering large colonies is lower for subadults with plumage more closely resembling that of adult males. In Harris sparrows, social dominance is signaled by black feathering on the crown and throat (Rohwer, 1977). The results of experiments in which the feathers of subordinates were dyed, and those of dominants bleached, were open to various interpretations. One such recent interpretation by Rohwer and Ewald (1981) does not postulate the operation of deception but instead considers the costs and benefits that could produce evolutionary stability for both dominants and subordinates. Paralleling this interpretation is the finding that dyed subordinates were attacked by other flock members because their black feathering was incongruous with their behavior (Rohwer and Rohwer, 1978). Research into the function of plumage variability in redpolls failed to support the deception hypothesis (Diamond, 1980). Instead, dominance is signaled by behavior, and plumage variability facilitates individual recognition. Similarly, results from American redstarts are not consistent with the deception hypothesis or an alternate hypothesis of selection for delayed maturation (Proctor-Gray and Holmes, 1981). However, in northern orioles, delayed plumage maturation is more plausibly accounted for by female mimicry than sexual selection (Flood, 1980). Territorial deception can take other forms, as in the pied flycatcher in which some males maintain two separate territories, thus duping a second, would-be monogamous female into laying and raising a clutch of eggs sired by him (Alatalo et al., 1981). Further in this vein, deception involving pseudofemale behavior is discussed below in Reproduction.

Dominance Hierarchies

The presumed selective advantages of dominance hierarchies have often been based on group arguments to the effect that the total amount of aggression for the group is minimized (a very totalitarian argument indeed!). On an individual selection basis, it has been assumed that the dominant individuals gain by preferential access to resources such as food and mates, which enhance their fitness, while subordinate individuals gain some benefits from belonging to the group, in terms of social feeding or defense, or at least by being on hand should openings higher in the hierarchy appear. Rarely, have these arguments been explicitly examined. In domestic fowl, the exemplar species for dominance hierarchies, Guhl and Allee (1944) reported that in unstable flocks undergoing reorganization, individuals pecked more, fed less, laid fewer eggs, and lost weight as compared to control flocks. The authors concluded with a group argument that dominance organization builds a better cooperative unit better fitted to compete with other flocks. In a subsequent paper, Guhl (1953) reported that high ranking hens had advantages including greater freedom of the pen and more access to food, water, nest boxes, and favorable roost locations. However, more recent research has found no function for hierarchies in terms of either resource access or group defense (Banks et al., 1979). It is not appropriate to generate excuses about chickens being domestic and therefore aberrant, and so the need for further investigation in this area is obvious. In other cases, however, the advantages of dominance can be seen. In red deer, dominant individuals have access to the best grazing areas (Appleby, 1980) and female gelada baboons have offspring in proportion to their dominance rank (Dunbar, 1980). Among elephant seals, males that are high ranking in the hierarchy perform most of the inseminations (LeBoeuf and Peterson, 1969). In *Leptothorax allardycei*, an ant unique for its dominance hierarchies, higher ranking individuals gain in liquid food exchange and egg-laying productivity (Cole, 1981).

In terms of recognition abilities, Barnard and Burk (1979, 1981) have considered different types of hierarchies that can evolve using different cues. They distinguish statistical hierarchies, resulting from asymmetries in fighting abilities, confidence hierarchies, involving decisions based on internal state, and assessment hierarchies, in which cues received from an opponent are used. The distinction between recognition of individuals and the use of simpler cues is thus an arbitrary one. In assessment hierarchies, individuals are selected both to emulate high status and to detect the true status of opponents (i.e., to detect cheats). Thus Barnard and Burk conclude that while individual recognition is not a prerequisite for dominance hierarchies, dominance hierarchies may be a driving force for the evolution of individual recognition. In a subsequent comment, Breed and Bekoff (1981) have pointed out, with illustrations from insects and mammals, that kin recognition may involve fine discriminations among individuals. In experimental work with platies, Zayan (1975) has shown how individual recognition can overcome the usual prior residency effect.

REPRODUCTION

Sexual Selection

The value of sexual recognition for reproduction is obvious. But even with sexual recognition problems overcome, not all potentially reproducing members of a population breed, and those that do generally do so assortatively (discussed below). Darwin (1871) defined sexual selection as "the advantage which certain individuals have over others of the same sex and species solely in respect of reproduction." Sexual selection can be intense in polygamous mating systems, such as leks and mating swarms, in which almost all females reproduce but only a fraction of males. Sexual selection is a topic of very great interest in contemporary biology (see, e.g., Blum and Blum, 1979; Campbell, 1972) and the present discussion will be limited to its impact on recognition abilities. Under sexual selection pressures, it is to be expected that animals will evolve the ability to choose mates of high fitness and that to be chosen confers enhanced fitness. As Fisher (1930) put it, "whenever appreciable differences exist in a species, which are in fact correlated with selective advantage, there will be a tendency to select also those individuals of the opposite sex which most clearly discriminate the difference to be observed, and which most decidedly prefer the more advantageous type." Evidence from fruitflies supporting this argument for at least one component of fitness has been presented by Partridge (1980). She demonstrated that the offspring of parents allowed to choose mates from a large group of potential mates had greater competitive success against a distinct mutant than did those of parents mated at random from the stock. Competitive success was measured from first instar larvae to adult flies and was approximately 4% higher in the offspring of "choice" parents over those of "no choice" parents. The discriminating cues and genetic mechanisms underlying this recognition behavior remain to be elucidated.

Sexual selection can operate either through intrasexual, generally male, competition, with winners gaining the females, or intersexual (epigamic) competition, with females choosing males. Often intrasexual competition leads to large males and hence size dimorphisms (e.g., elephant seals) whereas epigamic competition leads to bright colors and hence color dimorphisms (e.g., pheasants). Until recently, good evidence for epigamic selection was lacking, but is now available for several groups. In some scorpion flies females select mates providing large nuptial gifts of food (Alcock, 1979; Thornhill, 1980). Female bullfrogs choose relatively large males who defend high quality territories as reflected in lower embryo mortality prior to hatching (Howard, 1978). Female brown-headed cowbirds choose mates whose dominant status is recognized by their song (West et al., 1981). In red-winged blackbirds, females may even choose to have fewer offspring, sired by a polygynous male, than more sired by a relatively unsuccessful male, given that the reproductive ability of these offspring is relatively high (i.e., sexy fathers beget sexy sons) (Weatherhead and Robertson, 1979, 1981). Female johnny darter females choose mates who vigorously defend spawning sites (Grant, 1980; Figure 4.5) and guppy and damselfish females choose mates with high rates of courtship display (Farr, 1980; Schmale, 1981). These studies, together with many others from diverse species (e.g., wolf spiders: Uetz and Denterlein, 1979; prairie grouse: Sparling, 1981), are consistent with the hypothesis that females, who produce metabolically expensive eggs or young, tend to be choosier in mate choice than males, who churn out cheap sperm. However, it is experimentally difficult to untangle female choice and male choice.

Nevertheless, males can also be discriminating. Males of the amphipod *Gammarus duebenii* court only mature premolt females, ignoring females with unripe ovaries (Hartnoll and Smith, 1980). In two British freshwater isopods, males prefer females exhibiting a cue correlated with imminent oviposition and large brood size (Manning, 1975, 1980; Thompson and

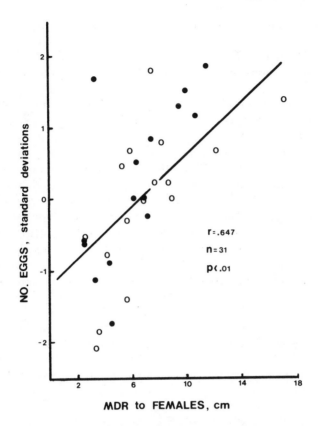

Figure 4.5. The number of eggs in the nest of a johnny darter increases with his maximum distance of response (MDR) to females (from Grant, 1980).

Manning, 1981). Small males do not attempt to guard females, whereas large males take over from small ones and guard females until copulation (Ridley and Thompson, 1979). Similarly, among baboons, dominant males consort with females during the period of the latter's reproductive cycle when pregnancy is most likely (Hausfater, 1975). "Save the last dance for me." In wood frogs and guppies, males preferentially court large females over small (Berven, 1981; Dussault and Kramer, 1981).

In general, recognition of ovulation can be expected to be advantageous to a female and her mate(s). It is therefore curious that human ovulation is not obviously recognizable. Burley (1979) has argued that this is a consequence of a hominid female tendency to avoid conception in biologically nonadaptive ways while Strassman (1981) has suggested that it has arisen in association with the evolution of paternal tendencies of less polygynous males. The validity of these arguments, and the actual extent to which ovulation is concealed in women, remain to be established.

The Coolidge effect (see Chapter 1, Sex and Mates), easy to understand proximately in terms of habituation in the male and different behavior in mated and unmated females, could be adaptive in that extra vigor with a new female could enhance fitness whereas additional effort with the same female would not. However, as Dewsbury (1981) has pointed out in his thorough review of this effect, its role in reproductive strategies, such as monogamy versus polygamy, requires further detailed study. A strategic approach to the function of the effect might well examine cases beyond mammals, such as male sweat bees, which show renewed sexual interest when presented with the odor of a different female (Barrows, 1975).

A frequent, important determinant in sexual selection is the age of a prospective mate. Cues for age include, beyond size, iris color in some birds (e.g., Australian babblers) and pelage color in mammals (e.g., silver-backed gorillas). Age is a predictor of ability to survive, of reproductive experience, and of reproductive value [the expected reproductive output of an individual (see Fisher, 1930) (Figure 4.6)], three key characters of a mate. In polygynous species, such as bullfrogs (Howard, 1978) and elephant seals (Cox and LeBoeuf, 1977), females prefer older, dominant males over younger ones. A similar preference is found in red-winged blackbirds in which experience at nest defense against long-billed marsh wrens is of major importance (Picman, 1980). In monogamous feral pigeons, although more experienced birds are preferred over less experienced ones as mates, birds over 7 years of age are discriminated against (Burley and Moran, 1979). Female mortality is higher than male mortality and hence a male is likely to outlive his first mate. Mate choice by inexperienced males is relatively inconsistent. Nevertheless, they are likely to gain breeding experience, with their first mate, which will enable them to mate advantageously later in life. Among humans, cosmetics serve to camouflage age discrepancies from the optimum for each sex.

It was stated above that sexual selection often leads to sexual dimorphism in species, with males being gaudy and conspicuous. As discussed in Chapter 3, Sexual and Filial Imprinting, a frequent, although not invariant, consequence of this dimorphism is that females are able to recognize males without experience whereas males require experience and subsequent imprinting for appropriate recognition. O'Donald (1980) has proposed a variety of genetic models for sexual selection and the related topic of assortative mating (discussed below). The data base for these models comes chiefly from O'Donald's research on the arctic skua. A critique of these models has been made by Taylor and Williams (1981).

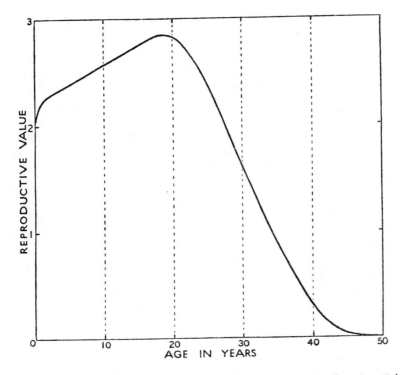

Figure 4.6. Original reproductive value function, for Australian women (from R. A. Fisher, 1930).

Recognition: Cuckolds, Pseudofemales, Errors, Strange Males, and Individuals

Given the selection pressure for opportunistic cuckoldry in many species, small wonder that it is the wise offspring who knows his father. [The term "kleptogamy" is used in place of "cuckoldry" by those with legitimate concerns about the introduction of anthropomorphic terms into the literature on social behavior. For instance, regarding the use of "rape" see Estep and Bruce (1981).] Recognition of cuckolds and adulteresses is thus an area of contact between recognition behavior and reproductive strategies. Cuckoldry is a risk in all internally fertilizing species, not least our own. Daly and Wilson (1982) found that in both spontaneous utterances at birth and solicited views, parents opined paternal resemblance much more often than maternal resemblance. This was particularly true of sons, as compared to daughters. The fact that mothers especially maintain this opinion was interpreted as an attempt to promote paternity confidence in their husbands.

Cuckoldry has been the focus of a number of avian studies. In laboratory studies, female doves that have associated with other males receive less courtship and more aggression from males than do previously isolated females (Zenone et al., 1979). However, the breeding experience of the birds, the behavior of the female, and the social complexities of the field situation are also important (Rissman, 1982). The changes in recognition responses of territorial male savannah sparrows can be understood in terms of cuckoldry pressure (Weatherhead and Robertson, 1980). Early in the breeding season, males are not hormonally prepared for copulation, and strongly attack both male and female stimulus dummies. Thus, while they are not able to cuckold other males themselves, they guard their mates against this possibility. During the 10 days of peak nest initiation, territorial males discriminate most strongly between stimulus dummies, presumably reflecting the dual strategy of protecting their own mates from other males while taking advantage of copulations with other receptive females when possible. Following this period, with his mate no longer at risk, territorial males can and do treat all stimulus dummies as females. Anticuckoldry mate guarding is found in lesser snow geese and mountain bluebirds but there is no consensus on the suggestion that in the latter species suspected adulteresses are driven away by their mates (Mineau and Cooke, 1979; Power, 1980; Power and Doner, 1980; Gowaty, 1981).

As discussed in Chapter 1, Sex and Mates, pseudofemale behavior may reflect behavioral "errors" due to high arousal. Such "errors" are informative about the proximate causal mechanisms that are operative. Pseudofemale behavior may also serve as an alternate reproductive strategy. Such an alternate strategy is employed by male scorpion flies (Thornhill, 1980). By mimicking females and thus attracting other males who bring prey items necessary for successful courtship, the mimics can rob the deluded males of their prizes and save themselves the effort of hunting. In some salamanders, males mimic females and so induce rivals to deposit spermatophores without fertilizing a female (Arnold, 1976). Pseudofemale behavior enables cuckoldry in several fish species such as the leaf fish (G.W. Barlow, 1967) and the bluegill sunfish (Dominey, 1981; Gross, 1980). Pseudofemale behavior enables a male to join a spawning pair and sneak in some fertilizations. Such pseudofemales thus belong to the class of sneakers, a class whose realized abundance continues to increase as more detailed study of reproductive social systems advances. Sneakers steal fertilizations rather than exhibiting the "normal" behavior of defending a nest site, or dominating in a hierarchy, and attracting females. Many sneakers do not trouble with female mimicry, but rather dash in and out to fertilize. The sneaker strategy can be foiled if the ability to discriminate eggs which one has fertilized from those fertilized by anothoer male is operative in nature. Such ability has been reported in pupfish in the laboratory (Loiselle, personal communication). One might also expect the evolution of sexual dimorphism to prevent female mimicry. However, in bluegills at least (Colgan et al., 1979) females may continue to be similar to males so that they are initially mistaken as males by nesting males. The females can then assess the aggressiveness of the male in defending his nest, and thus choose appropriately aggressive males. Hence, we may have males behaving like pseudofemales and females like pseudomales! In other species, pseudomale behavior may serve to draw attention. Domestic bulls are attracted by estrous cows who mount other cows. Overall, intraspecific deception appears to be as evolutionarily important as interspecific mimicry.

Recognition errors have also been invoked in another case of fish reproduction. McKaye (1977) reported that the cichlid *Cichlasoma nicaraguense* defends the offspring of a predator, *C. dovii*, and that this behavior is selected for because the predator in turn preys on competitors of *C. nicaraguense*. Coyne and Sohn (1978) suggested that the observed behavior was due to mistaken identity, but McKaye (1979) has reiterated his position. The finding that bagrid catfish defend young cichlids indicates that recognition errors are unlikely (McKaye and Oliver, 1980). Nevertheless, the scenario of reciprocal altruism described by McKaye requires certain key features, such as strong site attachment of the fishes involved, and it remains unclear which interpretation, if either, is valid. It has variously been suggested that mixed broods in cichlids are the result of fortuitous encounters between different species and an associated lack of recognition (Lewis, 1980), of brood parasitism (Ribbink, 1977; Ribbink et al., 1980), and of kidnapping to provide young other than one's own to predators (McKaye and McKaye, 1977; review by McKaye, 1981). Further studies are needed to distinguish these alternatives.

Errors in recognizing kin have been considered for Belding's ground squirrel (Sherman, 1980). As discussed in Groups above, individuals in this species are nepotistic in their alarm calling so that kin benefit. Since the ontogeny of sibling recognition takes time, mixing of littermates prior to this recognition ability can lead to errors in which related individuals are treated as unrelated and unrelated individuals are treated as related. Also, nonlittermate sisters, who do not meet prior to the disappearance of their mother, treat each other as unrelated, unlike such sisters who do associate through the mother. Both of these sources of recognition errors indicate the importance of social cues in kin recognition. Overall, cooperation is found between mothers and daughters, littermate sisters, and nonlittermate half-sisters (who have different fathers), but not between more distant relatives (Sherman, 1981).

Recognition of strange males is indicated by the Bruce effect (see Chapter 1, Species and Morphs). A possible function of the Bruce effect can be inferred from the observation that in at least some mammalian species (e.g., collared lemmings: Mallory and Brooks, 1978; lions: Bertram, 1975; Hanuman langurs: Hrdy, 1977a, 1977b) that live in groups in which there is considerable turnover in the breeding males, newly dominant males kill infants, thus bringing the females of the group into breeding condition more quickly. It may be that a female can cut her losses by aborting embryos whose likelihood of survival is slight and becoming pregnant by the new male (Labov, 1981a; Mallory and Brooks, 1980). Schwagmeyer (1979) has evaluated this and other suggestions on the function of the effect. For example, an explanation that the Bruce effect achieves exogamy (outbreeding) is contradicted by the finding that the effect is dependent on the genetic difference between the sire and blocking male, regardless of the genotype of the female. Schwagmeyer argues that the dependency of the effect on a number of situational contingencies implies that it may not be strictly male imposed, like infanticide, but rather reflect a female alternative for selecting a better mate. However, in house mice the social status of the male does not affect his ability to block pregnancy (Labov, 1981b). Blaustein (1981) has pointed out that females mating with males capable of blocking pregnancy will have similarly potent sons assuming a genetic basis to the ability. Females preferring such males are therefore at an advantage. The effect may, of course, have different functions in different species.

The advantages of individual recognition in a reproductive context has been discussed by several workers. Chemical discrimination of family membership in desert wood lice enables selective care by parents of the young of their own brood (Linsenmair, 1972). Individual recognition of the young enhances survival in leaf-nosed bats (Porter, 1979) and many avian species (e.g., Adelie penguins: Penney, 1968). Recognition of parents and siblings by young maintains the integrity of the family unit which promotes the growth of the offspring (e.g., ducks: Mattson and Evans, 1974; chickens: Evans and Mattson, 1972; Cowan and Evans, 1974). In swallows, recognition of young by parents becomes necessary only after fledging (Burtt, 1977). Prior to that time, attachment to the nest suffices. Several workers (e.g., Miller and Emlen, 1975) have advanced the general argument that recognition onset correlates with mobility of the offspring. However, Shugart (1977), discussing his results with Caspian terns, has suggested that an earlier onset of individual recognition enhances parental care since parents can respond to specific cues. In Galapagos fur seals and sea lions, mother–pup recognition enables the mother to raise selectively her own offspring while pups can avoid dangerous encounters with other females (Trillmich, 1981).

Recognition of the category "mother," their own or another, by young midas cichlids is adaptive since predation is high outside a school protected by a mother (Barnett, 1977a; McKaye and Barlow, 1976). The lack of reaction to males is appropriate since parental males spend more time defending the territory and less with the brood. A general recognition of femaleness, compared to a possible identification of individual mothers, is sufficient since it permits adoption into a new brood if separation from the maternal brood occurs. For their parts (as discussed above) parents may not recognize such young or may be at a selective advantage to adopt, or even kidnap, foreign young while distinguishing these from their own offspring.

Mate recognition has been shown to be advantageous in several species. Individual recognition of the mate by males of the monogamous marine shrimp *Hymenocera picta* is a consequence of the male strategy to enhance his reproductive efficiency (Seibt and Wickler, 1979). By being able to recognize his partner, he can selectively defend her against rivals and spend time with her, an investment that pays off with copulation when she becomes sexually receptive. During winter females of monogamous pairs in Bewick's swan flocks are more successful in agonistic encounters when with their mates than when separated (D. K. Scott, 1980). To a lesser extent, the same is true for males. In the kittiwake gull, there are strong fitness advantages to retaining the same mate (Coulson, 1966). As compared to females with new mates, females retaining the same mate breed earlier, lay more eggs, and have greater breeding success. Mate recognition is advantageous among long-lived, colonial snow petrels faced with a short breeding season (Guillotin and Jouventin, 1980). Among collared lemmings, a solitary species, individual recognition reduces aggression among potential mates (Huck and Banks, 1979). Mate recognition in the glandulocaudine fish *Corynopoma microlepis* serves an important function (Nelson, 1964). For courtship to be successful in this species, it must be preceded by the establishment of male dominance and be continuous over a long period of time. Individual recognition facilitates meeting these conditions. The next question, of course, is why the courtship has these characters.

Assortative Mating

In its broadest sense, assortative mating refers to nonrandom mating with respect to some character, whether genotypic or phenotypic. Just as genetic heritability must be specified with respect to some population, so assortative mating must be specified with respect to some character. Classical assortative mating involves polymorphic species (see Chapter 1, Species and Morphs) and may be positive (like preferring like, or homogamy) or negative (like preferring unlike, or heterogamy). Results from investigations reporting assortative mating in natural populations are given in Table 4.1. It should be noted, however, that mating in many populations with regard to many traits is random. Positive assortative mating patterns at the level of the population does not imply homogamic preferences at the level of the behavior of individuals. The observed population pattern could be the result of such processes as directional preferences, producing sexual selection, or clinal variation such that similar individuals inhabit the same locale when pairing occurs. [A cline is a geographical gradient in some character of a species (Huxley, 1939). An example of a behavioral cline is courtship behavior in domestic houseflies

Table 4.1. Results of Assortative Mating Studies

Species	Character	Source
Positive		
Spiders	Size	Rubenstein (personal communication)
European sparrow hawk	Age	Newton et al. (1979)
Kittiwake	Age	Coulson (1966)
Domestic fowl	Plumage	Lill (1968a, 1968b)
Swainson's hawk	Plumage	Dunkle (1977)
Western grebe	Plumage	Nuechterlein (1981a, 1981b)
Lesser snow goose	Plumage	Cooke et al. (1976)
Feral domestic pigeon	Plumage	Goodwin (1958)
White-crowned sparrow	Song dialect	Baker and Mewaldt (1978)
Thai gibbons	Pelage	Fooden (1969)
Humans	Several	Thiessen and Gregg (1980)
Midas cichlids	Color	Barlow and Rogers (1978)
Negative		
Bewick's swan	Bill shape	Bateson et al. (1980)
White-throated sparrow	Plumage	Lowther (1961)

(Bryant, 1980).] Cooke et al. (1976) have highlighted this problem with two hypotheses dealing with mate choice in snow geese. Under the preference hypothesis, birds choose according to familial color; under the prevalence hypothesis, they choose according to available potential mates. These hypotheses are not, of course, mutually exclusive. Burley (personal communication) illustrates the fallacy of inferring a process at one level (that of individual behavior) from data at another level (that of the population) with examples from birds and humans. Mating preferences can also be complicated by interacting factors. For instance, in the midas cichlid, spawning success is dependent on both the morph and size of the potential partner (Barlow et al., 1977). The experimental background of the test animals also influences mate preferences, as discussed in Chapter 3, Sexual and Filial Imprinting.

The functional aspects of assortative mating need to be considered in terms of inbreeding and local adaptation (Thiessen and Gregg, 1980). Inbreeding, the mating of individuals related by ancestry, is inevitable over generations in finite populations. The effective breeding population, which measures the effective size of the population in terms of its population genetics, is less than the nominal breeding population due to several factors. The relevant factor for the present discussion is assortative mating. Close inbreeding is deleterious and therefore regarded as the ultimate factor behind incest taboos in primates (Lumsden and Wilson, 1980; Pusey, 1980; review by Demarest, 1977), mice (Yana and McClearn, 1972), Florida scrub jays (Woolfenden, personal communication), prairie voles (McGuire and Getz, 1981), and, likely, snow geese (Cooke, personal communication). Field evidence for inbreeding depression comes from Oxford great tits. Survival of nestlings of mother–son and brother–sister pairs is lower than that of outbreeding pairs, although clutch size is not (Greenwood et al., 1978). However, work on other populations of this species has not found such depression (VanNoordwijk and Scharloo, 1981). Heinroth (1911) long ago suggested that incest avoidance prevented breeding in many anatid sibships. On the other hand, the assortative mating involving avian song dialects permits the evolution of adaptations to local conditions. In white-crowned sparrows, migration between two populations with different dialects is only a fifth of what is expected at random, due to aggression between males of different dialects (Baker and Mewaldt, 1978, 1981; Baker et al., 1981c). Bertram (1970) has argued that the greater responsiveness of Indian hill mynahs to calls of the same dialect, compared to those of a different dialect, is an extension of species recognition. By contrast, dialects ensure outbreeding in an insular population of New Zealand saddlebacks (Jenkins, 1978). In this long-lived semiflightless species, males move outside their own dialect area, presumably to avoid mating with close relatives. The balance between local adaptation and inbreeding must thus be examined in each population.

Against this background, the relevance, to the topic of assortative mating, of Bateson's (1978a, 1979) optimal discrepancy hypothesis for sexual imprinting is clear. Bateson argues that evolutionary pressures select for an optimal tradeoff between outbreeding and inbreeding, and that the balance between negative and positive assortative mating depends on how quickly the environment changes. He is able to link this hypothesis with general theory on the evolution of sexual imprinting, and to resolve apparent contradictions in the literature on mate selection. For instance, the finding that female mice show greatest interest in the odors of males of intermediate genetic relatedness (Gilder and Slater, 1978; D'Udine and Partridge, 1981) supports the hypothesis. Mate preferences in Japanese quail provide additional evidence (Bateson, 1980). Males raised with two females, and females with three males, prefer strangers over familiar birds. Birds raised in smaller groups found strangers unacceptably strange; those raised in larger groups were less likely to find strangers dissimilar from some group members. Further support comes from the finding that male and female quail prefer cousins to both siblings and unrelated conspecifics (Bateson, 1982). (Darwin, who married a cousin, would no doubt be delighted.)

Rare Male Effect

The most celebrated area of research involving recognition behavior in assortative mating is that of the rare male effect. Several studies involving seven species of fruit flies report that the mating success of males is frequency dependent with the rare type being favored (Ehrman, 1966; Spiess and Schwer, 1978; reviews by Ehrman and Parsons, 1976; Ehrman and Probber, 1978; Figure 4.7). The types may be genotypes or phenotypes such as the same strains raised on different diets. Reciprocal tests with different types being abundant or rare enable separation of frequency effects from type effects. Perhaps surprisingly, the genotype of the female does not influence the results. Experiments involving the circulation of air from areas containing males of the rare type indicate that olfaction is involved in the effective stimulus, a conclusion also supported by Hay (1972). It is possible that the ultimate function of such behavior is to avoid inbreeding and to enhance fitness via increased genetic variance in offspring. A proximate mechanism involving habituation to stimuli from the common type, leaving the rare type more exciting is also possible.

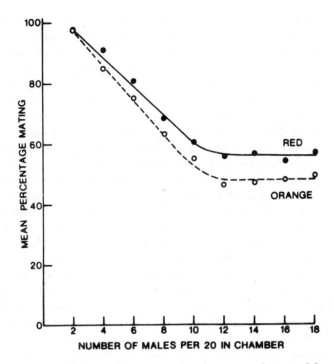

Figure 4.7. Rare male mating advantage in red- and orange-eyed *Dropsophila melanogaster* (from Spiess and Kruckeberg, 1980).

The rare male effect is controversial on both empirical and theoretical grounds. Turning first to empirical work, McKay (1978) was unable to detect, in a careful study involving several environments, any rare male effect in several strains of *Drosophila pseudoobscura*. Mating is also random among karyotypes of this species (Anderson and McGuire, 1978). Pot et al. (1980) reported no rare male effect in *D. melanogaster* with respect to genetic variants of the enzyme alcohol dehydrogenase. Whether males of the same species differ at only a single locus or represent different strains, mating is not frequency dependent in general (Markow, 1978; Markow et al., 1980). Houseflies variable in body and eye color do not show a rare male effect either (Childress and McDonald, 1973). Given the generally appropriate bias in the scientific literature against publishing negative results, one wonders how many other failures of replications, like Thomas Gray's "mute inglorious Milton," here may rest. Based on work with wing-clipped houseflies, Bryant et al. (1980) have suggested that such experimental sources of bias may be the basis of the effect. Even clipping each strain in alternate experiments does not remove such bias (Kence, 1981). Finally, reported results could suffer from the bias of aspirating fruit flies, which differ behaviorally, from different regions of their containers (Markow, 1980).

On the theoretical front, in a reanalysis of published data, O'Donald (1977, 1978) has argued "that a simple model of constant female preferences for particular phenotypes or genotypes is sufficient to explain a large body of data on frequency-dependent sexual selection in *Drosophila*." However, Spiess and Kruckeberg (1980) recently refuted this argument with data from *D. melanogaster*. They also suggest that the proximate behavioral mechanism in the female may not be habituation to stimuli from the majority type but rather avoidance of the cues of the first courting male, who on average will belong to the majority type. In Hawaiian populations of *D. silvestris*, variation in male tibial bristles is important in such sexual selection by females (Spiess and Carson, 1981). More generally, the analysis of selection data is beset with statistical difficulties (see, e.g., Goux and Anxolabehere, 1980). Finally, Lewontin (1974) has pointed out that "a generalized intrapopulation advantage for rare males with respect to almost any genotype could exist, if for no other reason than that every male is genotypically rare in a population with 10 percent heterozygosity and 40 percent polymorphism!"

Thus, the rare male effect in *Drosophila* is at best not robust, and the available data do not appear to require frequency-dependent judgmental powers on the part of females. Nevertheless, similar findings in other species (flour beetles: Sinnock, 1970; wasps: Grant et al., 1974, 1980; White and Grant, 1977; guppies: Farr, 1977) encourage further study. Experiments relating the laboratory findings to the natural situation, in which males are likely more genetically diverse (and hence all males are rare) and pheromones less concentrated, are warranted.

Evolutionary Consequences of Assortative Mating

Assortative mating can have a major impact on the evolution of a population. Such mating can arise due to imprinting and, if positive, can increase inbreeding in the population. Building on earlier general discussions (e.g., Cushing, 1941), quantitative models of this evolutionary impact have been considered in a number of papers (Mainardi et al., 1965b; Kalmus and Smith, 1966; Kemperman, 1967; Scudo, 1967; Seiger, 1967; Karlin, 1969; Seiger and Dixon, 1970; Matessi and Scudo, 1975; Campbell, 1980; Thiessen and Gregg, 1980; Geramita et al., 1982). Under the extreme assumption of complete imprinting, in which each morph mates only with its own type, the population becomes split into two noninterbreeding fractions, resulting in sympatric speciation (Kalmus and Smith, 1966; Seiger, 1967). Under the more reasonable assumption of partial imprinting, stable genetic polymorphisms can result. These results support Mayr's (1970) conclusion that "positive assortative mating can have very little importance as an evolutionary process unless it is exceedingly intense."

Models investigating the joint effects of imprinting and dispersion between populations produce trivial or stable genetic equilibria depending on the strength of imprinting and the initial genetic conditions (Seiger and Dixon, 1970). (In trivial equilibria, only one genotype persists over time.) If it is assumed that the preference resulting from the imprinting is determined by the phenotypes of relatives such as parents and siblings, morph fixation occurs if the preference is for the same morph (isophenogamy), but polymorphism evolves if the preference is for the opposite morph (heterophenogamy) (Mainardi et al., 1965b; Scudo, 1967; Matessi and Scudo, 1975). Phenotypic assortative mating accompanied by varying selection pressures can lead to polymorphic equilibria or equilibrium cycles (Campbell, 1980). Assortative mating in dimorphic snow geese is well modeled as the result of dispersion, initial population size and phase ratio, and coefficients of imprinting (reflecting the strength of preference for a mate of the same phase) (Geramita et al., 1982).

Assortative mating also influences clines (discussed above). Computer simulations indicate that assortative mating steepens the genotype frequency cline but does not affect the gene frequency cline (Endler, 1977). Assortative mating can evolve if genetic modifiers lower heterozygote fitness at major loci. Finally, Karlin (1978) has contrasted the tendency for assortative mating to produce genetic fixation with that of sexual selection to yield polymorphisms. Overall, sexual recognition behavior can be a strong force in the evolution of animal populations.

Coda

The parade, with shrikes duetting in the bush, killifish sniffing out cuckolded eggs, gulls incubating metal boxes, aromas of ants and armpits, babies responding to mum, and signature whistles from dolphins, has passed. What refrain echoes from this tragicomedy in four acts? Like that of any major behavioral topic, the analysis of recognition behavior offers many aspects and poses many problems. For the student of motivation, the existence of multiple causal systems for different types of recognition behavior requires the unraveling of internal and external causes and their interaction. The problem of identifying different recognition mechanisms is part of that of identifying the different drive systems which they subserve. For the student of communication, each modality must be examined for its dimentions and its channel capacity on each dimention. Both the sensory and motor modulation and apparatus of each species and its ecological appropriateness must be considered. For the student of ontogeny, analysis focuses on the shifting phenotype as maturational and experiential factors transform the behavioral repertoire and enhance recognition abilities. Such factors may act continuously over the lifetime of the animal or be of brief duration but lasting influence, such as imprinting stimuli. For the behavioral geneticist, the intricate interplay of genome and environment needs to be elucidated. As for behavioral genetics generally, the gap between genes and behavior is vast. Nevertheless, some problems, such as the genetic basis of kin recognition, invite investigation. For the functionalist, ingenuity is called for to avoid pious platitudes and instead demonstrate that various selection pressures have likely operated over evolutionary time to shape the observed recognition behavior and the social system for which it is adapted. Recognition behavior thus contributes many and long threads through the ethological tapestry.

Finally, it is important to examine the philosophical position of the present work. Like evolutionary trends, trends in science are most obvious over relatively long intervals. In 1775 the French ornithologist Lottinger atempted to imitate, as he thought, the Eruopean cuckoo by removing the eggs from 17 host nests and inserting an alien egg. To his dismay all hosts abandoned their nests. The difference between his failure and the success of the cuckoo he attributed to divine decree. The fact that a contemporary editor would not accept such an account reflects a scientific trend (*pace* creationists) and provides support for Comte's insight that societies pass from a theological through a metaphysical (for ethology, viz Lorenzian) to a positive (i.e., scientific) format. Because it is simple to dichotomize (recall "nature–nurture"), positions tend to be so characterized: Yin and Yang, nominalist and realist, classic and romantic, Apollonian and Dionysian, tough- and tender-minded, foxes and hedgehogs, two cultures, and generically Us and Them. Positions in fact are multivariate and are best appreciated through their similarities and differences (i.e., their similar or different loadings on the conceptual dimensions). The *Leitmotiv* of objective, quantitiative analysis has a long history.

Pythagoras's emphasis on mathematics and music has become the music of the spheres in the Voyager spacecraft. Leibniz searched for his *Characteristica universalis*, a general scientific language such that "if controversies were to arise, there would be no more need of disputation between two philosophers (or ethologists!) than between two accountants. For it would suffice to take their pencils in their hands, to sit down at their slates, and to say to each other (with a friend as witness, if they liked): Let us calculate." LaMettrie is the fountainhead for a thoroughly materialistic approach to behavior. Watson and Skinner have advanced James' principle that every difference must make a difference, a principle that serves as a cornerstone of contemporary experimental analysis. Schneirla's axiom that "no important term should be kept in use without frequent careful examination" hails back to Francis Bacon's idols of the marketplace, "either the names of things which have no existence . . . or the names of actual objects, but confused, badly defined, and hastily and irregularly abstracted from things," Wittgenstein's "what can be said at all can be said clearly, and what we cannot talk about we must pass over in silence," and Bridgman's "the concept is synonymous with the corresponding set of operations." While physics has its centimeter-gram-second system and chemistry its periodic table, ethology, like biology generally, lacks fundamental units. It is the central task of ethometrics to extract these units from behavioral data.

For the problematic analysis of self-recognition, or consciousness, the principal axis is that of richness, stretching from those who minimize their conceptual baggage with Occam's razor to those who protest, as did Boring, that "nature is notoriously prodigal. Why should we interpret only parsimoniously." But ontological reach cannot exceed epistemological grasp. Darwin observed that "experience shows the problem of the mind cannot be solved by attacking the citadel itself . . . we must bring some stable foundation to argue from." Such a foundation is provided by quantitative ethology which tackles the possibly knowable with the greatest clarity. As Ashby has argued, "science deals, and can deal, only with what one man can demonstrate to another. Vivid though consciousness may be to its possessor, there is as yet no method known by which he can demonstrate his experience to another. And until such a method, or its equivalent, is found, the facts of consciousness cannot be used in scientific method." Mental accounts are cast on to the Humean pyre not because they are false but because they are meaningless. If science does not, as Bronowski has warned, suffer a terrible loss of nerve, an ethometric approach will prosper research on recognition behavior. Because it is quantitative does not imply that it is uninteresting. Eddington once commented that a materialist must view his wife as a rather elaborate differential equation. Haldane retorted that there are dull differential equations just as there are dull wives.

References

Agren, G. 1976. Social and territorial behavior in the mongolian gerbil (*Meriones unguiculatus*) under semi-natural conditions. *Biol. Behav.* **1:** 276–285.

Ahearn, J. N. 1980. Evolution of behavioral reproductive isolation in a laboratory stock of *Drosophila silvestris. Experientia* **36:** 63–64.

Ahrens, R. 1954. Beitrag zur Entwicklung des Physiognomie- und Mimiker-kennens. 1 & 2. *Z. Exp. Angew. Psychol.* **2:** 412–454, 599–633.

Ainsworth, M. D. S. 1969. Object relations, dependency, and attachment: A theoretical review of the infant-mother relationship. *Child Dev.* **30:** 969–1025.

Alatalo, R. V., A. Carlson, A. Lundberg, and S. Ulfstrand. 1981. The conflict between male polygamy and female monogamy: The case of the pied flycatcher *Ficedula hypoleuca. Am. Nat.* **117:** 738–753.

Alcock, J. 1979. Selective mate choice by females of *Harpobittacus australis* (Mecoptera: Bittacidae). *Psyche* **86:** 213–217.

Alcock, J. 1981. Lek territoriality in the tarantula hawk wasp *Hemipepsis ustulata* (Hymenoptera: Pompilidae). *Behav. Ecol. Sociobiol.* **8:** 309–317.

Alexander, G., and D. Stevens. 1981. Recognition of washed lambs by Merino ewes. *Appl. Anim. Ethol.* **7:** 77–86.

Alexander, R. D. 1967. Acoustical communication in arthropods. *Annu. Rev. Entomol.* **12:** 495–526.

Alexander, R. D. 1975. Natural selection and specialized chorusing behavior in acoustical insects. In D. Pimental (ed.), *Insects, Science, and Society*, Academic, New York, pp. 35–77.

Allen, H. M. 1977. The response of willow grouse chicks to auditory stimuli. 1. Preference for hen grouse calls. *Behav. Proc.* **2:** 27–32.

Allen, H. M. 1979. The response of willow grouse chicks to auditory stimuli. 2. Synthesized brooding calls attract machine-incubated chicks. *Behav. Proc.* **4:** 23–33.

Allen, H. M. 1980.   The response of willow grouse chicks to auditory stimuli. 3. Recognition of the incubating hen's voice. *Behav. Proc.* **5**: 39–43.

Allen, P. P., and F. P. Mangles. 1938/1939.   Studies of the nesting behavior of the Black-crowned Night Heron. *Linn. Soc. N.Y. Proc.* **50/51**: 1–28.

Alleva, E., B. D'Udine, and A. Oliverio. 1981.   Effet d'une experience olfactive precoce sur les preferences sexuelles de deux souches de souris consanguines. *Biol. Behav.* **6**: 73–78.

Alley, R., and H. Boyd. 1950. Parent-young recognition in the coot *Fulica atra. Ibis* **92**: 46–51.

Alloway, T. M. 1980.   The origins of slavery in leptothoracine ants (Hymenoptera: Formicidae). *Am. Nat.* **115**: 247–261.

Altmann, M. 1963.   Naturalistic studies of maternal care in moose and elk. In H. L. Rheingold (ed.), *Maternal Behavior in Mammals,* Wiley, New York, Chap. 7, pp. 233–253.

Ambrose, J. A. 1961.   The development of the smiling response in early infancy. In B. M. Foss (ed.), *Determinants of Infant Behavior,* Vol. 1, Methuen, London, pp. 179–201.

Amlaner, C. J., Jr., and J. F. Stout. 1978.   Aggressive communication by *Larus glaucescens.* Part 6: Interactions of territory residents with a remotely controled, locomotory model. *Behaviour* **66**: 223–251.

Amsterdam, B. 1972.   Mirror self-image reactions before age two. *Dev. Psychobiol.* **5**: 297–305.

Amsterdam, B., and L. M. Greenberg. 1977.   Self-conscious behavior of infants: A videotape study. *Dev. Psychobiol.* **10**: 1–6.

Andelman, S. J. 1980.   Responses of gibbons to vocal playback experiments. *Am. Zool.* **20**: 854 (Abstr. 764).

Anderson, A. H., and A. Anderson. 1957.   Life history of the cactus wren. *Condor* **59**: 274–296.

Anderson, E., and L. Hubricht. 1938.   Hybridization in *Tradescantia.* 3. The evidence for introgressive hybridization. *Am. J. Bot.* **25**: 396–402.

Anderson, W. W., and P. R. McGuire. 1978.   Mating pattern and mating success of *Drosophila pseudoobscura* karyotypes in large experimental populations. *Evolution* **32**: 416–423.

Andersson, M. 1980.   Why are there so many threat displays? *J. Theor. Biol.* **86**: 773–781.

Anthouard, M. 1973. Au sujet d'une eventuelle reconnaissance intraspecifique et de ses consequences sur le comportement d'apprentissage chez le carassin soumis a un stimulus social. *Soc. Zool. Fran. Bull.* **98**: 557–562.

Appleby, M. C. 1980. Social rank and access in red deer stags. *Behaviour* **74**: 294–309.

Ardrey, R. 1966. *The Territorial Imperative.* Atheneum, New York, 390 + 12 pp.

Armitage, K. B. 1962. Social behaviour of a colony of the yellowbellied marmot (*Marmota flaviventris*). *Anim. Behav.* **10**: 319–331.

Armitage, K. B. 1965. Vernal behaviour of the yellow-bellied marmot (*Marmota flaviventris*). *Anim. Behav.* **13**: 59–68.

Armstrong, E. A. 1963. *A Study of Bird Song.* Oxford University Press, London, 335 + 15 pp.

Arnold, S. J. 1976. Sexual behavior, sexual interference and sexual defense in the salamanders *Ambystoma maculatum*, *Ambystoma tigrinum* and *Plethodon jondoni. Z. Tierpsychol.* **42**: 247–300.

Asbury, K., W. J. Matthews, and L. G. Hill. 1981. Attraction of *Notropis lutrensis* (Cyprinidae) to water conditioned by the presence of conspecifics. *Southwest Nat.* **25**: 525–528.

Aspey, W. P. 1971. Inter-species sexual discrimination and approach-avoidance conflict in two species of fiddler crabs, *Uca pugnax* and *Uca pugilator. Anim. Behav.* **19**: 669–676.

Assem, J. van den, and J. N. van den Molen. 1969. Waning of the aggressive response in the three-spined stickleback upon constant exposure to a conspecific. 1. A preliminary analysis of the phenomenon. *Behaviour* **34**: 286–324.

Auffenberg, W. 1965. Sex and species discrimination in two sympatric South American tortoises. *Copeia* **1965**: 335–342.

Averhoff, W. W., and R. H. Richardson. 1976. Reply: Pheromones vs. wings in *Drosophila* courtship. *Behav. Genet.* **6**: 97–98.

Averhoff, W. W., L. Ehrman, J. E. Leonard, and R. H. Richardson. 1979. Antennal signal receptors in *Drosophila* mating. *Biol. Z.* **98**: 1–12.

Awbrey, F. T. 1968. Call discrimination in female *Scaphiopus couchii* and *Scaphiopus hurterii. Copeia* **1968**: 420–432.

Axelrod, H. R., and W. E. Burgess. 1976. *African Cichlids of Lakes Malawi and Tanganyika,* 5th ed. Tropical Fish Hobbyist, Neptune City, 352 pp.

Baerends, G. P., and J. M. Baerends-VanRoon. 1950. An introduction to the ethology of cichlid fishes. *Behaviour Suppl.* **1**: 243 + 8 pp.

Baerends, G. P., and J. G. VanRhijn. 1975 The effect of colour in egg-recognition by the black-headed gull (*Larus ridibundus*) 1. *Koninkl. Nederl. Akad. Wetenschappen-Amsterdam. Ser. C Proc.* **78**: 1–20.

Bailey, K. 1978. Flehmen in the ring-tailed lemur (*Lemur cata*) *Behaviour* **65**: 309–319.

Bailey, W. J., and D. Robinson. 1971. Song as a possible isolating mechanism in the genus *Homorocoryphus* (Tettigonioidea, Orthoptera). *Anim. Behav.* **19**: 390–397.

Baker, M. C., and L. R. Mewaldt. 1978. Song dialects as barriers to dispersal in white-crowned sparrows, *Zonotrichia leucophrys nuttali. Evolution* **32**: 712–722.

Baker, M. C., and L. R. Mewaldt. 1981. Response to "Song dialects as barriers to dispersal: a re-evaluation." *Evolution* **35**: 189–190.

Baker, M. C., K. J. S. Nabors, and D. C. Bradley. 1981a. Early experience determines song dialect responsiveness of female sparrows. *Science* **214**: 819–821.

Baker, M. C., D. B. Thompson, and G. L. Sherman. 1981b. Neighbor/stranger song discrimination in white-crowned sparrows. *Condor* **83**: 265–267.

Baker, M. C., D. B. Thompson, G. L. Sherman, and M. A. Cunningham. 1981c. The role of male vs male interactions in maintaining population dialect structure. *Behav. Ecol. Sociobiol.* **8**: 65–69.

Ball, R. W., and D. L. Jameson. 1966. Premating isolating mechanisms in sympatric and allopatric *Hyla regilla* and *Hyla californiae. Evolution* **20**: 533–552.

Ballantyne, P. K., and P. W. Colgan. 1978a. Sound production during agonistic and reproductive behaviour in the pumpkinseed (*Lepomis gibbosus*), the bluegill (*L. marochirus*), and their hybrid sunfish. 1. Context. *Biol. Behav.* **3**: 113–135.

Ballantyne, P. K., and P. W. Colgan. 1978b. Sound production during agonistic and reproductive behaviour in the pumpkinseed (*Lepomis gibbosus*), the bluegill (*L. macrochirus*), and their hybrid sunfish. 2. Recipients. *Biol. Behav.* **3**: 207–220.

Ballantyne, P. K., and P. W. Colgan. 1978c. Sound production during agonistic and reproductive behaviour in the pumpkinseed (*Lepomis gibbosus*), the bluegill (*L. macrochirus*), and their hybrid sunfish. 3. Response. *Biol. Behav.* **3**: 221–232.

Balsano, J. S., K. Kucharski, E. J. Randle, E. M. Rasch, and P. J. Monaco. 1981. Reduction of competition between bisexual and unisexual females of *Poecilia* in notheastern Mexico. *Environ. Biol. Fishes* **6**: 39–48.

Bambridge, R. 1962. Early experience and sexual behavior in the domestic chicken. *Science* **136**: 259–260.

Banks, E. M., D. G. M. Wood-Gush, B. O. Hughes, and N. J. Mankovich. 1979. Social rank and priority of access to resources in domestic fowl. *Behav. Proc.* **4**: 197–209.

Baran, D., and S. E. Glickman. 1970. "Territorial marking" in the mongolian gerbil: A study of sensory control and function. *J. Comp. Physiol. Psychol.* **71**: 237–245.

Barash, D. P. 1974. Neighbor recognition in two "solitary" carnivores: The raccoon (*Procyon lotor*) and the red fox (*Vulpes fulva*). *Science* **185**: 794–796.

Barash, D. P. 1975. Behavioral individuality in the cichlid fish, *Tilapia mossambica*. *Behav. Biol.* **13**: 197–202.

Barlow, G. W. 1967. Social behavior of a South American leaf fish, *Polycentrus schomburgkii*, with an account of recurring pseudofemale behavior. *Am. Midl. Nat.* **78**: 215–324.

Barlow, G. W., and W. Rogers. 1978. Female midas cichlids' choice of mate in relation to parents' and to own color. *Biol. Behav.* **3**: 137–145.

Barlow, G. W., W. Rogers, and R. V. Cappeto. 1977. Incompatability and assortative mating in the midas cichlid. *Behav. Ecol. Sociobiol.* **2**: 49–59.

Barnard, C. J., and T. Burk. 1979. Dominance hierarchies and the evolution of "individual recognition." *J. Theor. Biol.* **81**: 65–73.

Barnard, C. J., and T. Burk. 1981. Individuals as assessment units—Reply to Breed and Bekoff. *J. Theor. Biol.* **88**: 595–597.

Barnett, C. 1977a. Chemical recognition of the mother by the young of the cichlid fish, *Cichlasoma citrinellum*. *J. Chem. Ecol.* **3**: 461–466.

Barnett, C. 1977b. Aspects of chemical communication with special reference to fish. *Biosci. Commun.* **3**: 331–392.

Barnett, C. 1981. The role of urine in parent–offspring communication in a cichlid fish. *Z. Tierpsychol.* **55**: 173–182.

Barrera, M. E., and D. Maurer, 1981. The perception of facial expression by the three-month-old. *Child Dev.* **52**: 203–206.

Barrette, C. 1977. The social behaviour of captive muntjacs *Muntiacus reevesi* (Ogilby 1839). *Z. Tierpsychol.* **43**: 188–213.

Barrette, C., and F. Messier. 1980. Scent-marking in free-ranging coyotes, *Canis latrans*. *Anim. Behav.* **28**: 814–819.

Barrows, E. M. 1975. Individually distinctive odors in an invertebrate. *Beh. Biol.* **15**: 57–64.

Barrows, E. M., W. J. Bell, and C. D. Michener. 1975. Individual odor differences and their social functions in insects. *Proc. Natl. Acad. Sci., U.S.A.,* **72**: 2824–2828.

Bartholomew, G. A. 1959. Mother-young relations and the maturation of pup behaviour in the Alaskan fur seal. *Anim. Behav.* **7**: 163–172.

Bateson, P. P. G. 1964. Effect of similarity between rearing and testing conditions on chicks' following and avoidance responses. *J. Comp. Physiol. Psychol.* **57**: 100–103.

Bateson, P. P. G. 1966. The characteristics and context of imprinting. *Biol. Rev.* **41**: 177–220.

Bateson, P. P. G. 1972. The formation of social attachments in young birds. *Proc. 15th Int. Ornithol. Congr.* pp. 303–315.

Bateson, P. P. G. 1973. Internal influences on early learning in birds. In R. A. Hinde and J. Stevenson-Hinde (eds.), *Constraints on Learning,* Academic, London, Chap. 5, pp. 101–116.

Bateson, P. P. G. 1977. Testing on observer's ability to identify individual animals. *Anim. Behav.* **25:** 247–248.

Bateson, P. 1978a. Sexual imprinting and optimal outbreeding. *Nature (London)* **273:** 659–660.

Bateson, P. P. G. 1978b. Early experience and sexual preferences. In J. B. Hutchison (ed.), *Biological Determinants of Sexual Behaviour,* Wiley, New York, Chap. 2, pp. 29–53.

Bateson, P. P. G. 1979. How do sensitive periods arise and what are they for? *Anim. Behav.* **27:** 470–486.

Bateson, P. 1980. Optimal outbreeding and the development of sexual preferences in Japanese quail. *Z. Tierpsychol.* **53:** 231–244.

Bateson, P. P. G. (ed.). 1982. *Mate Choice.* Cambridge University Press, Cambridge, England.

Bateson, P. P. G., and E. P. Reese. 1969. The reinforcing properties of conspicuous stimuli in the imprinting situation. *Anim. Behav.* **17:** 692–699.

Bateson, P., W. Lotwick, and D. K. Scott. 1980. Similarities between the faces of parents and offspring in Bewick's swan and the differences between mates. *J. Zool.* **191:** 61–74.

Baylis, J. R. 1976. A quantiative study of long-term courtship: 1. Ethological isolation between sympatric populations of the midas cichlid, *Cichlasoma citrinellum,* and the arrow cichlid, *C. zaliosum. Behaviour* **59:** 59–69.

Beach, F. A., and J. Jaynes. 1954. Effects of early experience upon the behavior of animals. *Psychol. Bull.* **51:** 240–263.

Beauchamp, G. K., and E. H. Hess. 1971. The effects of cross-species rearing on the social and sexual preferences of guinea pigs. *Z. Tierpsychol.* **28:** 69–76.

Beauchamp, G. K., B. R. Criss, and J. L. Wellington. 1979. Chemical communication in *Cavia:* Responses of wild (*C. aperea*), domestic (*C. porcellus*) and F_1 males to urine. *Anim. Behav.* **27:** 1066–1072.

Becker, P. H. 1976. Artkennzeichnende Gesangsmerkmale bei Winterund Sommergolhahnchen (*Regulus regulus, R. ignicapillus*). *Z. Tierpsychol.* **42:** 411–437.

Becker, P. H., G. Thielcke, and K. Wustenberg. 1980. Der Tonhohenverlauf ist entscheidend für das Gesangserkennen beim mitteleuropaischen Zilpzalp (*Phylloscopus collybita*). *J. Ornithol.* **121:** 229–224.

Beecher, M. D., M. R. Petersen, S. R. Zoloth, D. B. Moody, and W. C. Stebbins. 1979. Perception of conspecific vocalizations by Japanese macaques. *Brain Behav. Evol.* **16:** 443–460.

Beecher, M. D., I. M. Beecher, and S. Lumpkin. 1981a. Parent-offspring recognition in bank swallows. (*Riparia riparia*): 1. Natural history. *Anim. Behav.* **29**: 86–94.

Beecher, M. D., I. M. Beecher, and S. Hahn. 1981b. Parent–offspring recognition in bank swallows (*Riparia riparia*): 2. Development and acoustic basis. *Anim. Behav.* **29**: 95–101.

Beer, C. G. 1969. Laughing gull chicks: Recognition of their parents voices. *Science* **166**: 1030–1032.

Beer, C. G. 1970a. Individual recognition of voice in the social behavior of birds. *Adv. Stud. Behav.* **3**: 27–74.

Beer, C. G. 1970b. On the responses of laughing gull chicks (*Larus atricilla*) to the calls of adults. 1. Recognition of the voices of the parents. *Anim. Behav.* **18**: 652–660.

Beer, C. G. 1970c. On the response of laughing gull chicks (*Larus atricilla*) to the calls of adults. 2. Age changes and responses to different types of call. *Anim. Behav.* **18**: 661–677.

Beer, C. G. 1972. Individual recognition of voice and its development in birds. *Proc. 15th Int. Ornithol. Congr.*, pp. 339–356.

Beer, C. G. 1979. Vocal communication between laughing gull parents and chicks. *Behaviour* **70**: 118–146.

Bekoff, M. 1979. Scent-marking by free-ranging domestic dogs. Olfactory and visual components. *Biol. Behav.* **4**: 123–139.

Beletsky, L. D., S. Chao, and D. G. Smith. 1980. An investigation of song-based species recognition in the red-winged blackbird (*Agelaius phoniceus*). *Behaviour* **73**: 189–203.

Bennett, M. A. 1939. The social hierarchy in ring doves. *Ecology* **20**: 337–357.

Bennet-Clark, H. C., M. Dow, A. M. Ewing, A. Manning, and F. VonSchilcher. 1976. Courtship stimuli in *Drosophila melanogaster*. *Behav. Genet.* **6**: 93–95.

Bennet-Clark, H. C., Y. Leroy, and L. Tsacas. 1980. Species and sex-specific songs and courtship behaviour in the genus *Zaprionus* (Diptera-Drosophilidae). *Anim. Behav.* **28**:230–255.

Benzer, S. 1971. From the gene to behavior. *J. Am. Med. Assoc.* **218**: 1015–1022.

Berger, L. R., and J. D. Ligon. 1977. Vocal communication and individual recognition in the pinon jay, *Gymnorhinus cyanocephalus*. *Anim. Behav.* **35**: 567–584.

Bergman, G. 1946. Der Steinwalzer, *Arenaria i. interpres* (L.), in seiner Beziehung zur Umwelt. *Acta Zool. Fenn.* **47**: 1–152.

Bergmann, H.-H., S. Klaus. F. Muller, and J. Wiesner. 1975. Individualitat und Artspecifitat in den Gesangsstrophen einer Population des Haselhuhns (*Bonasa bonasia bonasia* L., Tetraoninae, Phasianidae). *Behaviour* **55**: 94–114.

Berlioz, J. 1933. L'elevage et l'hybridation du Bison au Canada. *Soc. Acclim. Paris Bull.* **80:** 47–53.

Bermant, G. 1963. Intensity and rate of distress calling in chicks as a function of social contact. *Anim. Behav.* **11:** 514–517.

Bernstein, I. S., and T. P. Gordon. 1979. Inter- and intra-specific sexual behavior in two species of macaque: A possible behavioral barrier to gene flow. *Behav. Proc.* **4:** 265–272.

Berryman, J. C. 1981. Guinea pig responses to conspecific vocalizations: Playback experiments. *Behav. Neurol Biol.* **31:** 476–482.

Berryman, J. C., and C. Fullerton. 1976. A developmental study of interactions between young and adult guinea pigs (*Cavia porcellus*). *Behaviour* **59:** 22–39.

Bertenthal, B. I., and K. W. Fischer. 1978. Development of self-recognition in the infant. *Dev. Psychol.* **14:** 44–50.

Bertram, B. C. R. 1970. The vocal behaviour of the Indian hill mynah, *Gracula religiosa. Anim. Behav. Monogr.* **3:** 81–192.

Bertram, B. C. R. 1975. The social system of lions. *Sci. Am.* **232(5):** 54–65.

Bertram, B. C. R. 1979. Ostriches recognise their own eggs and discard others. *Nature (London)* **279:** 233–234.

Berven, K. A. 1981. Mate choice in the wood frog, *Rana sylvatica. Evolution* **35:** 707–722.

Berwein, M. 1941. Beobachtungen und Versuche über das gesellige Leben von Elritzen. *Z. Vergl. Physiol.* **28:** 402–420.

Bethe, A. 1932. Vernachlassigte Hormone. *Naturwissenshaften* **20:**177–181.

Biben, M. 1980. Over-marking of alient conspecific odors by Mongolian gerbils. *Biol. Behav.* **5:** 139–145.

Bigelow, R. S. 1964. Song differences in closely related cricket species and their significance. *Aust. J. Sci.* **27:** 99–102.

Bigger, C. H. 1980. Interspecific and intraspecific acrorhagial aggressive behavior among sea anemones: A recognition of self and not-self. *Biol. Bull.* **159:** 117–134.

Birch, M. C. (ed.) 1974. *Pheromones.* Elsevier, New York, 495 + 21 pp.

Bjarvall, A. 1967. The critical period and the interval between hatching and exodus in mallard ducklings. *Behaviour* **28:** 141–148.

Blair, W. F. 1955. Mating call and stage of speciation in the *Microhyla olivacea-M. carolinensis* complex. *Evolution* **9:** 469–480.

Blair, W. F. 1968. Amphibians and reptiles. In T. A. Sebeok (ed.), *Animal Communication.* Indiana University Press, Bloomington, pp. 289–310.

Blair, W. F. 1974. Character displacement in frogs. *Am. Zool.* **14:** 1119–1125.

Blaustein, A. R. 1981.   Sexual selection and mammalian olfaction. *Am. Nat.* **117:** 1006–1010.

Blaustein, A. R., and R. K. O'Hara. 1981. Genetic control for sibling recognition? *Nature (London)* **290:** 246–248.

Blum, M. S., and N. A. Blum (eds.). 1979. *Sexual Selection and Reproductive Competition in Insects.* Academic Press, New York, 463 + 11 pp.

Boch, R., and R. A. Morse. 1974.   Discrimination of familiar and foreign queens by honeybee swarms. *Entomol. Soc. Am. Ann.* **67:** 709–711.

Bonner, T. P., and F. J. Etges. 1967.   Chemically mediated sexual attraction in *Trichinella spiralis. Exp. Parasitol.* **21:** 53–60.

Booij, C. J. H. 1982.   Biosystematics of the *Mullerianella* complex (Homoptera, Delphacidae), interspecific and geographic variation in acoustic behaviour. *Z. Tierpsychol.* **58:** 31–52.

Borden, J. H., J. R. Handley, J. A. Mclean, R. M. Silverstein, L. Chong, K. N. Slessor, B. D. Johnston, and H. R. Schuler. 1980.   Enantiomer-based specificity in pheromone communication by two sympatric *Gnathotrichus* species (Coleoptera: Scolytidae). *J. Chem. Ecol.* **6:** 445–456.

Borror, D. J. 1965.   Song variation in Maine song sparrows. *Wilson Bull.* **77:** 5–37.

Boughey, M. J., and N. S. Thompson. 1976. Species specificity and individual variation in the songs of the Brown Thrasher (*Toxostoma rufum*) and Catbird (*Dumetella carolinensis*). *Behaviour* **57:** 64–90.

Bourke, P. A. 1947.   Notes on the Horsfield Bush-lark. *Emu* **47:** 1–7.

Bowers, J. M., and B. K. Alexander. 1967.   Mice: Individual recognition by olfactory cues. *Science* **158:** 1208–1210.

Bowlby, J. 1980.   By ethology out of psycho-analysis: An experiment in inter-breeding. *Anim. Behav.* **28:** 649–656.

Brackbill, Y. 1958.   Extinction of the smiling response in infants as a function of reinforcement schedule. *Child Dev.* **29:** 115–124.

Bradbury, J. W. 1977.   Lek mating behavior in the hammer-headed bat. *Z. Tierpsychol.* **45:** 225–255.

Braddock, J. C. 1945.   Some aspects of the dominance-subordination relationship in the fish *Platypoecilus maculatus. Physiol. Zool.* **18:** 176–195.

Breed, M. D. 1981.   Individual recognition and learning of queen odors by worker honeybees. *Proc. Natl. Acad. Sci., U.S.A.* **78:** 2635–2637.

Breed, M. D., and M. Bekoff. 1981.   Individual recognition and social relationships. *J. Theor. Biol.* **88:** 589–593.

Breed, M. D., S. K. Smith, and B. G. Gall. 1980.   Systems of mate selection in a cockroach species with male dominance hierarchies. *Anim. Behav.* **28:** 130–134.

Bremond, J.-C. 1968a. Parametres physiques assurant la specificite du chant chez de pouillot siffleur (*Phylloscopus sibilatrix*). *Rev. Comp. Anim.* **3**: 97–98.

Bremond, J.-C. 1968b. Valeur specifique de la syntaxe dans le signal de defense territoriale du Troglodyte (*Troglodytes troglodytes*). *Behaviour* **30**: 66–75.

Bremond, J.-C. 1976. Specific recognition in the song of Bonelli's warbler (*Phylloscopus bonelli*). *Behaviour* **58**: 99–116.

Bremond, J.-C. 1978. Acoustic competition between the song of the wren (*Troglodytes troglodytes*) and the songs of other species *Behaviour* **65**: 89–98.

Brenowitz, E. A. 1982. Long-range communication of species identity in the song of the red-winged blackbird (*Agelaius phoeniceus*). *Behav. Ecol. Sociobiol.* **10**: 29–38.

Brian, M. V. 1973. Queen recognition by brood-rearing workers of the ant, *Myrmica rubra* L. *Anim. Behav.* **21**: 691–698.

Brian, M. V. 1974. Brood-rearing behaviour in small cultures of the ant *Myrmica rubra* L. *Anim. Behav.* **22**: 879–889.

Brian, M. V. 1975. Larval recognition by workers of the ant *Myrmica*. *Anim. Behav.* **23**: 745–756.

Bronson, F. H. 1971. Rodent pheromones. *Biol. Reprod.* **4**: 344–357.

Bronson, F. H., and B. E. Eleftheriou. 1963. Influence of strange males on implantation in the deermouse. *Gen. Comp. Endocrinol.* **3**: 515–518.

Brooke, M. de L. 1978. Sexual differences in the voice and individual vocal recognition in the manx shearwater (*Puffinus puffinus*). *Anim. Behav.* **26**: 622–629.

Brooks, R. J., and J. B. Falls. 1975a. Individual recognition by song in white-throated sparrows. 1. Discrimination of songs of neighbors and strangers. *Can. J. Zool.* **53**: 879–888.

Brooks, R. J., and J. B. Falls. 1975b. Individual recognition by song in white-throated sparrows. 3. Song features used in individual recognition. *Can. J. Zool.* **53**: 1749–1761.

Brosset, A. 1971. L' "imprinting" chez les Colombides—etude des modifications comportementales au cours de vieillisement. *Z. Tierpsychol.* **29**: 279–300.

Brown, J. L. 1963. Social organization and behavior of the Mexican jay. *Condor* **65**: 126–153.

Brown, J. L. 1964a. The evolution of diversity in avian territorial systems. *Wilson Bull.* **76**: 160–169.

Brown, J. L. 1964b. The integration of agonistic behavior in the Stellar's jay *Cyanocitta stelleri* (Gmelin). *Univ. Calif. Publ. Zool.* **60**: 223–328.

Brown, J. L. 1975. *The Evolution of Behavior*. Norton, New York, 761 + 19 pp.

Brown, J. L. 1978. Avian communal breeding systems. *Annu. Rev. Ecol. Syst.* **9**: 123–155.

Brown, L. 1981. Patterns of female choice in mottled sculpins (Cottidae, Teleostei). *Anim. Behav.* **29**: 375–382.

Brown, P. 1976. Vocal communication in the pallid bat, *Antrozous pallidus*. *Z. Tierpsychol.* **41**: 34–54.

Brown, R. E. 1977. Odor preference and urine-marking scales in male and female rats: Effects of gonadectomy and sexual experience on responses to conspecific odors. *J. Comp. Physiol. Psychol.* **91**: 1190–1206.

Brown, R. E. 1979. Mammalian social odors. *Adv. Stud. Behav.* **10**: 103–162.

Brown, W. L., Jr., and E. O. Wilson. 1956. Character displacement. *Syst. Zool.* **5**: 49–64.

Bruckner, G. H. 1933. Untersuchungen zu Tiersociologie, insbesonderer zur Anflosung der Familie. *Z. Psychol.* **128**: 1–110.

Bryant, E. H. 1980. Geographic variation in components of mating success of the housefly, *Musca domestica* L., in the United States. *Am. Nat.* **116**: 655–669.

Bryant, E. H., A Kence, and K. T. Kimball. 1980. A rare-male advantage in the housefly induced by wing clipping and some general considerations for *Drosophila*. *Genetics* **96**: 975–993.

Bubenik, A. B. 1965. Beitrag zur Geburtskunde und zu den Mutterkind-Beziehungen des Reh—(*Capreolus capreolus* L.) und Rotwildes (*Cervus elephus* L.). *Z. Saugetierk* **30**: 65–128.

Buckle, G. R., and L. Greenberg. 1981. Nest mate recognition in sweat bees (*Lasioglossum zephyrum*): Does an individual recognize its own odour or only odours of its nest mates? *Anim. Behav.* **29**: 802–809.

Buckely, P. A., and F. G. Buckley. 1972. Individual egg and chick recognition of adult royal terns (*Sterna maxima maxima*). *Anim. Behav.* **20**: 457–462.

Bullock, T. H. 1965. Physiological bases of behavior. In J. A. Moore (ed.), *Ideas in Evolution and Behavior*, Natural History, Garden City, N.Y. Chap. 16, pp. 449–482.

Burgess, J. W. 1979. Web-signal processing for tolerance and group predation in the social spider *Mallos gregalis* Simon. *Anim. Behav.* **27**: 157–164.

Burghardt, G. M., and M. Bekoff (eds.). 1978. *The Development of Behavior: Comparative and Evolutionary Aspects*. Garland, New York, 429 + 13 pp.

Burley, N. 1979. The evolution of concealed ovulation. *Am. Nat.* **114**: 835–858.

Burley, N. 1981a. Sex ratio manipulation and selection for attractiveness. *Science* **211**: 721–722.

Burley, N. 1981b. Mate choice by multiple criteria in a monogamous species. *Am. Nat.* **117**: 515–528.

Burley, N. 1982. Reputed bond attractiveness and sex manipulation in zebra finches. *Science* **215**: 423–424.

Burley, N., and N. Moran. 1979. The significance of age and reproductive experience in the mate preferences of feral pigeons, *Columba livia*. *Anim. Behav.* **27**: 686–698.

Burrows, W. H., and T. C. Byerly. 1938. The effect of certain groups of environmental factors upon the expression of broodiness. *Poult. Sci.* **17**: 324–330.

Burtt, E. H., Jr. 1977. Some factors in the timing of parent-chick recognition in swallows. *Anim. Behav.* **25**: 231–239.

Burtt, E. H., Jr. (ed.) 1979. *The Behavioral Significance of Color.* Garland, New York, 456 + 14 pp.

Buschinger, A., and T. M. Alloway. 1979. Sexual behaviour in the slave-making ant, *Harpagoxenus canadensis* M. R. Smith, and sexual pheromone experiments with *H. canadensis, H. americanus*)(Emery), and *H. sublaevis* (Nylander) (Hymenoptera; Formicidae). *Z. Tierpsychol.* **49**: 113–119.

Buschinger, A., W. Ehrhardt, and U. Winter. 1980. The organization of slave raids in dulotic ants—A comparative study (Hymenoptera; Formicidae). *Z. Tierpsychol.* **53**: 245–264.

Busse, K. 1977. Pragungsbedingte akustische Arterkennungsfahigkeit der Kuken der Fluss seeschwalben und Kustenseeschwalben *Sterna hirundo* L. und *S. paradisaea* Pont. *Z. Tierpsychol.* **44**: 154–161.

Busse, K., and Busse, K. 1977. Pragungsbedingte Bindung von Kustenseeschwalbenkuken (*Sterna paradisaea* Pont.) an die Eltern und ihre Fahigkeit, sie an der Stimme zu erkennen. *Z. Tierpsychol.* **43**: 287–294.

Butler, M., and D. A. Johnson. 1972. A test of individual recognition in bluegill sunfish using operant procedures. *Virg. J. Sci.* **23**: 149 (Abstr.).

Cairns, R. B. 1966a. Attachment behavior of mammals. *Psychol. Rev.* **73**: 409–426.

Cairns, R. B. 1966b. Development, maintenance and extinction of social attachment behavior in sheep. *J. Comp. Physiol. Psychol.* **62**: 298–306.

Caldwell, M. C., N. R. Hall, and D. K. Caldwell. 1971. Ability of an Atlantic bottlenosed dolphin to discriminate between, and potentially identify to individual, the whistles of another species, the spotted dolphin. *Cetology* **6**: 1–6.

Caldwell, M. C., D. K. Caldwell, and J. F. Miller. 1973. Statistical evidence for individual signature whistles in the spotted dolphin, *Stenella plagiodon. Cetology* **16**: 1–21.

Caldwell, R. L. 1979. Cavity occupation and defensive behaviour in the stomatopod *Gonodactylus festai:* Evidence for chemically mediated individual recognition. *Anim. Behav.* **27**: 194–201.

Cammaerts, M.-C., E.-D. Morgan, and R. Tyler. 1977. Territorial marking in the ant *Myrmica rubra* L. (Formicidae). *Biol. Behav.* **2**: 263–272.

Campanella, P. J., and L. L. Wolf. 1974. Temporal leks as a mating system in a temperate zone dragonfly (Odonata: Anisoptera). 1. *Plathemis lydia* (Drury). *Behaviour* **51**: 49–87.

Campbell, B. G. 1966. *Human Evolution.* Aldine, Chicago, 425 + 14 pp.

Campbell, B. G. (ed.). 1972. *Sexual Selection and the Descent of Man.* Aldine, Chicago, 378 + 10 pp.

Campbell, R. B. 1980. Polymorphic equilibria with assortative mating and selection in subdivided populations. *Theor. Pop. Biol.* **18:** 94–111.

Candland, D. K. 1969. Discriminability of facial regions used by the domestic chicken in maintaining the social dominance order. *J. Comp. Physiol. Psychol.* **69:** 281–285.

Candland, D. K., E. S. Blumer, and M. D. Mumford. 1980. Urine as a communicator in a New World primate, *Saimiri sciureus. Anim. Learn. Behav.* **8:** 486–480.

Capranica, R. R. 1966. Vocal response to natural and synthetic mating calls. *J. Acoust. Soc. Am.* **40:** 1131–1139.

Capranica, R. R., L. S. Frischkopf, and F. Nevo. 1973. Encoding of geographic dialects in the auditory system of the cricket frog. *Science* **182:** 1272–1275.

Carbaugh, B. T., M. W. Schein, and E. B. Hale. 1962. Effects of morphological variations of chicken models on sexual responses of cocks. *Anim. Behav.* **10:** 235–238.

Carmichael, M. S. 1980. Sexual discrimination by golden hamsters (*Mesocricetus auratus*). *Behav. Neural Biol.* **29:** 73–90.

Carpenter, C. C. 1960. Aggressive behaviour and social dominance in the six-lined racerunner (*Cnemidophorus sexlineatus*). *Anim. Behav.* **8:** 61–66.

Carr, W. J. 1974. Pheromonal sex attractants in the Norway rat. *Adv. Stud. Commun. Affect* **1:** 103–131.

Carr, W. J., and W. F. Caul. 1962. The effect of castration in rat upon the discrimination of sex odours. *Anim. Behav.* **10:** 20–27.

Carr, W. J., J. T. Hirsch, and J. M. Balazs. 1980a. Responses of male rats to odors from familiar vs novel females. *Behav. Neural Biol.* **29:** 331–337.

Carr, W. J., P. A. Zunino, and M. R. Landauer. 1980b. Responses by young house mice (*Mus musculus*) to odors from stressed vs. nonstressed adult conspecifics. *Psychon. Soc. Bull.* **15:** 419–421.

Carr, W. J., M. R. Landauer, and R. Sonsino. 1981. Responses by rats to odors from living versus dead conspecifics. *Behav. Neural Biol.* **31:** 67–72.

Carter, C. S., and J. N. Marr. 1970. Olfactory imprinting and age variables in the guinea-pig, *Cavia porcellus. Anim. Behav.* **18:** 238–244.

Caryl, P. G. 1979. Communication by agonistic displays: What can games theory contribute to ethology? *Behaviour* **68:** 136–169.

Caryl, P. G. 1981. Escalated fighting and the war of nerves: Games theory and animal combat. In P. P. G. Bateson and P. H. Klopfer (eds.), *Perspectives in Ethology*, Vol. 4, Plenum, New York, Chap. 10, pp. 199–224.

Caryl, P. G. 1982. Animal Signals: A reply to Hinde. *Anim. Behav.* **30:** 240–244.

Chamove, A. S., and H. F. Harlow. 1975. Cross-species affinity in three macaques. *J. Behav. Sci.* **2:** 311–316.

Chanel, J., and E. Vernet-Maury. 1963.   Reactions de discrimination olfactive et crise audiogene chez la souris. *Soc. Biol. Seances C.R.* **157**: 1020–1024.

Chase, R., K. Pryer, R. Bater, and D. Madison. 1978.   Responses to conspecific chemical stimuli in the terrestrial snail, *Achatina fulica* (Pulmonata: Sigmurethra). *Behav. Biol.* **22**: 302–315.

Cheke, A. S. 1969.   Mechanism and consequences of hybridization in sparrows *Passer. Nature (London)* **222**: 179–180.

Cheney, D. L., and R. M. Seyfarth. 1980.   Vocal recognition in free-ranging vervet monkeys. *Anim. Behav.* **28**: 362–367.

Cheng, K. M., R. N. Shaffner, R. E. Phillips, and F. B. Lee. 1978.   Mate preference in wild and domesticated (game-farm) mallards (*Anas platyrhynchos*): 1. Initial preference. *Anim. Behav.* **26**: 996–1003.

Cheng, K. M., R. N. Shaffner, R. E. Phillips, and F. B. Lee. 1979.   Mate preference in wild and domesticated (game-farm) mallards: 2. Pairing success. *Anim. Behav.* **27**: 417–425.

Cherfas, J. J., and A. Scott. 1981.   Impermanent reversal of filial imprinting. *Anim. Behav.* **29**: 301.

Chesler, P. 1969.   Maternal influence in learning by observation in kittens. *Science* **166**: 901–903.

Chesneaux, J. 1971.   *Secret Societies in China.* University of Michigan Press, Ann Arbor, 328 + 12 pp.

Chevalier-Skolnikoff, S., and F. E. Poirier (eds.). 1977.   *Primate Bio-Social Development.* Garland, New York, 636 + 19 pp.

Childers, W. F. 1967.   Hybridization of four species of sunfishes (Centrarchidae). *Ill. Nat. Hist. Surv. Bull.* **29**: 159–214.

Childress, D., and I. McDonald. 1973.   Tests for frequency-dependent mating in the housefly. *Behav. Genet.* **3**: 217–223.

Chiszar, D. 1978.   Lateral displays in the lower vertebrate: Forms, functions, and origins. In E. S. Reese and F. J. Lighter (eds.), *Contrasts in Behavior*, Wiley, New York, Chap. 4, pp. 105–135.

Chivers, D. J. 1976.   Communication within and between family groups of siamang (*Symphalangus syndactylus*). *Behaviour* **57**: 116–135.

Cinat-Tomson, H. 1926.   Die geschlectliche Zuchtwahl beim Wellensittich (*Melopsittacus undulatus* Shaw). *Biol. Z.* **46**: 543–552.

Clark, C. W., and J. M. Clark. 1980.   Sound playback experiments with southern right whales (*Eubalaena australis*). *Science* **207**: 663–665.

Clark, D. L., and J. E. Dillon. 1974.   Social dominance relationships between previously unacquainted male and female squirrel monkeys. *Behaviour* **50**: 217–231.

Clarke, J. R., F. V. Clulow, and F. Grieg. 1970.   Ovulation in the bank vole, *Clethriomomys glareolus. J. Reprod. Fertil.* **23**: 531.

Clulow, F. V., and J. R. Clarke. 1968.   Pregnancy block in *Microtus agrestis* an induced ovulator. *Nature (London)* **219**: 511.

Clulow, F. V., and P. E. Langford. 1971. Pregnancy block in the meadow vole, *Microtus pennsylvanicus*. *J. Reprod. Fertil.* **24:** 275–277.

Clutton-Brock, T. H., and S. D. Albon. 1979. The roaring of red deer and the evolution of honest advertisement. *Behaviour* **69:** 145–170.

Clutton-Brock, T. H., S. D. Albon, R. M. Gibson, and F. E. Guinness. 1979. The logical stag: Adaptive aspects of fighting in red deer (*Cervus elaphus* L.) *Anim. Behav.* **27:** 211–225.

Cohen, J. 1975. Cultural homology. *Science* **187:** 907–908.

Cole, B. J. 1981. Dominance hierarchies in *Leptothorax* ants. *Science* **212:** 83–84.

Cole, J. E., and J. A. Ward. 1970. An analysis of parental recognition by the young of the cichlid fish, *Etroplus maculatus* (Bloch). *Z. Tierpsychol.* **27:** 156–176.

Colgan, P., F. Cooke, and J. T. Smith. 1974. An analysis of group composition in assortatively mating populations. *Biometrics* **30:** 693–696.

Colgan, P. W., and M. R. Gross. 1977. Dynamics of aggression in male pumpkin-seed sunfish (*Lepomis gibbosus*) over the reproductive phase. *Z. Tierpsychol.* **43:** 139–151.

Colgan, P. W., W. A. Nowell, M. R. Gross, and J. W. A. Grant. 1979. Aggressive habituation and rim circling in the social organization of bluegill sunfish (*Lepomis macrochirus*). *Environ. Biol. Fishes* **4:** 29–36.

Collias, N. E. 1943. Statistical analysis of factors which make for success in initial encounters between hens. *Am. Nat.* **77:** 519–543.

Collias, N. E. 1952. The development of social behavior in birds. *Auk* **69:** 127–159.

Collias, N. E. 1956. The analysis of socialization in sheep and goats. *Ecology* **37:** 228–239.

Collins, H. L. 1965. Nurturing experiments with regard to "adult imprinting" and recognition of young in the cichlid species *Tilapia sparrmani* and *Aequidens latifrons*. Ph.D. thesis, Michigan State University, 88 + 8 pp.

Comfort, A. 1971. Likelihood of human pheromones. *Nature (London)* **230:** 432–433.

Conner, W. E., T. Eisner, R. K. Vander Meer, A. Guerrero, D. Ghiringelli, and J. Meinwald. 1980. Sex attractant of an arctiid moth (*Utetheisa ornatrix*): A pulsed chemical signal. *Behav. Ecol. Sociobiol.* **7:** 55–63.

Cooke, F. 1978. Early learning and its effect on population structure. Studies of a wild population of snow geese. *Z. Tierpsychol.* **46:** 344–358.

Cooke, F., and C. M. McNally. 1975. Mate selection and colour preferences in lesser snow geese. *Behaviour* **53:** 151–170.

Cooke, F., G. H. Finney, and R. F. Rockwell. 1976. Assortative mating in lesser snow geese (*Anser caerulescens*). *Behav. Genet.* **6:** 127–140.

Corbet, P. 1980. Biology of odonata. *Annu. Rev. Entomol.* **25:** 189–217.

Coss, R. G. 1978. Development of face aversion by the jewel fish (*Hemichromis bimaculatus*, Gill 1862). *Z. Tierpsychol.* **48:** 28–46.

Coss, R. G. 1979.   Delayed plasticity of instinct: Recognition and avoidance of 2 facing eyes by the jewel fish. *Dev. Psychobiol.* **12**: 335–345.

Coulon, J. 1975.   Les relations sociales chez le Cobaye domestique male. 1. Etude de la hierarchie sociale. *Behaviour* **53**: 183–199.

Coulson, G. M., and D. B. Croft. 1980.   Flehmen in Kangaroos. *Aust. Mammal.* **4**: 139–140.

Coulson, J. C. 1966.   The influence of the pair-bond and age on the breeding biology of the kittiwake gull *Rissa tridactyla. J. Anim. Ecol.* **35**: 269–279.

Cowan, P. J. 1974.   Selective responses to the parental calls of different individual hens by young *Gallus gallus:* Auditory discrimination learning versus auditory imprinting. *Behav. Biol.* **10**: 541–545.

Cowan, P. J., and R. M. Evans. 1974. Calls of different individual hens and the parental control of feeding behavior in young *Gallus gallus. J. Exp. Zool.* **188**: 353–360.

Cox, C. R., and B. J. LeBoeuf. 1977.   Female incitation of male competition: A mechanism for sexual selection. *Am. Nat.* **111**: 317–335.

Coyne, J. A., and J. J. Sohn. 1978.   Interspecific brood care in fishes: Reciprocal altruism or mistaken identity? *Am. Nat.* **112**: 447–450.

Crane, J. 1949.   Comparative biology of salticid spiders at Rancho Grande, Venezuela, Part 4: An analysis of display. *Zoologica* **34**: 159–214.

Crane, J. 1975.   *Fiddler Crabs of the World (Ocypodidae: Genus* Uca). Princeton Univ. Press, Princeton, New Jersey, 736 + 23 pp.

Crapon de Caprona, M. -D. 1980.   Olfactory communication in a cichlid fish, *Haplochromis burtoni. Z. Tierpsychol.* **52**: 113–134.

Crapon de Caprona, M. -D. 1982.   The influence of early experience on preferences for optical and chemical cues produced by both sexes in the cichlid fish *Haplochromis burtoni* (*Astatotilapia burtoni,* Greenwood 1979). *Z. Tierpsychol.* **58**: 329–361.

Crook, J. H., J. E. Ellis, and J. D. Goss-Custard. 1976.   Mammalian social systems: Structure and function. *Anim. Behav.* **24**: 261–274.

Cullen, E. 1957.   Adaptations in the kittiwake to cliff-nesting. *Ibis* **99**: 275–302.

Curio, E. 1959.   Vertaltensstudien am Trauerschnapper; Beitrage zur Ethologic und Okologie von *Muscicapa h. hypoleuca* Pallas. *Z. Tierpsychol. Suppl.* **3**: 118 pp.

Curio, E. 1976.   *The Ethology of Predation.* Springer-Verlag, Berlin, 250 + 10 pp.

Cushing, J. E. 1941.   Non-genetic mating preference as a factor in evolution. *Condor* **43**: 233–236.

Cushing, J. E., and A. O. Ramsay. 1949.   The non-heritable aspects of family uniting in birds. *Condor* **51**: 82–87.

Dagg, A. I., and D. E. Windsor. 1971.   Olfactory discrimination limits in gerbils. *Can J. Zool.* **49**: 283–285.

Daly, M., and M. Wilson. 1982. Whom are newborn babies said to resemble? *Ethol. Sociobiol.* in press.

Darwin, C. R. 1871. *The Descent of Man, and Selection in Relation to Sex,* 2 Vols. Murray, London, 423 + 8, 475 + 8 pp.

Darwin, C. R. 1872. *The Expression of the Emotions in Man and the Animals.* Murray, London, 374 + 6 pp.

Dathe, H. H. 1974. Untersuchungen zum phonotaktischen Verhalten von *Gryllus bimaculatus* (Insecta, Orthopteroidea). *Forma Functio* **7**: 7–20.

Davidson, R. J., and R. J. Davidson (eds.) 1980. *The Psychobiology of Consciousness.* Plenum, New York, 489 + 17 pp.

Davies, S., and R. Carrick. 1962. On the ability of crested terns, *Sterna bergii,* to recognize their own chicks. *Aust. J. Zool.* **10**: 171–177.

Davis, D. E. 1942. The phylogeny of social nesting habits in the Crotophaginae. *Q. Rev. Biol.* **17**: 115–134.

Davis, D. E. 1959. Territorial rank in starlings. *Anim. Behav.* **7**: 214–221.

Dawkins, R. 1976. *The Selfish Gene.* Oxford University Press, Oxford, 224 + 11 pp.

Dawkins, R., and J. R. Krebs. 1978. Animal signals: Information on manipulation? In J. R. Krebs and N. B. Davies (eds.), *Behavioural Ecology.* Blackwell, Oxford, pp. 282–309.

Dawkins, R., and J. R. Krebs. 1979. Arms races between and within species. *Proc. R. Soc. Lond. Ser. B* **205**: 489–511.

DeCasper, A. J., and W. P. Fifer. 1980. Of human bonding: Newborns prefer their mothers' voices. *Science* **208**: 1174–1176.

Delco, E. A., Jr. 1960. Sound discrimination by males of two cyprinid species. *Tex. J. Sci.* **12**: 48–54.

Demarest, W. J. 1977. Incest avoidance among human and nonhuman primates. In S. Chevalier-Skolnikoff and F. E. Poirier (eds.), *Primate Bio-social Development,* Garland, New York, Chap. 11, pp. 323–342.

Denenberg, V. H. 1969. The effects of early experience. In E. S. E. Hafez (ed.), *The Behaviour of Domestic Animals,* London, Bailliere, Tindall & Cassell, Chap. 6, pp. 95–130.

Denenberg, V. H. (ed). 1972. *The Development of Behavior.* Sinauer, Stamford, Connecticut, 483 + 9 pp.

Denenberg, V. H., L. J. Grota, and M. X. Zarrow. 1963. Maternal behaviour in the rat: Analysis of cross-fostering. *J. Reprod. Fertil.* **5**: 133–141.

DeVore, I. (ed.). 1965. *Primate behavior: Field studies of monkeys and apes.* Holt, Rinehart & Winston, New York, 654 + 14 pp.

Dewsbury, D. A. 1981. Effects of novelty on copulatory behavior: The Coolidge effect and related phenomena. *Psychol. Bull.* **89**: 464–482.

Diamond, M. L. 1980. Plumage variability in redpolls (*Carduelis flammea* and *C.*

hornemanni, L.): A test of Rohwer's status signalling hypothesis. M.Sc. thesis, University of Alberta, 127 + 14 pp.

Dietrich, K. 1981. Unterschiedliche Reaktionen von Weibchen des Japanischen Movchens (*Lonchura striata* var. *domestica*) auf Gesange verwandter und nicht verwandter Artgenossen. *Z. Tierpsychol.* **57**: 235–244.

Dilger, W. C. 1956. Hostile behavior and reproductive isolating mechanisms in the avian genera *Catharus* and *Hylocichla*. *Auk* **73**: 313–353.

Dilger, W. C. 1960. The comparative ethology of the African parrot genus *Agapornis*. *Z. Tierpsychol.* **17**: 649–685.

Dilger, W. C. 1962. The behavior of lovebirds. *Sci. Am.* **206(1)**: 88–98.

Dixon, A. K., and J. M. Mackintosh. 1975. The relationship between the physiological condition of female mice and the effects of their urine on the social behaviour of adult males. *Anim. Behav.* **23**: 513–520.

Dobzhansky, T., L. Ehrman, and P. A. Kastritsis. 1968. Ethological isolation between sympatric and allopatric species of the *obscura* group of *Drosophila*. *Anim. Behav.* **16**: 79–87.

Dominey, W. J. 1981. Maintenance of female mimicry as a reproductive strategy in bluegill sunfish (*Lepomis macrochirus*). *Environ. Biol. Fishes* **6**: 59–64.

Dooling, R., and M. Searcy. 1980. Early perceptual selectivity in the swamp sparrow. *Dev. Psychobiol.* **13**: 499–506.

Downes, J. A. 1969. The swarming and mating flight of diptera. *Annu. Rev. Entomol.* **14**: 271–298.

Dubos, R. 1971. In defense of biological freedom. In E. Tobach et al. (eds.), *The Biopsychology of Development*, Academic, New York, pp. 553–560.

D'Udine, B., and L. Partridge. 1981. Olfactory preferences of inbred mice (*Mus musculus*) for their own strain and for siblings: Effects of strain, sex and cross-fostering. *Behaviour* **78**: 314–324.

Duellman, W. E. 1967. Courtship isolating mechanisms in Costa Rican hylid frogs. *Herpetologica* **23**: 169–183.

Dunbar, I. F. 1978. Olfactory preferences in dogs: The responses of male and female beagles to conspecific urine. *Biol. Behav.* **3**: 273–286.

Dunbar, I., and M. Carmichael. 1981. The response of male dogs to urine from other males. *Behav. Neural Biol.* **31**: 465–470.

Dunbar, R. I. M. 1980. Determinants and evolutionary consequences of dominance among female gelada baboons. *Behav. Ecol. Sociobiol.* **7**: 253–265.

Dunham, D. W. 1978. Effect of chela white on agonistic success in a diogeid hermit crab (*Calcinus laevimanus*). *Mar. Behav. Physiol.* **5**: 137–144.

Dunkle, S. W. 1977. Swainson's hawks on the Laramie Plains, Wyoming. *Auk* **94**: 65–71.

Dunning, D. C., J. A. Byers, and C. D. Zanger. 1979. Courtship in two species of periodical cicadas, *Magicicada septendecim* and *Magicicada cassini*. *Anim. Behav.* **27**: 1073–1090.

Dussault, G. V., and D. L. Kramer. 1981. Food and feeding behavior of the guppy, *Poecilia reticulata* (Pisces: Poeciliidae). *Can. J. Zool.* **59**: 684–701.

Duvall, D. 1979. Western fence lizard (*Sceloporus occidentalis*) chemical signals. 1. Conspecific discriminations and release of a species-typical visual display. *J. Exp. Zool.* **210**: 321–325.

Duvall, D., R. Herskowitz, and J. Trupiano-Duvall. 1980. Responses of five-lined skinks (*Scincella lateralis*) to conspecific and interspecific chemical cues. *J. Herpetol.* **14**: 121–127.

Ehrman, L. 1964. Courtship and mating behavior as a reproductive isolating mechanism in *Drosophila*. *Am. Zool.* **14**: 147–153.

Ehrman, L. 1966. Mating success and genotype frequency in *Drosophila*. *Anim. Behav.* **14**: 332–339.

Ehrman, L., and P. A. Parsons. 1976. *The Genetics of Behavior*. Sinauer, Sunderland, Massachusetts, 390 + 8 pp.

Ehrman, L., and J. Probber. 1978. Rare *Drosophila* males: The mysterious matter of choice. *Am. Sci.* **66**: 216–222.

Eibl-Eibesfeldt, I. 1972. Similarities and differences between cultures in expressive movements. In R. A. Hinde (ed.), Nonverbal Communication, Cambridge University Press, Cambridge, pp. 297–314.

Eisenberg, J. F., and D. G. Kleiman. 1972. Olfactory communication in mammals. *Annu. Rev. Ecol. Syst.* **3**: 1–32.

Eisner, T., and F. G. Kafatos. 1962. Defence mechanisms of arthropods. 10. A phenomone promoting aggregation in an aposematic distasteful insect. *Psyche* **69**: 53–61.

Emerson, A. E. 1956. Ethospecies, ethotypes, and the evolution of *Apicotermes* and *Allognathotermes* (Isoptera, Termitidae). *Am. Mus. Nat. Hist. Novitates* **1771**: 31 pp.

Emlen, S. T. 1971. The role of song in individual recognition in indigo bunting. *Z. Tierpsychol.* **28**: 241–246.

Emlen, S. T. 1972. An experimental analysis of the parameters of bird song eliciting species recognition. *Behaviour* **41**: 130–171.

Emlen, S. T. 1976. Lek organization and mating strategies in the bullfrog. *Behav. Ecol. Sociobiol.* **1**: 283–313.

Emlen, S. T., and L. W. Oring. 1977. Ecology, sexual selection, and the evolution of mating systems. *Science* **197**: 215–223.

Emory, G. R., R. G. Payne, and M. R. A. Chance. 1979. Observations on a newly described usage of the primate play face. *Behav. Proc.* **4**: 61–71.

Endler, J. A. 1977. *Geographic Variation, Speciation and Clines*. Princeton University Press, Princeton, N.J.

Epstein, R., R. P. Lanza, and B. F. Skinner. 1981. "Self-awareness" in the pigeon. *Science* **212**: 695–696.

Erickson, C. J., and D. S. Lehrman. 1964. Effect of castration of male ring doves upon ovarian activity of females. *J. Comp. Physiol. Psychol.* **58**: 164–166.

Espmark, Y. 1964. Studies in dominance-subordination relationship in a group of semi-domestic reindeer (*Rangifer tarandus* L.) *Anim. Behav.* **12**: 420–426.

Espmark, Y. 1971. Individual recognition by voice in reindeer mother-young relationship. Field observations and playback experiments. *Behaviour* **40**: 295–301.

Espmark, Y. 1975. Individual characteristics in the calls of reindeer calves. *Behaviour* **54**: 50–59.

Estep, D. Q., and K. E. M. Bruce. 1981. The concept of rape in nonhumans: A critique. *Anim. Behav.* **29**: 1272–1273.

Estes, R. D. 1969. Territorial behavior of the wildebeest (*Connochaetes taurinus* Burchell, 1823). *Z. Tierpsychol.* **26**: 284–370.

Estes, R. D. 1974. Social organization of the African Bovidae. In V. Geist and F. Walther (eds.), *The Behavior of Ungulates and its Relation to Management.* Int. Union Conserv. Nature Nat. Resour., Morges, Switzerland, Paper 8, pp. 166–205.

Evans, L. T. 1951. Field study of the social behavior of the black lizard, *Ctenosaura pectinata. Am. Mus. Nat. Hist. Novitates* **1493**: 26 pp.

Evans, R. M. 1970a. Imprinting and mobility in young ring-billed gulls, *Larus delawarensis. Anim. Behav. Monogr.* **3**: 193–248.

Evans, R. M. 1970b. Parental recognition and the "mew call" in black-billed gulls (*Larus bulleri*). *Auk* **87**: 503–513.

Evans, R. M. 1980a. Development of behavior in seabirds: An ecological perspective. In J. Burger et al. (eds.), *Behavior of Marine Animals*, Vol. 4, *Marine Birds*, Plenum, New York, Chap. 8, pp. 271–322.

Evans, R. M. 1980b. Development of individual call recognition in young ring-billed gulls (*Larus delawarensis*): An effect of feeding. *Anim. Behav.* **28**: 60–67.

Evans, R. M., and S. Cosens. 1977. Selective control of peep vocalizations by familiar sound in young *Coturnix* quail. *Behaviour* **62**: 35–49.

Evans, R. M., and M. E. Mattson. 1972. Development of selective responses to individual maternal vocalizations in young *Gallus gallus. Can. J. Zool.* **50**: 777–780.

Evans, S. M. 1972. Specific distinctiveness in the calls of cordon bleus (*Uraeginthus* spp.; Estrildidae). *Anim. Behav.* **20**: 571–579.

Evans, W. E. 1967. Vocalization among marine mammals. In W. N. Tavolga (ed.), *Marine Bio-Acoustics*, Vol. 2, Pergamon, New York, pp. 159–186.

Ewbank, R., G. B. Meese, and J. E. Cox. 1974. Individual recognition and the dominance hierarchy in the domesticated pig. The role of sight. *Anim. Behav.* **22**: 473–480.

Ewer, R. F. 1968. *Ethology of Mammals.* Logos, London, 418 + 14 pp.

Ewert, D. N. 1980.   Recognition of conspecific song by the rufous-sided towbee. *Anim. Behav.* **28**: 379–386.

Ewing, A. W., and H. C. Bennet-Clark. 1968.   The courtship songs of *Drosophila*. *Behaviour* **31**: 288–301.

Ewing, L. S. 1972.   Hierarchy and its relation to territory in the cockroach *Nauphoeta cinerea*. *Behaviour* **42**: 152–174.

Fabricius, E. 1951.   Some experiments on imprinting phenomena in ducks. *Proc. 10th Int. Ornithol. Congr.*, 375–379.

Fabricius, E. 1964.   Crucial periods in the development of the following response in young nidifugous birds. *Z. Tierpsychol.* **21**: 326–337.

Fagan III, J. F. 1979.   The origins of facial pattern recognition. In M. H. Bornstein and W. Kessen (eds.), *Psychological Development from Infancy: Image to Intention*, Wiley, New York, Chap. 4, pp. 83–113.

Fagen, R. M. 1981.   *Animal Play Behavior*. Oxford University Press, Oxford, 684 + 18 pp.

Fairchild, L. 1981.   Mate selection and behavioral thermoregulation in Fowler's toads. *Science* **212**: 950–951.

Falls, J. B. 1963. Properties of bird song eliciting responses from territorial males. *Proc. 13th Int. Ornithol. Congr.*, **1**: 259–271.

Falls, J. B. 1969.   Functions of territorial song in the white-throated sparrow. In R. A. Hinde (ed.), *Bird Vocalizations*. Cambridge University Press, London, pp. 207–232.

Falls, J. B. 1978.   Bird song and territorial behavior. *Adv. Stud. Commun. Affect* **4**: 61–89.

Falls, J. B., and R. J. Brooks. 1965.   Studies on intraspecific individual recognition by song birds. *Am. Zool.* **5**: 225 (Abstr.).

Falls, J. B., and R. J. Brooks. 1975.   Individual recognition by song in white-throated sparrows. 2. Effects of location. *Can. J. Zool.* **53**: 1412–1420.

Falls, J. B., and L. G. D'Agincourt. 1981.   A comparison of neighbor-stranger discrimination in eastern and western meadowlarks. *Can. J. Zool.* **59**: 2380–2385.

Falls, J. B., and M. K. McNicholl. 1979.   Neighbor–stranger discrimination by song in male blue grouse. *Can. J. Zool.* **57**: 457–462.

Falt, B. 1981.   Development of responsiveness to the individual maternal "clucking" by domestic chicks (*Gallus gallus domesticus*). *Behav. Proc.* **6**: 303–317.

Farr, J. A. 1977.   Male rarity or novelty, female choice behavior, and sexual selection in the guppy, *Poecilia reticulata* Peters (Pisces: Poeciliidae). *Evolution* **31**: 162–168.

Farr, J. A. 1980.   Social behaviour patterns as determinants of reproductive success in the guppy, *Poecilia reticulata* Peters (Pisces: Poeciliidae). *Behaviour* **74**: 38–91.

Ferguson, G. W. 1966.   Releasers of courtship and territorial behaviour in the side-blotched lizard, *Uta stansburiana. Anim. Behav.* **14**: 89–92.

Ferguson, G. W. 1969.   Interracial discrimination in male side-blotched lizards, *Uta stansburiana. Copeia* **1969**: 188–189.

Ferguson, G. W. 1972.   Species discrimination by male side-blotched lizards, *Uta stansburiana* in Colorado. *Am. Midl. Nat.* **87**: 523–524.

Fernald, R. D. 1980.   Response of male cichlid fish, *Haplochromis burtoni*, reared in isolation to models of conspecifics. *Z. Tierpsychol.* **54**: 85–93.

Ferno, A., and S. Sjolander. 1973.   Some imprinting experiments on sexual preferences for colour variants in the platyfish (*Xiphophorus maculatus*). *Z. Tierpsychol.* **33**: 417–423.

Ferno, A., and S. Sjolander. 1976.   Influence of previous experience on the mate selection of two colour morphs of the convict cichlid, *Cichlasoma nigrofasciatum* (Pisces: Cichlidae). *Behav. Proc.* **1**: 3–14.

Ficken, M. S., and R. W. Ficken. 1969.   Responses of blue-winged warblers and golden-winged warblers to their own and the other species' songs. *Wilson Bull.* **81**: 69–74.

Ficken, M. S., and R. W. Ficken. 1973.   Effect of number, kind and order of song elements on playback responses of the golden-winged warbler. *Behaviour* **46**: 114–128.

Fielde, A. M. 1904.   The power of recognition among ants. *Biol. Bull.* **7**: 227–250.

Fischer, H. 1965.   Das Triumphgeschrei der Graugans (*Anser anser*). *Z. Tierpsychol.* **22**: 247–304.

Fisher, J. 1954.   Evolution and bird sociality. In J. S. Huxley et al. (eds.), *Evolution as a Process*, Allen & Unwin, London, pp. 71–83.

Fisher, R. A. 1930.   *The Genetical Theory of Natural Selection*. Clarendon, Oxford, 275 + 14 pp.

Fletcher, L. E., and D. G. Smith. 1978.   Some parameters of song important in conspecific recognition by gray catbirds. *Auk* **95**: 338–347.

Flood, N. J. 1980.   The adaptive significance of delayed plumage maturation in the northern oriole. M.Sc. thesis, University of Toronto. 191 + 8 pp.

Fooden, J. 1969.   Color phase in gibbons. *Evolution* **23**: 627–644.

Ford, E. B. 1964.   *Ecological Genetics*. Methuen, London, 335 + 15 pp.

Forester, D. C. 1973.   Mating call as a reproductive isolating mechanism between *Scaphiopus bombifrons* and *S. hammondii. Copeia* **1973**: 60–67.

Fricke, H. W. 1973.   Individual partner recognition in fish: Field studies on *Amphiprion bicinctus. Naturwissenschaften* **60**: 204–205.

Fricke, H. W., and S. Holzberg. 1974.   Social units and hermaphroditism in a pomacentrid fish. *Naturwissenschaften* **61**: 367–368.

Frings, H., M. Frings, J. Jumber, R. Busnel, J. Giban, and P. Gromet. 1958.   Reactions of American and French species of *Corvus* and *Larus* to recorded communication signals tested reciprocally. *Ecology* **39**: 126–131.

Fryer, G. 1977. Evolution of species flocks of cichlid fishes in African lakes. *Z. Zool. Syst. Evol. Forsch.* **15**: 141–165.

Fuller, J. L., and W. R. Thompson. 1978. *Foundations of Behavior Genetics.* Mosby, St. Louis, 533 + 8 pp.

Gahl, R. A. 1975. The shaking dance of honey bee workers: Evidence for age discrimination. *Anim. Behav.* **23**: 230–232.

Gallagher, J. 1976. 1976. Sexual imprinting: Effects of various regimes of social experience on mate preference in Japanese quail (*Coturnix coturnix japonica*). *Behaviour* **57**: 91–115.

Gallagher, J. E. 1977. Sexual imprinting: A sensitive period in Japanese quail (*Coturnix coturnix japonica*). *J. Comp. Physiol. Psychol.* **91**: 72–78.

Gallup, G. G., Jr. 1970. Chimpanzees: Self-recognition. *Science* **167**: 86–87.

Gallup, G. G., Jr. 1975. Towards an operational definition of self-awareness. In R. H. Tuttle (ed.), *Socioecology and Psychology of Primates*, Mouton, The Hague, pp. 309–341.

Gallup, G. G., Jr. 1977a. Absence of self-recognition in a monkey (*Macaca fascicularis*) following prolonged exposure to a mirror. *Dev. Psychobiol.* **10**: 281–184.

Gallup, G. G., Jr. 1977b. Self-recognition in primates: A comparative approach to the bidirectional properties of consciousness. *Am. Psychol.* **32**: 329–338.

Gallup, G. G., Jr. 1979a. Self-awareness in primates. *Am. Sci.* **67**: 417–421.

Gallup, G. G., Jr. 1979b. Self-recognition in chimpanzees and man: A developmental and comparative perspective. In M. Lewis and L. Rosenblum (eds.), *Genesis of Behavior*, Vol. 2, *The Child and Its Family*, Plenum, New York, pp. 107–126.

Gallup, G. G., Jr., M. K. McClure, S. D. Hill, and R. A. Bundy. 1971. Capacity for self-recognition in differentially reared chimpanzees. *Psychol. Rec.* **21**: 69–74.

Gallup, G. G., Jr., L. B. Wallnau, and S. D. Suarez. 1980. Failure to find self-recognition in mother–infant and infant–infant rhesus monkey pairs. *Folia Primatol.* **33**: 210–219.

Galton, F. 1908. *Memories of my Life.* Methuen, London, 339 + 8 pp.

Galusha, J. G., and J. F. Stout. 1977. Aggressive communication by *Larus glaucescens*. Part 4: Experiments on visual communication. *Behaviour* **62**: 22–235.

Gandolfi, G., R. Gandolfi, and F. LeMoli. 1973. Short-term individual recognition in *Padogobius martensi* (Teleostei, Gobiidae). *Lincei Rend. Sci. Fis. Mat. Nat.* **54**: 281–285.

Gehlbach, F. R. J. F. Watkins II, and J. C. Kroll. 1971. Pheromone trail-following studies of typhlopid, leptotyphlopid and colubrid snakes. *Behaviour* **40**: 282–294.

Geist, V. 1971. *Mountain Sheep: A study in Behavior and Evolution.* University of Chicago Press, Chicago, 383 + 15 pp.

George, W. 1981. Species-typical calls in the Ctenodactylidae (Rodentia). *J. Zool.* **195**: 39–52.

Gerald, J. W. 1970. Species isolating mechanisms in the genus *Lepomis*. Ph.D. thesis, Univ. Tex. at Austin, 75 + 5 pp.

Gerald, J. W. 1971. Sound production during courtship in six species of sunfish (Centrarchidae). *Evolution* **25**: 75–87.

Geramita, J. M., F. Cooke, and R. F. Rockwell. 1982. Assortative mating and gene flow in the lesser snow goose: A modelling approach. *Theor. Pop. Biol.*, in press.

Gerhardt, H. C. 1974a. Behavioral isolation of the tree frogs, *Hyla cinerea* and *Hyla andersonii*. *Am. Midl. Nat.* **91**: 424–433.

Gerhardt, H. C. 1974b. The vocalizations of some hybrid tree frogs: Acoustic and behavioral analyses. *Behaviour* **49**: 130–151.

Gerhardt, H. C. 1976. Significance of two frequency bands in long distance vocal communication in the green tree frog. *Nature (London)* **261**: 692–694.

Gerhardt, H. C. 1978. Mating call recognition in the green tree frog (*Hyla cinerea*): The significance of some fine-temporal properties. *J. Exp. Biol.* **74**: 59–73.

Gerhardt, H. C., and H. Schneider. 1980. Mating call discrimination by females of the tree frog *Hyla meridionalis* on Tenerife. *Behav. Proc.* **5**: 143–149.

Gerling, S. 1980. Gerbil pup preferences for parental odor cues. *Am. Zool.* **20**: 762 (Abstr. 194).

Getz, W. M. 1981. Genetically based kin recognition systems. *J. Theor. Biol.* **92**: 209–226.

Geyer, L. A. 1979. Olfactory and thermal influences on ultrasonic vocalization during development in rodents. *Am. Zool.* **19**: 420–431.

Geyer, L. A. 1981. Ontogeny of ultrasonic and locomotor responses to nest odors in rodents. *Am. Zool.* **21**: 117–128.

Gilder, P. M., and P. J. B. Slater. 1978. Interest of mice in conspecific male odours is influenced by degree of kinship. *Nature (London)* **274**: 364–365.

Gill, F. B., and W. E. Lanyon. 1964. Experiments on species discrimination in blue-winged warblers. *Auk* **81**: 53–64.

Gleason, K. K., and J. H. Reynierse. 1969. The behavioral significance of pheromones in vertebrates. *Psychol. Bull.* **71**: 58–73.

Gleeson, R. A. 1980. Pheromone communication in the reproductive behavior of the blue crab, *Callinectes sapidus*. *Mar. Behav. Physiol.* **7**: 119–134.

Goforth, W. R., and T. S.Baskett. 1965. Effects of experimental color marking on pairing of captive mourning doves. *J. Wildl. Manage.* **29**: 543–553.

Goldman, P. 1973. Song recognition by field sparrows. *Auk* **90**: 106–113.

Goodall, J. van L. 1968. The behaviour of free-living chimpanzees in the Gombe Stream Reserve. *Anim. Behav. Monogr.* **1**: 161–311.

Goodwin, D. 1958.   The existence and causation of colour-preferences in the pairing of feral and domestic pigeons. *Br. Ornithol. Club Bull.* **78:** 136–139.

Gorlick, D. L. 1976.   Dominance hierarchies and factors influencing dominance in the guppy *Poecilia reticulata* (Peters). *Anim. Behav.* **24:** 336–346.

Gorman, M. L. 1976.   A mechanism for individual recognition by odour in *Herpestes auropunctatus* (Carnivora: Viverridae). *Anim. Behav.* **24:** 141–145.

Gottlieb, G. 1966.   Species identification by avian neonates: Contributory effect of perinatal auditory stimulation. *Anim. Behav.* **14:** 282–290.

Gottlieb, G. 1968.   Species recognition in ground-nesting and hole-nesting ducklings. *Ecology* **49:** 87–95.

Gottlieb, G. 1971.   *Development of Species Identification in Birds.* University of Chicago Press, Chicago, 176 + 11 pp.

Gottlieb, G. 1974.   On the acoustic basis of species identification in wood ducklings (*Aix sponsa*). *J. Comp. Physiol. Psychol.* **87:** 1038–1048.

Gottlieb, G. 1975a.   Development of species identification in ducklings: 1. Nature of perceptual deficit caused by embryonic auditory deprivation. *J. Comp. Physiol. Psychol.* **89:** 387–399.

Gottlieb, G. 1975b.   Development of species identification in ducklings: 2. Experimental prevention of perceptual deficit caused by embryonic auditory deprivation. *J. Comp. Physiol. Psychol.* **89:** 675–684.

Gottlieb, G. 1975c.   Development of species identification in ducklings: 3. Maturational rectification of perceptual deficit caused by auditory deprivation. *J. Comp. Physiol. Psychol.* **89:** 899–912.

Gottlieb, G. 1978.   Development of species identification in ducklings: 4. Change in species-specific preception caused by auditory deprivation. *J. Comp. Physiol. Psychol.* **92:** 375–387.

Gottlieb, G. 1979.   Development of species identification in ducklings: 5. Perceptual differentiation in the embryo. *J. Comp. Physiol. Psychol.* **93:** 831–854.

Gottlieb, G. 1980a.   Development of species identification in ducklings. 6. Specific embryonic experience required to maintain species-typical perception in Peking ducklings. *J. Comp. Physiol. Psychol.* **94:** 579–587.

Gottlieb, G. 1980b.   Development of species identification in ducklings: 7. Highly specific early experience fosters species-specific perception in wood ducklings. *J. Comp. Physiol. Psychol.* **94:** 1019–1027.

Gottlieb, G. 1981.   Development of species identification in ducklings: 8. Embryonic versus post-natal critical period for the maintenance of species-typical perception. *J. Comp. Physiol. Psychol.* **95:** 540–547.

Gould, J. L. 1980.   The case for magnetic sensitivity in birds and bees (such as it is). *Am. Sci.* **68:** 256–267.

Gould, S. J. 1977.   *Ontogeny and Phylogeny.* Harvard University Press, Cambridge, Mass., 501 + 9 pp.

Gould, S. J. 1979. Sociobiology and the theory of natural selection. In G. W. Barlow and J. Silverberg (eds.), *Sociobiology: Beyond Nature/Nurture?*, Am. Assoc. Adv. Sci., Washington, D.C., Chap. 10, pp. 257–269.

Gould, S. J. 1981. Hyena myths and realities. *Nat. Hist.* **90(2)**: 16–24.

Gould, S. J., and R. C. Lewontin. 1979. The spandrels of San Marco and the Panglossian paradigm: A critique of the adaptationist programme. *Proc. R. Soc. London, Ser. B* **205**: 581–598.

Goux, J. M., and D. Anxolabehere. 1980. The measurement of sexual isolation and selection. A critique. *Heredity* **45**: 255–262.

Gowaty, P. A. 1981. Aggression of breeding eastern bluebirds (*Siala sialis*). *Anim. Behav.* **29**: 1013–1027.

Goz, H. 1941. Über den art- und individualgeruch bei fischen. *Z. Vergl. Physiol.* **29**: 1–45.

✗ Grabowski, U. 1941. Pragung eines Jungshafs auf den Menschen. *Z. Tierpsychol.* **4**: 326–329.

Graf, R., and M. Meyer-Holzapfel. 1974. Die Wirkung von Harnmarken auf Artgenossen beim Haushund. *Z. Tierpsychol.* **35**: 320–332.

Graham, J. M., and D. D. Thiessen. 1980. Social interactions in male gerbils, *Meriones unguiculatus*: Ultrasounds and open-field behavior. *Anim. Learn. Behav.* **8**: 502–504.

Grant, B., A. Snyder, and S. F. Glessner. 1974. Frequency-dependent mate selection in *Mormoniella vitripennis. Evolution* **28**: 259–264.

Grant, B., S. Burton, C. Contoreggi, and M. Rothstein. 1980. Outbreeding via frequency-dependent mate selection in the parasitoid wasp, *Nasonia* (=*Mormoniella*) *vitripennis* Walker. *Evolution* **34**: 983–992.

Grant, J. W. A. 1980. Territoriality, reproductive success, and mate choice in the johnny darter (*Etheostoma nigrum* Rafinesque). M. Sc. thesis, Queen's University at Kingston, Canada, 93 + 8 pp.

Grau, M. J. 1982. Kin recognition in white-footed deermice (*Peromyscus: leucopus*). *Anim. Behav.* **30**: 497–505.

Graves, J. A., and A. Whiten. 1980. Adoption of strange chicks by herring gulls, *Larus argentatus* L. *Z. Tierpsychol.* **54**: 267–278.

Green, C. D. 1966. Orientation of male *Heterodera rostochiensis* Woll. and *Heterodera schochtii* to their females. *Ann. Appl. Biol.* **58**: 327–339.

Green, S. 1975. Variation of vocal pattern with social situation in the Japanese monkey (*Macaca fuscata*): A field study. In L. A. Rosenblum (ed.), *Primate Behavior*, Vol. 4, Academic, New York, pp. 1–102.

Greenberg, B. 1963. Parental behavior and imprinting in cichlid fishes. *Behaviour* **21**: 127–144.

Greenberg, B., and G. K. Noble. 1944. Social behavior of the American chameleon (*Anolis carolinensis* Voigt). *Physiol. Zool.* **17**: 392–439.

Greenberg, L. 1979.   Genetic component of bee odor in kin recognition. *Science* **206:** 1095–1097.

Greenfield, M. D., and M. G. Karandinos. 1979.   Resource partitioning of the sex communication channel in clearwing moths (Lepidoptera: Sesiidae) of Wisconsin. *Ecol. Monogr.* **49:** 403–426.

Greenwood, P. J., P. H. Harvey, and C. M. Perrins. 1978.   Inbreeding and dispersal in the Great Tit. *Nature (London)* **271:** 52–54.

Greet, D. N. 1964.   Observations on sexual attraction and copulation in the nematode, *Panagrolaimus rigidus*, Schneider. *Nature (London)* **204:** 96–97.

Grier, J. B., S. A. Counter, and W. M. Shearer. 1967.   Prenatal auditory imprinting in chickens. *Science* **155:** 1692–1693.

Griffin, D. R. 1976.   *The Question of Animal Awareness*. Rockefeller University Press, New York, 135 + 8 pp.

Grosch, D. S. 1947.   The importance of antennae in mating reaction of male *Habrobracon*. *J. Comp. Physiol. Psychol.* **40:** 23–29.

Grosch, D. S. 1948.   Experimental studies of the mating reactions of the male *Habrobracon*. *J. Comp. Physiol. Psychol.* **41:** 188–195.

Gross, M. R. 1980.   Cuckoldry in sunfishes (*Lepomis:* Centrarchidae). *Can. J. Zool.* **57:** 1507–1509.

Grossfield, J. 1971.   Geographic distribution and light-dependent behavior in *Drosophila*. *Proc. Natl. Acad. Sci., U.S.A.* **68:** 2669–2673.

Grula, J. W., and O. R. Taylor, Jr. 1980.   The effect of X-chromosome inheritance on mate-selection behavior in the sulfur butterflies, *Colias eurytheme* and *C. philodice*. *Evolution* **34:** 688–695.

Gryzbowski, J. A. 1979.   Responses of barn swallows to eggs, young, nests, and nest sites. *Condor* **81:** 236–246.

Gubernick, D. J. 1980.   Maternal 'imprinting' or maternal 'labelling' in goats? *Anim. Behav.* **28:** 124–129.

Gubernick, D. J. 1981.   Mechanisms of maternal 'labelling' in goats. *Anim. Behav.* **29:** 305–306.

Gubernick, D. J., K. C. Jones, and P. H. Klopfer. 1979.   Maternal 'imprinting' in goats? *Anim. Behav.* **27:** 314–315.

Guhl, A. M. 1942.   Social discrimination in small flocks of the common domestic fowl. *J. Comp. Psychol.* **34:** 127–148.

Guhl, A. M. 1953.   Social behavior of the domestic fowl. *Kans. Agric. Exp. Stn. Tech. Bull.* **73:** 3–48.

Guhl, A. M., and W. C. Allee. 1944.   Some measurable effects of social organization in flocks of hens. *Physiol. Zool.* **17:** 320–347.

Guhl, A. M., and G. J. Fischer. 1969.   The behaviour of chickens. In E. S. E. Hafez (ed.), *The Behaviour of Domestic Animals*, 2nd ed., Bailliere, Tindall & Cassell, London, Chap. 16, pp. 515–553.

Guhl, A. M., and L. L. Ortman. 1953. Visual patterns in the recognition of individuals among chickens. *Condor* **55:** 287–298.

Guillotin, M., and P. Jouventin. 1980. Le petrel des nieges a Pointe Geologie. *Gerfaut* **70:** 51–72.

Guiton, P. 1958. The effect of isolation on the following response of brown leghorn chicks. *Proc. R. Phys. Soc. Edin.* **27:** 9–14.

Guiton, P. 1959. Socialization and imprinting in Brown Leghorn chicks. *Anim. Behav.* **7:** 26–34.

Guiton, P. 1961. The influence of imprinting on the agonistic and courtship responses of the Brown Leghorn cock. *Anim. Behav.* **9:** 167–177.

Guiton, P. 1962. The development of sexual responses in the domestic fowl in relation to the concept of imprinting. *Zool. Soc. Lond. Symp.* **8:** 227–234.

Guiton, P. 1966. Early experience and sexual object-choice in the Brown Leghorn. *Anim. Behav.* **14:** 534–538.

Gunn, D. L. 1975. The meaning of the term 'klinokinesis.' *Anim. Behav.* **23:** 409–412.

Gwinner, E. 1961. Beobachtungen über die Aufzucht und Jugendentwicklung des Weidenlaubsangers. *J. Ornithol.* **102:** 1–23.

Gwinner, E. 1964. Untersuchungen uber das Ausdrucks- und Sozialverhalten des Kolkraben (*Corvus corax corax* L.) *Z. Tierpsychol.* **21:** 657–748.

Gwinner, E., and J. Kneutgen. 1962. Uber die biologische Bedeutung der "zweckdienlichen" Anwendung erlernter Laute bei Vogeln. *Z. Tierpsychol.* **19:** 692–696.

Gyger, M., and F. Schenk. 1980. Effet des traces d'un congenere sur la production d'ultrasons du mulot sylvestre (*Apodemus sylvaticus*, L.) *Behav. Proc.* **5:** 311–322.

Haaf, R. A., and R. Q. Bell. 1967. A facial dimension in visual discrimination by human infants. *Child Dev.* **38:** 893–899.

Haeson, W., and H. Wijffels. 1967. Experimenteel onderzoek naar de mogelijkheid van "observational learning" bij de vis *Cichlasoma meeki* (Pisces, Cichlidae). *Psychol. Belg.* **7:** 45–57.

Hafez, E. S. E. (ed.). 1969. *The Behaviour of Domestic Animals*, 2nd ed., Bailliere, Tindall & Cassell, London, 647 + 12 pp.

Hahn, M. E., Jr., and E. C. Simmel. 1968. Individual recognition by natural concentrations of olfactory cues in mice. *Psychon. Sci.* **12:** 183–184.

Hahn, M. E., and P. Tumolo. 1971. Individual recognition in mice: How is it mediated? *Ecol. Soc. Am. Bull.* **52:** 53–54.

Hailman, J. P. 1967. The ontogeny of an instinct. *Behaviour Suppl.* **15:** 159 + 7 pp. pp.

Hailman, J. P. 1977. *Optical Signals*. Indiana University Press, Bloomington, 362 + 19 pp.

Hailman, J. C., and P. H. Klopfer. 1962. On measuring "critical learning periods" in birds. *Anim. Behav.* 10: 233–234.

Haken, H. (ed.). 1979. *Pattern Formation by Dynamic Systems and Pattern Recognition*. Springer-Verlag, New York, 306 + 8 pp.

Hale, E. B. 1957. Breed recognition in the social interaction of domestic fowl. *Behaviour* 10: 240–253.

Halpin, Z. T. 1976. The role of individual recognition by odors in the social interactions of the Mongolian gerbil (*Meriones unguiculatus*). *Behaviour* 58: 117–130.

Halpin, Z. T. 1980. Individual odors and individual recognition: Review and commentary. *Biol. Behav.* 5: 233–248.

Hamilton, W. D. 1964. The genetical evolution of social behaviour. 1 & 2. *J. Theor. Biol.* 7: 1–16, 17–52.

Hamilton, W. D. 1971. Geometry for the selfish herd. *J. Theor. Biol.* 31: 295–311.

Hansen, E. W. 1976. Selective responding by recently separated juvenile rhesus monkeys to the calls of their mothers. *Dev. Psychobiol.* 9: 83–88.

Hardeland, R. 1972. Species differences in the diurnal rhythmicity of courtship behaviour within the *melanogaster* group of the genus *Drosophila*. *Anim. Behav.* 20: 170–174.

Harmon, L. D. 1973. The recognition of faces. *Sci. Am.* 229(5): 70–82.

Harrington, F. H., and L. D. Mech. 1979. Wolf howling and its role in territory maintenance. *Behaviour* 68: 207–249.

Harrington, J. E. 1976a. Discrimination between individuals by scent in *Lemur fulvus*. *Anim. Behav.* 24: 207–212.

Harrington, J. E. 1976b. Olfactory communication in *Lemur fulvus*. In R. D. Martin et al. (eds.), *Prosimian Behaviour*, Duckworth, London, pp. 331–346.

Harrington, J. E. 1976c. Recognition of territorial boundaries by olfactory cues in mice (*Mus musculus* L.) *Z. Tierpsychol.* 41: 295–306.

Harrington, J. E. 1977. Discrimination between males and females by scent in *Lemur fulvus*. *Anim. Behav.* 25: 147–151.

Harris, M. A., and J. O. Murie. 1982. Responses to oral gland scents from different males in Columbian ground squirrels. *Anim. Behav.* 30: 140–148.

Harris, M. P. 1970. Abnormal migration and hybridization of *Larus argentatus* and *L. fuscus* after interspecies fostering experiments. *Ibis* 112: 488–498.

Harrison, C. J. O. 1968. Egg mimicry in British cuckoos. *Bird Study* 15: 22–28.

Hartley, J. C., D. J. Robinson, and A. C. Warne. 1974. Female response song in the ephippigerines *Steropleurus stali* and *Platystalus obvius* (Orthoptera, Tettigoniidae). *Anim. Behav.* **22**: 382–389.

Hartnoll, R. G., and S. M. Smith. 1980. An experimental study of sex discrimination and pair formation in *Gammarus duebenii* (Amphipoda). *Crustaceana* **38**: 253–264.

Haskins, C. P. 1978. Sexual calling behavior in highly primitive ants. *Psyche* **85**: 407–415.

Hasler, A. D., A. T. Scholz, and R. M. Horvall. 1978. Olfactory imprinting and homing in salmon. *Am. Sci.* **66**: 347–355.

Hausfater, G. 1975. Dominance and reproduction in baboons (*Papio cynocephalus*): A quantitative analysis. *Contrib. Primatol.* **7**: 1–150.

Hay, D. A. 1972. Recognition by *Drosophila melanogaster* of individuals from other strains or cultures: Support for the role of olfactory cues in selective mating. *Evolution* **26**: 171–176.

Hay, D. A. 1976. The behavioral phenotype and mating behavior of two inbred strains of *Drosophila melanogaster*. *Behav. Genet.* **6**: 161–170.

Hay, T. G. 1978. Filial imprinting in the convict cichlid fish *Cichlasoma nigrofasciatum*. *Behaviour* **65**: 138–160.

Hayes, K. J., and C. H. Nissen. 1971. Higher mental functions in a home-raised chimpanzee. In A. M. Schrier and F. Stollnitz (eds.), *Behavior of Non-human Primates*, Academic, New York, Chap. 2, pp. 59–115.

Hazlett, B. A. 1969. "Individual" recognition and agonistic behaviour in *Pagurus bernardus*. *Nature (London)* **22**: 268–269.

Healey, M. C. 1967. Aggression and self-regulation of population size in deermice. *Ecology* **48**: 377–392.

Heaton, B. H. 1972. Prenatal auditory discrimination in the wood duck (*Aix sponsa*). *Anim. Behav.* **20**: 421–424.

Hebb, D. O. 1949. *Organization of Behavior*. Wiley, New York, 335 + 19 pp.

Hediger, H. 1942. *Wildtiere in Gefangenschaft—Ein Grundiss der Tiergartenbiologie*. Schwabe, Basle, 205 pp.

Heimburger, N. 1959. Das Markierungsverhalten einiger Caniden. *Z. Tierpsychol.* **16**: 104–113.

Heinroth, O. 1911. Beitrage zur Biologie, namentlich Ethologie und Psychologie der Anatiden. *Int. Ornithol. Kongr. Verh.* **5**: 589–702.

Helversen, D. von. 1972. Gesang des Mannchens und Lautschema des Weibchens bei der Feldheuschrecke, *Chorthippus biguttulus* (Orthoptera, Acrididae). *J. Comp. Physiol.* **81**: 381–422.

Helversen, D. von, and W. Wickler. 1971. Uber den Duettgesang des afrikansichen Drongo *Dicrurus adsimilis* Bechstein. *Z. Tierpsychol.* **29**: 301–321.

Helversen, O. von. 1979. Angeborenes Erkennen akustischer Schlusselreize. *Dtsch. Zool. Ges. Verh.* **72**: 42–59.

Hennessy, D. F. 1980. Early olfactory determinants of adult responsiveness to social status odors in *Mus musculus. J. Mammal.* **61**: 520–524.

Herrnstein, R. J., and P. A. DeVilliers. 1980. Fish as a natural category for people and pigeons. *Psychol. Learn. Motiv.* **14**: 59–95.

Hersher, L., A. U. Moore, and J. B. Richmond. 1958. Effect of postpartum separation of mother and kid on maternal care in the domestic goat. *Science* **128**: 1342–1343.

Hersher, L., J. B. Richmond, and A. U. Moore. 1963a. Modifiability of the critical period for the development of maternal behavior in sheep and goats. *Behaviour* **20**: 311–320.

Hersher, L., J.B. Richmond, and A. U. Moore. 1963b. Maternal behavior in sheep and goats. In H. L. Reingold (ed.), *Maternal Behavior in Mammals*, Wiley, New York, Chap. 6, pp. 203–232.

Hess, E. H. 1957. Effects of meprobamate on imprinting in waterfowl. *Ann. N.Y. Acad. Sci.* **67**: 724–732.

Hess, E. H. 1973. *Imprinting.* Van Nostrand, New York, 472 + 15 pp.

Hess, E. H. 1975. The role of pupil size in communication. *Sci. Am.* **233(5)**: 110–119.

Hill, K. G., J. J. Loftus-Hills, and D. F. Cartside. 1972. Premating isolation between the Australian field crickets, *Teleogryllus commodus* and *T. oceanicus. Aust. J. Zool.* **20**: 153–163.

Hinde, R. A. (ed.). 1969. *Bird Vocalizations.* Cambridge University Press, Cambridge, 394 + 16 pp.

Hinde, R. A. 1970. *Animal Behaviour*, 2nd ed. McGraw-Hill, New York, 876 + 16 pp.

Hinde, R. A. 1981. Animal signals: Ethological and games-theory approaches are not incompatible. *Anim. Behav.* **29**: 535–542.

Hinde, R. A., and J. Stevenson-Hinde (eds.). 1973. *Constraints on Learning.* Academic, London, 488 + 15 pp.

Hindman, J. L. 1981. Attachment in chicks: Effects of companion species on social preferences. *Dev. Psychobiol.* **14**: 13–18.

Hochbaum, H. A. 1959. *The Canvasback on a Prairie Marsh*, 2nd ed. Stackpole, Harrisburg, Penn., 207 + 7 pp.

Hoffman, H. S. 1978. Laboratory investigations of imprinting. In G. M. Burghardt and M. Bekoff (eds.), *The Development of Behavior: Comparative and Evolutionary Aspects*, Garland, New York, Chap. 10, pp. 203–212.

Hoffman, H. S., and P. DePaulo. 1977. Behavioral control by an imprinting stimulus. *Am. Sci.* **65**: 58–66.

Hoffman, H. S., and A. L. Ratner. 1973. Effects of stimulus and environmental familiarity on visual imprinting on newly hatched ducklings. *J. Comp. Physiol. Psychol.* **85**: 11–19.

Hoffman, H. S., L. A. Eiserer, and D. Singer. 1972. Acquisition of behavioral control by a stationary imprinting stimulus. *Psychon. Sci.* **26**: 146–148.

Hoffman, M. D. 1981. Kin recognition and preference in *Peromyscus leucopus*: Innate recognition or social familiarity. M. Sc. thesis, University of Missouri at St. Louis.

Hoglund, L. B., and M. Astrand. 1973. Preferences among juvenile char (*Salvelinus alpinus* L.) to intraspecific odours and water currents studied with the fluvariun technique. *Drottningholm Inst. Freshwater Res. Rep.* **53**: 21–30.

Hoglund, L. B., A. Bohman, and N. -A. Nilsson. 1975. Possible odour responses of juvenile arctic char (*Salvelinus alpinus* (L.)) to three other species of subarctic fish. *Drottningholm Inst. Freshwater Res. Rep.* **54**: 21–35.

Hold, B., and M. Schleidt. 1977. The importance of human odour in non-verbal communication. *Z. Tierpsychol.* **43**: 225–238.

Holldobler, B. 1971. Communication between ants and their guests. *Sci. Am.* **224(3)**: 86–93.

Holldobler, B. 1976a. Recruitment behavior, home range orientation and territoriality in harvester ants, *Pogonomyrmex. Behav. Ecol. Sociobiol.* **1**: 3–44.

Holldobler, B. 1976b. The behavioral ecology of mating in harvester ants (Hymenoptera: Formicidae: *Pogonomyrmex*). *Behav. Ecol. Sociobiol.* **1**: 405–423.

Holldobler, B., and C. P. Haskins. 1977. Sexual calling behavior in primitive ants. *Science* **195**: 793–794.

Holldobler, B., and E. O. Wilson. 1970. Recruitment trails in the harvester ant *Pogonomyrmex badius. Psyche* **77**: 385–399.

Holldobler, B., and E. O. Wilson. 1977. Colony-specific territorial pheromone in the African weaver ant *Oecophylla longinoda* (Latreille). *Proc. Natl. Acad. Sci, U.S.A.* **74**: 2072–2075.

Holldobler, B., and M. Wust. 1973. Ein Sexualpheromon bei der Pharaomeise *Monomorium pharaonis* (L.) *Z. Tierpsychol.* **32**: 1–9.

Hoogland, J. L., and P. W. Sherman. 1976. Advantages and disadvantages of bank swallow (*Riparia riparia*) coloniality. *Ecol. Monogr.* **46**: 33–58.

Hopkins, C. D. 1972. Sex differences in electric signaling in an electric fish. *Science* **176**: 1035–1037.

Hopkins, C. D. 1974a. Electric communication: Functions in the social behavior of *Eigenmannia virescens. Behaviour* **50**: 270–305.

Hopkins, C. D. 1974b. Electric communication in the reproductive behavior of *Sternopygus macrurus* (Gymnotoidei). *Z. Tierpsychol.* **35**: 518–535.

Hopkins, C. D., and A. H. Bass. 1981. Temporal coding of species recognition signals in an electric fish. *Science* **212**: 85–87.

Howard, D. F., and W. R. Tschinkel. 1976. Aspects of necrophoric behavior in the red imported fire ant, *Solenopsis invicta. Behaviour* **56**: 157–180.

Howard, J. W. 1974.   Dominance and relation to coloration in green sunfish, *Lepomis cyanellus. Behav. Biol.* 12: 559–565.

Howard, R. D. 1978.   The evolution of mating strategies in bullfrogs, *Rana catesbeiana. Evolution* 32: 850–871.

Howard, W. E., and J. T. Emlen. 1942.   Intercovey social relationships in the valley quail. *Wilson Bull.* 54: 162–170.

Howe, N. R., and Y. M. Shiekh. 1975.   Anthopleurine: A sea anemone alarm pheromone. *Science* 189: 386–388.

Howe, R. J. 1974.   Marking behaviour of the Bahaman hutia (*Geocapromys ingrahami*). *Anim. Behav.* 22: 645–649.

Howells, T. H., and D. O. Vine. 1940.   The innate differential in social learning. *J. Abnorm. Soc. Psychol.* 35: 537–548.

Hoy, R. R. 1974.   Genetic control of acoustic behavior in crickets. *Am. Zool.* 14: 1067–1080.

Hoy, R. R., J. Hahn, and R. C. Paul. 1977.   Hybrid cricket auditory behavior: Evidence for a genetic coupling in animal communication. *Science* 195: 82–83.

Hrdy, S. B. 1977a.   Infanticide as a primate reproductive strategy. *Am. Sci.* 65: 40–49.

Hrdy, S. B. 1977b.   Letters to the editor. *Am. Sci.* 65: 266, 268.

Hubbs, C. E., and E. A. Delco, Jr. 1960.   Mate preference in males of four species of gambusiine fishes. *Evolution* 14: 145–152.

Hubbs, C., and E. A. Delco, Jr. 1962.   Courtship preferences of *Gambusia affinis* associated with the sympatry of the parental populations. *Copeia* 1962: 396–400.

Huck, U. W., and E. M. Banks. 1979.   Behavioral components of individual recognition in the collared lemming (*Dicrostonyx groenlandicus*). *Behav. Ecol. Sociobiol.* 6: 85–90.

Huck, U. W., and E. M. Banks. 1980a.   The effects of cross-fostering on the behaviour of two species of North American lemmings, *Dicrostonyx groenlandicus* and *Lemmus trimucronatus*: 1. Olfactory preferences. *Anim. Behav.* 28: 1046–1052.

Huck, U. W., and E. M. Banks. 1980b.   The effect of cross-fostering on the behaviour of two species of North American lemmings, *Dicrostonyx groenlandicus* and *Lemmus trimucronatus*: 2. Sexual behaviour. *Anim. Behav.* 28: 2053–1062.

Hughes, B. O., D. G. M. Wood-Gush, and R. Morley Jones. 1974.   Spatial organization in flocks of domestic fowls. *Anim. Behav.* 22: 438–445.

Humphrey, N. K. 1980.   Nature's psychologists. In D. D. Josephson and V. S. Ramachandra (eds.), *Consciousness and the Physical World*, Pergamon, Oxford, Chap. 4, pp. 57–80.

Humphrey, N. 1982.   Consciousness: A just-so story. *New Scientist* **95**: 474–477.

Hunsaker, D. 1962.   Ethological isolating mechanisms in the *Sceloporus torquatus* group of lizards. *Evolution* **16**: 62–74.

Hutchison, R. E., J. G. Stevenson, and W. H. Thorpe. 1968.   The basis for individual recognition by voice in the sandwich tern (*Sterna sandvicensis*). *Behaviour* **32**: 150–157.

Huxley, C. R., and R. Wilkinson. 1979.   Duetting and vocal recognition by Aldabra white-throated rails *Dryolimnas cuvieri aldabranus*. *Ibis* **121**: 265–273.

Huxley, J. S. 1914.   The courtship-habits of the Great Crested Grebe (*Podiceps cristatus*); with an addition to the theory of sexual selection. *Proc. Lond. Zool. Soc.* **35**: 491–562.

Huxley, J. S. 1939.   Clines: An auxiliary method in taxonomy. *Bijdr. Dierk.* **27**: 491–520.

Huxley, J. S. (ed.). 1961.   *The Humanist Frame.* Allen & Unwin, London, 432 pp.

Huxley, J. S. (ed.). 1966.   A discussion on ritualization of behaviour in animals and man. *Philos. Trans. R. Soc. London, Ser. B* **251**: 247–526.

Iersel, J. J. A. van. 1953.   An analysis of the parental behaviour of the male three-spined stickleback (*Gasterosteus aculeatus* L.) *Behaviour Suppl.* **3**: 159 + 7 pp.

Immelmann, K. 1969.   Song development in the zebra finch and other estrildid finches. In R. H. Hinde (ed.), *Bird Vocalizations*, Cambridge University Press, Cambridge, pp. 61–74.

Immelmann, K. 1972.   The influence of early experience upon the development of social behaviour in estrildine finches. *Proc. 15th Int. Ornithol. Congr.*, pp. 316–338.

Immelmann, K. 1975a.   Ecological significance of imprinting and early learning. *Annu. Rev. Ecol. Syst.* **6**: 15–37.

Immelmann, K. 1975b.   The evolutionary significance of early experience. In G. Baerends et al. (eds.), *Function and Evolution in Behaviour*, Oxford University Press, Oxford, Chap. 11, pp. 243–253.

Impekhoven, M. 1973.   The response of incubating laughing gulls (*Larus atricilla* L.) to calls of hatching chicks. *Behaviour* **46**: 94–113.

Impekhoven, M. 1976.   Responses of laughing gull chicks (*Larus atricilla*) to parental attraction- and alarm-calls, and effects of prenatal auditory experience on the responsiveness of such calls. *Behaviour* **56**: 250–278.

Ingersoll, D. W., and C. -T. Lee. 1980.   Belontiidae chemosignal activity: Interspecific attraction and perceived chemosignal similarity. *Behav. Neural Biol.* **29**: 463–472.

Ingold, P. 1973.   Zur lautlichen Beziehung des Elters zu seinem Kueken bei Tordalken (*Alca tarda*). *Behaviour* **45**: 154–190.

Jacobson, M. 1972.   *Insect Sex Pheromones*. Academic, New York, 382 + 12 pp.

Jaeger, R. G. 1981.   Dear enemy recognition and the costs of aggression between salamanders. *Am. Nat.* **117**: 962–974.

Jaeger, R. G., and W. F. Gergits. 1979.   Intra- and interspecific communication in salamanders through chemical signals on the substrate. *Anim. Behav.* **27**: 150–156.

Jaisson, P. 1975.   L'impregnation dans l'ontgenese des comportements de soins aux cocons chez la jeune fourmi rousse (*Formica polyctera* Forst). *Behaviour* **52**: 1–37.

Jaisson, P., and D. Fresneau. 1978.   The sensitivity and responsiveness of ants to their cocoons in relation to age and methods of measurement. *Anim. Behav.* **26**: 1064–1071.

James, M. 1959.   Flicker: An unconditioned stimulus for imprinting. *Can J. Psychol.* **13**: 59–67.

James, M. 1962.   Imprinting with visual flicker: Effects of testosterone cyclopentylproprionate. *Anim. Behav.* **10**: 341–346.

James, W. 1890.   *The Principles of Psychology*, 2 Vols., Holt, New York, 689 + 12, 688 + 6 pp.

Janequin, C. 1965.   *Chansons Polyphoniques*, Vol. 2, A. T. Merritt and F. Lesure (eds.), Remparts, Monaco, 230 pp.

Janetos, A. C. 1980. Strategies of female mate choice: A theoretical analysis. *Behav. Ecol. Sociobiol.* **7**: 107–112.

Janetos, A. C., and B. J. Cole. 1981. Imperfectly optimal animals. *Behav. Ecol. Sociobiol.* **9**: 203–209.

Jansson, A. 1973.   Stridulation and its significance in the genus *Cenocorixa* (Hemiptera, Corixidae). *Behaviour* **46**: 1–36.

Jay, P. 1963.   Mother-infant relations in langurs. In H. L. Rheingold (ed.), *Maternal Behavior in Mammals*, Wiley, New York, Chap. 9, pp. 282–304.

Jaynes, J. 1957.   Imprinting: The interaction of learned and innate behavior. 2. The critical period. *J. Comp. Physiol. Psychol.* **50**: 6–10.

Jaynes, J. 1976.   *The Origin of Consciousness in the Breakdown of the Bicameral Mind*. Houghton Mifflin, Boston, 467 + 7 pp.

Jenkins, P. F. 1978.   Cultural transmission of song patterns and dialect development in a free-living bird population. *Anim. Behav.* **26**: 50–78.

Jensen, G. D. 1965. Mother-infant relationship in the monkey *Macaca nemestrina*: Development of specificity of maternal response to an infant. *J. Comp. Physiol. Psychol.* **59**: 305–308.

Jenssen, T. A. 1970.   Female responses to filmed displays of *Anolis nebulosus* (Sauria, Iguanidae). *Anim. Behav.* **18**: 640–647.

Johnson, C. 1966.   Species recognition in the *Hyla versicolor* complex. *Tex. J. Sci.* **18**: 361–364.

Johnson, L. K. 1941.   Nesting behavior of the Atlantic murre. *Auk* **58:** 153–163.

Johnson, L. K., and S. P. Hubbell. 1975.   Contrasting foraging strategies and coexistence of two bee species on a single resource. *Ecology* **56:** 1398–1406.

Johnson, R. P. 1973.   Scent marking in mammals. *Anim. Behav.* **21:** 521–535.

Johnson, V. R., Jr. 1977.   Individual recognition in the banded shrimp *Stenopus hispidus* (Olivier). *Anim. Behav.* **25:** 418–428.

Johnston, J. W., Jr., D. G. Moulton, and A. Turk (eds.). 1970.   *Advances in Chemoreception*, Vol. 1, *Communication by Chemical Signals*. Appleton-Century-Crofts, New York, 412 + 10 pp.

Johnston, R. E. 1975.   Scent marking by male golden hamsters (*Mesocricetus auratus*). 3. Behavior in a semi-natural environment. *Z. Tierpsychol.* **37:** 213–221.

Johnston, R. E. 1980.   Responses of male hamsters to odors of females in different reproductive states. *J. Comp. Physiol. Psychol.* **94:** 894–904.

Johnston, T. D., and G. Gottlieb. 1981a.   Visual preferences of imprinted ducklings are altered by the maternal call. *J. Comp. Physiol. Psychol.* **95:** 663–675.

Johnston, T. D., and G. Gottlieb. 1981b.   Development of visual species identification in ducklings: What is the role of imprinting? *Anim. Behav.* **29:** 1082–1099.

Jones, R. B., and N. W. Nowell. 1974.   The urinary aversive pheromone of mice: Species, strain and grouping effects. *Anim. Behav.* **22:** 187–191.

Jones, T. P. 1966.   Sex attraction and copulation in *Pelodera teres*. *Nematologica* **12:** 518–522.

Jonge, G. de. 1980.   Response to con- and heterospecific male odours by the voles *Microtus agrestis, M. arvalis* and *Clethrionomys glareolus* with respect to competition for space. *Behaviour* **73:** 277–303.

Jouventin, P., G. Pasteur, and J. P. Cambefort. 1977.   Observational learning of baboons and avoidance of mimics: Explanatory tests. *Evolution* **31:** 214–218.

Jouventin, P., M. Guillotin, and A. Cornet. 1979.   Le chant du manchot empereur et sa signification adaptive. *Behaviour* **70:** 231–250.

Jurgens, U. 1979.   Vocalization as an emotional indicator. A neuroethological study in the squirrel monkey. *Behaviour* **69:** 88–117.

Jutsum, A. R., T. S. Saunders, and J. M. Cherrett. 1979.   Intraspecific aggression in the leaf-cutting ant *Acromyrmex octospinosus*. *Anim. Behav.* **27:** 839–844.

Kalkowski, W. 1967.   Olfactory bases of social orientation in the white mouse. *Folia Biol. (Krakow)* **15:** 69–87.

Kalmus, H. 1955.   The discrimination by the nose of the dog of individual human odours and in particular the odours of twins. *Br. J. Anim. Behav.* **3:** 25–31.

Kalmus, M., and S. M. Smith. 1966.   Some evolutionary consequences of pegmatypic mating systems (imprinting). *Am. Nat.* **100:** 619–635.

Kamper, G., and M. Dambach. 1981. Response of the cercus-to-giant inter-neuron system in crickets to species-specific song. *J. Comp. Physiol.* **141**: 311–317.

Kaplan, J. N. 1978. Olfactory recognition of mothers by infant squirrel monkeys. In D. J. Chivers and J. Herbert (eds.), *Recent Advances in Primatology*, Vol. 1. Academic, London, pp. 103–105.

Kaplan, J., and M. Russell. 1974. Olfactory recognition in the infant squirrel monkey. *Dev. Psychobiol.* **7**: 15–19.

Kaplan, J. N., D. Cubiciotti, and W. K. Redican. 1977. Olfactory discrimination of squirrel monkey mothers by their infants. *Dev. Psychobiol.* **10**: 447–453.

Karlin, S. 1969. *Equilibrium Behavior of Population Genetic Models with Non-random Mating.* Gordon & Breach, London, 163 pp.

Karlin, S. 1978. Comparison of positive assortative mating and sexual selection models. *Theor. Pop. Biol.* **14**: 281–312.

Karlson, P., and A. Butenandt. 1959. Pheromones (ectohormones) in insects. *Annu. Rev. Entomol.* **4**: 39–58.

Kassel, J., and R. E. Davis. 1975. Early behavioral experience and adult social behavior in the paradise fish, *Macropodus opercularis* L. *Behav. Biol.* **15**: 343–351.

Katzir, G. 1981a. Aggression by the damselfish *Dascyllus aruanus* L. towards conspecifics and heterospecifics. *Anim. Behav.* **29**: 835–841.

Katzir, G. 1981b. Visual aspects of species recognition in the damselfish *Dascyllus aruanus* L. (Pisces, Pomacentridae). *Anim. Behav.* **29**: 842–849.

Kaufman, J. H. 1967. Social relations of adult males in a free-ranging band of rhesus monkeys. In S. A. Altmann (ed.), *Social Communication among Primates*, University of Chicago Press, Chicago, Chap. 6, pp. 73–98.

Keenleyside, M. H. A. 1955. Some aspects of the schooling behaviour of fish. *Behaviour* **8**: 183–248.

Keenleyside, M. H. A. 1967. Behavior of male sunfishes (genus *Lepomis*) towards females of three species. *Evolution* **21**: 688–695.

Keevin, T. M., Z. T. Halpin, and N. McCurdy. 1981. Individual and sex-specific odors in male and female eastern chipmunks (*Tamias striatus*). *Biol. Behav.* **6**: 329–338.

Keller, H. *Midstream. My Later Life.* Greenwood, New York, 362 + 23 pp.

Kemperman, J. H. B. 1967. On systems of mating. 1 & 2. *Koninkl. Nederl. Akad. Wetenschappen—Amsterdam. Ser. A 70 (3) Indag. Math.* **29**: 245–304.

Kence, A. 1981. The rare-male advantage in *Drosophila*: A possible source of bias in experimental design. *Am. Nat.* **117**: 1027–1028.

Kennett, C. B., and F. E. McKay. 1980. Learning as an isolating mechanism in *Poeciliopsis lucida* males. *Am. Zool.* **20**: 854 (Abstr. 763).

Kessler, S. 1966. Selection for and against ethological isolation between *Drosophila pseudoobscura* and *Drosophila persimilis*. *Evolution* **20**: 634–645.

Keverne, E. B. 1978. Olfactory cries in mammalian sexual behaviour. In J. B. Hutchison (ed.) *Biological Determination of Sexual Behaviour*, Wiley, New York, Chap. 22, pp. 727–763.

Kilham, P., P. H. Klopfer, and H. Oelke. 1968. Species identification and colour preferences in chicks. *Anim. Behav.* **16**: 238–244.

Kimsey, L. S. 1980. The behaviour of male orchid bees (Apidae, Hymenoptera, Insecta) and the question of leks. *Anim. Behav.* **28**: 996–1004.

King, A. P., and M. J. West. 1977. Species identification in the North American cowbird: Appropriate responses to abnormal song. *Science* **195**: 1002–1004.

King, A. P., M. J. West, and D. H. Eastzer. 1980. Song structure and song development as potential contributors to reproductive isolation in cowbirds (*Molothrus ater*). *J. Comp. Physiol. Psychol.* **94**: 1028–1039.

King, J. A. 1955. Social behavior, social organization and population dynamics in a black-tailed prairie dog town in the Black Hills of South Dakota. *Univ. Mich. Lab. Vert. Biol.* **67**: 1–123.

King, J. A. 1963. Maternal behavior in *Peromyscus*. In H. L. Rheingold (ed.), *Maternal Behavior in Mammals*, Wiley, New York, Chap. 2, pp. 58–93.

King, M. G. 1965. The effect of social context on dominance capacity of domestic hens. *Anim. Behav.* **13**: 132–133.

Kirkman, F. B. 1937. *Bird Behaviour: A Contribution Based Chiefly on a Study of the Black-headed Gull*. Nelson, London, 232 + 15 pp.

Kleiman, D. G., and J. F. Eisenberg. 1973. Comparison of canid and felid social systems from an evolutionary perspective. *Anim. Behav.* **21**: 637–659.

Klinghammer, E. (ed.). 1975. *The Behavior and Ecology of Wolves*. Garland, New York, 588 + 17 pp.

Klint, T. 1975. Sexual imprinting in the context of species recognition in female mallards. *Z. Tierpsychol.* **38**: 385–392.

Klint, T. 1978. Significance of mother and sibling experience for mating preferences in the mallard (*Anas platyrhynchos*). *Z. Tierpsychol.* **47**: 50–60.

Klint, T. 1980. Influence of male nuptial plumage on mate selection in the female mallard (*Anas platyrhynchos*). *Anim. Behav.* **28**: 1230–1238.

Klopfer, P. H. 1970. Discrimination of young in galagos. *Folia Primatol* **13**: 137–143.

Klopfer, P. H. 1971. Mother love: What turns it on? *Am. Sci.* **59**: 404–407.

Klopfer, P. H. 1973. *Behavioral Aspects of Ecology*, 2nd ed. Prentice-Hall, Englewood Cliffs, N. J., 200 + 21 pp.

Klopfer, P. H., and J. Gamble. 1966. Maternal "imprinting" in goats: The role of chemical senses. *Z. Tierpsychol.* **23**: 588–592.

Klopfer, P. H., and J. P. Hailman. 1964.   Perceptual preferences and imprinting in chicks. *Science* **145**: 1333–1334.

Klopfer, P. H., and M. S. Klopfer. 1968.   Maternal "imprinting" in goats: Fostering of alien young. *Z. Tierpsychol.* **25**: 862–866.

Klopfer, P. H., D. K. Adams, and M. S. Klopfer. 1964.   Maternal "imprinting" in goats. *Proc. Natl. Acad. Sci., U.S.A.* **52**: 911–914.

Kneutgen, J. 1964.   Uber die kunstliche Auslosbarkeit des Gesangs der Schama-drossel (*Copsychus malabaricus*). *Z. Tierpsychol.* **21**: 124–128.

Kolb, A. 1977.   Wie erkennen sich Mutter und Junges des Mausohrs, *Myotis myotis*, bei der Ruckkehr vom Jagdflug wieder? *Z. Tierpsychol.* **44**: 423–431.

Konishi, M., and F. Nottebohm. 1969.   Experimental studies on the ontogeny of avian vocalization. In R. H. Hinde (ed.), *Bird Vocalizations*, Cambridge University Press, Cambridge, Chap. 2, pp. 29–48.

Kop, P. P. A. M., and B. A. Heuts. 1973.   An experiment on sibling imprinting in the jewel fish *Hemichromis bimaculatus* (Gill 1862, Cichlidae). *Rev. Comp. Anim.* **7**: 63–76.

Koref-Santibanez, S. 1963.   Courtship and sexual isolation in five species of the *mesophragmatica* group of the genus *Drosophila*. *Evolution* **17**: 99–106.

Kosswig, C. 1947.   Selective mating as a factor for speciation in Cichlid fish of East African lakes. *Nature (London)* **159**: 604–605.

Koutnik, D. L. 1980.   Submissive signalling in mule deer. *Anim. Behav.* **28**: 312–313.

Kovach, J. K. 1979.   Genetic influences and genotype-environment interactions in perceptual imprinting. *Behaviour* **68**: 31–60.

Kovach, J. K., E. Fabricius, and L. Falt. 1966.   Relationship between imprinting and perceptual learning. *J. Comp. Physiol.* **61**: 449–454.

Kozlowa, E. V. 1947.   On the spring life and breeding habits of the pheasant (*Phasianus colchicus*) in Tadjikistan. *Ibis* **89**: 423–429.

Kramer, B., F. Kirschbaum, and H. Markl. 1981.   Species specificity of electric organ discharges in a sympatric group of gymnotoid fish from Manaus (Amazonas). *Adv. Physiol. Sci.* **31**: 195–219.

Kramer, D. L. 1973.   Parental behaviour in the blue gourami *Trichogaster trichopterus* (Pisces, Belontiidae) and its induction during exposure to varying numbers of conspecific eggs. *Behaviour* **47**: 14–32.

Krebs, J. R. 1971.   Territory and breeding density in the great tit, *Parus major* L. *Ecology* **52**: 2–22.

Krebs, J. R. 1977.   The significance of song repertoires: The Beau Geste hypo-thesis. *Anim. Behav.* **25**: 475–478.

Krebs, J. R., and D. E. Kroodsma. 1980.   Repertoires and geographical variation in bird song. *Adv. Stud. Behav.* **11**: 143–177.

Kroodsma, D. E. 1976. The effect of large song repertoires on neighbor "recognition" in male song sparrows. *Condor* **78**: 97–99.

Kroodsma, D. E. 1977. A re-evaluation of song development in the song sparrow. *Anim. Behav.* **25**: 390–399.

Kroodsma, D. E. 1978. Aspects of learning in the ontogeny of bird song: Where, from whom, when, how many, which, and how accurately? In G. M. Burghardt & M. Bekoff (eds.), *The Development of Behavior: Comparative and Evolutionary Aspects*, Garland, New York, Chap. 11, pp. 215–230.

Kroodsma, D. E., and R. Pickert. 1980. Environmentally dependent sensitive periods for avian vocal learning. *Nature (London)* **288**: 477–479.

Kruijt, J. P. 1962. Imprinting in relation to drive interactions in Burmese Red Jungle Fowl. *Zool. Soc. Lond. Symp.* **8**: 219–226.

Kruijt, J. P. 1964. Ontogeny of social behaviour in Burmese Red Jungle Fowl (*Gallus gallus spadiceus*). *Behaviour Suppl.* **12**: 209 + 9 pp.

Kruijt, J. P. (ed.). 1972. Symposium on development of behaviour in birds. *Proc. 15th Int. Ornithol. Congr.*, pp. 281–362.

Kuhme, W. 1963. Chemische ausgeloste Brutpflege- und Schwarmreaktionen bei *Hemichromis bimaculatus* (Pisces). *Z. Tierpsychol.* **20**: 688–704.

Kuhn, T. S. 1971. *The Structure of Scientific Revolutions*, 2nd ed., University of Chicago Press, Chicago, 210 + 12 pp.

Kukuk, P. F., M. D. Breed, A. Sobti, and W. J. Bell. 1977. The contributions of kinship and conditioning to nest recognition and colony member recognition in a primitvely eusocial bee, *Lasioglassum zephyrum* (*Hymenoptera: Halictidae*). *Behav. Ecol. Sociobiol.* **2**: 319–327.

Kumari, S., and I. Prakash. 1981. Behavioural responses of *Meriones hurrianae* (Jerdon) to conspecific sebum of ventral sebaceous gland. *Biol. Behav.* **6**: 255–263.

Kuo, Z. Y. 1930. The genesis of the cat's response towards the rat. *J. Comp. Psychol.* **11**: 1–35.

Kuo, Z. Y. 1967. *The Dynamics of Behavior Development*. Random House, New York, 240 + 12 pp.

Labov, J. B. 1981a. Pregnancy blocking in rodents: Adaptive advantages for females. *Am. Nat.* **118**: 361–371.

Labov, J. B. 1981b. Male social status, physiology, and ability to block pregnancies in female house mice (*Mus musculus*). *Behav. Ecol. Sociobiol.* **8**: 287–291.

Lack, D. 1939. The behaviour of the robin. Part 1. The life-history, with special reference to aggressive behaviour, sexual behaviour, and territory. Part 2. A partial analysis of aggressive and recognitional behaviour. *Zool. Soc. Lond. Proc.* **109A**: 169–219.

Lack, D. 1945. The Galapagos finches (Geospizinae): A study in variation. *Calif. Acad. Sci. Occas. Pap.* **21**: 1–151.

Lade, B. I., and W. H. Thorpe. 1964.   Dove songs as innately coded patterns of specific behaviour. *Nature (London)* **202**: 366–368.

Ladewig, J., and B. L. Hart. 1980.   Flehmen and vomeronasal organ function in male goats. *Physiol. Behav.* **24**: 1067–1071.

Lall, A. B. 1981.   Vision tuned to species bioluminescence emission in firefly *Photinus pyralis. J. Exp. Zool.* **216**: 317–319.

Lall, A. B., H. H. Seliger, W. H. Biggley, and J. E. Lloyd. 1980.   Ecology of colors of firefly bioluminescence. *Science* **210**: 560–562.

Lambert, D. M. 1982.   Male recognition in members of the *Drosophila nasuta* complex. *Anim. Behav.* **30**: 438–443.

Lamprecht, J. 1970.   Duettgesang beim Siamang, *Symphalangus syndactylus* (Hominoidea, Hylobatinae). *Z. Tierpsychol.* **27**: 186–204.

Lamprecht, J. 1979.   Field observations on the behaviour and social system of the bat-eared fox *Otocyon megalotis* Desmarest. *Z. Tierpsychol.* **49**: 260–284.

Land, M. F. 1969.   Movements of the retimae of jumping spiders (Salticidae: Dendrodryphantinae) in response to visual stimuli. *J. Exp. Biol.* **51**: 471–493.

Landauer, M. R., E. M. Banks, and C. S. Carter. 1978.   Sexual and olfactory preferences of marine and experienced male hamsters. *Anim. Behav.* **26**: 611–621.

Landauer, M. R., S. Liu, and N. Goldberg. 1980.   Responses of male hamsters to the ear gland secretions of conspecifics. *Physiol. Behav.* **24**: 1023–1026.

Lang, H. H. 1980.   Surface wave discrimination between prey and nonprey by the back swimmer *Notonecta glauca* L. (Hemiptera, Heteroptera). *Behav. Ecol. Sociobiol.* **6**: 233–246.

Langley, P. A., T. W. Coates, and D. A. Carlson. 1982.   Sex recognition pheromone in the tsetse fly *Glossina pallidipes* Austen. *Experientia* **38**: 473–475.

Lanyon, W. E. 1963.   Experiments on species discrimination in *Myiarchus* flycatchers. *Am. Mus. Nat. Hist. Novitates* **2126**: 16 pp.

Larson, R. J. 1980.   Territorial behavior of the black and yellow rockfish and gopher rockfish (Scorpaenidae, *Sebastes*). *Mar. Biol.* **58**: 111–122.

Lashley, K. S. 1915.   Notes on the nesting activities of the noddy and sooty terns. *Carnegie Inst. Wash. Publ.* **211**: 61–83.

LeBlanc, M. A., and M. F. Bouissou. 1981.   Mise au point d'une epreuve destinee a l'etude de la reconnaissance du jeune par la mere chez le cheval. *Biol. Behav.* **6**: 283–290.

LeBouef, B. J., and R. S. Peterson. 1969.   Social status and mating activity in elephant seals. *Science* **163**: 91–93.

Lee, C. T. 1970.   Reactions of mouse fighters to male and female mice, intact or deodorized. *Am. Zool.* **10**: 486. (Abstr. 65)

LeMagnen, J. 1952.   Les phenomenes olfacto-sexuels chez le rat blanc. *Arch. Sci. Physiol.* **6**: 295–331.

Lemaire, F. 1977. Mixed song, interspecific competition and hybridisation in the reed and marsh warblers. (*Acrocephalus scirpaceus* and *palustris*). *Behaviour* 36: 215–240.

Lemon, R. E. 1967. The response of cardinals to songs of different dialects. *Anim. Behav.* 15: 538–545.

Lemon, R. E. 1968a. Coordinated singing by black-crested titmice. *Can. J. Zool.* 46: 1163–1167.

Lemon, R. E. 1968b. The relation between organization and function of song in cardinals. *Behaviour* 32: 158–178.

Lemon, R. E. 1971. Differentiation of song dialects in cardinals. *Ibis* 113: 373–377.

Lemon, R. E., and A. Herzog. 1969. The vocal behaviour of cardinals and pyrrhuloxias in Texas. *Condor* 71: 1–15.

LeNeindre, P., and J. -P. Garel. 1976. Existence d'une periode sensible pour l'establissement du comportement maternal de la vache apres la mise-bas. *Biol. Behav.* 1: 217–221.

Leroy, Y. 1964a. Analyse de la transmission des divers parametres des signaux acoustiques chez les hybrides interspecifiques de grillons (Orthoptera, Ensiferes). *Proc. 12th Int. Congr. Entomol.*, p. 339.

Leroy, Y. 1964b. Transmission du parametre frequence dans le signal acoustique des hybrides F_1 et $P \times F_1$, de deux Grillons: *Teleogryllus commodus* Walker et *T. oceanicus* LeGuillou (Orthopteres, Ensiferes). *C.R. Acad. Sci. Paris* 259: 892–895.

Lethmate, J., and G. Ducker. 1973. Untersuchungen zum Selbsterkennen im Spiegel bei Orang-Utans und einigen anderen Affenarten. *Z. Tierpsychol.* 33: 248–269.

Leuthold, W. 1966. Variations in territorial behavior of Uganda kob *Adenota kob thomasi* (Newmann). *Behaviour* 27: 215–258.

Levinson, S. E., and M. Y. Liberman. 1981. Speech recognition by computer. *Sci. Am.* 244(4): 64–76.

Lewis, D. S. C. 1980. Mixed species broods in Lake Malawi cichlids: An alternate to the cuckoo theory. *Copeia* 1980: 874–875.

Lewontin, R. C. 1974. *The Genetic Basis of Evolutionary Change.* Columbia University Press, New York, 346 + 14 pp.

Liechti, P. M., and W. J. Bell. 1975. Brooding behavior of the Cuban burrowing cockroach *Byrsotria fumigata* (Blaberidae, Blattaria). *Insectes Soc.* 22:35–46.

Light, L. L., S. Hollander, and F. Kayra-Stuart. 1981. Why attractive people are harder to remember. *Pers. Soc. Psychol. Bull.* 7: 269–276.

Liley, N. R. 1966. Ethological isolating mechanisms in four sympatric species of poeciliid fishes. *Behaviour Suppl.* 13: 197 + 6 pp.

Liley, N. R. 1982. Chemical communication in fish. *Can. J. Fish. Aquat. Sci.* 39: 22–35.

Lill, A. 1968a. An analysis of sexual isolation in the domestic fowl: 1. The basis of homogamy in males. *Behaviour* **30**: 107–126.

Lill, A. 1968b. An analysis of sexual isolation in the domestic fowl: 2. The basis of homogamy in females. *Behaviour* **30**: 127–145.

Lill, A. 1974a. Sexual behavior of the lek-forming white-bearded manakin (*Manacus manacus trinitatis* Hartert). *Z. Tierpsychol.* **36**: 1–36.

Lill, A. 1974b. Social organization and space utilization in the lek-forming white-bearded manakin, *M. manacus trinitatis* Hartert. *Z. Tierpsychol.* **36**: 513–530.

Lill, A., and D. G. M. Wood-Gush. 1965. Potential ethological isolating mechanisms and assortative mating in the domestic fowl. *Behaviour* **25**: 16–45.

Lindsay, D. R. 1965. The importance of olfactory stimuli in the mating behaviour of the ram. *Anim. Behav.* **13**: 75–78.

Lindsay, D. R., and I. C. Fletcher. 1968. Sensory involvement in the recognition of lambs by their dams. *Anim. Behav.* **16**: 415–417.

Lindzey, G., D. D. Thiessen, and A. Tucker. 1968. Development and hormonal control of territorial marking in the male Mongolian gerbil (*Meriones unguiculatus*). *Dev. Psychobiol.* **1**: 97–99.

Linsenmair, K. E. 1972. Die Bedeutung familien spezifischer "Abzeichen" für den Familienzusammenhalt bei der sozialen Wustenassel *Hemilepistus reamuri* Audouin u. Savigny (Crustacea, Isopoda, Oniscoridea). *Z. Tierpsychol.* **31**: 131–162.

Linsenmair, K. E., and C. Linsenmair. 1971. Paarbildung und paarzusammenhalt bei der monogamen Wustenassel *Hemilepistus reaumuri* (Crustacea, Isopoda, Oniscoidea). *Z. Tierpsychol.* **29**: 134–155.

Littlejohn, M. J. 1959. Call differentiation in a complex of seven species of *Crinia* (Anura, Leptodactylidae). *Evolution* **13**: 452–468.

Littlejohn, M. J. 1964. Geographic isolation and mating call differentiation in *Crinia signifera. Evolution* **18**: 262–266.

Littlejohn, M. J. 1965. Premating isolation in the *Hyla ewingi* complex (Anura: Hylidae). *Evolution* **19**: 234–243.

Littlejohn, M. J. 1969. The systematic significance of isolating mechanisms. In Int. Conf. Syst. Biol. (ed.), *Systematic Biology*, Nat. Acad. Sci. Publ. 1692, Washington, D.C., pp. 459–482.

Littlejohn, M. J. 1971. A reappraisal of mating call differentiation in *Hyla cadaverina* (=*Hyla californiae*) and *Hyla regilla. Evolution* **25**: 98–102.

Littlejohn, M. J., and J. J. Loftis-Hills. 1968. An experimental evaluation of premating isolation in the *Hyla ewingi* complex. *Evolution* **22**: 659–663.

Littlejohn, M. J., and T. C. Michaud. 1959. Mating call discrimination by females of Strecker's chorus frog (*Pseudacris strecheri*). Tex. J. Sci. **11**: 86–92.

Littlejohn, M. J., and R. S. Oldham. 1968. *Rana pipiens* complex: Mating call structure and taxonomy. *Science* **162**: 1003–1005.

Littlejohn, M. J., and G. F. Watson. 1974. Mating call discrimination and phonotaxis by females of the *Crinia laevis* complex (Anura: Leptodactylidae). *Copeia* **1974**: 171–175.

Littlejohn, M. J., M. J. Fouquette, and C. Johnson. 1960. Call discrimination by female frogs of the *Hyla versicolor* complex. *Copeia* **1960**: 47–49.

Lloyd, J. E. 1966. Studies on the flash communication system in *Photinus* fireflies. *Univ. Mich. Mus. Zool. Misc. Publ.* **130**: 95 pp.

Lloyd, J. E. 1971. Bioluminescent communication in insects. *Annu. Rev. Entomol.* **16**: 97–122.

Lloyd, J. E. 1980. Male *Photuris* fireflies mimic sexual signals of their females' prey. *Science* **210**: 669–671.

Lobb, S. M. 1972. Aspects of the social behaviour, ecology and anatomy of the hairy crab *Pilumnus hirtellus* (L.), Ph.D. thesis, University of Reading, U.K.

Loiselle, P. V., and G. W. Barlow. 1978. Do fishes lek like birds? In E. S. Reese and F. J. Lighter (eds.), *Contrasts in Behavior.* Wiley-Interscience, New York, Chap. 2, pp. 31–75.

Lorenz, K. Z. 1970, 1971. *Studies in Animal and Human Behaviour,* 2 Vols. Methuen, London, 403 + 20, 366 + 24 pp.

Lorenz, K. Z. 1966. *On Aggression.* Methuen, London, 273 + 13 pp.

Lorenz, K. Z. 1974. Analogy as a source of knowledge. *Science* **185**: 229–234.

Lorenz, K. Z., and N. Tinbergen. 1957. Taxis and instinctive action in the egg-retrieving behavior of the greylag goose. In C. H. Schiller (ed.), *Instinctive Behavior.* International Universities, New York, Pt. 2, Chap. 3, pp. 176–208.

Lott, D. F., and J. H. Hopwood. 1972. Olfactory pregnancy-block in mice (*Mus musculus*): An unusual response acquisition paradigm. *Anim. Behav.* **20**: 263–267.

Lowe, M. E. 1956. Dominance-subordinance relationships in the crawfish *Cambarellus shufeldtii. Tulane Univ. Stud. Zool.* **4**: 139–170.

Lowther, J. K. 1961. Polymorphism in the white-throated sparrow, *Zonotrichia albicollis* (Gmelin). *Can. J. Zool.* **39**: 281–292.

Lumsden, C. J., and E. O. Wilson. 1980. Gene-culture translation in the avoidance of sibling incest. *Proc. Natl. Acad. Sci., U.S.A.* **77**: 6248–6250.

Lumsden, C. J., and E. O. Wilson. 1981. *Genes, Mind, and Culture.* Harvard University Press, Cambridge, 428 + 12 pp.

MacGinitie, G. E. 1939. The natural history of the blind goby, *Typhlogobius californiensis* (Steindachner). *Am. Midl. Nat.* **21**: 489–505.

MacKay-Sim, A., and D. G. Laing. 1981a. Rats' responses to blood and body odors of stressed and non-stressed conspecifics. *Physiol. Behav.* **27**: 503–510.

MacKay-Sim, A., and D. G. Laing. 1981b. The source of odors from stressed rats. *Physiol. Behav.* **27**: 511–513.

Mackinnon, J. 1974. The behaviour and ecology of wild orang-utans (*Ponge pygmaeus*). *Anim. Behav.* **22:** 3–74.

Mackintosh, J. H. 1973. Factors affecting the recognition of territory boundaries in mice (*Mus musculus*). *Anim. Behav.* **21:** 464–470.

Mackintosh, N. J. 1974. *The Psychology of Animal Learning.* Academic, London, 730 + 14 pp.

Maeda, N., and T. Hidaka. 1979. Ethological function of the parr marks in a Japanese trout, *Oncorhynchus masou* f. *ishikawai. Zool. Mag.* **88:** 34–42.

Maier, R. A. 1964. The role of the dominance-submission ritual in social recognition of hens. *Anim. Behav.* **12:** 59.

Mainardi, D., M. Marson, and A. Pasquali. 1965a. Causation of sexual preferences of the house mice. The behaviour of mice reared by parents whose odour was artificially altered. *Atti. Soc. Ital. Sci. Nat. Mus. Civ. Stor. Nat. Milano* **104:** 325–338.

Mainardi, D., F. M. Scudo, and D. Barbieri. 1965b. Assortative mating based on early learning: Population genetics. *Acta Bio-medica* **36:** 583–605.

Mallory, F. F., and R. J. Brooks. 1978. Infanticide and other reproductive strategies in the collared lemming, *Dicrostonyx groenlandicus. Nature (London)* **273:** 144–146.

Mallory, F. F., and R. J. Brooks. 1980. Infanticide and pregnancy failure: Reproductive strategies in the female collared lemming (*Dicrostonyx groenlandicus. Biol. Reprod.* **22:** 192–196.

Mallory, F. F., and F. V. Clulow. 1977. Evidence of pregnancy failure in the wild meadow vole, *Microtus pennsylvanicus. Can. J. Zool.* **55:** 1–17.

Manning, A. 1959. The sexual behaviour of two sibling *Drosophila* species. *Behaviour* **15:** 123–145.

Manning, J. T. 1975. Male discrimination and investment in *Asellus aquaticus* (L.) and *A. meridianus* Racovitza (Crustacea: Isopoda). *Behaviour* **55:** 1–14.

Manning, J. T. 1980. Sex ratio and optimal male time investment strategies in *Asellus aquaticus* (L.) and *A. meridianus* Racovitza. *Behaviour* **74:** 264–273.

Markow, T. A. 1978. A test for rare male mating advantage in coisogenic strains of *Drosophila melanogaster. Genet. Res.* **32:** 123–127.

Markow, T. A. 1980. Rare male advantages among *Drosophila* of the same laboratory strain. *Behav. Genet.* **10:** 553–556.

Markow, T. A. 1981a. Mating preferences are not predictive of the direction of evolution in experimental populations of *Drosophila. Science* **213:** 1405–1407.

Markow, T. A. 1981b. Courtship behavior and control of reproductive isolation between *Drosophila mojavensis* and *Drosophila arizonensis. Evolution* **35:** 1022–1026.

Markow, T. A., R. C. Richmond, L. Mudler, I. Sheer, S. Roman, C. Laetz, and L.

Lorenz. 1980. Testing for rare male mating advantages among various *Drosophila melanogaster* genotypes. *Genet. Res.* **35**: 59–64.

Marks, H. L., T. B. Siegel, and C. Y. Kramer. 1960. The effect of comb and wattle removal on the social organisation of mixed flocks of chickens. *Anim. Behav.* **8**: 192–196.

Marler, P. 1960. Bird songs and mate selection. In W. E. Lanyon & W. N. Tavolga (eds.), *Animal Sounds and Communication*, Am. Inst. Biol. Sci., Washington, D.C., pp. 348–367.

Marler, P. 1970. Birdsong and speech development: Could there be parallels? *Am. Sci.* **58**: 669–673.

Marler, P. 1973. A comparison of vocalizations of red-tailed monkeys and blue monkeys, (*Cercopithecus ascanius* and *C. mitis*) in Uganda. *Z. Tierpsychol.* **33**: 223–247.

Marler, P., and L. Hobbett. 1975. Individuality in a long-range vocalization of wild chimpanzees. *Z. Tierpsychol.* **38**: 97–109.

Marler, P., and P. Mundinger. 1971. Vocal learning in birds. In H. Moltz (ed.), *The Ontogeny of Vertebrate Behavior*, Academic, New York, pp. 389–450.

Marler, P., and P. Mundinger. 1975. Vocalizations, social organization and breeding biology of the twite, *Acanthus flavirostris. Ibis* **117**: 1–17.

Marler, P., and M. Tamura. 1964. Culturally transmitted patterns of vocal behavior in sparrows. *Science* **164**: 1483–1486.

Marples, G., and A. Marples. 1934. *Sea Terns or Sea Swallows.* Country Life, London, 227 + 12 pp.

Martin, E. M., and J. L. Ruos. 1976. Wild red-shouldered hawks readily accept additional nestlings. *Raptor Res.* **10**: 88.

Martin, G. B., and R. D. T. Clark. 1982. Distress crying in neonates: Species and peer specificity. *Dev. Psychol.*, in press.

Martof, B. S., and E. F. Thompson. 1964. A behavioral analysis of the mating call of the chorus frog, *Pseudacris triseriata. Am. Midl. Nat.* **71**: 198–209.

Mason, J. R., and R. F. J. Reidinger. 1981. Effects of social facilitation and observational learning on feeding behavior of the red-winged blackbird (*Agelaius phoeniceus*). *Auk* **98**: 778–784.

Mason, W. 1979. Ontogeny of social behavior. In P. Marler and J. G. Vandenbergh (eds.), *Social Behavior and Communication. Handbook of Behavioral Neurobiology*, Vol. 3, Plenum, New York, Chap. 1, pp. 1–28.

Matessi, C., and F. M. Scudo. 1975. The population genetics of assortative mating based on imprinting. *Theor. Pop. Biol.* **7**: 306–337.

Matthews, W. A., and G. Hemmings. 1963. A theory concerning imprinting. *Nature (London)* **198**: 1183–1184.

Mattson, M. E., and R. M. Evans. 1974. Visual imprinting and auditory-discrimination learning in young of the canvas-back and semi-parasitic redhead (Anatidae). *Can. J. Zool.* **52**: 421–427.

Maynard Smith, J. 1964.   Group selection and kin selection. *Nature (London)* **201**: 1145–1147.

Maynard Smith, J. 1976.   A comment on the red queen. *Am. Nat.* **110**: 325–330.

Maynard Smith, J. 1979.   Game theory and the evolution of behaviour. *Proc. R. Soc. London, Ser. B* **205**: 475–488.

Mayr, E. 1950.   The role of the antennae in the mating behavior of female *Drosophila. Evolution* **4**: 149–154.

Mayr, E. 1970.   *Populations, Species, and Evolution.* Harvard University Press, Cambridge, Mass., 453 + 15 pp.

McArthur, P. D. 1982.   Mechanisms and development of parent-young vocal recognition in the pinon jay (*Gymnorhinus cyanocephalus*). *Anim. Behav.* **30**: 62–74.

McBride, G. 1964.   Social discrimination and subflock structure in the domestic fowl. *Anim. Behav.* **12**: 264–267.

McCann, L. I., and C. C. Carlson. 1982.   Effect of cross-rearing on species identification in zebra fish and pearl danios. *Dev. Psychobiol.* **15**: 71–74.

McCann, L. I., and J. J. Matthews. 1974.   The effects of lifelong isolation on species identification in zebra fish (*Brachydanio rerio*). *Dev. Psychobiol.* **7**: 159–163.

McCann, L. I., D. J. Koehn, and N. J. Kline. 1971.   The effects of body size and body markings on nonpolarized schooling behavior of zebra fish (*Brachydanio rerio*). *J. Psychol.* **79**: 71–75.

McCarty, R., and C. H. Southwick. 1977.   Cross-species fostering: Effects on the olfactory preference of *Onychomys torridus* and *Peromyscus leucopus. Behav. Biol.* **19**: 255–260.

McClintock, M. K. 1971.   Menstrual synchrony and suppression. *Nature (London)* **229**: 244–245.

McDonald, D. L., and L. G. Forslund. 1978.   The development of social preferences in the voles *Microtus montanus* and *Microtus canicaudus*: Effects of cross-fostering. *Behav. Biol.* **22**: 497–508.

McDougall, W. 1923.   *An Outline of Psychology.* Methuen, London, 456 + 16 pp.

McDougall, W., and K. McDougall. 1927.   Notes on instinct and intelligence in rats and cats. *J. Comp. Psychol.* **7**: 145–175.

McGavin, M. 1978.   Recognition of conspecific odors by the salamander *Plethodon cinereus. Copeia* **1978**: 356–358.

McGregor, P. K. 1980.   Song dialects in the corn bunting (*Emberiza calandra*). *Z. Tierpsychol.* **54**: 285–297.

McGuire, M. R., and L. L. Getz. 1981.   Incest taboo between sibling *Microtus ochrogaster*. *J. Mammal* **62**: 213–215.

McHugh, T. 1958.   Social behavior of the American buffalo (*Bison bison bison*). *Zoologica* **43**: 1–40.

McKay, F. E. 1971.   Behavioral aspects of population dynamics in unisexual–bisexual *Poeciliopsis* (Pisces: Poeciliidae). *Ecology* **52**: 778–790.

McKay, L. R. 1978.   A reanalysis of the rare male effect in *Drosophila pseudoobscura*. M. Sc. thesis, Queen's University at Kingston, Canada, 71 + 9 pp.

McKaye, K. R. 1977.   Defense of a predator's young by a herbivorous fish: An unusual strategy. *Am. Nat.* **111**: 301–315.

McKaye, K. R. 1979.   Defense of a predator's young revisited. *Am. Nat.* **114**: 595–601.

McKaye, K. R. 1981.   Natural selection and the evolution of interspecific brood care in fishes. In R. D. Alexander and D. W. Tinkle (eds.), *Natural Selection and Social Behavior*, Chiron, New York, Chap. 10, pp. 173–183.

McKaye, K. R., and G. W. Barlow. 1976.   Chemical recognition of young by the midas cichlid, *Cichlasoma citrinellum*. *Copeia* **1976**: 276–282.

McKaye, K. R., and N. M. McKaye. 1977.   Communal care and kidnapping of young by parental cichlids. *Evolution* **31**: 674–681.

McKaye, K. R., and M. K. Oliver. 1980.   Geometry of a selfish school: Defence of cichlid young by bagrid catfish in Lake Malawi, Africa. *Anim. Behav.* **28**: 1287.

McPhail, J. D. 1978.   Sons and lovers: The functional significance of sexual dichromism in a fish, *Neoheterandria tridentiger* (Garman). *Behaviour* **64**: 329–339.

Mech, L. D. 1970.   *The Wolf: The Ecology and Behavior of an Endangered Species.* Natural History, New York, 384 + 20 pp.

Mehler, J., J. Bertoncini, M. Barriere, and D. Jassik-Gerschenfeld. 1978.   Infant recognition of mother's voice. *Perception* **7**: 491–497.

Meikle, D. B., and S. H. Vessey. 1981.   Nepotism among rhesus monkey brothers. *Nature (London)* **294**: 160–161.

Meltzoff, A. N., and M. K. Moore. 1977.   Imitation of facial and manual gestures by human neonates. *Science* **198**: 75–78.

Meltzoff, A. N., and M. K. Moore. 1979.   Interpreting "imitative" responses in early infancy. *Science* **205**: 217–219.

Messmer, E., and I. Messmer. 1956.   Die Entwicklung der Lautausserungen und einiger Verhaltensweisen der Amsel (*Turdus merula merula* L.) unter natürlichen Bedingungen und nach Einzelaufzucht in schalldichten Raumen. *Z. Tierpsychol.* **13**: 341–441.

Meudec, M. 1978.   Response to and transport of brood by workers of *Tapinoma erraticum* (Formicidae: Dolichoderinae) during nest disturbance. *Behav. Proc.* **3**: 199–209.

Michael, R. P., and E. B. Keverne. 1968. Pheromones in the communication of sexual status in primates. *Nature (London)* **218**: 746–749.

Michael, R. P., E. B. Keverne, and R. W. Bonsall. 1971. Pheromones: Isolation of male sex attractants from a female primate. *Science* **172**: 964–966.

Michaud, T. C. 1962. Call discrimination by females of the chorus frogs, *Pseudacris clarki* and *Pseudacris nigrita. Copeia* **1962**: 213–215.

Michener, C. D. 1966. Interaction among workers from different colonies of sweat bees (Hymenoptera, Halictidae). *Anim. Behav.* **14**: 126–129.

Michener, G. R. 1973. Field observations on the social relationships between adult female and juvenile Richardson's ground squirrels. *Can. J. Zool.* **51**: 33–38.

Michener, G. R. 1974. Development of adult-young identification in Richardson's ground squirrels. *Dev. Psychobiol.* **7**: 375–384.

Michener, G. R., and D. H. Sheppard. 1972. Social behavior between adult female Richardson's ground squirrels (*Spermophilus richardsonii*) and their own and alien young. *Can. J. Zool.* **50**: 1343–1349.

Miehlbradt, J., and D. Newmann. 1976. Reproduktive Isolation durch optische Schwarmmarken bei den sympatrischen *Chironomus thummi* und *Ch. piger. Behaviour* **58**: 272–297.

Milinski, M. 1977a. Experiments on the selection by predators against spatial oddity of their prey. *Z. Tierpsychol.* **43**: 311–325.

Milinski, M. 1977b. Do all members of a swarm suffer the same predation? *Z. Tierpsychol.* **45**: 373–388.

Milinski, M., and C. Lowenstein. 1980. On predator selection against abnormalities of movement. A test of an hypothesis. *Z. Tierpsychol.* **53**: 325–340.

Miller, D. B. 1979a. Long-term recognition of father's song by female zebra finches. *Nature (London)* **280**: 389–391.

Miller, D. B. 1979b. The acoustic basis of mate recognition by female zebra finches (*Taeniopygia guttata*). *Anim. Behav.* **27**: 376–380.

Miller, D. B. 1980. Maternal vocal control of behavioral inhibition in mallard ducklings (*Anas platyrhynchos*). *J. Comp. Physiol. Psychol.* **94**: 606–623.

Miller, D. B., and G. Gottlieb. 1976. Acoustic features of wood duck (*Aix sponsa*) maternal calls. *Behaviour* **57**: 260–280.

Miller, D. B., and G. Gottlieb. 1978. Maternal vocalizations of mallard ducks (*Anas platyrhynchos*). *Anim. Behav.* **26**: 1178–1194.

Miller, D. E., and J. T. Emlen. 1975. Individual chick recognition and family integrity in the ring-billed gull. *Behaviour* **52**: 124–144.

Miller, N. E., and J. Dollard. 1941.   *Social Learning and Imitation*. Yale University Press, New Haven, Conn., 341 + 14 pp.

Miller, R. J. 1979.   Agonistic behavior in fishes and terrestrial vertebrates. In E. S. Reese and F. J. Lighter (eds.), *Contrasts in Behavior*, Wiley, New York, Chap. 10, pp. 281–311.

Milligan, M. 1966.   Vocal responses of white-crowned sparrows to recorded songs of their own and another species. *Anim. Behav.* **14**: 356–361.

Milligan, M. M., and J. Verner. 1971. Inter-populational song dialect discrimination in the white-crowned sparrow. *Condor* **73**: 208–213.

Mills, M., and E. Melhuish. 1974.   Recognition of mother's voice in early infancy. *Nature (London)* **252**: 123–124.

Mineau, P., and F. Cooke. 1979.   Rape in the lesser snow goose. *Behaviour* **70**: 280–291.

Miranda, S. B., and R. L. Fantz. 1974.   Recognition and memory in Down's syndrome and normal infants. *Child Dev.* **45**: 651–660.

Mitchell, G. D., H. F. Harlow, G. A. Griffin, and G. W. Moller. 1967.   Repeated maternal separation in the monkey. *Psychon. Sci.* **8**: 197–198.

Moehlman, P. D. 1979.   Jackal helpers and pup survival. *Nature (London)* **277**: 382–383.

Moltz, H. 1963.   Imprinting: an epigenetic approach. *Psychol. Rev.* **70**: 123–138.

Moltz, H., and T. M. Lee. 1981.   The maternal pheromone of the rat: Identity and functional significance. *Physiol. Behav.* **26**: 301–306.

Moltz, H., and L. J. Stettner. 1961.   The influence of patterned-light deprivation on the critical period for imprinting. *J. Comp. Psychol.* **54**: 279–283.

Morgan, C. L. 1909.   *An Introduction to Comparative Psychology*, 2nd ed. Scott, London, 386 + 14 pp.

Morgan, P. D., C. A. P. Boundy, G. W. Arnold, and D. R. Lindsay. 1975.   The roles played by the senses of the ewe in the location and recognition of lambs. *Appl. Anim. Ethol.* **1**: 139–150.

Morley, A. 1942.   Effects of baiting on the Marsh Tit. *Br. Birds* **35**: 261–266.

Morris, D. 1955.   The causation of pseudofemale and pseudomale behaviour. *Behaviour* **8**: 46–57.

Morris, D. 1956.   The feather postures of birds and the problem of the origin of social signals. *Behaviour* **9**: 75–113.

Morris, D. 1979.   *Animal Days*. Cape, London, 275 + 9 pp.

Morris, R. L., and C. J. Erickson. 1971.   Pair bond maintenance in the ring dove (*Streptopelia risoria*). *Anim. Behav.* **19**: 398–406.

Morsbach, G., and C. Bunting. 1979.   Maternal recognition of their neonates' cries. *Dev. Med. Child Neurol.* **21**: 178–185.

Moseley, L. J. 1979.   Individual auditory recognition in the least tern (*Sterna albifrons*). *Auk* **96**: 31–39.

Mountfort, G. 1957. *The Hawfinch.* Collins, London, 176 + 12 pp.

Mugford, R. A., and N. N. Nowell. 1971. The preputial glands as a source of aggression-promoting odors in mice. *Physiol. Behav.* **6**: 247–249.

Mueller, H. C. 1980. Comments on the recognition of offspring by raptors. *Raptor Res.* **14**: 20–21.

Muller-Schwarze, D. 1971. Pheromones in black-tailed deer (*Odocoileus hemionus columbianus*). *Anim. Behav.* **19**: 141–152.

Muller-Schwarze, D. 1972. Social significance of forehead rubbing in black-tailed deer (*Odocoileus hemionus columbianus*). *Anim. Behav.* **20**: 788–797.

Muller-Schwarze, D., and R. M. Silverstein (eds.). 1979. *Chemical Signals, Vertebrates and Aquatic Invertebrates.* Plenum, New York, 445 + 10 pp.

Mundinger, P. C. 1970. Vocal imitation and individual recognition of finch calls. *Science* **168**: 480–482.

Mundinger, P. C. 1979. Call learning in the carduelinae: Ethological and systematic considerations. *Syst. Zool.* **28**: 270–283.

Munro, J., and J. Bedard. 1977a. Creche formation in the common eider. *Auk* **94**: 759–771.

Munro, J., and J. Bedard. 1977b. Gull predation and creching behaviour in the common eider. *J. Anim. Ecol.* **46**: 799–810.

Murphy, M. R. 1978. Oestrous turkish hamsters display lordosis toward conspecific males but attack heterospecific males. *Anim. Behav.* **26**: 311–312.

Murphy, M. R., and G. E. Schneider. 1970. Olfactory bulb removal eliminates mating behavior in the male golden hamster. *Science* **167**: 302–304.

Murray, B. G. J. 1981. The origins of adaptive interspecific territorialism. *Biol. Rev.* **56**:1–22.

Mykytowycz, R. 1968. Territorial working by rabbits. *Sci. Am.* **218(5)**: 116–126.

Mykytowycz, R. 1972. The behavioural role of the mammalian skin glands. *Naturwissenschaften* **59**: 133–139.

Myrberg, A. A., Jr. 1964. An analysis of the preferential care of eggs and young by adult cichlid fishes. *Z. Tierpsychol.* **21**: 53–98.

Myrberg, A. A., Jr. 1966. Parental recognition of young in cichlid fishes. *Anim. Behav.* **14**: 565–571.

Myrberg, A. A., Jr. 1975. The role of chemical and visual stimuli in the preferential discrimination o fyoung by the cichlid fish *Cichlasoma nigrofasciatum* (Gunther). *Z. Tierpsychol.* **37**: 274–297.

Myrberg, A. A., Jr. 1980. Sensory mediation of social recognition processes in fishes. In J. E. Bardach et al. (eds.), *Fish Behavior and its Use in the Capture and Culture of Fishes,* Int. Cent. Living Resour. Manage., Manila, pp. 146–178.

Myrberg, A. A., Jr., and J. Y. Spires. 1972. Sound discrimination by the bicolor damselfish, *Eupomacentrus partitus. J. Exp. Biol.* **57**: 727–735.

Narda, R. D. 1968. Experimental evaluation of the stimuli involved in sexual isolation among three members of the *ananassae* species subgroup (*Sophophora*, *Drosophila*). *Anim. Behav.* **16:** 117–119.

Neill, W. T. 1964.   Isolating mechanisms in snakes. *Flor. Acad. Sci. Q. J.* **27:** 333–347.

Nelson, K. 1964.   Behavior and morphology in the glandulocaudine fishes (Ostariophysi, Characidae). *Univ. Calif. Publ. Zool.* **75:** 59–152.

Newcombe, C. P., and G. F. Hartman. 1980.   Visual signals in the spawning behaviour of rainbow trout. *Can. J. Zool.* **58:** 1751–1757.

Newton, G., and S. Levine (eds.) 1968.   *Early Experience and Behavior.* Thomas, Springfield, Illinois, 785 + 12 pp.

Newton, I., M. Marquiss, and D. Moss. 1979.   Habitat, female age, organochlorine compounds and breeding of European sparrowhawks. *J. Appl. Ecol.* **16:** 777–793.

Nice, M. M. 1937.   Studies in the life history of the song sparrow. 1. A population study of the song sparrow. *Linn. Soc. N.Y. Trans.* **4:** 1–247.

Nice, M. M. 1943.   Studies in the life history of the song sparrow. 2. The behavior of the song sparrow and other passerines. *Linn. Soc. N.Y. Trans.* **6:** 1–328.

Nicolai, J. 1956.   Zur Biologie und Ethologie des Gimpels (*Pyrrhula pyrrhula* L.). *Z. Tierpsychol.* **13:** 93–132.

Nicolai, J. 1959.   Familien tradition in der Gesangsentwicklung des Gimpels (*Pyrrhula pyrrhula*). *J. Ornithol.* **100:** 39–46.

Nicolai, J. 1964.   Der Brutparasitismus der Viduinae als ethologisches Problem. Pragungsphanomene als Faktoren der Rassen- und Artbildung. *Z. Tierpsychol.* **21:** 129–204.

Nicolai, J. 1967.   Rassen- und Artbildung in der Viduinengattung *Hypochera*. *J. Ornithol.* **108:** 309–319.

Nicolai, J. 1968.   Die Schnabelfarbung als potentieller Isolationsfaktor zwischen *Pytilia phoenicoptera* Swainson und *Pytilia lineata* Heuglin (Familie: Estrildidae). *J. Ornithol.* **109:** 450–461.

Noakes, D. L. G., and G. W. Barlow. 1973.   Cross-fostering and parent-offspring responses in *Cichlasoma citrinellum* (Pisces, Cichlidae). *Z. Tierpsychol.* **33:** 147–152.

Noble, G. K. 1934.   Sex recognition in the sunfish, *Eupomotis gibbosus* (Linne). *Copeia* **1934:** 151–154.

Noble, G. K. 1936.   Courtship and sexual selection of the flicker (*Colaptes auratus lutus*). *Auk* **53:** 269–282.

Noble, G. K. 1937.   The sense organs involved in the courtship of *Storeria*, *Thamnophis* and other snakes. *Am. Mus. Nat. Hist. Bull.* **73:** 673–725.

Noble, G. K., and B. Curtis. 1939.   The social behavior of the jewel fish, *Hemichromis bimaculatus* Gill. *Am. Mus. Nat. Hist. Bull.* **76:** 1–46.

Noble, G. K., and E. J. Farris. 1929.   The method of sex recognition in the wood frog, *Rana sylvatica* LeConte. *Am. Mus. Nat. Hist. Novitates* **363:** 17 pp.

Noble, G. K., and D. S. Lehrman. 1940. Egg recognition by the Laughing Gull. *Auk* **57**: 22–43.

Noble, G. K., and W. Vogt. 1935. An experimental study of sex recognition in birds. *Auk* **52**: 278–286.

Noble, G. K., and M. Wurm. 1943. Social behavior of the laughing gull. *Ann. N.Y. Acad. Sci.* **45**: 179–220.

Noirot, C., P. E. Howse, and G. LeMasne (eds.). 1975. *Pheromones and Defensive Secretions in Social Insects.* Lab. Zool., Dijon, 245 + 8 pp.

Noirot, E. 1969. Changes in responsiveness to young in the adult mouse: 5. Priming. *Anim. Behav.* **17**: 542–546.

Noirot, E., and M. P. M. Richards. 1966. Maternal behaviour in virgin female golden hamsters: Changes consequent upon initial contact with pups. *Anim. Behav.* **24**: 1–6.

Nolte, D. J., I. R. May, and B. M. Thomas. 1970. The gregarisation pheromone of locusts. *Chromosoma* **29**: 462–473.

Nolte, D. J., S. H. Eggers, and I. R. May. 1973. A locust pheromone: Locustol. *J. Insect Physiol.* **19**: 1547–1554.

Norman, D. O. 1977. A role for plumage color in mute swan (*Cygnus olor*) parent-offspring interactions. *Behaviour* **62**: 314–321.

Norton-Griffiths, M. 1969. The organization, control and development of parental feedings in the oystercatcher (*Haematopus ostralegus*). *Behaviour* **34**: 55–114.

Nottebohm, F. 1970. Ontogeny of bird song. *Science* **167**: 950–956.

Nuechterlein, G. L. 1981a. Variations and multiple functions of the advertising display of western grebes. *Behaviour* **76**: 289–317.

Nuechterlein, G. L. 1981b. Courtship behavior and reproductive isolation between western grebe color morphs. *Auk* **98**: 335–349.

Nyby, J., C. J. Wysocki, G. Whitney, and G. Dizinno. 1977. Pheromonal regulation of male mouse ultrasonic courtship (*Mus musculus*). *Anim. Behav.* **25**: 333–341.

O'Donald, P. 1977. Mating advantage of rare males in models of sexual selection. *Nature (London)* **267**: 151–154.

O'Donald, P. 1978. Reply to Spiess and Ehrman. *Nature (London)* **272**: 189.

O'Donald, P. 1980. *Genetic Models of Sexual Selection.* Cambridge University Press, Cambridge, 250 + 12 pp.

Oester, P. T., and J. A. Rudinsky. 1979. Acoustic behaviour of the three sympatric species of *Ips* (Coleoptera: Scolytidae) co-inhabiting Sitka spruce. *Z. Angew. Entomol.* **87**: 398–412.

O'Hara, R. K., and A. R. Blaustein. 1981. An investigation of sibling recognition in *Rana cascadae* tadpoles. *Anim. Behav.* **29**: 1121–1126.

Ohguchi, O. 1981. Prey density and selection against oddity by three-spined sticklebacks. *Z. Tierpsychol. Suppl.* **23**: 79 pp.

Ohta, A. T. 1978. Ethological isolation and phylogeny in the grimshawi species complex of Hawaiian *Drosophila*. *Evolution* **32**: 485–492.

Ono, Y. 1955. Experimental studies of intraspecific recognition in *Oryzias latipes*. *Kagawa Univ. Fac. Arts Lib. Educ. Mem. Pt.* 2, **17**: 1–38.

Oppenheimer, J. R., and E. C. Oppenheimer. 1973. Preliminary observations of *Cebus nigrivittatus* (Primates: Cebidae) on the Venezuelan llanos. *Folia Primatol.* **19**: 409–436.

Otte, D. 1972. Simple *versus* elaborate behavior in grasshoppers. An analysis of communication in the genus *Syrbula*. *Behaviour* **42**: 291–322.

Otte, D., and W. Cade. 1976. On the role of olfaction in sexual and interspecies recognition in crickets (*Acheta* and *Gryllus*) (Othoptera, Gryllidae). *Anim. Behav.* **24**: 1–116.

Palmer, R. S. 1941. A behavior study of the common tern. *Boston Soc. Nat Proc.* **42**: 1–119.

Parkes, A. S., and H. M. Bruce. 1961. Olfactory stimuli in mammalian reproduction. *Science* **134**: 1049–1054.

Parr, A. E. 1937. On self-recognition and social reaction in relation to biomechanics, with a note on terminology. *Ecology* **18**: 321–323.

Parsons, P.A. 1973. *Behavioural and ecological genetics: A study in Drosophila.* Clarendon, Oxford, 223 + 6 pp.

Partridge, B. L., N. R. Liley, and N. E. Stacey. 1976. The role of pheromones in the sexual behavior of the goldfish. *Amin. Behav.* **24**: 291–299.

Partridge, L. 1980. Mate choice increases a component of offspring fitness in fruit flies. *Nature (London)* **283**: 290–291.

Parzefall, J. 1973. Attraction and sexual cycle of Poeciliids. In J. H. Schroder (ed.),*Genetics and Mutagenesis of Fish*, Springer-Verlag, New York, pp. 177–183.

Patterson, F. 1978. Conversations with a gorilla. *Natl. Geogr.* **154**: 438–465.

Patterson. I. J., A. Gilboa, and D. J. Tozer. 1982. Rearing other people's young: Brood-mixing in the shelduck *Tadorna tadorna. Anim. Behav.* **30**: 199–202.

Paul, R. 1976. Acoustic response to chemical stimuli in ground crickets. *Nature (London)* **263**: 404–405.

Payman, B. C., and H. H. Swanson. 1980. Social influence on sexual maturation and breeding in the femal Mongolian gerbil (*Meriones unguiculatus*). *Anim. Behav.* **28**: 528–535.

Payne, R. B. 1971. Duetting and chorus singing in African birds. *Ostrich Suppl.* **9**: 125–146.

Payne, R. B. 1973a. Behavior, mimetic songs and song dialects, and relationships of the parasitie indigo birds (*Vidua*) of Africa. *Ornithol. Monogr.* **11**: 333 + 6 pp.

Payne, R. B. 1973b. Vocal mimicry of the paradise whydahs (*Vidua*) and response of female whydahs to the songs of their hosts (*Pytilia*) and their mimics. *Anim. Behav.* **21**: 762–771.

Payne, R. B. 1977. The ecology of brood parasitism in birds. *Annu. Rev. Ecol. Syst.* **8**: 1–28.

Payne, R. S., and S. McVay. 1971. Songs of humpback whales. *Science* **173**: 585–597.

Peek, F. W. 1972a. An experimental study of the territorial function of vocal and visual displays in the male red-winged blackbird (*Agelaius phoeniceus*). *Anim. Behav.* **20**: 112–118.

Peek, F. W. 1972b. The effect of tranquilization upon territory maintenance in the male red-winged blackbird (*Agelaius phoeniceus*). *Anim. Behav.* **20**:119–122.

Peeke, H. V. S., and M. J. Herz (eds.). 1973. *Habituation*, 2 Vols. Academic, New York, 290 + 11, 216 + 11 pp.

Peeke, H. V. S., and A. Veno. 1973. Stimulus specificity of habituated aggression in the stickleback (*Gasterosteus aculeatus*). *Behav. Biol.* **8**: 427–432.

Peeke, H. V. S., and A. Veno. 1976. Response independent habituation of territorial aggression in the three-spined stickleback (*Gasterosteus aculeatus*). *Z. Tierpsychol.* **40**: 53–58.

Peeke, H. V. S., M. H. Figler, and N. Blankenship. 1979. Retention and recovery of habituated territorial aggressive behavior in the three-spined stickleback (*Gasterosteus aculeatus* L.): The roles of time and nest construction. *Behaviour* **69**: 171–182.

Penney, R. L. 1968. Territorial and social behavior in the Adelie penguin. In O. L. Austin Jr. (ed.), *1968 Antarctic Bird Studies*, Vol. 12., Am. Geophys. Union, Washington, D.C., pp 83–131.

Perdeck, A. C. 1958. The isolating value of specific song patterns in two sibling species of grasshoppers (*Chorthippus brunneus* Thunb. and *C. biguttulus* L.). *Behaviour* **12**: 1–75.

Perret, D. I., E. T. Rolls, and W. Caan. 1979. Temporal lobe cells of the monkey with visual responses selective for faces. *Neurosci. Lett. Suppl.* **3**: 358.

Pesaro, M., M. Balsamo, G. Gandolfi, and P. Tongiorgi. 1981. Discrimination among different kinds of wate rin juvenile eels, *Anguilla anguilla* (L.). *Monit. Zool. Ital.* (*N.S.*) **15**: 183–191.

Peters, R. P., and L. D. Mech. 1975. Scent-marking in wolves. *Am. Sci.* **63**: 628–637.

Peters. S. S., W. A. Searcy, and P. Marler. 1980. Species song discrimination in choice experiments with territorial male swamp and song sparrows. *Anim. Behav.* **28**: 393–404.

Peterson, N. 1960.   Control of behavior by presentation of an important stimulus. *Science* **132**: 1395–1396.

Petrinovich, L. 1974.   Individual recognition of pup vocalization by northern elephant seal mothers. *Z. Tierpsychol.* **34**: 308–312.

Petrinovich, L., and T. L. Patterson. 1979.   Field studies of habituation: 1. Effect of reproductive condition, number of trials, and different delay intervals on responses of the white-crowned sparrow. *J. Comp. Physiol. Psychol.* **93**: 337–350.

Petrinovich, L., and T. L. Patterson. 1981.   The responses of white-crowned sparrows to songs of different dialects and subspecies. *Z. Tierpsychol.* **57**: 1–14.

Petrinovich, L., and H. V. S. Peeke. 1973.   Habituation to territorial song in the white-crowned sparrow (*Zonotrichia leucophrys*). *Behav. Biol.* **8**: 743–748.

Pfeiffer, W. 1977.   The distribution of fright reaction and alarm substance cells in fishes. *Copeia* **1977**: 653–665.

Pfungstt. O. 1965.   *Clever Hans, the Horse of Mr. Von Osten.* Holt, Rinehart and Winston, New York, 274 + 39 pp.

Picciolo, A. R. 1964.   Sexual and nest discrimination in anabantid fish of the genus *Colisa* and *Trichogaster. Ecol. Mongr.* **34**: 53–76.

Picman, J. 1980.   Behavioral interactions between red-winged blackbirds and long-billed marsh wrens and their role in the evolution of redwinged polygynous mating systems. Ph.D. thesis, Univ. British Columbia, 345 pp.

Pinckney, G. A., and L. E. Anderson. 1967.   Rearing conditions and sociability in *Lebistes reticulatus. Psychon. Sci.* **9**: 591–592.

Pleszczynska, W. 1980.   Interspecific and intraspecific song discrimination by *Zonotrichia albicollis* and *Z. leucophrys. Can. J. Zool.* **58**: 1433–1438.

Poindron, P., and M. J. Carrick. 1976.   Hearing recognition of the lamb by its mother. *Anim. Behav.* **24**: 600–602.

Poindron, P., and P. LeNeindre. 1980.   Endocrine and sensory regulation of maternal behavior in the ewe. *Adv. Stud. Behav.* **11**: 75–119.

Poindron, P., P. LeNeindre, I. Raksanyi, G. Trillat, and P. Orgeur. 1980.   Importance of the characteristics of the young in the manifestation and establishment of maternal behavior in sheep. *Reprod. Nutr. Dev.* **20**: 817–826.

Pollack, G. S. 1982.   Sexual differences in cricket calling song recognition. *J. Comp. Physiol.* **146**: 217–221.

Pollack, G. S., and R. R. Hoy. 1979.   Temporal pattern as a cue for species-specific calling song recognition in crickets. *Science* **204**: 429–432.

Poole, T. B., and H. D. R. Morgan. 1975.   Aggressive behaviour of male mice (*Mus musculus*) towards familiar and unfamiliar opponents. *Anim. Behav.* **23**: 470–479.

Popper, K. R., and J. C. Eccles. 1977.   *The Self and Its Brain.* Springer, New York, 597+ 16 pp.

Porter, F. L. 1979. Social behavior in the leaf-nosed bat, *Carollia perspicillata*. 2. Social communication. *Z. Tierpsychol.* **50**: 1–8.

Porter, R. H., and J. A. Czaplicki. 1974. Responses of water snakes (*Natrix r. rhombifera*) and garter snakes (*Thamnophis sirtalis*) to chemical cues. *Anim. Learn. Behav.* **2**: 129–132.

Porter, R. H., and J. D. Moore. 1982. Human kin recognition by olfactory cues. *Physiol. Behav.* **27**: 493–495.

Porter, R. H., and M. Wyrick. 1979. Sibling recognition in spiny mice (*Acomys cahirinus*): Influence of age and isolation. *Anim. Behav.* **27**: 761–766.

Porter, R. H., M. Wyrick, and J. Pankey. 1978. Sibling recognition in spiny mice (*Acomys cahirinus*). *Behav. Ecol. Sociobiol.* **3**: 61–68.

Porter, R. H., S. A. Cavallavo, and J. D. Moore. 1980. Developmental parameters of mother-offspring interactions in *Acomys cahirinus*. *Z. Tierpsychol.* **53**: 153–170.

Porter, R. H., J. D. Moore, and D. M. White. 1981a. Food sharing by sibling vs nonsibling spiny mice (*Acomys cahirinus*). *Behav. Ecol. Sociobiol.* **8**: 207–212.

Porter, R. H., V. J. Tepper, and D. M. White. 1981b. Experimental influences on the development of huddling preferences and "sibling" recognition in spiny mice. *Devl. Psychobiol.* **14**: 375–382.

Pot, W., W. VanDelden, and J. P. Kruijt. 1980. Genotypic differences in mating success and the maintenance of the alcohol dehydrogenase polymorphism in *Drosophila melanogaster*: No evidence for overdominance or rare genotype mating advantage. *Behav. Genet.* **10**: 43–58.

Potter, J. H. 1949. Dominance relations between different breeds of domestic hens. *Physiol. Zool.* **22**: 261–280.

Potter, J. H., and W. C. Allee. 1953. Some effects of experiences with breeds of *Gallus gallus* L. on behavior of hens towards strange individuals. *Physiol. Zool.* **26**: 147–161.

Power, H. W. 1980. On bluebird cuckoldry and human adultery. *Am. Nat.* **116**: 705–709.

Power, H. W., and C. G. P. Doner. 1980. Expeiments on cuckoldry in the mountain bluebird. *Am. Nat.* **116**: 689–704.

Pratt, C. L., and G. P. Sackett. 1967. Selection of social partners as a function of peer contact during rearing. *Science* **155**: 1133–1135.

Prevet, J. P., and C. D. MacInnes. 1980. Family and other social groups in snow geese. *Wildl. Monogr.* **71**: 46 pp.

Proctor-Gray, E., and R. T. Holmes. 1981. Adaptive significance of delayed attainment of plumage in male American redstarts: Tests of two hypotheses. *Evolution* **35**: 742–751.

Provost, E. 1979. Etude de la fermeture de la societe de Fourmis chez diverses especes de *Leptothorax* et chez *Camponotus lateralis* (Hymenopteres *Formicidae*). *C.R. Acad. Sci. Paris* **288**: 429–432.

Pruzan, A. 1976. Effects of age, rearing and mating experiences on frequency dependent sexual selection in *Drosophila pseudoobscura*. *Evolution* **30**: 130–145.

Pusey, A. E. 1980. Inbreeding avoidance in chimpanzees. *Anim. Behav.* **28**: 543–552.

Pyburn, W. F. 1955. Species discrimination in two sympatric lizards, *Sceloporus olivaceus* and *S. poinsetti*. *Tex. J. Sci.* **7**: 312–315.

Quadagno, D. M., and E. M. Banks. 1970. The effect of reciprocal cross fostering on the behaviour of two species of rodents, *Mus musculus* and *Baiomys taylori ater*. *Anim. Behav.* **18**: 379-390.

Quadagno, D. M., H. E. Shubeita, J. Deck, and D. Francoeur. 1981. Influence of male social contacts, exercise and all-female living conditions on the menstrual cycle. *Psychoneuroendocrinology* **6**: 239–244.

Raber, H. 1948. Analysis des Balzverhalten eines domestizierten Truthahns (*Meleagris*). *Behaviour* **1**: 237–266.

Radesater, T. 1976. Individual sibling recognition in juvenile Canada geese (*Branta canadensis*). *Can. J. Zool.* **54**: 1069–1072.

Radesater, T., and A. Ferno. 1979. On the function of the eye-spots in agonistic behaviour in the fire-mouth cichlid (*Cichlasoma meeki*). *Behav. Proc.* **4**: 5–13.

Raitt, R. J., and J. W. Hardy. 1970. Relationships between two partly sympatric species of thrushes (*Catharus*) in Mexico. *Auk* **87**: 20–57.

Ralls, K. 1971. Mammalian scent marking. *Science* **171**: 443–449.

Ramsay. A. O. 1951. Familial recognition in domestic birds. *Auk* **68**: 1–16.

Ramsay. A. O. 1961. Behaviour of some hybrids in the mallard group. *Anim. Behav.* **9**: 104–105.

Ramsay. A. O., and E. H. Hess. 1954. A laboratory approach to the study of imprinting. *Wilson Bull.* **66**: 196–206.

Randall, J. A. 1981. Olfactory communication at sandbathing loci by sympatric species of kangaroo rats. *J. Mammal.* **62**: 12–19.

Rasa, O. A. E. 1977. The ethology and sociology of the dwarf mongoose (*Helogale undulata rufula*). *Z. Tierpsychol.* **43**: 337–406.

Rashevsky, N. 1960. *Mathematical Biophysics*, 3rd ed., 2 Vols. Dover, New York, 488 + 26, 462 + 12 pp.

Ratner, S. C. 1961. The effects of learning to be submissive on status in the peck order of domestic fowl. *Anim. Behav.* **9**: 34–37.

Ratner, A. M., and H. S. Hoffman. 1974. Evidence for a critical period for imprinting in khaki campbell ducklings (*Anas platyrhynchos domesticus*). *Anim. Behav.* **22**: 249–255.

Raveling, D. G. 1970. Dominance relationships and agonistic behavior of Canada geese in winter. *Behaviour* **37**: 291–319.

Raw, A. 1975. Territoriality and scent marking by *Centris* males (Hymenoptera, Anthophoridae) in Jamaica. *Behaviour* **54**: 311–321.

Rechten, C. 1980. A note on the reproductive colouration of the cichlid fish *Etroplus maculatus*. *Z. Tierpsychol.* **52**: 135–140.

Redican, W. K. 1975. Facial expressions in nonhuman primates. In L.A. Rosenblum (ed.), *Primate Behavior*, Vol. 4, Academic, New York, pp. 103–194.

Reese, E. S. 1975. A comparative field study of the social behavior and related ecology of reef fishes of the family Chaetodontidae. *Z. Tierpsychol.* **37**: 37–61.

Rence, B., and W. Loher. 1977. Contact chemoreceptive sex recognition in the male cricket *Teleogryllus commodus*. *Physiol. Entomol.* **2**: 225–236.

Rensch, B. 1925. Verhalten von Singvogeln bei Aenderung Geleges. *Ornithol. Monatsbr.* **33**: 169–173.

Reynierse, J. H. 1967. Aggregation formulation in planaria, *Phagocata gracilis* and *Cura foremani*: Species differentiation. *Anim. Behav.* **15**: 270–272.

Ribbink, A. J. 1972. The behaviour and brain function of the cichlid fish *Hemihaplochromis philander*. *Zool. Afr.* **7**: 21–41.

Ribbink, A. J. 1977. Cuckoo among Lake Malawi cichlid fish. *Nature (London)* **267**: 243–244.

Ribbink, A. J., A. C. Marsh, B. Marsh, and B. J. Sharp. 1980. Parental behaviour and mixed broods among cichlid fish of Lake Malawi. *S. Afr. J. Zool.* **15**: 1–6.

Richards, D. G. 1979. Recognition of neighbors by associative learning in rufus-sided towhees. *Auk* **96**: 688–693.

Ridley, M., and A. Grafen. 1981. Are green beard genes outlaws? *Anim. Behav.* **29**: 954–955.

Ridley, M., and D. J. Thompson. 1979. Size and mating in *Asellus aquaticus* (Crustacea: Isopoda). *Z. Tierpsychol.* **51**: 380–397.

Riechert, S.E. 1978. Games spiders play: Behavioral variability in territorial disputes. *Behav. Ecol. Sociobiol.* **3**: 135–162.

Rissman, E. F. 1982. Detection of cuckoldry in ring doves. *Anim. Behav.*, in press.

Ritter, F. J. (ed.). 1979. *Chemical Ecology: Odour Communication in Animals*. Elsevier, New York, 427 + 14 pp.

Robel, R. J., and W. B. Ballard, Jr. 1974. Lek social organization and reproductive success in the greater prairie chicken. *Am. Zool.* **14**: 121–128.

Roberts, B. 1940. The breeding behavior of penguins with special reference to *Pygoscelis papua* (Forster). *Br. Graham Land Expedition, 1934–1937, Sci. Rep.* **1**: 195–254.

Robertson, C. M. 1979. Aspects of sexual discrimination by female Siamese fighting fish (*Betta splendens* Regan). *Behaviour* **70**: 323–326.

Robertson, C. M., and P. F. Sale. 1975.   Sexual discrimination in the Siamese fighting fish (*Betta splendens* Regan). *Behaviour* 54: 1–25.

Robinson, M. H., and B. Robinson. 1980.   Comparative studies of the courtship and mating behavior of tropical araneid spiders. *Pac. Insects Monogr.* 36: 218 pp.

Roeder, J. -J. 1978.   Marking behaviour in genets (*G. genetta* L.): Seasonal variations and relation to social status in males. *Behaviour* 67: 149–156.

Roeder, J. -J. 1980.   Marking behaviour and olfactory recognition in genets (*Genetta genetta* L., Carnivora-Viverridae). *Behaviour* 72: 200–210.

Roell, A. 1978.   Social behaviour of the jackdaw, *Corvus monedula*, in relation to its niche. *Behaviour* 64: 1–124.

Roelofs, W. L., and R. T. Carde. 1977.   Responses of lepidoptera to synthetic sex pheromone chemicals and their analogues. *Annu. Rev. Entomol.* 22: 377–405.

Rohwer, S. 1977.   Status signaling in Harris sparrows: Some experiments in deception. *Behaviour* 61: 107–129.

Rohwer, S. 1978a.   Parent cannibalism of offspring and egg raiding as a courtship strategy. *Am. Nat.* 112: 429–440.

Rohwer, S. 1978b.   Passerine subadult plumages and the deceptive acquisition of resources: Test of a critical assumption. *Condor* 80: 173–179.

Rohwer, S., and P. W. Ewald. 1981.   The cost of dominance and advantage of subordination in a badge signaling system. *Evolution* 35: 441–454.

Rohwer, S., and D. M. Niles. 1979.   The subadult plumage of male purple martins: Variability, female mimicry and recent evolution. *Z. Tierpsychol.* 51: 282–300.

Rohwer, S., and F. C. Rohwer. 1978.   Status signalling in Harris sparrows: Experimental deceptions achieved. *Anim. Behav.* 26: 1012–1022.

Rohwer, S., S. D. Fretwell, and R. C. Tuckfield. 1976.   Distress screams as a measure of kinship in birds. *Am. Midl. Nat.* 96: 418–430.

Rohwer, S., S. D. Fretwell, and D. M. Niles. 1980.   Delayed maturation in passerine plumages and the deceptive acquisition of resources. *Am. Nat.* 115: 400–437.

Rooke, I. 1979.   The social behaviour of the honeyeater, *Phydidonyris novaehollandiae*. Ph.D. thesis, University of Western Australia. 233 + 8 pp.

Ropartz, P. 1968.   The relation between olfactory stimulation and aggressive behaviour in mice. *Anim. Behav.* 16: 97–100.

Roper, T. J., and E. Polioudakis. 1977.   The behaviour of Mongolian gerbils in a semi-natural environment, with special reference to ventral marking, dominance and sociality. *Behaviour* 61: 207–237.

Rose, R., and K. Casper. 1980.   Pheromonal recognition of the female crayfish, *Procambarus clarkii. Am. Zool.* 20: 853 (Abstr. 757).

Rosenblatt, J. S. 1967.   Nonhormonal basis of maternal behavior in the rat. *Science* **156**: 1512–1514.

Rosenblum, L. A., and S. Alpert. 1977.   Response to mother and stranger: A first step in socialization. In S. Chevalier-Skolnikoff and F.E. Poirier (eds.), *Primate Bio-social Development*, Garland, New York, Chap. 15, pp. 463–477.

Rosenfeld, S. A., and G. W. VanHoesen. 1979.   Face recognition in the rhesus monkey. *Neuropsychologia* **17**: 503–509.

Ross, N. M., and G. J. Gamboa. 1981.   Nestmate discrimination in social wasps (*Polistes metricus*, Hymenoptera: Vespidae). *Behav. Ecol. Sociobiol.* **9**: 163–165.

Rossetto, K., M. A. Roy, and J. LeRoy. 1980.   Innate predisposition for a species identity in *Cavia porcellus*? *Am. Zool.* **20**: 854 (Abstr. 762).

Roth, L. M., and E. R. Willis. 1952.   A study of cockroach behaviour. *Am. Midl. Nat.* **47**: 66–129.

Rothman, R. J., and L. D. Mech. 1979.   Scent-marking in lone wolves and newly formed pairs. *Anim. Behav.* **27**: 750–760.

Rothstein, S. I. 1975.   Mechanisms of avian egg-recognition: Do birds know their own eggs? *Anim. Behav.* **23**: 268–278.

Rothstein, S. I. 1978.   Mechanisms of avian egg-recognition: Additional evidence for learned components. *Anim. Behav.* **26**: 671–677.

Rothstein, S. I. 1980.   Reciprocal altruism and kin selection are not clearly separable phenomena. *J. Theor. Biol.* **87**: 255–261.

Rowell, T. E. 1961.   Maternal behaviour in non-maternal golden hamsters (*Mesocricetus auratus*). *Anim. Behav.* **9**: 11–15.

Rowell, T. E. 1972.   Agonistic sounds of the rhesus monkey (*Macaca mulatta*). *Zool. Soc. Lond. Symp.* **8**: 91–96.

Rowley, I. 1980.   Parent–offspring recognition in a cockatoo, the galah, *Cacatua roseicapilla*. *Aust. J. Zool.* **28**: 445–456.

Roy, M. A. (ed.), 1980.   *Species Identity and Attachment*. Garland, New York, 414 + 13 pp.

Ruddy, L. L. 1980.   Discrimination among colony mates' anogenital odors by guinea pigs (*Cavia procellus*). *J. Comp. Physiol. Psychol.* **94**: 767–774.

Russell, M. J. 1976.   Human olfactory communication. *Nature (London)* **260**: 520–522.

Russock, H. I., and M. W. Schein. 1977.   Effect of age and experience on the filial behaviour of *Tilapia mossambica* fry (Pisces: Cichlidae). *Behaviour* **61**: 276–303.

Russock, H. I., and M. W. Schein. 1978.   Effect of socialization on adult social preferences in *Tilapia mossambica* (*Sarotherodon mossambicus*); Pisces: Cichlidae. *Anim. Behav.* **26**: 148–159.

Rust, M. K. 1976.   Quantitative analysis of male responses released by female sex pheromones in *Periplaneta americana*. *Anim. Behav.* **24**: 681–685.

Rutowski, R. L. 1981.   Sexual discrimination using visual cues in the checkered white butterfly (*Pieris protodice*). *Z. Tierpsychol.* **55**: 325–334.

Ryan, M .J. 1980a.   Female mate choice in a neotropical frog. *Science* **209**: 523–525.

Ryan, M. J. 1980b.   The reproductive behavior of the bullfrog (*Rana catesbeiana*). *Copeia* **1980**: 108–114.

Saglio, P. 1979.   Interactions sociales chez les poissons: Les pheromones. *Fran. Piscic. Bull.* **273**: 173–184.

Sales, G. D. 1972a   Ultrasound and aggressive behaviour in rats and other small mammals. *Anim. Behav.* **20**: 88–101.

Sales, G. D. 1972b.   Ultrasound and mating behaviour in rodents with some observations on other behavioural situations. *J. Zool.* **168**: 149–164.

Salzen, E. A. 1970.   Imprinting and environmental learning. In L. R. Aronson et al. (eds.), *Development and Evolution of Behavior*, Freeman, San Francisco, pp. 158–178.

Salzen, E. A. and C. C. Meyer. 1967.   Imprinting: Reversal of a preference established during the critical period. *Nature (London)* **215**: 785–786.

Salzen, E. A., and W. Sluckin. 1959.   The incidence of the following response and the duration of responsiveness in domestic fowl. *Anim. Behav.* **7**: 172–179.

Sambraus, H. H., and D. Sambraus. 1975.   Pragung von Nutztieren auf Menschen. *Z. Tierpsychol.* **38**: 1–17.

Samson, F. B. 1978.   Vocalizations of Cassin's finch in northern Utah. *Condor* **80**: 203–210.

Sanavio, E., and U. Savardi. 1980.   Observational learning in Japanese quail. *Behav. Proc.* **5**: 355–361.

Sandegren, F. E. 1976.   Agonistic behavior in the male Northern elephant seal. *Behaviour* **57**: 136–158.

Schaffer, H. R., and P. E. Emerson. 1964.   The development of social attachments in infancy. *Soc. Res. Child Dev. Monogr.* **29**(3): 77 pp.

Schaller, G. B. 1972.   *The Serengeti Lion.* University of Chicago Press, Chicago, 480+ 12 pp.

Schein, M. W. 1963.   On the irreversibility of imprinting. *Z. Tierpsychol.* **20**: 462–467.

Schein, M. W., and E. B. Hale. 1959.   The effect of early social experience on male sexual behavior of androgen injected turkeys. *Anim. Behav.* **7**: 189–200.

Schilcher, F. von. 1976.   The function of pulse song and sine song in the courtship of *Drosophila melanogaster*. **Anim. Behav.** **24**: 622–625.

Schilcher, F. von, and M. Dow. 1977.   Courtship behavior in *Drosophila*. Sexual isolation or sexual selection? *Z. Tierpsychol.* **43**: 304–310.

Schilling, A. 1976. A study of marking behaviour in *Lemur catta*. In R. D. Martin et al. (eds.), *Prosimian Behaviour*, Duckworth, London, pp. 347–362.

Schjelderup-Ebbe, T. 1921. Beitrage zur Sozialpsychologie des Haushuhns. *Z. Psychol.* **88**: 225–252.

Schjelderup-Ebbe, T. 1922. Soziale Verhaltnisse bei Vogeln. *Z. Psychol.* **90**: 106–107.

Schjelderup-Ebbe, T. 1935. Social behavior in birds. In C. Murchison (ed.), *Murchison's Handbook of Social Psychology*, Clark University Press, Worcester, Mass., Chap. 20, pp. 947–972.

Schleidt, M. 1980. Personal odor and nonverbal communication. *Ethol. Sociobiol.* **1**: 225–231.

Schleidt, W. M. 1964. Uber die Spontaneitat von Erbkoordinationen. *Z. Tierpsychol.* 21: 235–256.

Schleidt, W. M. 1976. On individuality: The constituents of distinctiveness. In P. P. G. Gateson and P. H. Klopfer (eds.), *Perspectives in Ethology*, Vol. 2, Plenum, New York, Chap. 8, pp. 299–310.

Schleidt, W. M., M. Schleidt, and M. Magg. 1960. Storung der Mutter-kind-Beziehung bei Truthuhnern durch Gehorverlust. *Behaviour* **16**: 254–260.

Schloeth, R. 1958. Über die Mutter-kind-Beziehungen beim halbwilden Camargue-Rid. *Saugetierkund. Mitt.* **6**: 145–150.

Schmale, M. C. 1981. Sexual selection and reproductive success in males of the bicolor damselfish, *Eupomacentrus partitus* (Pisces: Pomacentridae). *Anim. Behav.* **29**: 1172–1184.

Schmutz, J. K., S. M. Schmutz, and D. A. Boag. 1980. Coexistence of three species of hawks (*Buteo* spp.) in the prairie-parkland ecotone. *Can. J. Zool.* **58**: 1075–1089.

Schneirla, T. C. 1941. Social organization in insects as related to individual function. *Psychol. Rev.* **48**: 465–486.

Schneirla, T. C. 1971. *Army Ants* (H. R. Topoff, ed.), Freeman, San Francisco, 349 + 20 pp.

Schneirla, T. C., and J. S. Rosenblatt. 1961. Behavioral organization and genesis of the social bond in insects and mammals. *Am. J. Orthopsychiat.* **31**: 223–253.

Schubert, G. 1971. Experimentelle Untersuchungen über die art kennzeichnenden Parameter im Gesang des Zilpzalps, *Phylloscopus c. collybita* (Veillot). *Behaviour* **38**: 289–314.

Schulman, A. H. 1972. Transfer of behavior controlled by an imprinted stimulus via brain homogenate injections in turkeys. *Psychon. Sci.* **27**: 48–50.

Schultze-Westrum, T. 1965. Innerartliche Verstandigung durch Dufte beim Gleitbeutler *Petaurus breviceps papuanus* Thomas (Marsupialia, Phalangeridae). *Z. Vergl. Physiol.* **50**: 151–220.

Schutz, F. 1965. Sexuelle Pragung bei Anatiden. *Z. Tierpsychol.* **22**: 50–103.

Schutz, F. 1971. Pragung des Sexualverhaltens von Enten und Gansen durch

Sozialeindrucke wahrend der Jugendphase. *J. Neuro-visc. Rel. Suppl.* **10**: 339–357.

Schwagmeyer, P. L. 1979. The Bruce effect: An evaluation of male/female advantages. *Am. Nat.* **114**: 932–938.

Scott, D. K. 1980. Functional aspects of the pair bond in winter in Bewick's swans (*Cygnus columbianus bewickii*). *Behav. Ecol. Sociobiol.* **7**: 323–327.

Scott, J. P. (ed.). 1978. *Critical Periods.* Dowden, Hutchinson, & Ross, Stroudsberg, Penn., 383 + 18 pp.

Scott, J. P., and J. L., Fuller. 1974. *Dog Behavior. The Genetic Basis.* University of Chicago Press, Chicago, 468 + 18 pp.

Scott, J. P., J. M. Stewart, and V. J. DeGhett. 1974. Critical periods in the organization of systems. *Dev. Psychobiol.* **7**: 489–513.

Scudo, F. 1967. L'accoppiamento assortativo basato sul fenotipo di parenti. Alcune conseguenze in popolazioni. *Inst. Lombardo Rend. Sc.* **101B**: 435–455.

Searcy, W. A., and P. Marler. 1981. A test for responsiveness to song structure and programming in female sparrows. *Science* **213**: 926–928.

Searcy, W. A., P. Marler, and S. S. Peters. 1981a. Species song discrimination in adult female song and swamp sparrows. *Anim. Behav.* **29**: 997–1003.

Searcy, W. A., P. D. McArthur, S. S. Peters, and P. Marler. 1981b. Response of male song and swamp sparrows to neighbor, stranger, and self songs. *Behaviour* **77**: 152–163.

Seibt, U., and W. Wickler. 1972. Individuen-Erkennen und Partnerbevorzugung bei der Garnele *Hymenocera picta* Dana. *Naturwissenschaften* **59**: 40–41.

Seibt, U., and W. Wickler. 1977. Duettieren als Revier-Anzeige bei Vogeln. *Z. Tierpsychol.* **43**: 180–187.

Seibt, U., and W. Wickler. 1979. The biological significance of the pair-bond in the shrimp *Hymenocera picta. Z. Tierpsychol.* **50**: 166–179.

Seiger, M. B. 1967. A computer simulation study of the influence of imprinting on population structure. *Am. Nat.* **101**: 47–57.

Seiger, M. B., and R. D. Dixon. 1970. A computer simulation study of the effects of two behavioral traits on the genetic structure of semi-isolated populations. *Evolution* **24**: 90–97.

Seitz, A. 1940. Die Paarbildung bei einigen Cichliden. 1. Die Paarbildung bei *Astatotilapia strigigena* Pfeffer. *Z. Tierpsychol.* **4**: 40–84.

Serpell, J. 1981a. Duets, greetings and triumph ceremonies: Analogous displays in the parrot genus *Trichoglossus. Z. Tierpsychol.* **55**: 268–283.

Serpell, J. A. 1981b. Duetting in birds and primates: A question of function. *Anim. Behav.* **29**: 963–965.

Serrier, J. 1979. Electric organ discharge specificity and social recognition in mormyrids (Pisces). *Neurosci. Lett. Suppl.* **3**: 62.

Sexton, O. J., and E. H. Hess. 1968. A pheromone-like dispersant affecting the local distribution of the European house cricket, *Acheta domestica. Biol. Bull.* **134:** 490–502.

Shaw, E. 1960. The development of schooling behavior in fishes. *Physiol. Zool.* **33:** 79–86.

Shaw, E. 1961. The development of schooling in fishes. 2. *Physiol. Zool.* **34:** 263–272.

Shaw, E. 1962. Environmental conditions and the appearance of sexual behavior in the platyfish. In E. L. Bliss (ed.), *Roots of Behavior,* Harper, New York, Chap. 8, pp. 123–141.

Sherman, P. W. 1977. Nepotism and the evolution of alarm calls. *Science* **197:** 1246–1253.

Sherman, P. W. 1980. The limits of ground squirrel nepotism. In G. W. Barlow and J. Silverberg (eds.), *Sociobiology: Beyond Nature/Nurture?,* Am. Assoc. Adv. Sci., Washington, D.C., Chap. 20, pp. 505–544.

Sherman, P. W. 1981. Kinship, demography, and Belding's ground squirrel nepotism. *Behav. Ecol. Sociobiol.* **8:** 251–259.

Sherrod, L. 1974. The role of sibling associations in the formation of social and sexual companion preferences in ducks (*Anas platyrhynchos*): An investigation of the 'primacy versus recency' question. *Z. Teirpsychol.* **34:**247–264.

Shillito Walser, E. 1980. Maternal recognition and breed identity in lambs living in a mixed flock of Jacob, Clun Forest and Dalesbred sheep. *Appl. Anim. Ethol.* **6:** 221–231.

Shillito Walser, E., and G. Alexander. 1980. Mutual recognition between ewes and lambs. *Reprod. Nutr. Devel.* **20:** 807–816.

Shillito Walser, E., P. Hague, and E. Walters. 1981. Vocal recognition of recorded lambs' voices by ewes of three breeds of sheep. *Behaviour* **78:** 260–272.

Shiovitz, K. A. 1975. The process of species-specific song recognition by the indigo bunting, *Passerina cyanea,* and its relationship to the organization of avian acoustical behavior. *Behaviour* **55:** 128–179.

Shiovitz, K. A., and R. E. Lemon. 1980. Species identification of song by indigo buntings as determined by responses to computer generated sounds. *Behaviour* **74:** 167–199.

Shipley, C., M. Hines, and J. S. Buchwald. 1981. Individual differences in threat calls of northern elephant seals. *Anim. Behav.* **29:** 12–19.

Shipley, W. U. 1963. The demonstration in the domestic guinea pig of a process resembling classical imprinting. *Anim. Behav.* **11:** 470–474.

Shorey, H. H. 1973. Behavioral responses to insect pheromones. *Annu. Rev. Entomol.* **18:** 349–380.

Shorey, H. H. 1976. *Animal Communication by Pheromones.* Academic, New York, 167 + 8 pp.

Shorey, H. H., and R. J. Bartell. 1970. Role of a volatile female sex pheromone in stimulating male courtship behavior in *Drosophila melanogaster*. *Anim. Behav.* **18:** 159–164.

Shugart, G. W. 1977. The development of chick recognition by adult Caspian Terns. *Colonial Waterbird Gp. Conf. Proc.*, pp. 110–117.

Shuvalov, V. F., and A. V. Popov. 1973a. Study of the significance of some parameters of calling signals of male crickets *Gryllus bimaculatus* for phonotaxis of females. *J. Evol. Biochem. Physiol.* **9:** 152–156.

Shuvalov, V. F., and A. V. Popov. 1973b. The importance of rhythmic calling song pattern of males of the genus *Gryllus* for phonotaxis of females. *Zool. Zh.* **52:** 1179–1185.

Siegel, P. B., and D. C. Hurst. 1962. Social interactions among females in dubbed and undubbed flocks. *Poult. Sci.* **41:** 141–145.

Simpson, J. 1979. The existence and physical properties of pheromones by which worker honeybees recognize queens. *J. Apicult. Res.* **18:** 233–249.

Simpson, M. J. A. 1968. The display of the Siamese fighting fish, *Betta splendens*. *Anim. Behav. Monogr.* **1:** 1–73.

Simpson, M. J. A. 1973. Social displays and the recognition of individuals. In P. P. G. Bateson and P. H. Klopfer (eds.), *Perspectives in Ethology*, Vol. 1, Plenum, New York, Chap. 7, pp. 225–279.

Sinnock, P. 1970. Frequency dependence and mating behavior in *Tribolium castaneum*. *Am. Nat.* **104:** 469–476.

Sjolander, S., and A. Ferno. 1973. Sexual imprinting on another species in a cichlid fish, *Haplochromis burtoni*. *Rev. Comp. Anim.* **7:** 77–81.

Skutch, A. F. 1945. Life history of the allied woodhewer. *Condor* **47:** 85–94.

Slater, A. E. 1951. Biological problems of space flight. A report of Professor Haldane's lecture to the Society on April 7, 1951. *Br. Interplanetary Soc. J.* **10:** (July 4, 1951): 154–158.

Slater, P. J. B. 1978. Beau Geste has problems. *Anim. Behav.* **26:** 304.

Slater, P. J. B. 1981a. Chaffinch song repertoires: Observations, experiments and a discussion of their significance. *Z. Tierpsychol.* **56:** 1–24.

Slater, P. J. B. 1981b. Individual differences in animal behavior. In P. P. G. Bateson and P. H. Klopfer (eds.), *Perspectives in Ethology*, Vol. 4, Plenum, New York, Chap. 2, pp. 35–49.

Slobodkin, L. B. 1978. Is history a consequence of evolution? In P. P. G. Bateson and P. H. Klopfer (eds.), *Perspectives in Ethology*, Vol. 3, Plenum, New York, Chap. 10, pp. 233–255.

Sluckin, W. 1964. *Imprinting and Early Learning*. Methuen, London, 147 + 10 pp.

Sluckin, W. 1970. *Early Learning in Man and Animal*. Allen & Unwin, London, 123 pp.

Smith, D. G. 1972. The role of the epaulets in the red-winged blackbird (*Agelaius phoeniceus*) social system. *Behaviour* **41:** 251–268.

Smith, D. G. 1976. An experimental analysis of the function of red-winged blackbird song. *Behaviour* **56:** 136–156.

Smith, D. G. 1979. Male singing ability and territory integrity in red-winged blackbirds (*Agelaius phoeniceus*). *Behaviour* **68:** 197–206.

Smith, F. V. 1960. Towards a definition of the stimulus situation for the approach response of the domestic chick. *Anim. Behav.* **8:** 197–200.

Smith, F. V. 1965. Instinct and learning in the attachment of lamb and ewe. *Anim. Behav.* **13:** 84–86.

Smith, F. V., and P. A. Hoyes. 1961. Properties of the visual stimuli for the approach response in the domestic chick. *Anim. Behav.* **9:** 159–166.

Smith, F. V., C. Van-Toller, and T. Boyes. 1966. The critical period in the attachment of lambs and ewes. *Anim. Behav.* **14:** 120–125.

Smith, N. G. 1966. Evolution of some arctic gulls (*Larus*): An experimental study of isolating mechanisms. *Am. Ornithol. Union Monogr.* **4:** 99 pp.

Smith, R. J. F. 1982. The adaptive significance of the alarm substance–fright reaction system. In T. J. Hara (ed.), *Chemoreception in Fishes*, Elsevier, Amsterdam, Chap. 18, pp. 327–342.

Smith, W. J. 1977. *The Behavior of Communicating.* Harvard University Press, Cambridge, Mass., 545 + 8 pp.

Smith, W. J., S. L. Smith, E. C. Oppenheimer, J. G. de Villa, and F. A. Ulmeni. 1973. Behavior of a captive population of black-tailed prairie-dogs. Annual cycle of social behavior. *Behaviour* **46:** 189–220.

Snapp, B. D. 1969. Recognition of maternal calls by parentally naive *Gallus gallus* chicks. *Anim. Behav.* **17:** 440–445.

Snow, B. K. 1963. The behaviour of the shag. *Br. Birds* **56:** 77–103, 164–186.

Snowden, C. T., and J. Cleveland. 1980. Individual recognition of contact calls by pygmy marmosets. *anim. Behav.* **28:** 717–727.

Snyder, N. F. R., and H. A. Snyder. 1971. Pheromone-mediated behaviour of *Fasciolaria tulipa. Anim. Behav.* **19:** 257–268.

Snyder, N., and H. Snyder. 1978. Alarm substance of *Diadema antillarum. Science* **168:** 276–278.

Sokolov, V. E., K. L. Lyapunova, A. V. Surov, and S. A. Krashnin. 1979. The dependence of social behaviour of the Norway rats (*Rattus norvegicus*) from sex and physiological state of the "stranger." *Zool. Zh.* **58:** 724–730.

Solignac, M. 1981. Isolating mechanisms and modalities of speciation in the *Jaera albifrons* species complex (Crustacea, Isopoda). *Syst. Zool.* **30:** 387–405.

Sonneman, P., and S. Sjolander. 1977. Effects of cross fostering on the sexual imprinting of the female zebra finch *Taeniopygia guttata. Z. Tierpsychol.* **45:** 337–348.

Spalding, D. 1873.   Instinct with original observations on young animals. *Macmillan's Mag.* **27**: 282–293. (Reprinted in 1954 *Br. J. Anim. Behav.* **2**: 1–11.)

Spanier, E. 1979.   Aspects of species recognition by sound in four species of damselfishes, genus *Eupomacentrus* (Pisces: Pomacentridae). *Z. Tierpsychol.* **51**: 301–316.

Sparling, D. W. 1981.   Communication in prairie grouse. 2. Ethological isolating mechanisms. *Behav. Neural. Biol.* **32**: 487–503.

Spiess, E. B., and H. L. Carson. 1981.   Sexual selection in *Drosophila silvestris* of Hawaii. *Proc. Natl. Acad. Sci., U.S.A.* **78**: 3088–3092.

Spiess, E. B., and J. F. Kruckeberg. 1980.   Minority advantage of certain eye color mutants of *Drosophila melanogaster*. 2. A behavioral basis. *Am. Nat.* **115**: 307–327.

Spiess, E. B., and W. A. Schwer. 1978.   Minority mating advantage of certain eye color mutants of *Drosophila melanogaster*. 1. Multiple-choice and single-female tests. *Behav. Genet.* **8**: 155–168.

Spieth, H. T. 1958.   Behavior and isolating mechanisms. In A. Roe and G. G. Simpson (eds.), *Behavior and Evolution*, Yale University Press, New Haven, Conn., pp. 363–389.

Spieth, H. T. 1974.   Courtship behavior in *Drosophila. Annu. Rev. Entomol.* **19**: 385–405.

Spooner, J. D. 1964.   The Texas bush katydid—Its sounds and their significance. *Anim. Behav.* **12**: 235–244.

Stacey, P. B., and D. Chiszar. 1978.   Body color pattern and the aggressive behavior of male pumpkinseed sunfish (*Lepomis gibbosus*) during the reproductive season. *Behaviour* **64**: 271–297.

Steele, R. G., and M. H. A. Keenleyside. 1971.   Mate selection in two species of sunfish (*Lepomis gibbosus* and *L. megalotis peltastes*). *Can. J. Zool.* **49**: 1541–1548.

Stehn, R. A., and M. E. Richmond. 1975.   Male induced pregnancy termination in the prairie vole, *Microtus ochrogaster. Science* **187**: 1211–1213.

Stein, R. C. 1963.   Isolating mechanisms between populations of Traill's flycatchers. *Proc. Am. Philos. Soc.* **107**: 21–50.

Stevenson, J. G., R. E. Hutchison, J. Hutchison, B. C. R. Bertram, and W. H. Thorpe. 1970.   Individual recognition by auditory cues in the Common tern (*Sterna hirundo*). *Nature (London)* **226**: 562–563.

Stout, J. F. 1963.   The significance of sound production during the reproductive behaviour of *Notropis analostanus* (family Cyprinidae). *Anim. Behav.* **11**: 83–92.

Stout, J., and R. McGhee. 1980.   Preferences for parameters of the calling song by female crickets *Acheta domesticus. Am. Zool.* **20**: 853 (Abstr. 758).

Strassmann, B. I. 1981. Sexual selection, paternal care, and concealed ovulation inhumans. *Ethol. Sociobiol.* **2**: 31–40.

Stratton, G. E. 1979. Courtship behavior, acoustic communication, and reproductive isolation in two sibling species of wolf spiders (Araneae: Lycosidae). M. Sc. thesis, University of Cincinnati, Ohio.

Stratton, G. E., and G. W. Uetz. 1981. Acoustic communication and reproductive isolation in two species of wolf spiders. *Science* **214**: 575–577.

Strayer, F. F. 1976. Learning and imitation as a function of social status in macaque monkeys (*Macaca nemestrina*). *Anim. Behav.* **24**: 835–848.

Struhsaker, T. T. 1967. Auditory communication among vervet monkeys (*Cercopithecus aethiops*). In S. A. Altmann (ed.), *Social Communication among Primates*, University of Chicago Press, Chicago, Chap. 16, pp. 281–324.

Tavolga, W. N. 1958. The significance of underwater sounds produced by males of the gobiid fish, *Bathygobius soporator*. *Physiol. Zool.* **31**: 259–271.

Tavolga, W. N. (ed.). 1976. *Sound Reception in Fishes*. Benchmark Papers in Animal Behavior, Vol. 7. Dowden, Hutchinson & Ross, Stroudsberg, Penn., 317 + 13 pp.

Tavolga, W. N. (ed.). 1977. *Sound Production in Fishes*. Benchmark Papers in Animal Behavior, Vol. 9. Dowden, Hutchinson & Ross, Stroudsberg, Penn., 363 + 13 pp.

Taylor, P. D., and G. C. Williams. 1981. Commentary: On the modeling of sexual selection. *Q. Rev. Biol.* **56**: 305–313.

Terami, H. 1977. Analyses of the social hierarchy in the cichlid, *Pelmatochromis pulcher*. 5. Recognition of the sexual partner. *Zool. Mag.* **87**: 520.

Terhune, J. M., M. E. Terhune, and K. Ronald. 1979. Location and recognition of pups by adult female harp seals. *Appl. Anim. Ethol.* **5**: 375–380.

Theberge, J. B., and J. B. Falls. 1967. Howling as a means of communication in timber wolves. *Am. Zool.* **7**: 331–338.

Thielcke, G. 1962. Versuche mit Klangattrappen zur Klarung der Verwandtschaft der Baumlaufer *Certhia familiaris* L., *C. brachydactyla* Brehm und *C. americana* Bonaparte. *J. Ornithol.* **103**: 266–271.

Thielcke, G. 1969. Geographic variation in bird vocalizations. In R. A. Hinde (ed.), *Bird Vocalizations*, Cambridge University Press, Cambridge, Chap. 14, pp. 311–339.

Thielcke, G., and H. Thielcke. 1970. Die sozialen Funktionen verschiedener Gesangsformern des Sonnenvogels (*Leiothrix lutea*). *Z. Tierpsychol.* **27**: 177–185.

Thielcke-Poltz, H., and G. Thielcke. 1960. Akustisches Lernen verschieden alter schallisolierter Amseln (*Turdus merula* L.) und die Entwicklung erlernter

Motive ohne und mit kunstlichen Einfluss von Testosteron. *Z. Tierpsychol.* **17:** 211–244.

Thiessen, D. D. 1971. Reply to Wilcock on gene action and behavior. *Psychol. Bull.* **75:** 103–105.

Thiessen, D. D., and B. Gregg. 1980. Human assortative mating and genetic equilibrium: An evolutionary perspective. *Ethol. Sociobiol.* **1:** 111–140.

Thiessen, D. D., and M. Rice. 1976. Mammalian scent gland marking and social beahvior. *Psychol. Bull.* **83:** 505–539.

Thiessen, D. D., and P. Yahr. 1977. *The Gerbil in Behavioral Investigations: Mechanisms of Territoriality and Olfactory Communication.* University of Texas Press, Austin, 224 + 21 pp.

Thiessen, D. D., G. Lindzey, S. L. Blum, and P. Wallace. 1970. Social interactions and scent marking in the mongolian gerbil (*Meriones unguiculatus*). *Anim. Behav.* **19:** 505–513.

Thompson, D. H., and J. T. Emlen. 1968. Parent-chick individual recognition in the Adelie penguin. *Antarct. J.* **3:** 132.

Thompson, D. J., and J. T. Manning. 1981. Mate selection by *Asellus* (Crustacea: Isopoda). *Behaviour* **78:** 178–187.

Thompson, D. W. 1961. *On Growth and Form,* 2nd ed. Macmillan, New York, 1116 + 4 pp.

Thompson, N. S. 1969. Individual identification and temporal patterning in the cawing of common crows. *Commun. Behav. Biol.* 09690044.

Thompson, W. L. 1969. Song recognition by territorial male buntings (*Passerina*). *Anim. Behav.* **17:** 658–663.

Thornhill, R. 1980. Sexual selection in the black-tipped hanging fly. *Sci. Am.* **242(6):** 162–172.

Thorp, J. H., and K. S. Ammerman. 1978. Chemical communication and agonism in the crayfish, *Procambarus acutus acutus. Am. Midl. Nat.* **100:** 471–474.

Thorpe, W. H. 1963. *Learning and Instinct in Animals,* 2nd ed. Harvard University Press, Cambridge, Mass., 558 + 10 pp.

Thorpe, W. H. 1972. Duetting and antiphonal songs in birds. *Behav. Suppl.* **18:** 197 + 10 pp.

Thorpe, W. H., and J. Hall-Craggs. 1976. Sound production and perception in birds as related to the general principles of pattern perception. In P. P. G. Bateson and R. A. Hinde (eds.), *Growing Points in Ethology,* Cambridge University Press, Cambridge, Chap. 5, pp. 171–189.

Thresher, R. E. 1976. Field experiments on species recognition by the threespot damselfish *Eupomacentrus planifrons* (Pisces: Pomacentridae). *Anim. Behav.* **24:** 562–569.

Thresher, R. E. 1979. The role of individual recognition in the territorial behaviour of the threespot damselfish, *Eupomacentrus planifrons*. *Mar. Behav. Physiol.* **6**: 83–93.

Tinbergen, N. 1935. Field observations of East Greenland birds. 1. The behaviour of the red-necked phalarope (*Phalaropus lobatus* L.) in spring. *Ardea* **24**: 1–42.

Tinbergen, N. 1939. Field observations of East Greenland birds. 2. The behavior of the snow bunting (*Plectrophenax nivalis subnivalis* (Brehm)) in spring. *Linn. Soc. N.Y. Trans.* **5**: 1–94.

Tinbergen, N. 1951. *The Study of Instinct*. Oxford University Press, Oxford, 228 + 12 pp.

Tinbergen, N. 1953. *The Herring Gull's World*. Collins, London, 255 + 16 pp.

Tinbergen, N., G. J. Brockhuysen, F. Feekes, J. C. W. Houghton, H. Kruuk, and E. Szulc. 1962. Egg shell removal by the black-headed gull, *Larus ridibundus* L.; a behaviour component of camouflage. *Behaviour* **19**: 74–117.

Tobin, T. R. 1981. Pheromone orientation: Role of internal control mechanisms. *Science* **214**: 1147–1149.

Todd, J. H. 1971. The chemical language of fishes. *Sci. Am.* **224(5)**: 98–108.

Todd, J. H., J. Atema, and J. E. Bardach. 1967. Chemical communication in social behavior of a fish, the yellow bullhead (*Ictalurus natalis*). *Science* **158**: 672–673.

Todd, J. T., L. S. Mark, R. E. Shaw, and J. B. Pittenger. 1980. The perception of human growth. *Sci. Am.* **242(2)**: 132–144.

Todt, D. 1975. Effect of territorial conditions on the maintenance of pair contract in duetting birds. *Experientia* **31**: 648–649.

Tomlinson, K. A., and E. O. Price. 1980. The establishment and reversibility of species affinities in domestic sheep and goats. *Anim. Behav.* **28**: 325–330.

Traniello, J. F. A. 1980. Colony specificity in the trail pheromone of an ant. *Naturwissenschaften* **67**: 361–362.

Tretzel, E. 1965. Artkennzeichnende und reaktionsauslosende Komponeten im Gesang der Heidelerche (*Lullula arborea*). *Dtsch. Zool. Ges. Jena Verh.* **1965**: 367–380.

Trillmich, F. 1976. Learning experiments on individual recognition in budgerigars (*Melopsittacus undulatus*). *Z. Tierpsychol.* **41**: 372–395.

Trillmich, F. 1981. Mutual mother-pup recognition in Galapagos fur seals and sea lions: Cues used and functional significance. *Behaviour* **78**: 21–42.

Trivers, R. L. 1971. The evolution of reciprocal evolution. *Q. Rev. Biol.* **46**: 35–57.

Tschantz, B. 1968. Trottellummen. *Z. Tierpsychol. Suppl.* **4**: 103 pp.

Tschanz, B. 1979. Helfer-Beziehungen bei Trottellummen. *Z. Tierpsychol.* **49**: 10–34.

Turner, J. R. G. 1978. Why male butterflies are non-mimetic: Natural selection, sexual selection, group selection, modification and sieving. *Linn. Soc. Biol. J.* **10**: 385–432.

Tyack, P. 1981. Interactions between singing Hawaiian humpback whales and conspecifics nearby. *Behav. Ecol. Sociobiol.* **8**: 105–116.

Uetz, G. W., and G. Denterlein. 1979. Courtship behavior, habitat, and reproductive isolation in *Schizocosa rovneri*. Uetz and Dondale (Araneae: Lycosidae). *J. Arachnol.* **7**: 121–128.

Usuki, H. 1977. Underwater observations and experiments on pair formation and related behaviours of the apogonid fish *Apogon notatus* (Houttuyn). *Kyoto Univ. Seto Mar. Biol. Lab.* **23**: 223–243.

VanHooff, J. A. R. A. M. 1967. The facial displays of the catarrhine monkeys and apes. In D. Morris (ed.), *Primate Ethology*, Aldine, Chicago, Chap. 2, pp. 7–68.

VanNoordwijk, A. J., and W. Scharloo. 1981. Inbreeding in an island population of the great tit. *Evolution* **35**: 674–688.

VanRhijn, J. G. 1973. Behavioural dimorphism in male ruffs, *Philomachus pugnax* (L.). *Behaviour* **47**: 153–229.

VanRhijn, J. G. 1980. Communication by agonistic displays: A discussion. *Behaviour* **74**: 284–293.

Van Rhiijn, J. G., and R. Vodegel. 1980. Being honest about one's intentions: An evolutionarily stable strategy for animal conflicts. *J. Theor. Biol.* **85**: 623–641.

Van Someren, V. G. L. 1944. Some aspects of behaviour of nesting birds. *Ibis* **86**: 226–228.

VanTets, G. F. 1965. A comparative study of some social communication patterns in the pelecaniformes. *Am. Ornithol. Union Monogr.* **2**: 88 pp.

VanValen, L. 1973. A new evolutionary law. *Evol. Theory* **1**: 1–30.

Vaz-Ferreira, R., and F. Achaval. 1979. Relacion y reconcimiento materno-filial en *Otaria flavescens* (Shaw) 'lobo de un pelo', y reacciones de los machos subadultos onte los cachorros. *Acta Zool. Lilloana* **35**: 295–302.

Vehrencamp, S. L. 1977. Relative fecundity and parental effort in communally nesting anis, *Crotophaga sulcirostris*. *Science* **197**: 403–405.

Verberne, G. 1976. Chemocommunication among domestic cats, mediated by the olfactory and vomeronasal senses. 2. The relation between the function of Jacobson's organ (vomeronasal organ) and flehmen behaviour. *Z. Tierpsychol.* **42**: 113–128.

Verberne, G., and J. DeBoer. 1976. Chemocommunication among domestic cats, mediated by the olfactory and vomeronasal senses. 1. Chemocommunication. *Z. Tierpsychol.* **42**: 86–109.

Verberne, G., and P. Leyhausen. 1976. Marking behaviour of some Viverridae and Felidae; Time-interval analysis of the marking pattern. *Behaviour* **58**: 192–253.

Vestal, B. M., and J. J. Hellack. 1978. Comparison of neighbor recognition in two species of deer mice (*Peromyscus*). *J. Mammal.* 59:339–346.

Victoria, J. K. 1972. Clutch characteristics and egg discriminative ability of the African village weaverbird *Ploceus cucullatus. Ibis* 114: 367–376.

Vidal, J. -M. 1975. Influence de la privation sociale et de "l'autoperception" sur le comportement sexual du coq domestique. *Behaviour* 52: 57–83.

Vidal, J. -M. 1980. The relations between filial and sexual imprinting in the domestic fowl: Effects of age and social experience. *Anim. Behav.* 28: 880–891.

Volkman, N. J., K. F. Zemanek, and D. Muller-Schwarze. 1978. Antorbital and forehead secretions of black-tailed deer (*Odocoileus hemionus columbianus*): Their role in age-class recognition. *Anim. Behav.* 26: 1098–1106.

VonRautenfeld, D. B. 1978. Bemerkungen zur Austauschbarkeit von Kuken der Silbermowe (*Larus argentatus*) nach der ersten Lebenswoche. *Z. Tierpsychol.* 47: 180–181.

VonUexkull, J. 1957. A stroll through the world of animals and men. In C. H. Schiller's (ed.), *Instinctive Behavior*, International Universities, New York, Pt. 1, pp. 5–80.

Waddington, C. H. 1940. *Organisers and Genes.* Cambridge University Press, Cambridge, 160 + 10 pp.

Wade, T. D. 1976. The effect of strangers on rhesus monkey groups. *Behaviour* 56: 194–214.

Waldman, B. 1981. Sibling recognition in toad tadpoles: The role of experience. *Z. Tierpsychol.* 56: 341–358.

Waldman, B., and K. Adler. 1979. Toad tadpoles associate preferentially with siblings. *Nature (London)* 282: 611–613.

Waldron, I. 1964. Courtship sound production in two sympatric sibling *Drosophila* species. *Science* 144: 191–193.

Walker, T. J. 1957. Specificity in the response of female tree crickets (Orthoptera, Gryllidae, Oecanthinae) to calling songs of the males. *Ann. Entomol. Soc. Am.* 50: 626–636.

Wallace, A. R. 1889. *Darwinism.* Macmillan, London, 494 + 16 pp.

Wallace, B. 1973. Misinformation, fitness, and selection. *Am. Nat.* 107: 1–7.

Wallace, B., and N. Felthousen. 1965. Mating interference: A new test of sexual isolation. *Evolution* 19: 552–555.

Wallace, P. 1977. Individual discrimination of humans by odor. *Physiol. Behav.* 19: 577–579.

Walsh, J. P., and W. R. Tschinkel. 1974. Brood recognition by contact pheromone in the red imported fire ant, *Solenopsis invicta. Anim. Behav.* 22: 695–704.

Walter, M. J. 1973. Effects of parental colouration on the mate preference of offspring in the zebra finch, *Taeniopygia guttata castanotis* Gould. *Behaviour* **46:** 154–173.

Walther, F. R. 1978.   Quantitative and functional variations of certain behaviour patterns in male Thomson's gazelle of different social status. *Behaviour* **65:** 212–240.

Warriner, C. C., W. B. Lemmon, and T. S. Ray. 1963.   Early experiences as a variable in mate selection. *Anim. Behav.* **11:** 221–224.

Waser, P. M. 1976.   Individual recognition, intragroup cohesion and intergroup spacing: Evidence from sound playback to forest monkeys. *Behaviour* **60:** 28–74.

Wassersug, R., and C. M. Hessler. 1971.   Tadpole behaviour: Aggregation in larval *Xenopus laevis. Anim. Behav.* **19:** 386–389.

Watanabe, M., and Y. Tamoto. 1981.   The motivation of the care for offsprings in the cichlid *Sarotherodon mossambicus. Proc. Jpn. Acad.* **57B:** 266–270.

Watson, J. B. 1908.   The behavior of noddy and sooty terns. *Carnegie Inst. Wash. Publ.* **103:** 187–255.

Watson, M. 1969.   Significance of antiphoral song in the eastern whipbird, *Psophodes olivaceus. Behaviour* **35:** 157–178.

Weatherhead, P. J., and R. J. Robertson. 1979.   Offspring quality and the polygyny threshold: "The sexy son hypothesis." *Am. Nat.* **113:** 201–208.

Weatherhead, P. J., and R. J. Robertson. 1980.   Sexual recognition and anti-cuckoldry behaviour in savannah sparrows. *Can. J. Zool.* **58:** 991–996.

Weatherhead, P. J., and R. J. Robertson. 1981.   In defense of the "sexy son" hypothesis. *Am. Nat.* **117:** 349–356.

Weber, P. G., and S. P. Weber. 1976.   The effect of female color, size, dominance and early experience upon mate selection in male convict cichlids, *Cichlasoma nigrofasciatum* Günther (Pisces, Cichlidae). *Behaviour* **56:** 116–135.

Weeden, J. S., and J. B. Falls. 1959.   Differential responses of male ovenbirds to recorded songs of neighboring and more distant individuals. *Auk* **76:** 343–351.

Weigel, P. D., and E. V. Hanson. 1980.   Observational learning and the feeding behavior of the red squirrel *Tamiasciurus hudsoniscus*: The ontogeny of optimization. *Ecology* **61:** 213–218.

Weigel, R. M. 1979.   The facial expressions of the brown capuchin monkey (*Cebus apella*). *Behaviour* **68:** 250–276.

Weller, M. W. 1959.   Parasitic egg laying in the redhead (*Aythya americana*) and other North American anatidae. *Ecol. Monogr.* **29:** 333–365.

Weller, M. W. 1968.   The breeding biology of the parasitic black-duck. *Living Bird* **7,** 169–207.

Wellington, J. L., K. J. Byrne, G. Preti, G. K. Beauchamp, and A. B. Smith III. 1979.   Perineal scent gland of wild and domestic guinea pigs. *J. Chem. Ecol.* **5:** 737–751.

Wells, K. D. 1977. The social behaviour of anuran amphibians. *Anim. Behav.* **25:** 666–693.

Wells, K. D., and B. J. Greer. 1981. Vocal responses to conspecific calls in a neotropical hylid frog, *Hyla ebraccata. Copeia* **1981:** 615–624.

Wells, M. J. 1978. *Octopus.* Chapmann & Hall, London, 417 + 13 pp.

Wessel, J. P., and W. H. Leigh. 1941. Studies in the flock organization of the white-throated sparrow. *Wilson Bull.* **53:** 222–230.

West, M. J., A. P. King, and D. H. Eastzer. 1981. The cowbird: Reflections on development from an unlikely source. *Am. Sci.* **69:** 57–66.

White, H. C., and B. Grant. 1977. Olfactory cues as a factor in frequency-dependent mate selection in *Mormoniella vitripennis. Evolution* **31:** 829–835.

White, S. J. 1971. Selective responsiveness by the gannet to played-back calls. *Anim. Behav.* **19:** 125–131.

White, S. J., and R. E. C. White. 1970. Individual voice production in gannets. *Behaviour* **37:** 40–54.

White, S. J., R. E. C. White, and W. H. Thorpe. 1970. Acoustic basis for individual recognition in the gannet. *Nature (London)* **225:** 1156–1158.

Whitman, C. L. 1919. The behavior of pigeons. *Carnegie Inst. Wash. Publ. 257*, 3: 161 + 11 pp.

Whitney, C. L., and J. R. Krebs. 1975. Mate selection in Pacific tree frogs. *Nature (London)* **255:** 325–326.

Whittle, N. 1981. Reactions of tigers to the scent of conspecifics. *J. Zool.* **194:** 263–265.

Wickler, W. 1967. Socio-sexual signals and their intra-specific imitation among primates. In D. Morris (ed.), *Primate Ethology,* Aldine, Chicago, pp. 69–147.

Wickler, W. 1968. *Mimicry in Plants and Animals.* McGraw-Hill, New York, 255 pp.

Wickler, W. 1972. Aufbau und Paarspezifitat des Gesangduettes von *Laniarius funebris* (Aves, Passeriformes, Laniidae). *Z. Tierpsychol.* **30:** 464–476.

Wickler, W. 1973. Artunterschiede im Duettgesang zwischen *Trachyphonus d'arnaudii usambiro* und den anderen Unterarten von *T. d'arnaudii. J. Ornithol.* **114:** 123–128.

Wickler, W. 1980. Vocal dueting and the pair bond. 1. Coyness and partner commitment. A hypothesis. *Z. Tierpsychol.* **52:** 201–209.

Wickler, W., and U. Seibt. 1980. Vocal dueting and the pair bond. 2. Unison dueting in the African forest weaver, *Symplectes bicolor. Z. Tierpsychol.* **52:** 217–226.

Wickler, W., and D. Uhrig. 1969. Bettelrufe, Antwortszeit und Rassenunterschiede im Begrussungsduett des Schmuckbartvogels *Trachyphonus d'arnaudii. Z. Tierpsychol.* **26:** 651–661.

Wilcock, J. 1971. Gene action and behavior: A clarification. *Psychol. Bull.* **75:** 106–108.

Wilcox, R. S. 1972.   Communication by surface waves. *J. Comp. Physiol.* **80:** 255–266.

Wilcox, R. S. 1979.   Sex discrimination in *Gerris remigis*: Role of a surface wave signal. *Science* **206:** 1325–1327.

Wiley, R. H. 1974.   Evolution of social organization and life-history patterns among grouse. *Q. Rev. Biol.* **49:** 201–227.

Wiley, R. H., and M. S. Wiley. 1977.   Recognition of neighbor's duets by stripe-backed wrens, *Camplorhynchus nuchalis. Behaviour* **62:** 10–34.

Williams, E. E., and A. S. Rand. 1977.   Species recognition, dewlap function and faunal size. *Am. Zool.* **17:** 261–270.

Williams, M. 1974.   Creching behaviour of the shelduck *Tadorna tadorna* L. *Ornis Scand.* **5:** 131–143.

Williams, M. M., and E. Shaw. 1971.   Modifiability of schooling behavior in fishes: The role of early experience. *Am. Mus. Novitates* **2448:** 19 pp.

Wilson, E. O. 1962.   Chemical communication among workers of the fire ant *Solenopsis saevissima* (Fr. Smith): The organization of mass-foraging. *Anim. Behav.* **10:** 134–147.

Wilson, E. O. 1971.   *The Insect Societies.* Harvard University Press, Cambridge, Mass., 548 + 10 pp.

Wilson, E. O. 1975.   *Sociobiology.* Harvard University Press, Cambridge, Mass., 697 + 9 pp.

Wilson, J. R., R. E. Kueln, and F. A. Beach. 1963.   Modification in the sexual behavior of male rats produced by changing the stimulus female. *J. Comp. Physiol. Psychol.* **56:** 636–644.

Winston, M. L., and S. Jacobson. 1978.   Dominance and effects of strange conspecific on aggressive interactions in the hermit crab *Pagurus longicarpus* (Say). *Anim. Behav.* **26:** 184–191.

Witt, P. N., and J. S. Rovner (eds.). 1982.   *Spider Communication.* Princeton University Press. 440 + 9 pp.

Wittenberger, J. F. 1979.   The evolution of mating systems in birds and mammals. In P. Marler and J. G. Vandenbergh (eds.), *Handbook of Behavioral Neurobiology,* Vol. 3, *Social Behavior and Communication,* Plenum, New York, Chap. 6, pp. 271–349.

Wolski, T. R., K. A. Houpt, and R. Aronson. 1980.   The role of the senses in mare-foal recognition. *Appl. Anim. Ethol.* **6:** 121–138.

Wood, D., and J. M. Ringo. 1980.   Male mating discrimination in *Drosophila melanogaster, D. simulans* and their hybrids. *Evolution* **34:** 320–329.

Wood, M. T. 1977.   Social grooming patterns in two levels of monozygotic twin dairy cows. *Anim. Behav.* **25:** 635–642.

Wooller, R. D. 1978.   Individual vocal recognition in the kittiwake gull, *Rissa tridactyla* (L.) *Z. Tierpsychol.* **48:** 68–86.

Worsley, A. 1974a. Long-term effects of imprinting exposure upon breed discriminatory behaviour in chickens. 1. Imprinting to peers ("peerprinting"). *Z. Tierpsychol.* **35**: 1–9.

Worsley, A. 1974b. Long-term effects of imprinting exposure upon breed discriminatory behaviour in chickens. 2. Imprinting to the dam ("damprinting"). *Z. Tierpsychol.* **35**: 10–22.

Wrede, W. L. 1932. Versuche uber den Artduft der Elritzen. *Z. Vergl. Physiol.* **17**: 510–519.

Wu, H. M. H., W. G. Holmes, S. R. Medina, and G. P. Sackett. 1980. Kin preference in infant *Macaca nemestrina. Nature (London)* **285**: 225–227.

Wunderle, J. M., Jr. 1978 Differential response of territorial yellowthroats to the songs of neighbors and non-neighbors. *Auk* **95**: 389–395.

Wunderle, J. M. J. 1979. Components of song used for species recognition in the common yellowthroat. *Anim.Behav.* **27**: 982–996.

Yahr, P. 1977. Social subordination and scent-marking in male mongolian gerbils (*Meriones unguiculatus*). *Anim. Behav.* **25**: 292–297.

Yamazaki, F., and K. Watanabe. 1979. The role of steroid hormones in sex recognition during spawning behavior of the goldfish, *Carassius auratus. Proc. Indian Nat. Sci. Acad.* **45B**: 505–511.

Yamazaki, K., E. A. Boyse, V. Mike, H. T. Thaler, B. J. Mathieson, J. Abbott, J. Boyse, Z. A. Zayas, and L. Thomas. 1976. Control of mating preferences in mice by genes on the major histocompatibility complex. *J. Exp. Med.* **144**: 1324–1335.

Yana, J., and G. E. McClearn. 1972. Assortative mating in mice and the incest taboo. *Nature (London)* **238**: 281–282.

Yarrow, L. J. 1967. The development of focused relationships during infancy. In J. Hollmuth (ed.), *Exceptional Infants,* Vol. 1, *The Normal Infant.* Special Child Publ., Seattle, pp. 427–442.

Yasukawa, K. 1981. Song repertoires in the red-winged blackbird (*Agelaius phoeniceus*). A test of the Beau Geste hypothesis. *Anim. Behav.* **29**: 114–124.

Yerkes, R. M. 1943. *Chimpanzees, a Laboratory Colony.* Yale University Press, New Haven, Conn., 321 + 15 pp.

Yom-Tov, Y. 1976. Recognition of eggs and young by the carrion crow (*Corvus corone*). *Behaviour* **59**: 247–251.

Yom-Tov, Y. 1980. Intraspecific nest parasitism in Birds. *Biol. Rev.* **55**: 93–108.

Young, A. J. 1971. Studies on the acoustic behaviour of certain orthoptera. *Anim. Behav.* **19**: 727–743.

Young, P. T. 1943. *Emotion in Man and Animal.* Wiley, New York, 422 + 13 pp.

Zajonc, R. B. 1971. Attraction, affiliation, and attachment. In J. F. Eisenberg and W. S. Dillon (eds.), *Man and Beast: Comparative Social Behavior,* Smithson. Inst., Washington, D.C., Chap. 4, pp. 141–179.

Zajonc, R. B., W. R. Wilson, and D. W. Rajecki. 1975. Affiliation and social discrimination produced by brief exposure in day-old domestic chicks. *Anim. Behav.* **23:** 131–138.

Zayan, R. C. 1974.   Le role de la reconnaissance individuelle dans la stabilite des relations hierarchiques chez *Xiphophorus* (Pisces, Poeciliidae). *Behaviour* **49:** 268–312.

Zayan, R. C. 1975.   Defense du territoire et reconnaissance individuelle chez *Xiphophorus* (Pisces, Poeciliidae). *Behaviour* **52:** 266–312.

Zenone, P. G., M. E. Sims, and C. J. Erickson. 1979.   Male ring dove behavior and the defense of genetic paternity. *Am. Nat.* **114:** 615–626.

Zentall, T. R., and J. M. Levine. 1972.   Observational learning and social facilitation in the rat. *Science* **178:** 1220–1221.

Zimmer, U. E. 1982.   Birds react to playback of recorded songs by heart rate alteration. *Z. Tierpsychol.* **58:** 25–30.

Zippel, M. P., and C. Langescheid. 1973.   Chemical transfer of a dummy reaction released in young mouthbreeding fish, *Tilapia nilotica* during the critical period from imprinted donors into unimprinted recipients after the critical period. In H. P. Zippell (ed.), *Memory and Transfer of Information,* Plenum, New York, pp. 451–470.

Zippelius, H. M. 1972.   Die Karawanen bildung bei Feld- und Hausspitzmaus. *Z. Tierpsychol.* **30:** 305–320.

Zouros, E., and C. J. d'Entremont. 1980.   Sexual isolation among populations of *Drosophila mojavensis*: Responses to pressure from a related species. *Evolution* **34:** 421–430.

Author Index

Names in the Author Index are primary author's names only. Please refer to the Reference Section for the full listing of authors' names.

Species Index

Subject Index